Business and Professional Communication:
Plans, Processes, and Performance

James R. DiSanza

Idaho State University

Nancy J. Legge

Idaho State University

Allyn and Bacon

Boston ▪ London ▪ Toronto ▪ Sydney ▪ Tokyo ▪ Singapore

For Alexis and Jacob

Vice President, Editor-in-Chief: Paul A. Smith
Series Editor: Karon Bowers
Editorial Assistant: Jennifer Becker
Marketing Manager: Jackie Aaron
Editorial Production Service: Chestnut Hill Enterprises, Inc.
Manufacturing Buyer: Megan Cochran
Cover Administrator: Jennifer Hart
Electronic Composition: Omegatype Typography, Inc.

Copyright © 2000 by Allyn & Bacon
A Pearson Education Company
160 Gould Street
Needham Heights, Massachusetts 02494

Internet: www.abacon.com

Between the time web site information is gathered and then published, some sites may have closed. Also, the transcription of URLs can result in typographical errors. The publisher would appreciate notification where these occur so that they may be corrected in subsequent editions.

Library of Congress Cataloging-in-Publication Data
DiSanza, James R.
    Business and professional communication : plans, processes, and
performance / by James R. DiSanza and Nancy J. Legge.
        p.   cm.
    Includes bibliographical references and index.
    ISBN 0-205-29585-1
    1. Business communication.   2. Communication in organizations.
3. Communication in management.   4. Interpersonal communication.
I. Legge, Nancy J.   II. Title.
    HF5718.D59   1999
    658.4'5—dc21   99-26282
                                                                CIP

Printed in the United States of America

10   9   8   7   6   5   4   3   2   1   04   03   02   01   00   99

CONTENTS

Dyadic and Group Communication

8 Creating and Using Visual Aids   184

Types of Business and Professional Presentations

9 Technical Presentations   204

PREFACE

Business and Professional Communication: Plans, Processes, and Performance began with a request that created a problem. In 1994, the Idaho State University College of Business conducted a survey of companies that had hired recent business graduates. The survey results showed that College of Business students needed to improve their oral and written communication skills. Although business students were already required to take a basic course in oral communication, the business faculty wanted them to also take a more advanced course in business and professional communication. They asked the communication department to structure a business and professional communication course that was presentation oriented but did not repeat material from the basic oral communication requirement.

The problem was that none of us in the communication department could find textbooks or course outlines for a presentation-oriented business and professional course that emphasized communication skills and did not repeat significant units covered in most public speaking courses. It was obvious that we needed to develop new content and unique assignments for the course. Working with other faculty members, we developed new assignments; wrote lectures, exercises, and discussion questions; and created evaluation instruments for learning modules on interpersonal politics, technical communication, risk communication, and crisis communication. These materials have been refined through three years of practical instruction in our service course here at Idaho State University.

Lacking a textbook for our unique course, we decided to see whether we could find a publisher willing to take a chance on a different approach to the business and professional communication course. Fortunately, the answer was "Yes." Through a development process that lasted four years, we tried to include the most up-to-date content available. We avoided rehashing theories from management and social psychology, focusing instead on the basic communication skills required in any business or professional career. Finally, we included chapters not found in any other business communication textbook on interpersonal politics, technical communication, risk communication, and crisis communication. When faithfully applied, the skills described in this book can improve any student's chances for professional employment and advancement. Perhaps this book is a reflection of the often-given advice that employees should look for opportunities in everyday problems. If so, then the development of the book serves as an example of its content. In any event, we believe that our product can help you change your professional problems into opportunities.

Writing a book is never an individual accomplishment. Without the help of a variety of people this project could not have been accomplished. We would like to thank our parents, Yvonne and Richard and JoAn and Norm, for their constant words of support and encouragement. The book has been enriched by the enthusiasm and pedagogical suggestions made by our wonderful colleagues at Idaho

State University including John Gribas, Bob Rouse, Andra Hansen, Jackie Czere-pinski, and Charles Heisler. We appreciate the support of our chair, Bruce Loebs, who has given us much free time from administrative duties over the years and always expressed his interest in and encouragement of this project.

We would also like to thank the dean of the College of Arts and Sciences at Idaho State University, Victor Hjelm, for his constant belief in the importance of communication in a liberal arts curriculum. The dean of the College of Business at Idaho State University, William Stratton, has consistently supported our ideas for the Business and Professional course, and to him and his faculty we owe a great debt of gratitude. Thanks also go to George Ziegelmueller at Wayne State University, a friend and fellow Allyn and Bacon author, who had sage words of advice to offer us one August afternoon. Finally, thanks to Noelle Tangredi for her artistic talents and advice.

We extend much gratitude to our editor, Karon Bowers, her assistant, Scout Reilly, and all the other good people at Allyn and Bacon for their much needed-editorial assistance and support. They and the following reviewers had the unenviable task of slugging through less than ideal drafts prior to the book's publication: Susan Opt, University of Houston-Victoria; Tracy Russo, University of Kansas; Lauren Arnold, University of Pittsburgh-Johnstown; Patrice Buzzanell, Northern Illinois University; Russell Church, Middle Tennessee State University; Richard Crable, California State University-Sacramento; and Raymie McKerrow, Ohio University.

James R. DiSanza
Nancy J. Legge
Idaho State University

1 The Role of Communication in Business and the Professions

The new millennium is here and with it enormous changes in business and professional life. Global competition, international trade, the environmental movement, rising health care costs, new technologies, reductions in the size and scope of government, and constant pressure for increased productivity are just a few of the changes that have accelerated at the close of the twentieth century. Despite these rapid changes, many people agree on one thing: A person's success in a business or professional career depends in large measure on the ability to communicate with others. Let's look at some of the contributions communication makes to employee motivation, productivity, organizational change, and individual career success.

Communication is crucial to employee motivation. There is a consensus among professionals that "truly effective communication does not occur until the employees understand how the 'big picture' affects them and their jobs. Changes in the economy, among competitors in the industry, or in the company as a whole, must be translated into implications for each plant, job, and employee."[1] Letting employees know how their efforts were successful in landing an important account not only instills pride but provides information about the kinds of efforts that succeed at the organization. Even bad news can motivate employees. In a study of communication practices in business, researchers found that "the company with the highest bad-news to good-news ratio appeared to be performing very well, in terms of employee satisfaction and economic performance."[2] As the researcher explained, when bad news is candidly reported, problems can be solved or reduced before they are company threatening. In addition, reporting bad news makes good news more believable.

Whereas good communication provides a motivating work environment, ineffective communication often leads to a drop in the quality and quantity of work, higher absenteeism, and higher staff turnover.[3] According to Mike Greene and Mike Hollister, partners in Greene, Hollister, Inc., a Boca Raton, Florida, management consulting firm, "You can tell when communication is awry. Employees start leaving early...and behaving irresponsibly, even though you've done a good job of hiring."[4] Michael Dennis, a credit manager, says, "more open and frequent communication will build bridges between you and your subordinates, resulting in a happier and more productive work environment."[5] A healthy communication environment means that employees enjoy going to work because it is satisfying and they like to share ideas with their coworkers and supervisors. As such, effective communication improves employee motivation and morale, which are essential for organizational productivity.

Effective communication is also important to managing organizational change. Faced with increased global competition, downsizing, restructuring, and the constant need to cut costs, U.S. corporations are making major changes to enhance productivity in every aspect of their business. Moreover, government agencies are not immune from these pressures: As of 1998, the federal government employed 62,000 fewer employees than in 1990.[6] Remaining employees face greater pressures for efficiency and productivity than ever before. Although this can be beneficial for companies and agencies, the changes can be wrenching for employees. Downsizing and restructuring threaten jobs, business relationships, and employee security.[7] Effective communication is one way to reconcile the competing needs of organizational change and employee security. A study of ten leading U.S. companies revealed that "organizations can convert employees' concerns into support for major changes if they effectively address employees' fears about restructuring and reorganization. On the other hand, if communication is inadequate, employees will be more resistant to change."[8]

To ensure creativity in a competitive environment, employees must be able to exchange mundane news. As one manager suggests, "Most employees are more interested in their company than you suspect."[9] Innovativeness is spurred when people from different parts of an organization talk casually, compare notes on problems, and work together to create new solutions and opportunities. Casual conversation isn't meaningless gossip; rather, problems are often solved as people exchange information. Organizations in which people are free to communicate and feel safe in doing so are more creative than in places where communication is hindered by strict supervision and distrust.

Finally, effective communication is vital for new management models. Total quality management, total quality improvement, flattened hierarchies, employee empowerment, and self-directed work teams all require effective communication for success. One business consultant suggests that, within the next ten years, over 90 percent of all firms will adopt some form of new management practice. Effective communication is the key to making these processes work.[10]

Effective communication is also essential for individual career success. According to W. H. Weiss, an industrial consultant, "no single aspect of the supervisor's job can contribute to career success as much as being an effective communicator."[11] Researchers Beverly Sypher and Theodore Zorn conducted a study of the relationship between communication skills and upward mobility in an East Coast insurance company. They found that "Persons with more developed [communication] abilities tended to be found at higher levels in the organizational hierarchy and tended to be promoted more often than persons with less developed abilities."[12] A study of job competencies showed that oral communication was more important than written communication for entry-level job seekers in business. The specific skills preferred by managers in this study include following instructions, listening skills, conversation skills, giving feedback, communicating with the public, meeting skills, presentation skills, handling customer complaints, and conflict-resolution skills.[13]

Despite the emphasis on communication by many companies, employees often lack these skills. A survey of 470 human resource executives rated communication as the most critical employee shortcoming. Managers of training departments consistently cite communication as one of the most critical areas for additional employee development.[14] Seattle-based consultant John Jensen believes that, "poor communication skills are more the rule than the exception in companies."[15] When business students now in the working world were asked which skills they wished they had been taught in college, they cited public speaking, how to present technical information, listening, writing, small-group communication, problem-solving communication, and persuasion.[16]

Perhaps communication skills are ignored because they are considered soft skills—"touchy-feely indulgences, less critical to business success than 'hard' technical skills."[17] Professionals are taught technical information vital to their field but are not taught how to communicate that information. One health professional wrote, "the most consistent problem that I have experienced in my career of working with industrial hygienists, safety professionals, environmental engineers, and other technical specialists...is a persistent and serious failing of technical people to communicate well."[18] Business consultant Robert Gedaliah says the attitude that communication skills are soft skills is nonsense. "Communication skills are the nuts and bolts of everything. For success in hard skills, we must educate people in soft skills."[19] As we move into the next century, communication skills will be the key to achieving your own professional aspirations.

But what exactly is communication and how does it function? We will answer these questions by defining communication in two parts: First, we will define and explain the concept of meaning, and then we will explain how messages flow between communicators. This leads us to the two overarching goals of most business and professional communication: shared meaning and ambiguity. We then discuss three axioms of effective communication and close the chapter with a discussion of the stages of learning necessary to improve your communication skills.

What Is Communication?

As previously indicated, the term "communication" has become an important one for people in business and industry. When pressed to define exactly what the term means, however, many managers are at a loss. What exactly is communication? For our purposes, **communication** is an exchange of messages between individuals for the purpose of creating or influencing the meaning that others assign to events. To fully understand our definition of communication it is first necessary to understand our definition of "meaning"; then we will explain how messages are exchanged between communicators.

Meaning

Meanings are interpretations we develop for particular experiences. For example, going to a job interview is an experience that some relish and others despise. The difference is in the interpretation or meaning that each person associates with the activity.[20] The meaning that we give an event is not carried by the event itself; rather, events gain particular meanings as people converse about them. For example, most people hate the game-playing and intrigue associated with organizational politics. Nevertheless, in Chapter 3 we argue that the strategic thinking in organizational politics can be enjoyable. If you are convinced, your interpretation of organizational politics will have changed. As such, the meaning of any situation not only varies from person to person but can change for individuals over time, based on their communication with others.

As you might guess from the discussion, **shared meaning** occurs when two people share agreement in their interpretation of an experience or event.[21] Shared meaning may develop independently—for example, when two people learn that they both hate job interviews. More frequently, we attempt to negotiate shared meaning with others through communication. When business people talk about effective communication they usually mean communication that creates shared meaning between people. For example, sales people work to persuade potential buyers to share their assessment of a product's value. On the other hand, **ambiguity** is the opposite of shared meaning. It occurs when a message sender achieves a low correspondence between his or her intent and the receiver's interpretation.[22] Although business people tend to emphasize the

Communication is an exchange of messages for the purpose of creating or influencing meaning.
Credit: Kevin C. Wellard

importance of shared meaning, ambiguity plays an important role in a variety of professional communication contexts, including organizational politics and organizational crises.

Communication creates or influences shared meaning through the use of signs and symbols. **Signs** are involuntary expressions of emotion, and are usually nonverbal rather than verbal cues. Facial expressions, eye contact, posture, gesture, and vocal variations are all examples of nonverbal signs. Signs are involuntary because they are not normally under conscious control. When angry, you do not need to think about raising your voice, scowling, and slamming your fist. These cues are exhibited as a natural extension of your anger. As such, signs usually illustrate and emphasize the verbal portion of a message, although they can contradict a message, producing ambiguity and confusion for the listener.

Symbols, on the other hand, are voluntary expressions that stand for or represent something else. Symbols are voluntary because the choice of whether and how to express yourself symbolically is more conscious than is the case for signs. Letters are symbols because they stand for certain sounds. Words are symbols because they stand for objects, ideas, or states of mind. Symbols are necessary because my picture of a tree cannot be transmitted to you directly. Instead, our culture has agreed that the word "tree" stands for objects with roots, a trunk, branches, and leaves or needles. If my use of the word "tree" creates a corresponding picture of a similar tree in the your head, then this symbol has created shared meaning. If, however, when I use the word "tree" I am thinking of a Joshua tree, a variety common in the desert Southwest, but the word makes you think of a maple tree, the symbol has been only partly successful in helping us share meaning. However, sharing meaning is never as simple as selecting the one correct symbol to represent an idea. Effective communicators consider the logical and psychological meanings of their symbols.

To create shared meaning the communicator must consider the logical relationship between a symbol and the thing it represents. This involves selecting the right words to stand for the objects, events, or states of mind to which the speaker is referring. Although tools such as dictionaries aid this selection, the chore is complicated by the fact that almost every word has more than one definition. If I said, in response to the CEO's motivational presentation, "The boss's rhetoric is quite nice," this could be taken in two ways depending on my meaning for the term "rhetoric." In one meaning, rhetoric is the art or science of using words effectively, thus my comment is a compliment. If, on the other hand, I meant rhetoric as artificial eloquence, showiness, and unnecessary elaboration of language and literary style, then my comment is an ironic insult. Multiple definitions increase the beauty and power of language, but do so at the cost of precision.

In addition to the sheer number of definitions for each symbol, the fact that they are abstract further complicates the possibility of shared meaning. As we said above, symbols are not the things they represent; rather, they stand in the place of those things. Although this may seem to be an obvious point, it leads to less obvious complications. The fact that symbols are abstractions (removed from the thing they represent) is sometimes depicted as a ladder of possibilities.[23]

At the bottom of the ladder in Figure 1.1 is an event, an employee's lateness for work. The statements above the line are symbolic, meaning they are representations of the actual event. As we climb the ladder of abstraction we increase the power of our description, moving from describing three events to describing the employee's general approach to work. But, that increase in power also increases the ambiguity of the description. All language operates on a continuum that at one end may be highly precise but only minimally descriptive, and at the other end is broader but more ambiguous.

In addition to the logical properties of language, psychological meanings must also be considered. Psychological meanings are the private associations that individuals have for a symbol. For example, although the dictionary definition for the term

	You are a poor worker.
	You have a poor attitude toward your work.
Symbols	Your poor attitude is reflected in poor attendance.
	You have been late a variety of times this month.
	You have been late three times this month.

An Event	Late for work three times.

FIGURE 1.1   The Ladder of Abstraction

"radiation" focuses exclusively on the emission of a wave or particle from an unstable substance such as plutonium, the psychological meanings some people have for radiation include accident, cancer, death, and so forth. These idiosyncratic meanings remind us that ambiguity lurks in the use of any symbol. If shared meaning is an important goal, then communicators must take account of psychological meanings.

Signs and symbols have enormous influence on the meanings people give events. (Remember that events do not have meanings.) People use symbols and signs to label or relabel events, thereby changing the meaning the event has for others. For example, a car dealer in Cleveland sells used Cadillacs, but does not refer to the automobiles as "used." Obviously, the label "used" lacks the class and cache desired by a Cadillac buyer. Instead, the dealer sells "previously owned" Cadillacs, hoping, no doubt, to remove the negative stigma (interpretation) associated with a "used car." Looking at another example, "road rage" refers to aggressive driving and is said to be a national disaster that has increased the number of accidents, injuries, and deaths on American highways. In 1997, there were over 4,000 media stories that used the terms "road rage" and "epidemic" in the same article. However, writing in the *Atlantic Monthly*, Michael Fumento argues that "there was not—there is not—the least statistical or other scientific evidence of more-aggressive driving on our nation's roads."[24] He suggests that the "epidemic" is inspired not by real statistics, but by the power of the label itself. Quoting David Murray, director of the Statistical Assessment Service in Washington D.C., Fumento suggests that, once a phenomenon picks up a label, the label tends to be applied to more things: "There has always been a degree of aggression while driving, but what did we used to call it? Nothing. Now that we have a name, we look for things that seem to be similar and build a pathology."[25] Nevertheless, the label "road rage" has greatly influenced our perceptions about the aggressiveness of American drivers. History is rife with moments when people change a label, hoping to persuade others to think differently about something.

Almost all persuasion is based on the ability of signs and symbols to label or relabel events for others. This persuasive function is vital for a variety of professional goals, including sales presentations and crisis communication. Through the use of signs and symbols people attempt to influence and manage meaning for others in organizations. Let's examine how signs and symbols are combined into messages.

The Flow of Messages

Many models of communication emphasize the flow of messages between people. This makes sense since messages are the most visible part of communication. However, the emphasis on the flow of messages encourages us to think of communication as a simple act, similar to throwing a football or shipping a package. When I throw a football or ship a package, it arrives in almost exactly the same condition as it left my hands. Ideas, however, are not thrown or shipped between people, and what is sent never corresponds perfectly with what is received. We have attempted to avoid these simplifications in the model of the message transmission process in Figure 1.2.

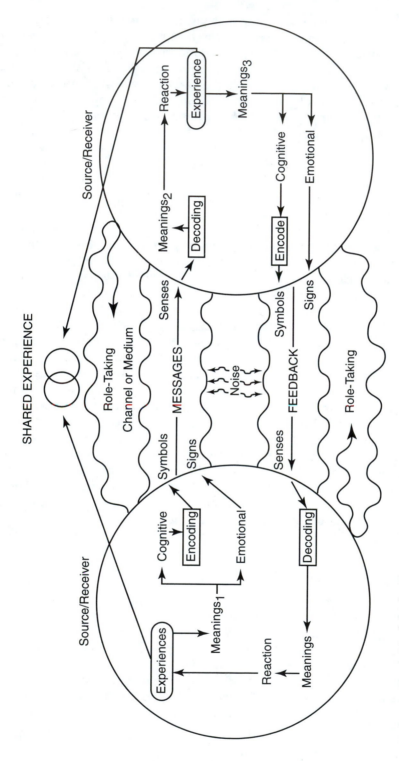

FIGURE 1.2   A Model of Message Transmission

Adapted from a model by Christopher L. Johnstone, The Pennsylvania State University. Reprinted with permission.

The model depicts two large circles that represent **source/receivers,** people that send and receive messages. Because communication is a circular process, we could begin anywhere in the model, but for convenience sake we will begin with the left source/receiver. In the upper left quadrant of the circle is **experience,** which is anything that happened to us in the past. For two people to communicate they must share some experience. The overlapping circles in the top-center of the model represent the amount of experience that the two communicators share. The greater the **shared experience** between people, the easier it is for them to share meaning. For example, talking to someone from another country can be difficult because you don't share a language. In addition, basic values, attitudes, and interpretations may be different enough to interfere with the ability to communicate. Moving back to the left source/receiver, follow the arrow from experience to meaning. As we stated above, meanings are the interpretations or attitudes we assign to our experiences. The subscript "1" after meanings emphasizes that these are unique to the individual and cannot be transmitted whole to another person.

For purposes of simplicity, meanings can be classified into two categories, cognitive and emotional. **Emotional meanings** are feelings such as sadness, surprise, and curiosity. Feelings are usually expressed directly in the form of signs, although it is also possible to put feelings into words, such as, "I feel great about this project." As we said before, signs are involuntary emotional expressions that are usually nonverbal. On the other hand, **cognitions** are ideas, and before these can be sent they must be encoded into symbols. **Encoding** is the process of selecting symbols to stand for or represent cognitions. When trying to share meaning, we select symbols that we hope represent similar meanings in the receiver. We have covered some of the complexities of this selection process.

Messages are composed of signs and symbols that travel along a **channel.** Common channels for oral communication include audio, visual, and tactile channels. **Noise** can interfere with the communication anywhere in the channel and tends to produce ambiguity. **Physical noise** is any concrete interference with the process of communication, such as the speaker's talking too fast, a construction crew that is working in the next room, or children crying in the audience. **Psychological noise** is any internal interference with listening, such as a bias against the speaker or her point of view.

After the message completes its passage along the channel it encounters the sense organs of the other source/receiver. The message is **decoded,** meaning that the receiver selects meanings to attach to the signs and symbols. It is important to emphasize that meanings are not sent; rather, the receiver selects meaning from within herself and attaches that meaning to the message. This is the reason for the subscript "2" behind meanings. The message then becomes part of the receiver's experience, which the receiver may further examine and interpret.

Once a message is fully interpreted, this meaning becomes part of a new message that includes both cognitive and emotional components. The cognitive components are encoded into symbols, and the emotional components are emitted as signs that travel along a channel. These are received by the first source/receiver through the senses, decoded, and then interpreted to create a new meaning.

The return message is referred to as feedback. **Feedback** includes information about how the first message was received. For example, a person who shakes his or her head no and frowns while you finish a proposal is indicating how the message was received. Technically, when two people meet, everything after the initial utterance is feedback because it is, in part, a response to a speaker's previous message. Feedback is valuable for sharing meaning because it allows us to estimate the degree of shared meaning that exists between speakers. Quizzical looks, for example, are a sign that the speaker has not succeeded in the quest to share meaning.

The wavy lines from each source/receiver indicate the ability to view one's own communication from the point of view of the other person; to put yourself in the other person's shoes, so to speak. This form of **role-taking** involves anticipating a reaction to a message rather than waiting for the person's feedback.[26] Thus, role-taking can help a speaker anticipate difficulties or objections and develop ways to overcome these problems prior to actually speaking. As such, role-taking also serves to reduce ambiguity and increases the chances of sharing meaning.

By representing the flow of messages, the model depicts the components and processes of communication. Encoding and decoding are complicated and, depending on how they are handled by communicators, serve to increase either shared meaning or ambiguity. Noise can interfere with message transmission, increasing the likelihood of ambiguity. Shared experience, feedback, and role-taking facilitate the process of shared meaning. We will refer to elements of this model throughout the rest of the book.

Goals of Communication

The model presented in this chapter suggests two overarching goals for communication in business and the professions. These goals are the foundation for the material in later chapters, and we will refer to them repeatedly throughout the book.

Shared Meaning Is the Objective of Most Business and Professional Communication

As we have noted, shared meaning results when there is a high correspondence between the intent of the sender and the receiver's interpretation. When consultants, for example, talk about converting employee fears about restructuring into support for needed changes, or discuss the importance of corporate values, they are encouraging managers to create shared meaning. Self-directed work teams and total quality improvement depend on creating shared objectives among employees. Selling a product or service also requires shared meaning. Informing other people about safety or environmental procedures depends on the ability to share information accurately. In short, shared meaning is vital to a variety of organizational functions and goals.

However, shared meaning is not an "either–or" proposition; it exists on a continuum. At the low end of the continuum is **contractual shared meaning.**[27] In this form of sharing, two parties each give up something they would rather not part with to get something valuable from the other person. For example, salespeople might not want to put forth extra effort to exceed sales quotas, but do so in order to receive a bonus at the end of the month. Similarly, organizations do not want to spend money on bonuses but do so to increase sales. Contractual shared meaning does not require that employees agree with the organization's sales goals or the choices of products it markets. All that is required is for each party to give up something in order to receive something else that cannot be achieved alone.

For example, despite their importance, safety regulations are notoriously difficult to enforce in manufacturing operations. Employees see regulations as excessive, and the demands of the job encourage drift from adherence. However, rewarding safe workers and punishing unsafe workers improve compliance regardless of whether the employee thinks the regulations are important. This minimal form of shared meaning is the basis of many professional interactions, and we will discuss it more fully in the chapters on interpersonal and group communication.

A second kind of shared meaning represents relatively greater correspondence between sender and receiver, and we refer to this as **consensual shared meaning.**[28] When parties share consensus they agree about basic objectives and values. If an employee follows safety precautions because she believes they protect both the employee and the organization, she is expressing a point of view shared by the plant management. Consensual shared meaning is the basis for most persuasive communication and is covered in the chapters on persuasive proposals and sales communication. Although it is safe to say that shared meaning is an important goal for business and professional communicators, there are times when ambiguity is valuable.

Ambiguity Is the Objective of Some Business and Professional Communication

As we indicated in our model, ambiguity is a constant presence in the communication process. Ambiguity occurs when there is little overlap between a sender's intent and a receiver's interpretation. It is a myth, however, to believe that effective communication must always be clear. Several scholars suggest that ambiguity can serve important strategic functions in organizations.

Ambiguity is useful to leaders developing group or organizational mission statements. Ambiguous mission statements provide a sense of shared direction while leaving room for individual interpretation.[29] Ford's "Quality Is Job 1" assertion clearly sets company direction but leaves employees free to develop their own means to achieve quality. The motivating function of ambiguity is evident in a situation involving a small, nonprofit radio station. The station was run largely by community volunteers, and when the DJs became insulting, sponsors threatened the station with closure if it didn't improve. Their jobs on the line, the DJs were met by the managerial staff, who proclaimed that the station's new mission was "professionalism," although they never defined what they meant by the term. As the year progressed, different definitions of professionalism emerged. Management tended to define professionalism as technical skills such as choosing the right music for public service announcements. The staff tended to define professionalism as attitudes such as formality, consideration for audience sensibilities, and responsibility.[30] Despite the fact that no single definition of professionalism emerged, individuals were motivated to meet their own standards. As a result, on-air incidents fell to zero, and the sponsors ceased their threats. We will discuss a leader's use of ambiguity as a motivational technique in the chapter on groups and teams.

Ambiguity also plays a vital role in organizational crisis communication. In circumstances in which a clear apology creates unacceptably high legal liabilities, an ambiguous apology may be warranted. We cover the methods and ethical implications of the ambiguous apology in the chapter on crisis communication. Although less vital than shared meaning, ambiguity serves important functions in professional settings.

Precepts of Effective Communication

Despite the complexity of communication and its variability across different contexts, there are several precepts for effectiveness that are true in almost any situation.

The Most Powerful Communication is Multichannel and Multidirectional

Oral communication is more powerful and more influential than written communication, in part because it is multichannel and multidirectional. Whereas writing engages only the visual channel, oral communication employs both aural and visual channels, making it more engaging. While writing can be multidirectional over time, oral communication is simultaneously multidirectional, stimulating more involvement than in written messages.

Gone are the days when a monthly newsletter reflects sufficient managerial communication. A 1992 study of in-house newsletters showed that only 16 percent of surveyed employees said the newsletter was a helpful communication tool, compared with 45 percent of employees in 1980.[31] Employees expect managers to understand and utilize various communication methods and channels. Informal conversation, regular team meetings, and formal presentations are increasingly valued by employees. These should be augmented by older technologies such as newsletters and by new information technologies such as e-mail and videoconferencing. In addition, oral presentations can be made more powerful through the use of appealing visual aids, covered in Chapter 8.

Effective Communication Involves More Listening Than Talking

When people suggest that "we need to communicate more or better," many take that as a signal that they need to "talk more." But as our model of communication suggests, decoding is one of the most error-prone elements in the communication process. Decoding skills are synonymous with effective listening, and listening is one of the most overlooked ways to improve communication.[32] Ken Blanchard, coauthor of the *One Minute Manager,* wrote that although many think of listening as a "commonplace skill," it is not valued or practiced nearly to the extent it should be in business.[33] Chapter 3 covers material on listening and feedback in organizations.

Effective Communication Is Audience Centered

The audience is vital to the success of all communication. This was illustrated at a recent communication conference. The event's keynote speaker, a former TV anchorwoman, suggested that communication skills—which she defined as how to hold a camera, how to put on make-up, how to choose a sports coat—should not be taught in college. Such skills, she argued, were cosmetic and have nothing to do with covering the news. Had she done any research on her audience, however, she would have known that conference-goers did not share her definition of communication and that her comments could be perceived as an insult.

In the professions, people communicate to accomplish goals. If these goals could be achieved individually, people wouldn't bother with communication. Thus, we communicate to get a desired response from an audience. What does the audience know about the topic? Do they have a positive or negative attitude toward it? How did they arrive at that attitude? Knowing the answers to such questions can help a communicator adjust the content and delivery of the message, increasing the likelihood of the desired response.

The communication model indicates two methods of adapting to the audience. By paying attention to feedback, a communicator can adapt to better suit the audience. Does the audience need you to slow down? Have you lost your supervisor during a complicated explanation? Are you addressing the real concerns of your client? By paying attention to feedback, a communicator can answer such questions and make appropriate adjustments.

Role-taking is another means of assessing the audience. While role-taking, a communicator imagines how others will react to his message. Ling, for example, owns a small landscaping company and wants to get a contract at the new shopping mall. After sketching out his sales pitch to the mall's management team, he attempts to imagine the members' concerns about or objections to his proposal. Are they concerned about quality? Is cost a concern? Will they want to know about liability insurance? Are they concerned about the small size of the company? The answers to these questions will help Ling adjust his content to address relevant concerns. Effective role-taking allows communicators to adapt to feedback prior to actual interaction, thereby increasing the chances that receivers will respond in the desired way. Another term for role-taking is audience analysis, which we cover extensively in Chapter 6. The last section of this chapter explains how people learn and improve complex communication skills.

Communication Competence

Our goal in writing this book is to explain the variety and complexity of communication that you are likely to encounter in your career. However, understanding is only the beginning of the learning process. If you are to succeed, you must be able to apply your knowledge to specific situations. As we have noted, people communicate to accomplish individual, group, and organizational goals that they cannot accomplish alone. Therefore, **competent communication** is the ability to interact with others in such a way that mutual goals are accomplished. Providing applicable knowledge to help you become a more competent communicator is our objective.

To provide applicable knowledge, we have attempted to steer a course between two hazards. On the one side is the hazard of oversimplification. No one can provide a list of five steps to outstanding team leadership or ten "never-fail" sales pitches. Whereas some teams require a watchful eye and constant feedback, this approach would inhibit a more motivated and creative group. Likewise, some managers base their buying decisions solely on their trust in the salesperson, while others ignore credibility and focus on quantitative information about the product. This variety of responses makes communication an art rather than a science. It also means that simple prescriptions will not be effective. The other hazard to avoid is the problem of too much abstraction. While esoteric management and communication theories provide useful descriptions of events, they rarely help with specific solutions. To improve your communication competence you need specific suggestions.

Because every person, group, and audience is different, we will teach you to analyze your audience for their present knowledge, problems, attitudes toward your topic, and preferred style. With this analysis, you will find it easier to select the most appropriate strategies to achieve your goals. To increase your repertoire of effective communication strategies we have taken what we consider to be the best and most innovative communication theories and distilled these into suggestions for effectively responding to audience needs. In this way we have attempted to provide applicable knowledge without dangerous simplification or banal generalities.

We have also decided to focus almost exclusively on oral communication in this book. Although business writing is a vital area of study, it is our opinion that oral communication is more influential than writing in organizational decision making. According to Joel D. Whalen, business professor at DePaul University, "My experience and the experience of thousands of my graduate students and business associates shows that oral communication is more important than written in influencing business decisions. It is used more often, and more executives make most of their decisions about people and plans based on oral communication."[34] Given the significance of oral communication for both organizational and individual success, and the apparent poor communication skills of many employees, learning the material in this book will prove a worthy investment for your career.

Happily, the ability to communicate competently is not genetic; it can be improved with practice. However, the process of becoming a competent communicator is not as simple as learning basic facts. Learning complicated skills proceeds through four stages.

The first stage is **unconscious incompetence.** At this stage a person is unaware of making mistakes or performing at less than optimal levels.[35] Such people are probably frustrated with their limited success but blame others for their failures, not realizing that the real source of the problem is inadequate communication skills.

How could we be so unaware of skills that we use everyday? The process of sinking repeatedly used knowledge from conscious to unconscious levels provides useful mental economy. It allows us to perform routine skills without thinking about them, thus saving our limited conscious attention for other tasks. This works for a variety of complex skills such as riding a bicycle, typing, driving, speaking, and listening. For example, when you first learned to ride a bicycle, conscious thought was necessary to control the steering, balancing, and braking operations. After a time, however, the program for bicycle-riding was absorbed into less conscious levels of your mind and you could (and probably still can) perform the activity without much thought. The riding process is said to be a habit.[36] The same process works for communication skills. We learn most of our rudimentary communication activities such as word choice and listening very early in life. As such, these skills are so habituated they don't require conscious thought. But, if our communication habits are ineffective, we continue to perform them without awareness of the need to improve; and if we are to change bad habits, they must become conscious again.

The next level of learning is **conscious incompetence.** In this case, a person is made aware of the fact that habits and practices are not effective and that there is room for improvement.[37] Teachers or managers often play a role in raising our awareness of ineffective habits. This stage is often an uncomfortable one for students or employees because they discover that things they never thought of before are hindering their performance.

In **conscious competence,** a person attempts to improve the deficient skill.[38] Improvement requires conscious and concerted effort to repeatedly enact the preferred behavior. This is equivalent to learning to ride a tandem bicycle. If you have ever tried it, a tandem bicycle requires a host of new operations to coordinate and balance the efforts of two riders. Old habits (for example, trying to steer from the second seat) must be unlearned and new ones learned. Riding the tandem will require as much conscious effort as it took to learn to ride a regular bicycle. The more a pair practices, the easier riding will become. Ultimately, the new procedures and operations will sink back down to an unconscious level, becoming habits. Likewise, new communication skills can be learned through consistent conscious effort. According to Sprague and Stuart, "The absence of such [conscious] vigilance is likely to mean a regression to more comfortable but less competent patterns."[39] Improving communication skills requires vigilant effort. With perseverance, the awkwardness of the new behavior diminishes, as does the need for self-monitoring, and the person progresses to the fourth stage of learning.

The fourth level of learning is **unconscious competence**.[40] At this level, the person has integrated the new, more effective skills thoroughly enough that he or she need not devote conscious attention to enacting them. The new and improved skills are habituated. Our goal for this book is to help students identify ineffective business and professional communication skills and begin to implement improvements. Although a single class in any subject is not enough to move everyone to unconscious competence with every skill, it can point out skills that require improvement and encourage movement toward that level.

Summary

Despite enormous changes in business and the professions at the close of the twentieth century, most people agree that effective communication is vital for both individual and organizational success. Communication is crucial to employee morale, and morale is related to productivity. Effective communication is also relevant to managing rapid organizational change. New management models such as total quality management and the self-directed work team also require effective communication. Further, effective communication is vital for individual career success.

Communication is the exchange of messages between individuals for the purpose of creating or influencing the meaning that others assign to events. Meanings are interpretations or attitudes we develop for particular experiences. It is important to remember that events do not have a particular meaning, rather, meaning is given to events by people. Changes in the meaning of an event usually come through communication with others. Shared meaning occurs when two people agree in their interpretation of an event. Ambiguity is the opposite of shared meaning. It occurs when a message sender achieves a low correspondence between his intent and the receiver's interpretation.

Meanings are created and influenced through signs and symbols. Signs are involuntary (usually nonverbal) emotional expressions. Symbols are voluntary expressions that stand for or represent something else. Language is a form of symbolic communication. Effective use of language means considering the logical and psychological meanings for symbols. We use signs and symbols to influence the meanings that other people assign to events.

The communication model depicts source/receivers who wish to share their experiences. Emotional meanings are expressed involuntarily through signs, whereas cognitive meanings are encoded into symbols and sent in a message through a channel. Noise is any physical or psychological interference with the message, and it contributes to ambiguity. The message is decoded by the receiver when he selects meanings from within himself to attach to the signs and symbols. This meaning is always somewhat different from the meaning that the original person intended to communicate. The return message is referred to as feedback. Role-taking is the ability of communicators to put themselves in the position of the other person to anticipate their reaction to a message. Paying attention to feedback and careful role-taking can improve shared meaning.

Shared meaning is the goal of most business and professional communication. Shared meaning exists on a continuum that ranges from the contractual shared meaning, the most minimal form, to consensual shared meaning. Ambiguity, on the other hand, is sometimes useful in business and professional communication. Ambiguity can provide a sense of unity while allowing for individual creativity and innovativeness.

Multichannel, multidirectional communication is more powerful than single-channel, linear communication. Managers should employ a number of communication strategies and channels for the greatest effect. Effective listening can improve the ability to accurately decode messages. Finally, effective communication is audience centered, meaning that a communicator must adapt to the receiver's needs and preferences for greatest effect.

Communication competence is the ability of a communicator to interact with others in such a way that mutual goals are accomplished. Learning new communication skills involves a four-step process that proceeds through unconscious incompetence, conscious incompetence, conscious competence, and unconscious competence.

QUESTIONS FOR DISCUSSION

1. Can you think of an instance of communication in which a misunderstanding occurred because someone didn't take account of the logical or psychological meaning of a term or phrase? What were the consequences of this misunderstanding? What could have been done to prevent the misunderstanding?

2. In the communication model, what happens to individuals who do not pay attention to feedback? Can you provide an example of this kind of miscommunication? What were the consequences of this problem?

3. Have you ever had a job in which you shared consensus with most managerial decisions and actions? If so, how did your approach to this job differ from other jobs when you were merely fulfilling a contractual agreement?

4. Describe some of the things managers do to encourage consensual shared meaning among employees. Are these techniques effective? Why or why not?

5. Can you think of any other precepts of effective communication in business and professional settings? Are there any that you would eliminate from the list because they do not apply in various situations?

6. Identify a skill that you have acquired by tracing its acquisition through the four stages of skill development cited in this chapter. What level of competence do you have now in this skill?

ACTIVITIES AND EXERCISES

1. The following exercise should help illustrate the idea that events do not have a particular meaning. In class or with a small group of your friends, take a few moments to describe the following diagram in a page of written prose.[41] When you are finished, compare the results of your descriptions.

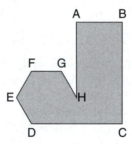

Each description represents a different way of interpreting or giving meaning to the object. Communication theorist Gregory Bateson notes that people can take different descriptive tactics toward the object. While some take an analogic approach, describing the object as a boot, or even a toilet, others talk about the object as a combination of an incomplete rectangle and a hexagon. Another group may attempt an operational description and start at one point of the object, usually an angle, and describe how to draw the object by moving one line at a time until it is completed. There is nothing in the object itself that dictates how it will be described. The description is imposed on it by each individual. In another exercise, think of someone setting off a bomb in a large manufacturing operation. What are the various meanings that the perpetrator, organization members, and the community might apply to such an act?

2. In this chapter we suggested that symbols are used to influence the meanings that people apply to events. The following quotes present two opinions about the safety of irradiated foods. Advocates of irradiation argue that exposing fruits, vegetables, and meats to doses of radiation kills harmful pests and bacteria more effectively and more safely than chemical-based pesticides. Dissenters claim the process is dangerous.

> The vault has concrete walls twelve to twenty feet thick. A door in the vault opens, and food enters on a conveyor belt. The door closes behind it. A shutter opens, and rods of radioactive cobalt 60, the waste products from nuclear reactors, or rods of cesium 137, the waste products of atomic-bomb construction, rise out of a bed of water. The food is exposed to a radioactive dose of 100,000 rads.

The rods go back down into the water, and the shutter closes. The door opens, the food leaves. Now it is ready for you to eat.[42]

Now from a proponent of food irradiation.

Not even the most ardent food-irradiation opponent argues that the process makes food radioactive, but, as radiation chemistry has shown, irradiation does create tiny numbers of molecules know as radiolytic products—formed when the ionizing energy from a radioactive isotope or a linear accelerator splits food molecules, creating new ones.[43]

How is the word choice and sentence structure in each quotation designed to influence your interpretation of food irradiation? Point to specific words or sentences and the effect they are designed to have on your attitude. Does either of these quotations influence your attitude toward food irradiation? Why or why not?

3. Prepare the following exercise for a friend or a small group in class. Using a plastic cup and straightedge, draw a fairly complicated geometric design on a single piece of paper. The design can include some circles, squares, and lines that connect them in fairly complicated ways. Now draw a second design that approximates the first in its level of complexity. Take this design to your friend and have him or her reproduce each under the following two conditions. In the first condition, sit back-to-back and give the person the directions necessary to reproduce the design on a sheet of paper. The person reproducing the design is not allowed to look at you or utter any sound while reproducing the design. In the second condition, the person can now face you and try to reproduce the design and is allowed to interrupt the process to ask questions and seek more information. However, under no circumstances should the person reproducing the design show his or her paper to the person giving directions. Under which condition was the design better reproduced? Why is the design usually closer to the original in the second condition? What does this exercise illustrate about the importance of feedback for effective communication?

NOTES

1. Young, M., and J. E. Post, "Managing to Communicate, Communicating to Manage: How Leading Companies Communicate with Employees," *Organizational Dynamics* 22, 1 (1993): 41.

2. Ibid., 39.

3. Dennis, M. C., "Effective Communication Will Make Your Job Easier," *Business Credit* 97 (1995): 45.

4. Nelton, S., "Face To Face," *Nation's Business,* November 1995, 22.

5. Dennis, 45.

6. Wessel, D., "In March to a Surplus, Government Changed In Many Small Ways," *The Wall Street Journal,* 3 February 1998, A1 & A11.

7. Young and Post.

8. Ibid., 31.

9. Weiss, W. H., "Handling Communication Problems," *Supervision,* March 1994, 19.

10. Martin, S., "The Role of Nonverbal Communications in Quality Improvement," *National Productivity Review,* Winter 1995/96, 27–39.

11. Weiss, 17.

12. Sypher, B. D., and T. E. Zorn, "Communication-Related Abilities and Upward Mobility: A Longitudinal Investigation," *Human Communication Research* 12 (1986): 420.

13. Maes, J. D., T. G. Weldy, and M. L. Icenogle, "A Managerial Perspective: Oral Communication Competency Is Most Important for Business Students in the Workplace," *The Journal of Business Communication* 34 (1997): 67–80.

14. Brown, R. M., "Rethinking the Approach to Communication Training," *Technical Communication* 41 (August 1994): 406–415.

15. Jensen, J., "Ten Days to Better Communication," *Executive Female*, March/April 1993, 70.

16. Curtis, D. B., J. L. Winsor, and R. D. Stephens, "National Preferences In Business and Communication Education," *Communication Education* 38 (1989): 6–14.

17. McNerney, D. J., "Improve Your Communication Skills," *HRFocus*, October 1994, 22.

18. Mansdorf, Z., "Communication—The Key To Success," *Occupational Hazards*, May 1993, 85.

19. McNerney, 22.

20. DiSanza, J. R., "Shared Meaning as a Sales Inducement Strategy: Bank Teller Responses to Frames, Reinforcements, and Quotas," *The Journal of Business Communication* 30 (1993): 133–180.

21. Harris, L., and V. E. Cronen, "A Rules-Based Model for the Analysis and Evaluation of Organizational Communication," *Communication Quarterly* 27 (1979): 12–28.

22. Eisenberg, E. M., "Ambiguity as Strategy in Organizational Communication," *Communication Monographs* 51 (1984): 227–242.

23. Hayakawa, S. I., *Language in Action* (New York: Harcourt, Brace and Company, 1942).

24. Fumento, M., "'Road Rage' Versus Reality," *The Atlantic Monthly*, August 1998, 12.

25. Ibid., 14.

26. Blumer, H., "Symbolic Interaction," in *Interdisciplinary Approaches to Human Communication*, ed. by W. Budd and B. D. Ruben (Rochelle Park, CA: Hayden, 1979), 135–153.

27. DiSanza.

28. Ibid.

29. Eisenberg.

30. Embree, E. F., "The Uses/Abuses of Ambiguity: Staff Responses to Omission and Contradiction at a Student Radio Station" (M. A. thesis, Idaho State University, 1995).

31. Sonnenberg, F., "Internal Communication: Turning Talk into Action," *Supervisory Management*, September 1992, 8–9.

32. Taylor, G. R., "Getting Results Through Good Communication," *Business Credit*, November/December 1990, 44.

33. Blanchard, K., "New Communication Skills, New roles in the '90s," *Supervisory Management*, July 1991, 2.

34. Whalen, J. D., *I See What You Mean: Persuasive Business Communication* (Beverly Hills, CA: Sage, 1996), 117–118.

35. Sprague, J., and D. Stuart, *The Speaker's Handbook* (Fort Worth: Harcourt Brace, 1996).

36. DiSanza, J. R., "The Role of Consciousness in Interpersonal Communication: Pedagogical Implications for the Introductory Course" (ERIC Document Reproduction Service No. ED 341 098), February 1991.

37. Sprague and Stuart.

38. Ibid.

39. Ibid., 14.

40. Ibid.

41. Bateson, G., *Mind and Nature: A Necessary Unity* (Toronto: Bantam Books, 1979), 5.

42. Gibbs, G., "Zap, Crackle, Pop. Irradiated foods aren't coming; they're here." *The Progressive*, September 1987, 22.

43. Leslie, J. "Food Irradiation." *The Atlantic*, September 1990, 28.

CHAPTER

2 The Employment Interview

Belma was nervous and fidgeted with her briefcase strap for a moment. She couldn't stop thinking about how much was riding on the upcoming meeting. The door to the inner office opened and a woman came out and introduced herself. Belma thought the woman friendly, but not overly so. She had probably held several similar discussions throughout the morning. Belma followed her into the office and took a seat at the table. She accepted the offer of hot coffee, but worried that it might only make her more nervous. The woman sat down and said, "So, tell me a little about yourself."

So began Belma's job interview with a chemical manufacturing firm. What do employers want in a job applicant? How should Belma—or anyone else in an employment interview—conduct herself to make the best possible impression? The **employment interview** is one of the most common forms of interpersonal contact in the modern organization. Whether getting a first job with a company or getting a new job within the same company, most people experience some form of employment interview. Although the world of job searches is rapidly changing, the employment interview remains the primary tool for recruiting, hiring, and placing new employees in business, military, and government organizations.[1] This chapter explains the three phases of an employment interview: the pre-interview stage, the interview itself, and the post-interview stage.

As we are writing this book, the current job market is excellent for prospective candidates. Thus, some interviewers must convince prospective candidates that their organization is a desirable place at which to work.[2] Whether the present job market in your field is open or tight, remember that the majority of interviewers are interested in recruiting the most talented people to their organizations. Understanding that interviewers are also interested in recruiting may help you approach the interview less as an interrogation than as an exchange of information. Just as the recruiter's job is to "sort out" the most desirable candidates, the interviewee's job is to "sort out" the most desirable organization. Keeping this recruitment aspect in mind may help you relax a bit better than Belma and to perform your best during the interview.

The secret to every stage of the employment interview is role-taking. As you recall from Chapter 1, role-taking is the ability to put yourself in the shoes of the interviewer and understand his or her primary needs and concerns. Once these needs and concerns are understood, the interviewee highlights aspects of experience and education that meet the organization's needs and address the interviewer's concerns. Throughout this chapter we emphasize the importance of research to understand the organization's needs. Knowing the organization allows a candidate to adapt the resume, the cover letter, and responses in the interview to the specific organization. Audience-centered candidates create specific messages for specific organizations. They are more likely to get job offers than are candidates that run the same routine for every organization to which they apply. Remember the importance of role-taking and audience adaptation as you read this chapter.

The Pre-Interview Stage

In the **pre-interview stage** job candidates must *secure* an interview. This involves research, formulating a resume, and writing a cover letter. Rushing through these stages will prevent you from obtaining an interview. Although they are sometimes tedious, appropriate research and a top-notch resume and cover letter mean the difference between being noticed and unemployment or underemployment. Success depends on taking pre-interview preparation seriously.

Research

One of the most frequent questions college students ask as they look toward graduation is: "Where do I find a job?" Often, people hear about position openings through word of mouth. But what happens if you don't have contacts in your field or feel sheepish about "blowing your own horn?" There are some obvious starting places for any job search, including such old stand-bys as classified advertisements in a local newspaper. But there is a wealth of other resources available to most college students. The career center at your university is an excellent starting point for finding field-specific job openings. In addition, one can find a variety of multipurpose job search resources on the Internet (see Figure 2.1).

FIGURE 2.1   Doing Job Research On The Internet

General Employment Sources	Types of Information Offered
• Adam's JobBank Online	Information on job search skills as well as job listings
• America's Job Bank	Service of the U.S. Department of Labor and state employment agencies
• BridgePath	Free job and internship announcements to students via e-mail
• Career Magazine	Information about upcoming job fairs, articles related to job searches, career links, and recruiter information
• Career Mosaic	Job listings, employer profiles, career fairs, networking opportunities, and tips about resume writing and interviewing
• Career Net	A warehouse of links to job posting sites, employers, businesses, and other sites related to job searches
• Chronicle of Higher Education	Job listings inside and outside of academe including teaching, administrative, and professional positions
• College Grad Job Hunter	Useful job-search articles and job listings
• Cyber Fairs	Calendar advertising upcoming job fairs
• HelpWanted.com	Searchable database for job listings
• JobBank USA	Offers Job MetaSearch, which allows you to search for jobs in a number of employment databases
• JobWeb	Maintained by the National Association of Colleges and Employers; boasts Catapult as its main job search feature
• The Monster Board	Offers numerous job-search resources for all levels of job seekers
• Online Career Center	Allows job seekers to do keyword searches in its job-listing database
• On-Trac Employment Resource	Provides virtually comprehensive listings of WWW employment resources

Enter the name of any of the sources in Figure 2.1 into a search engine and conduct job research from the comfort of the nearest computer terminal. Keep the following advice in mind when doing an Internet job search. If possible, contact the source by telephone once you have retrieved information from the Internet to ensure that the information is up-to-date and reliable. Second, save time by finding a focus and sticking to it. Avoid getting sidetracked by attractive options that you are not yet qualified to fill. Once you have found positions for which you are qualified, it is important to learn more about the specific organization.

Investigating the prospective organization provides a number of advantages for job seekers. First, it allows you to tailor your resume and cover letter specifically to the position for which you are applying. As we have mentioned, information that is adapted to the specific organization makes you stand out from other candidates who submit generic cover letters and resumes. Researching the company also helps you decide if the organization and its culture match your career goals. Finally, research provides a base of knowledge from which questions can be asked and to which information can be added. In the end, such preparation communicates interest and enthusiasm that impresses most employers.

There are a number of resources you may use to help you find information about a specific organization. Consult company profiles in the College Placement Council's (CPC) *Job Choices, Standard and Poor's Register, Dun and Bradstreet Million Dollar Directory,* and *Moody's Directories.* Visit or call the Chamber of Commerce where the company is headquartered. You may also call the company directly and talk with someone in public relations and/or human relations. If appropriate, inquire with trade associations about the organization. Finally, many organizations and agencies have Web pages on the Internet (refer to Chapter 7 for specific methods of research on the Internet).

When researching an organization, the goal is to obtain basic information concerning the services/products offered, competitors, age and size, growth pattern, reputation, divisions and subsidiaries, location(s), sales/assets/earnings, and new products or projects. This information will help you answer such common interview questions as: "What do you know about us?" or "How do you feel about our company?" Figure 2.2 provides a form that you may adapt to compile information about the company. When you find a company with a suitable position that matches your goals, interests, and qualifications, you should proceed to apply for the job.

Most job ads request that an applicant submit a resume and cover letter (also called a "letter of application"). You should prepare your application materials with great care. It is widely agreed that a well-written resume and cover letter can open the door for a job candidate as certainly as a badly written resume and cover letter will close that door.[3] Resumes provide the reader with an understanding of your work experiences and abilities at a glance. Often, candidates are "judged"—selected or rejected for a job—in thirty seconds or less, based on their resume. A resume is often read to "weed out" clearly unqualified candidates. This means that resume readers may search for reasons to take you out of the running. Thus, the resume should be flawless and carefully written to highlight your assets

FIGURE 2.2   Sample Form for Compiling Information When Researching an Organization

Prospective Job Title: _____

Contact Person: _____

Contact Person's Title: _____

Company: _____

Address: _____

Telephone: _____

Research Source: _____

Size/Age of the Company: _____

Location(s): _____

Services/Products: _____

Growth Pattern: _____

Divisions/Subsidiaries: _____

Sales/Assets/Earnings: _____

New Products/Projects: _____

Reputation: _____

Compensation/Benefit Policies: _____

My Questions about the Company: _____

_____

_____

_____

_____

and help you stay in the "potential" pile. Successful candidates view their resumes as extensions of themselves; they are conscious of its construction and content, and ensure that both the resume and cover letter project an accurate and favorable image. Although there are few hard and fast rules about writing resumes and cover letters, we can provide the following suggestions.

The Resume

A **resume** is a one-page (usually) description of your skills, education, and work experience. The biggest mistake most people make when preparing their resume is to borrow a friend's resume, an instructor's model, or a sample from a computer program or a placement office, then change the information on the form by inserting their own details. The problem with this all-too-typical approach is that the categories on the model resume do not suit the individual's experiences, skills, or abilities. Generic resumes usually end up in the "weed out" pile. The best advice we can offer to those who are tempted to copy another form is: Don't do it! Formulaic resumes do not fulfill the key criterion of a resume: demonstrating your unique assets! Rather than copying another's resume, a candidate should begin with a blank sheet of paper and consider the three parts of a resume: headings, leads, and descriptions. Although the specific information each individual brings to his or her resume will vary, there are some general guidelines one should follow for each of the three parts.

Headings.   The **heading** is the category under which specific information is classified. Headings are the flags that signal individual areas of accomplishment. As such, the headings on your resume should be different from headings on your friend's resume. Typical headings for graduating seniors include: "Career Objective," "Education," "Work Experience," "Honors and Awards," "Computer Skills," "Language Abilities," "Professional Memberships or Accreditations," and "Leadership Activities."

Headings should be concisely phrased and highlighted with boldfacing and/ or capital letters, so they are the first place an employer's eyes are drawn. You would be surprised at how many resumes include categories that do not fit the individual. For example, creating an entire category called "Honors and Awards" to cover one award from high school only draws attention to one's weakness. On the other hand, the candidate who has language abilities or computer skills should create headings that draw attention to these desirable traits.

In what order should headings be listed? The candidate's name is the first heading on the resume. Your name should be at the top of the resume, either centered or left justified. It should "stand out" from the address and phone numbers listed after your name. The next heading depends on your abilities and experiences. If you have a clear "Career Objective" that is concisely phrased and fits the job, this should follow your name. If you do not know your objective, however, omit it rather than include something vague. Thus, "An internship in local news programming" may be an objective that is specific and tailored to the position—hence worth including, but "An entry level job leading to advancement" is vague and unpersuasive. Leave it off if it doesn't advance your case for employment.

If you are applying for a job in sales and have worked in retail sales for a number of years, you may consider a heading such as "Sales Experience," and make that the first heading after your name. If, on the other hand, you do not have much work experience, you may want to begin with "Education," demonstrating that you have completed a relevant degree.

Although the specific headings depend on your experiences and abilities, there are some headings that should not appear on a professional resume. For instance, you should avoid including personal information such as race, gender, age, date of birth, health, height, weight, marital status, number and ages of children, and religious affiliation. It's unlawful for an employer to base a decision on personal information, and including it on a resume gives the prospective employer more information than needed. Any information that is not directly related to your qualifications for the job should be omitted. Finally, salary information should be omitted. If an application requires you to insert "salary," you should write "negotiable." Stating a salary range could put you out of the running by making you appear "unaware" of market realities or inflexible in your requirements. As a general rule, omit information that is not strictly job-related because it may be used to "weed you out" of the candidate pool.

Leads. The next category of information on a resume is the lead. **Leads** consist of the first information on each new line under the heading and should include the most important information for any individual entry. For example, under the heading "Education," it is generally more important to lead with your degree than with the institution from which you received the degree. The institution is usually less important than the fact and focus of the degree. For example, an ineffective lead appears below:

Education

University of Montana, Missoula, Montana, May 1999. Bachelor of Business Administration, emphasis in Marketing.

This entry does little to draw attention to the unique traits and assets of the individual. Instead of focusing on the person, this entry focuses on the school. A better lead should draw attention to the individual's assets:

Education

Bachelor of Business Administration, emphasis in **Marketing.** Minor in **Computer Information Systems.** University of Montana, Missoula, Montana, May 1999.

Leads should include the most revealing information about you. For headings such as "Related Work Experience," lead with the title of the position you held rather than the name of the company (which does not emphasize your role). For instance, a poor lead may look like this:

Work Experience

City of Tacoma, Chamber of Commerce, Summer Intern in Public Relations Department. Summer 1998.

Rather than emphasizing the individual, this lead focuses on the city. There is nothing to draw one's attention to the information presented. A better lead, using the same information appears below:

Work Experience

Intern in Public Relations, Chamber of Commerce, Tacoma, Washington. Summer 1998.

Many resume models lead with the date, emphasizing the inclusive dates of employment rather than what the individual did during that time. This approach should be used only in those instances when the duration of employment is the most important aspect of the job, a very rare situation. To emphasize leads appropriately, use boldface or underlines. Finally, avoid using abbreviations. Don't write B.B.A. and force the reader to stop and decipher what it may mean. Tell the reader what it means to begin with.

Descriptions.   **Descriptions** include all the information that follows the lead. Read the following entry taken from a resume:

> Yellowstone Natural Adventures. West Yellowstone, MT. Summers 1997–1999. Worked as a summer guide for white-water rafting trips in Yellowstone National Park. Duties included interacting with tourists, instructing them in proper safety guidelines and equipment use, giving presentations about the park, and overseeing proper campsite set up and breakdown.

Although this entry includes some interesting information, much of it is lost in the description because the emphasis is on the "duties performed" rather than on what the individual's experience brings to future work environments. Now, read another description of the same job and note the differences:

> *Instructor/Leader,* Yellowstone Natural Adventures, West Yellowstone, Montana. Served as a white-water guide for five extended trips each summer into Yellowstone National Park area. Instructed 15–20 participants on each trip in safety guidelines and proper use of marine and flotation equipment. Supervised three assistants to ensure that proper procedures were carried out in all areas of camping, rafting, and managing natural resources. Recognized by supervisors as outstanding with "Summer Employee of the Year" Award in both 1998 and 1999. Summers 1997–1999.

What is the difference between these two entries? Detail and action. The best descriptions use **action words** and specific **quantification** (when possible) to delineate what you did in the position. To make it more active, change the ending of a word with "ion" or "ing" to an "ed." The emphasis then shifts from the act to the individual who performs the act (that's you). A common description that is not very dynamic may read: "duties included supervision of hourly and part-time employees." An improved description says: "supervised five employees." Whenever possible, omit phrases that promote listing—"duties were" or "responsibilities included"—and find active verbs that better describe what you did. Figure 2.3 provides a list of useful action words to describe your transferable skills and experiences.

FIGURE 2.3 Action Words

accelerated	consolidated	established	launched	prioritized	streamlined
accomplished	contained	evaluated	led	processed	summarized
achieved	contributed	expanded	licensed	provided	supervised
administered	controlled	fabricated	logged	reconciled	supplied
advanced	converted	filed	maintained	recorded	supported
analyzed	coordinated	financed	managed	rehabilitated	surveyed
approved	corrected	finished	marketed	reinforced	systemized
arranged	corresponded	formulated	mediated	related	tallied
assigned	counseled	generated	moderated	relayed	taught
assisted	credited	guided	modified	reorganized	tested
authored	critiqued	headed	negotiated	reported	trained
billed	debated	hired	nominated	researched	transferred
budgeted	decided	increased	obtained	restored	translated
calculated	delegated	identified	opened	revised	transported
catalogued	delivered	implemented	organized	revitalized	trimmed
chaired	demonstrated	improved	originated	routed	tutored
changed	designed	informed	overhauled	saved	typed
classified	dispatched	initiated	participated	scheduled	upgraded
closed	displayed	inspected	performed	screened	utilized
collected	documented	instituted	persuaded	secured	validated
communicated	earned	integrated	pinpointed	selected	verified
completed	educated	inventoried	planned	serviced	won
conceived	encouraged	investigated	prescribed	simplified	worked
conducted	enlisted	issued	presented	solidified	wrote

Good descriptions focus on transferable skills rather than merely relating job duties in laundry-list fashion. Your descriptions should demonstrate the skills, abilities, and experiences that employers seek. Consider that employers seek individuals who are effective communicators, self-motivated and trustworthy employees, who can complete projects effectively and work well with others. Your descriptions should highlight the skills employers find important and that are transferable. Figure 2.4 includes a summary of "Do" and "Don't" advice for constructing resumes. Once you have constructed and typed your resume, you need to produce a final copy for the printing process.

Resume Format.   Reread the resume several times and be sure to ask others to provide feedback and to proofread the resume. Also make sure that your headings are consistently formatted, that the leads emphasize you rather than the institution or the date, and that the descriptions are accurate and reflect your skills and abilities. Phrasings should be consistent and parallel, and you should

FIGURE 2.4   Resume writing tips

Your resume could open the door to a great job. However, your resume could also prevent that door from ever opening. It is a fact that in 30 seconds or less, you are "judged"—selected or rejected for a job—based on your resume. You should view your resume as an extension of yourself. You should be conscious of its construction and content, ensuring that it projects an accurate and favorable image of yourself.

There are few hard and fast rules for resume writing, but here are some suggestions for writing them.

DO...	DON'T...
Include information that is relevant to your experiences and abilities. • Name (no need for middle) • Address and phone numbers • Job objective (optional) • Education: degree, date, school, GPA optional (and only if over 3.0) • Employment history: job title, company, location, dates, responsibilities • Professional affiliations • Honors and activities • Computer/language skills	Include irrelevant information... • "Resume" or other document title • Availability • Personal information (age, birth date, marital status, height, pictures, religion, health, etc.) • Salary desired • References listed
Always use action verbs to describe what you did. • Example: "Supervision" becomes "Supervised" • Emphasize abilities and experiences • Show how they are relevant and/or transferable	Offer a simple laundry list of duties or responsibilities.
Use consistency in writing structure and style.	Be inconsistent in structure or style.
Write words out in full.	Use contractions.
Make the document visually appealing. • Be sure it is aesthetically balanced. • Use white space skillfully	Be concerned only with getting the information somewhere on the document.
Individualize your resume. • Consciously think about the form and content • Be aware of headings and leads and their placement • Consider what is most important and then prioritize and emphasize it	Copy a resume format from someone else or a generic format.
Be specific about identifying and clarifying projects, successes, supervising experiences.	Offer only vague descriptions of jobs or activities.
Have a flawless resume.	Make typographical errors or "correct" errors manually.
Use professional-looking, high quality paper. • At least 25% cotton. • Use neutral, classy resume paper (off white, ivory, etc.)	Use ordinary typing paper or use colored, flashy paper to be "different" and stand out.

avoid using any abbreviations. Finally, try to keep your resume to one page, because a brief scan doesn't allow the reader to get past the first page anyway.

Although it may be tempting to print your resume on brightly colored paper to help it stand out from the others, remember that many readers dismiss resumes that are on different paper (such as fluorescent orange, neon blue) or have fancy borders because they reflect an individual who is unprofessional or inexperienced. Select professional-looking, high-quality resume paper that is white, off-white, light beige, ivory, or light blue. Paper should have at least a 25 percent cotton fiber content. Your resume should be printed on an easy-to-read laser printer and copied by a professional. Employers want to hire people who understand the importance of professionalism.[4] Figure 2.5 includes two sample resumes, one of which is good, the other poor. Examine these resumes for their strengths and weaknesses.

Scannable Resumes. One final consideration must be addressed before we move on to cover letters. A **scannable resume** is one that an optical scanner can read and retrieve from its database. Many companies request scannable resumes because they save time and allow for easy access to critical information. If a company seeks an applicant with specific qualifications, the computer can analyze the resumes in the database and retrieve those that fulfill the specific qualifications.

Scannable resumes differ from traditional resumes in three ways. First, the scannable resume includes "no frills." That means that you should use simple, basic fonts—for example, Times Roman—and the font should be 12 to 14 point because computers have difficulty reading smaller type. Also, although you may want to boldface headings and leads, avoid using italics, underlining, shading, or special symbols because computer programs have difficulty deciphering these characters.

Second, unlike completing a regular resume, the use of jargon and abbreviations is important in scannable resumes. Computer scanning programs are instructed to search for position-related jargon and skills. Also, resumes should list phone numbers without parentheses for area codes.

Finally, an important difference in scannable resumes is the emphasis on **keywords.** Nouns in the form of keywords, such as "customer service," or "accounts receivable," need to be emphasized more than such action words as "supervised," "scheduled," or "ordered" used on a regular resume. With scannable resumes, computers search the database for keywords, not verbs, in order to identify which candidate has the required background and experience. Keywords can be utilized in two ways. First, develop a section heading "Keyword Summary" immediately following your contact data. Include 15–20 key words that are related to your background and experience. Second, add keywords to the descriptions of your scannable resume. Finally, include keywords in the cover letter, since this is also scanned along with the resume. Use synonyms for keywords that are repeated frequently.

If you are unsure about appropriate keywords in your field, try reading other job listings for similar positions and include the nouns listed in these ads.

Allison Lucas
30682 Elmtree Lane
Phillipsburg, PA 16832
(814) 785–0964

Retail Experience

Sales Associate.   Macy's Apparel, Pittsburgh, Pennsylvania. August 1996–Present.

- Work 20+ hours a week while going to school full time.
- Assist customers with clothing purchases, make recommendations, and provide creative options in women's and children's clothing departments.
- Design and build displays for new items every week. Seek feedback and institute suggestions for displays.
- Manage inventory by tabulating stock and inventory control sheets in the two largest departments in the store.
- Train part-time workers during the season rush. Last year was promoted to train all incoming sales associates in a two-hour training session, "Assisting customers with selections and purchases."
- Commended by supervisor for "superior levels of customer service" in recent performance assessment.

Grocery Supervisor.   Buttrey Food & Drug, Phillipsburg, Pennsylvania. December 1994–July 1996.

- Supervised stock clerks in the produce department. Oversaw 7 part-time employees and 1 full-time worker.
- Scheduled work assignments for 8 people.
- Ordered and received produce, oversaw pricing of produce items, and ensured products were high quality. Produce orders involved a $5,000 weekly budget.
- Designed and implemented displays of items. Christmas display of "produce stocking" won "spirit of Christmas" award for the city in 1994.

FIGURE 2.5   Sample Resumes

Cashier.   Buttrey Food & Drug, Phillipsburg, Pennsylvania. September 1993–December 1994.

- Engaged in positive customer relations with 100 customers per day.
- Balanced a cashier drawer of $3000+/daily.

Stocking Clerk.   Buttrey Food & Drug, Phillipsburg, Pennsylvania. August 1992–August 1993.

- Stocked shelves and inventory in frozen foods.
- Cited by management for efficiency.
- Asked to apply for promotion as cashier.

Education

Bachelor of Business Administration. Major in **Marketing.** University of Pittsburgh. December 1999.

- 3.6 Grade Point Averge.
- Dean's List, College of Business: Fall 1997, Spring 1998, Fall 1998, Spring 1999.

FIGURE 2.5   Continued

ALLISON LUCAS
30682 ELMTREE LANE
PHILLIPSBURGH, PA 16832
(814) 785-0964

OBJECTIVE:

To find an entry-level marketing position leading to sales or marketing management.

EDUCATION:

December, 1999. University of Pittsburgh, Pittsburgh, Pennsylvania.
B.B.A. Major in <u>Marketing</u>
<u>HONORS:</u> Member of Dean's List, College of Business
Fall 1997, Spring 1998, Fall 1998, Spring 1999
3.6 GPA in major; 3.25 Cumulative GPA

EXPERIENCE:

Aug. 1996–Present. MACY'S APPAREL, Pittsburgh, Pennsylvania.
Sales Associate.
Learning the basic skills of salesmanship. Responsible for assisting customers, displays, and inventory control. Commended by supervisors for superior levels of customer service.

Dec. 1994–July 1996. BUTTREY FOOD & DRUG, Phillipsburg, Pennsylvania.
Grocery Supervisor.
Received management training in the areas of supervision, scheduling of work assignments, ordering stock, receiving merchandise, pricing, displays, bookkeeping, and customer relations. Reason for leaving: needed to reduce working hours to pursue a bachelor's degree to supplement work experience.

Sept. 1993–Dec.1994. BUTTREY FOOD & DRUG. Phillipsburg, Pennsylvania.
Cashier/Stocking Clerk.
Learned the basics of stocking, ordering, and merchandising. Received cashier training and developed customer service

FIGURE 2.5   Continued

skills. Reason for leaving: promoted to supervisor in produce department.

Aug. 1992–Aug.1993. BUTTREY FOOD & DRUG. Phillipsburg, Pennsylvania. Stocking Clerk.

Responsible for stocking, inventory control, and display in the frozen food department. Cited by management for efficiency. Reason for leaving: promotion to cashier clerk.

REFERENCES:

Confidential references available through Career Center, Box 8108, University of Pittsburgh, Pittsburgh, PA, 17852, or by request.

FIGURE 2.5   Continued

Consult trade journals or professional associations in your own and related fields(s) to identify the key terms and phrases. Finally, human resources representatives are well-versed in the keywords companies are searching for. Figure 2.6 presents a sample of a scannable resume.

The Cover Letter

Once your resume is complete, you should compose your cover letter. A **cover letter** should be viewed as your chance to explain and highlight how your abilities, skills, and experiences listed on your resume fit the job requirements. Each cover letter should be adapted to the specific job ad for which you are applying. An effective cover letter convinces the reader that you deserve a "second look" by being granted an interview. Writing a persuasive cover letter involves identifying the needs of the potential employer (role-taking) and then selecting relevant aspects of your resume to demonstrate that you can fulfill those needs. Your cover letter should include three parts: an introduction, a body, and a conclusion.

The introduction of your cover letter should begin with a concise statement of the position for which you are applying. You might also state your immediate job objectives or your educational experience, and then preview the traits you have that match the job requirements. The goal of the introduction is to attract attention and encourage the employer to continue reading.

The body of the letter should include two to three paragraphs. The first paragraph should show employers that you have the background, the training, and the qualifications they need. Let employers know that you want to work for their organization and why. Point out how your key assets are relevant to the position for which you want to be considered. Keep in mind that the employer's needs should be emphasized, not your wants. In the second paragraph, stress your relevant accomplishments. Don't repeat what is on the resume word for word, but show specific examples from your background/education or work experience that demonstrate your ability to meet the requirements in the ad. Use the third paragraph to detail your interests and how they match the organization's needs. Again, emphasize how you can be an asset to the organization rather than how much you would like to work for them. Read the following excerpts from the body of a cover letter for a position in sales. Which is best?

Letter 1: As you can see by my resume, I have significant sales experience.

Letter 2: For the last three years I have acquired significant sales experience working at Lamar's Apparel in Pocatello, Idaho.

Letter 3: Your first job requirement emphasizes the need for sales experience. As my resume indicates, I have spent the last three years acquiring significant sales experience at Lamar's Apparel. My position has taught me the basics of sales. I assist customers, display merchandise, and oversee inventory control. In the past six months I have been promoted twice because of my sales abilities. And I recently attended a weekend Sales

Allison Lucas
30682 Elmtree Lane
Phillipsburg, PA 16832
(814) 785-0964

KEYWORDS

Customer Service. Supervisor. Trainer. Retail Sales. Sales Representative. Display designer. Inventory control. Accounts receivable. Dependable. Self-motivated.

CAREER OBJECTIVE

Seeking challenging position in sales or marketing management. 5 years' experience in retail sales. Management and supervisory experience. Consistently met or exceeded all job expectations. Given added responsibility of training all new seasonal hires. Dependable, self-motivated, and responsible.

EDUCATION

BACHELOR OF BUSINESS ADMINISTRATION, MAJOR IN MARKETING. University of Pittsburgh, Pennsylvania, Spring 1999. Dean's List Fall 1997 on. 3.6 Grade Point Average.

QUALIFICATIONS SUMMARY

JOB PERFORMANCE:

- Consistently met or exceeded retails sales quotas.
- Balanced variety of tasks including customer relations, product display, and inventory control.
- Responsible for $3000+ daily
- Commended by supervisor for "superior levels of customer service" in recent performance assessment.

(Continued)

FIGURE 2.6 Sample of a Scannable Resume

TRAINER/SUPERVISOR:
- Trained part-time/seasonal workers in retail sales techniques.
- Supervised 8 employees at every level including schedules, ordering, displays, and employee relations.

MOTIVATION:
- Worked 20+ hours a week to put self through school. Maintained high GPA and excellent work references.
- Promoted in every organization because of consistent track record and strong work ethic.

WORK HISTORY

MACY'S APPAREL, PITTSBURGH, PENNSYLVANIA
- Sales Associate-Retail Sales. Responsibilities include assisting customers, designing and building clothes displays, inventory control, balancing ledgers. 1996–present.

BUTTREY FOOD & DRUG, PHILLIPSBURG, PENNSYLVANIA. August 1992–August 1993.
- Began as stocking clerk, promoted to cashier, then supervisor of the produce department.
- Managed and trained 8 employees. Responsible for inventory, purchasing, and balancing $5,000 weekly budget.

FIGURE 2.6   Continued

Retreat to learn advanced sales techniques. I have already begun to implement some of these in my current job. As you can see, I have significant experience to offer your firm.

Sample three is best because it specifies why the applicant fulfills the job requirements. The reader is able to understand "how" the requirement is met by this applicant, and by being specific, the writer demonstrates that he has significant sales experience

The final section of a cover letter is the close. You should articulate that you would like an interview. Be assertive, but do not suggest that you will call to set up an interview. Convey the impression that you know the employer must do the inviting. Close the letter appropriately—"Sincerely" or "Yours Truly" are appropriate. Include your signature, your typed name, and a current address, phone number, and e-mail address where you can be reached. The employer who must search for contact information may decide not to bother. Also, since resumes and cover letters may get separated, it's important that your contact information is included on both. Examine the sample cover letter in Figure 2.7.

As with your resume, your cover letter should be flawless. Proofread it several times and be sure that others read it as well. Your cover letter should be on the same paper as your resume and mailed in an 8 × 12 envelope so that it isn't folded. Folded resumes and cover letters can be difficult to read and stack. The packet should also include additional information that the job ad requests such as transcripts, portfolios, or writing samples.

The Interview Stage

Ideally, your resume and cover letter will lead to a phone call requesting an **interview.** Typically, candidates are not hired until they have at least one in-house interview—and usually several. In-house interviews can be nerve-wracking if you are new to the job-seeking experience. Knowing that there are certain things you can expect, however, may make the process less daunting. A recent survey of over 2,000 organizations revealed some interesting and consistent patterns in the ways that interviews are arranged. Most organizations initiate contact with a candidate by telephone, and some follow the phone call with a letter that confirms the date, time, and arrangements made during the phone call. Surprisingly, more than one-third of the organizations brought between five and ten candidates to their company for each position. This differs markedly from the common belief that only the top two or three candidates are interviewed. In addition, more than 70 percent of the companies surveyed arrange and pay for the travel, meals, and hotel accommodations for the candidate. Most in-house interviews are conducted by "teams" of interviewers to ensure that the candidate meets a wide spectrum of employees, from potential colleagues to supervisors. Almost all interviews also include an informational meeting with someone in human resources.[5]

November 1, 1999

Mr. James Dylan
Personnel Manager
Moondance Sales
26 Wall Street
Chicago, IL 60611

Dear Mr. Dylan:

This letter is my application for the sales associate position advertised in the October 30 edition of the *Wall Street Journal.* I am currently a sales associate at Macy's, where I work part-time while I finish my degree, a Bachelor of Business Administration with a major in marketing. I will graduate with honors in December, 1999. My career goal is to have a sales position that will lead to opportunities in training and management. My experience and enthusiasm make me an excellent candidate for your position.

Your job requires someone with sales experience. As you can tell by the enclosed resume, I have been working as a sales associate for three years. During that time, I have had significant experience dealing with all types of customers—from very satisfied ones to very frustrated ones—and have been asked to help in selecting entire wardrobes for some people. My experiences in sales have taught me the importance of dealing with each customer on his/her own terms—and to avoid making blanket assumptions. My personal touch with customers has been successful. I was recently recognized by the store's manager as "superior in customer service." My approach to sales will be an asset to Moondance Sales, a company known for its one-on-one sales style.

In addition to being experienced in sales, I am highly motivated—your second job qualification. I began as a stock clerk in a local grocery store chain, and learned the job so thoroughly that I was asked if I'd like to

FIGURE 2.7 Sample Cover Letter

expand my skills to be cashier. Once I learned that job, I became supervisor of a whole department in the store. At each step, I enjoyed my job and worked to do it well and with great enthusiasm. My interests paid off and my motivation became clear as I worked my way up in that organization to a managerial position.

In sum, I possess the traits that you require in a sales associate and believe that my experiences make me an excellent candidate for your position. I would be an asset to Moondance Sales because of my experience in the same sales techniques that Moondance is known for, and because I have the initiative and the drive to be an effective sales associate.

As you can see on the enclosed resume, I have a number of other credentials that would be helpful to Moondance. I am genuinely interested in your company, as your creative and innovative approach to sales has always been a model that I have studied in developing my sales techniques. I appreciate your consideration for the position and hope to hear from you soon. Please contact me at (814) 785–0964 to arrange an interview. I look forward to hearing from you.

Sincerely,

Allison Lucas

Allison Lucas
30682 Elmtree Lane
Phillipsburg, PA 16832
(814) 785-0964

FIGURE 2.7   Continued

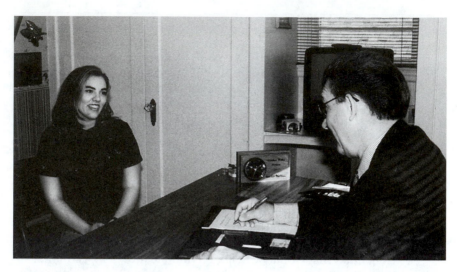

Getting a job requires effective verbal and nonverbal communication. Credit: Caryn Elliot.

How will you distinguish yourself from as many as ten other candidates for a position? Candidates must make a positive, lasting impression that communicates confidence, competence, and professionalism. Be aware that both your actions and your words help to create that all-important impression.

Presenting Yourself in an Employment Interview: Nonverbal Dimensions

Whether or not it is fair, you will be judged by how you present yourself in an interview.[6] Your **nonverbal communication** is an important part of the interview process. This section discusses nonverbal self-presentation skills, including dress and body cues.

The interview is not the time to make a personal statement about the way you dress. Interviewees should respect and adapt to the interviewer's expectations. Although professional dress and appropriate style may vary slightly depending on the job, work environment, and geographical region, there are several commonalties to remember.

For men, a conservative business suit is almost always the rule. A well-tailored suit will go a long way in helping you present yourself professionally and confidently. The additional expense invested in a quality suit will pay tremendous dividends in making a positive first impression and will also make you feel good, enhancing confidence. Acceptable colors continue to be darker shades, including grays, navy blue, and black. Pattern designs may be worn only if they are subtle. In warmer climates, lighter shades of blue, gray, and even tan may be acceptable. A plain white or off-white shirt is never a bad choice. Other soft colors or designs may be acceptable if they look subtle and conservative rather than flashy. The same goes for neckties; think in terms of conservative, subtle patterns.

For women, a conservative business suit is the best way to present a professional image. Studies show that women have a wider range of colors to select from when considering "professional dress." Although grays and blues are standard, women can often wear bright colors (red, bright blues, green) without appearing unprofessional. Women should wear blouses that are not too revealing nor too frilly. Stockings should be flesh-toned. Finally, shoes should be sensible heels that are polished if not new.

Both men and women should be well groomed. Make sure your clothes are ironed and clean, hair trimmed and styled, and fingernails groomed. Avoid flashy and excessive jewelry and cologne or perfume that is too strong. In sum, moderation is almost always the key for the professional interview. You want to appear confident, professional, conscientious, and reliable.

Aside from your dress, nonverbal body cues can convey a positive or negative image. One of the first nonverbal traits that executives seek in prospective employees is punctuality. Candidates who do not arrive for the interview on time—and preferably five minutes early—rarely get a job offer. Greet office workers and interviewers with a firm handshake and direct eye contact. Get pen and paper out when you sit down and write down the name of the person interviewing you; have your interview questions within reach, ready to ask when given the opportunity. In addition, employers cited nonverbal qualities such as friendliness, appropriate eye contact, enthusiasm, and confidence as key to their extending a job offer to interviewees.[7] Now that you've made it this far, what should you say in an interview?

Presenting Yourself in an Employment Interview: Verbal Dimensions

Although employers do consider nonverbal behaviors, studies indicate that the most important factor in receiving a second interview or the job offer involves the candidate's **answers** to questions.[8] This section will discuss typical questions and strategies for answering those questions.

The first thing to do is prepare for common interview questions. Figure 2.8 lists common questions interviewers like to ask.

Answering questions is easier if you follow a four-step procedure: (1) state your answer briefly, (2) explain your statement with an additional two to three sentences, (3) provide some concrete example or testimony to support your claim, and (4) reconnect your answer to the original question. To see this four-step process in action, consider the follow excerpt:

INTERVIEWER: How does your previous experience relate to this position?

CANDIDATE: I just completed an internship at a local television station that required skills similar to this position. As a production assistant, I worked

FIGURE 2.8   Typical Interview Questions

1. Why don't you tell me about yourself?
2. What are your career goals? Where would you like to be in ten years?
3. Why did you decide to go into this field?
4. Why do you feel that you will be successful in this position?
5. What supervisory or leadership roles have you had?
6. How do you spend your spare time?
7. Which course did you like the best and why? the least and why?
8. Why are your grades low?
9. How does your previous experience relate to this position?
10. Why are you looking for this type of position—and why with us?
11. What are your strengths?
12. What are your weaknesses?
13. What will your references say about you?
14. What sort of pay do you expect to receive?
15. Why should I hire you?

closely with the producer to prepare every 6:00 news broadcast. Although I started out doing clerical work, in a few weeks I was making decisions about who should be interviewed, what questions should be included, and which news to prioritize. My experiences in the internship have taught me to be an effective communicator, and I have developed excellent oral and written communication skills. I learned to carry out and complete daily and monthly projects. And my position taught me to make good decisions under pressure. Good communication skills, project development, and experience with making tough decisions are precisely the traits required for this position.

This candidate followed the four-step procedure for answering an interview question. And although it is difficult for individuals to speak bluntly about themselves, it is precisely this sort of response that distinguishes the strongest candidates from the others.

Federal and state laws clearly regulate the kinds of questions that a person can and cannot ask during an employment interview. Although there are no limits on the kinds of information an interviewee can present, providing direct answers to illegal questions can create a problem for the candidate. See the Ethics Brief in this section for more information about illegal interview questions and how to respond to them.

Now that you know about questions and answers, we can talk about proved techniques for answering questions. Specifically, successful candidates make reference to the company, support their claims, actively participate in the process, exhibit natural but enthusiastic delivery, and ask good questions.[9] Each of these tips represents a way to adapt to the interviewer's expectations.

Ethics Brief

Since the passage of the civil rights act of 1964, employment screening interviews have been subject to federal and state equal opportunity employment laws. These laws are based on the belief that all persons—regardless of race, gender, national origin, religion, age, or marital status—should be able to compete equally for a job. Employers may refuse to hire candidates who are not qualified, but they may not base a hiring decision on factors other than skills, experience, and education. These are the only legal factors for selecting employees.

Although laws differ from state to state, it is illegal for employers to ask questions in the following areas: national origin/birthplace, age, race or ethnic background, religious affiliation, marital status, general physical condition, or voluntary affiliations such as clubs, fraternities, or sororities. Scrupulous interviewers avoid these areas and address questions directly to job qualifications.

What should a job candidate do if asked an illegal interview question? Unfortunately, there is no easy answer. Some people ask illegal interview questions out of malice. If you believe the question is malicious and you have decided that you wouldn't want to work for the employer, then simply refusing to answer the question is the best solution. This effectively ends the interview, which is what you wanted anyway. More often, interviewers ask illegal questions out of ignorance, which poses a problem for the interviewee. Refusing to answer the question will embarrass the interviewer and effectively end the interview. Answering the question puts the interviewee at risk, as the interviewer may use the information to discriminate against the candidate.

Fredric M. Jablin and Craig D. Tengler have developed a creative way to respond to illegal questions that keeps the interview and the chances of employment with the interviewer's organization alive.* Rather than answering or refusing to answer the question, Jablin and Tengler suggest answering the concern behind the question rather than the question itself. According to Jablin and Tengler, most illegal inquiries are related to gender and specifically discriminate against women. Most such questions ask women about their marital or family plans, apparently trying to screen out candidates who might be too dedicated to their families to manage career responsibilities. Such questions as, "Do you have plans for having children?" or "What happens if your husband gets transferred or needs to relocate?" are common. These questions clearly express the concern that the woman's family will come before her career. Creative responses address this concern, rather than directly answering the question: "I don't know at present. I plan on a career and believe my career will be successful with or without a family," or "My husband's career will not interfere with my career."† Or, when asked about working for someone younger than you, a candidate could respond, "My previous employer will tell you that I get along well with my coworkers and am able to subordinate my interests to the larger goals of the team."

Addressing the concern behind the question rather than the question itself is an ethical and personally advantageous way to manage the illegal interview question. Prepare yourself for an interview by thinking about answers to questions in each of the illegal areas. Be able to provide an answer that addresses the concern without destroying the interview. The job opening you save may be your own.

*Jablin, F. M., and C. D. Tengler, "Facing Discrimination in On-Campus Interviews." *Journal of College Placement,* Winter 1982, 58–61.

†Ibid.

Successful Candidates Refer to the Organization. Interviewees who make specific references to the company make a better impression than candidates who speak in vague and general terms about their goals or the company's objectives. For example, one study found that unsuccessful candidates admitted that they didn't know what they wanted to do for their careers and were "unable to find anything out" about the organization. One unsuccessful candidate said, "I really don't know what I want to do or where I'll be in five years. I thought I could give retail sales a try, though."[10]

Successful candidates, on the other hand, are specific in their career goals. They also make clear their desire to work for the organization. Thus, in a successful interview, a candidate suggested, "I really like how your company blends public relations techniques with marketing approaches in its sales division." Such answers require extensive research about the prospective employer.

Successful Candidates Support Their Claims. Successful candidates support their claims with a variety of personal examples, illustrations, comparisons/contrasts, statistics, and testimonies from colleagues or employers.[11] A successful candidate may state, in response to the question, "What would your references say about you?":

> My references would recommend me because I do quality work. I always give my best in my jobs and don't watch the clock. If a project requires me to put in more time than I'm scheduled for, I will put in the extra hours to ensure that it is done well. I don't want my name associated with things that aren't high quality. My summer employer for the last four years said that I was the best worker he's ever had—full-time or summertime. And I think my work paid off for him; three of the accounts I got last summer are now loyal clientele at his firm. So, I think my references would say that I'm the kind of worker they would be happy to hire.

Aside from following the four-step procedure for answering, this candidate used concrete evidence, testimony, and statistics to support her claims. Compare that use of evidence with an unsuccessful candidate who spoke ambiguously in response to the same question:

> I think that, well, my references would say they liked me. I got along well with the people I work with. I always enjoyed going to work.

If they support their claims at all, unsuccessful candidates use only personal experiences and do not elaborate on their brief answers. By answering with details and specifics, candidates appear more prepared, more experienced, and hence, more desirable to the employer.

Successful Candidates Are Active Participants in the Process. Successful interviewees speak more, elaborate on their answers, and ask follow-up questions. In short, they are active participants in the interview process. At the end of the interview, successful candidates provide summaries of their relevant qualifications and how they relate to the employer's needs.[12] Unsuccessful candidates, in contrast, can be classified as passive participants; they need to be prodded to expand upon their answers, they fail to have a dialogue with the interviewer, and they provide no summary statement at the end of the interview.

Successful Candidates Have Natural But Enthusiastic Delivery.   Unsuccessful candidates speak in monotone, are soft-spoken, and use few gestures. They display nervous habits such as playing with their hair, laughing at inappropriate times, scratching their noses, and avoiding eye contact by staring at the wall, the floor, or the desk. In short, unsuccessful candidates emphasize their nervousness rather than their interest, abilities, and enthusiasm. In sharp contrast, successful candidates speak quickly and use variety in their pitch, volume, and rate. They smile when discussing themselves and gesture naturally. They display good listening skills by looking at the interviewer and nodding when the interviewer is talking.[13] Successful candidates portray an image that is professional, competent, dynamic, and enthusiastic.

Successful Candidates Ask Good Questions.   Most interviews include an opportunity for the candidate to ask questions about the position or the company. Many interviewers believe that the questions a candidate asks are more revealing than their answers to questions. And, although it's hard to list the kinds of questions one should ask, there are some questions that should not be asked. First, never ask a question that is answered in the materials supplied by the employer. To do so indicates that you have not read the information carefully. Rather, refer in advance to the information provided. Also, don't ask about salary or fringe benefits. Such questions communicate that you are more interested in pay than in the position, or in vacation time than in working. Salary discussions should wait until a job offer is made.

Remember that a job interview is an "information exchange," and you should find out as much about the organization as possible to determine if it is a good match with your goals and abilities. The most successful candidates ask questions about training and career expansion programs available at the company, about the kinds of clientele the organization handles, and first-person questions of the interviewer. For example, one question that impressed a recruiter was, "What is the most rewarding thing you have experienced working for this company?" It is imperative that candidates develop several (four to five) questions tailored to specific company goals. Successful candidates also ask questions that place them in the position. Thus, rather than asking, "What are the expectations for this position?" a successful candidate asks, "What expectations do you have for me in my first year in this position?" Good questions communicate that the candidate is thoughtful, prepared, and interested in the organization. Figure 2.9 presents a list of questions that one candidate prepared before an interview. Use the suggestions as a springboard for formulating your own questions.

FIGURE 2.9   Sample Questions to Ask Interviewers

1. Where are people who formerly held the position for which I am applying?
2. Can you tell me about _____[a specific]_____ product line? or about specific clientele?
3. Can you tell me about training programs and opportunities for continued growth sponsored by the company?
4. What are the typical avenues of advancement in the organization?
5. Can you clarify what your expectations of me in this job are?
6. Tell me about evaluation procedures. How often am I evaluated and what form do the evaluations take?
7. What is the thing you enjoy the most about working for the organization?
8. What is the one thing you would change about the company if you were able?
9. Where do you think this organization will be in ten years?
10. What is the atmosphere like in the office in which I will work?

The Post-Interview Stage

The interview may be complete, but the interview process is not over. The first thing you should do after the interview is send a thank-you note to the organization, specifically the person who conducted the interview. About 42 percent of employers view candidates who send thank-you notes more favorably than those who do not send them.[14] In the note, refer to the interview, provide any additional information that was requested in the interview, summarize your qualifications, and reiterate your interest in the position. If you decide you don't want the job, thank the individual and the organization for their time and inform them of your decision. If you are still interested in the job, let them know. Figure 2.10 provides a sample thank-you letter. Don't copy this letter; use it as a guide for an individualized note. The post-interview process includes getting a job offer, salary negotiations, and dealing with rejection.

Getting the Job Offer

Let's assume that the interview goes well and you receive a job offer from the company. It's time to determine if you still want the position and if the offer is desirable. Organizations usually give a candidate five to seven days to consider an offer. Consider the issues that are most critical to you both personally and professionally. If you have researched the company and asked the right questions during the interview, you have a head start on this assessment process. Consider

December 9, 1999

Mr. James Dylan
Personnel Manager
Moondance Sales
26 Wall Street
Chicago, IL 60611

Dear Mr. Dylan:

Thank you for the opportunity to interview with you last Monday, December 8, to discuss the position of sales associate at Moondance Sales. I was pleased to hear you discuss the future of Moondance Sales and its projected growth plan. I also was excited to hear you talk about the innovations your sales teams are developing with its new product line, "Flowers on the Wall." Moondance Sales is a company with which I would like to be associated.

I was especially pleased to learn that I would be able to use my sales experience and my interest and experience with creative design in my position with your company. My current position as sales associate has allowed me to interact with a number of customers and I understand that a good sales associate must tailor the sales approach to the specific needs of the specific customer. The fact that I have been recognized by my superiors as superior in customer service speaks to my ability to be adaptable.

I would also like to mention that since our meeting yesterday, I have been informed that I have been selected as one of two sales associates to attend the national conference in Orlando, Florida. This award typically goes to full-time employees, but my supervisor told me that he wanted to recognize the "significant contribution" I have made as a sales associate. I plan to attend several workshops at the conference that are tailored to developing and promoting new product lines—information that I hope may be used to develop similar products to "Flowers on the Wall."

Again, thank you for considering me for the position. I look forward to hearing from you soon.

Sincerely,

Allison Lucas

Allison Lucas
30682 Elmtree Lane
Phillipsburg, PA 16832
(814) 785-0964

FIGURE 2.10   Sample Thank-You Letter

the company's objectives, activities, professional and personal atmosphere, and location, including cost of living and cultural and recreational opportunities. Also ask yourself if you will be happy in the job itself. Finally, consider opportunities for continued learning and growth within the organization. If there are few opportunities for promotion, will you become bored with the job after a short time? Do your best to picture the "real" expectations of the job, and compare those with your own desires and goals.

Salary Negotiation

Salary negotiations come hand in hand with some job offers. Prepare for negotiation by learning about the industry's standard salaries for your position. You can learn about industry standards for compensation by talking with people in similar positions, consulting classified ads, or consulting sources such as *Business Week's Guide to Careers, CPC Salary Survey,* and *The Wall Street Journal's Business Employment Weekly.*

Consider also the benefits the position offers, including health coverage, expense accounts, profit sharing/stock plans, bonuses, retirement funds, life insurance, and vacation time. Such benefits can distinguish great jobs from ordinary ones.

The organization usually opens negotiation with a written offer that the candidate can accept or reject. Requests for more than the original offer should be based on the candidate's advanced education or skills, or industry standards. Both sides usually trade offers until a mutually satisfactory figure is reached. A candidate's tenacity should be based on his or her options. If, for example, one candidate has been looking for work for six months, and the company's offer is the only one he has received, he ought to curb his tenacity and would probably be wise to accept something close to the organization's original offer. On the other hand, a candidate who has two or more offers is in a much stronger bargaining position. Such a candidate can press the organization harder than the first, knowing that if the organization ceases negotiation she can accept one of the other offers. A candidate who has higher offers from other organizations should mention them, which might induce the organization to up its offer. However, this kind of power play may also convince the organization that the candidate is unwinnable and cause it to cease negotiation.

If you accept the position, do so with a contact over the phone and follow up by signing the documents provided by the firm. If you decide to reject the job offer, it is a common courtesy to write a formal letter of rejection. Maintain professional decorum with this letter. Do not burn bridges or make a negative final impression. Typically, your letter should let the employer know the reason for your rejection in a tactful and general way. If you do not want to live in the city where the company is located, avoid insult. For example, "I am turning down your offer to take a position working for a company near my hometown, where my family still resides." Be sure that your explanation is honest, but tactful. Thank the employer for considering you and for the courtesies extended. Letters of acceptance and rejection are vital aspects of professional life. They communicate that you are a quality individual.

Dealing with Rejection

More often than not, candidates are not offered a job. Although it is hard to avoid viewing a **rejection** personally, try to keep the rejection of your candidacy separate from the rejection of you personally. There are several things candidates can do to keep rejections in perspective.

First, try to get feedback. There are a number of reasons for rejection, some are very good reasons, while others are not. Be polite and diplomatic and suggest that you would like to learn from this experience. Ask if there is something that the employer could tell you that may help you in future interviews.

Second, send a thank-you note anyway. Don't ruin your future chances by acting angry or hurt. By displaying the professional attitude that employers seek you keep your options open for the future.

Third, seek support. Don't keep your rejection "hidden" because you are embarrassed about it. Talk to family and friends who can lend an ear and keep you motivated. Talk about it for a few minutes and then move on. Don't dwell on the bad news for too long.

Finally, use the rejection as a learning experience. Consider that you attained valuable interview experience, that you were able to reevaluate your priorities and career options, and that you learned a great deal about yourself and your professional life. If you view the interview process as an opportunity to learn more about yourself and your career options, even a rejection can become a valuable learning opportunity.

Everyone meets with some rejection, but it doesn't have to be a major setback unless you view it that way. Remember that it only takes one offer to get a position, and this offer usually comes after several rejections. Employment interviews are communication events. Every stage of the interview allows you to communicate that you are the kind of employee that the organization would benefit from hiring.

Summary

The employment interview is the primary tool for recruiting and hiring new employees. The best interviewees are able to adapt their skills and experience to the employer's needs and concerns. The pre-interview stage starts when the candidate begins researching jobs through personal contacts, classified ads, the university's career center, and the Internet. Once positions are located, the candidate must research the company to understand its needs and concerns.

Most job ads require that the candidate submit a resume and cover letter. Candidates should avoid fitting their information into someone else's format. A heading is a category under which specific information is classified. Candidates should develop headings that relate to their specific skills, education, and experience. A lead consists of the first information on each line under the heading. Only the most important information should be included in the lead. Descriptions provide important detail about educational or work experience. A scannable resume is one that can be read into a computerized database. Scannable resumes should emphasize key words from the field or industry.

The cover letter represents a chance to highlight specific skills and abilities that fit the organization's needs. The cover letter includes an introduction, body, and conclusion and should specify why the applicant fulfills the organization's requirements.

In the interview stage, the candidate meets and talks with members of the prospective organization. The nonverbal dimensions of the interview consist of dress and body cues. Answering questions is the interview's primary verbal component. Strong answers follow a four-step procedure: state an answer briefly, explain the answer, provide concrete examples to support the answer, and reconnect the answer to the original question. Research suggests that successful candidates make reference to the company, support their claims, are active participants in the process, exhibit enthusiasm, and ask good questions.

In the post-interview stage, the candidate should send a thank-you letter to the contact in the organization. Candidates should take their time to carefully evaluate any job offer. Salary negotiations should wait until after an offer is received. Any request for more money should be based on the candidate's exceptional skills and experience, or comparisons to similar jobs in the industry. A candidate with more than one offer can be more assertive in salary negotiations. However, more often than not, candidates are not offered a job. Rejection is a very common part of any search. Avoid taking rejection personally. Instead, try to learn from the experience so the next interview is more successful.

QUESTIONS FOR DISCUSSION

1. Examine the list of tips for resume writing in Figure 2.4. Given your experience in employment interviews, are there any tips you could add to this list? Are there other resume writing practices that you would clearly warn against?

2. As a class, examine Allison Lucas's poor resume in Figure 2.5. Identify the various features of that resume that are inappropriate or unpersuasive. What content changes would you make to improve this resume? What changes would you make in the form and layout of the resume to improve its appearance?

3. Discuss the improvements made to Allison Lucas's first resume in Figure 2.5. In what ways does this resume represent an improvement over the second?

4. Discuss the suggestions for the nonverbal and verbal dimensions of an interview presented in this chapter. Are there any additional suggestions you would add to our list? Develop a list of additional nonverbal and body cues that candidates should be aware of during an interview. Develop a list of additional verbal cues that candidates should be aware of.

ACTIVITIES AND EXERCISES

1. Practice your interview research skills by completing the following exercise. Select a local company that employs people in your field and research the organization, using the techniques discussed in this chapter. As you develop information, fill out a form on the organization modeled after that in Figure 2.2. Were you able to find enough information to complete the form? If not, what other avenues can you use to complete your research?

2. Use your university's career center, the Internet, or some other source to find a job ad for a position you could apply for now or immediately after you graduate. Following the guidelines in this chapter, write a resume and cover letter for that position. Make sure that your resume is error free and includes creative headings, leads, and descriptions. Make the cover letter persuasive by writing it for the specific job ad. Submit your resume and cover letter to a group of your classmates and have them evaluate them based on the guidelines offered in this chapter. Make changes in your resume and cover letter so that they are ready when you want to apply for your next job.

3. Take the resume that you created in the above exercise and make it scannable. Emphasize key words and phrases relevant to your field and the job ad you used above. Submit your scannable resume to your classmates for evaluation and make the improvements they suggest on your final copy. This resume is now ready, should you ever need it.

4. Take the list of typical interview questions in Figure 2.8 and prepare answers to five of the toughest questions on that list. Follow the four-step process for answering questions as outlined in this chapter. Review your answers with your instructor or colleagues in your class. What suggestions do they offer for improving your answers? Incorporate those suggestions into a revised response. Preparing answers prior to the interview will make you feel more confident and ready to handle even the toughest inquiry.

NOTES

1. Baker, H. G., and M. S. Spier, "The Employment Interview: Guaranteed Improvement In Reliability," *Public Personnel Management* 19 (Spring 1990): 85–90.

2. Ralston, S. M., and R. Brady, "The Relative Influence of Interview Communication Satisfaction on Applicants' Recruitment Interview Decisions," *The Journal of Business Communication* 31 (1994): 61–77.

3. Adams, R. L., *Adams Job Almanac* (Holbrook, MA: Adams Media Corporation, 1996).

4. Heinemann, K. G. "What Do Today's Employers Want From Job Applicants?" *Technological Horizons in Education Journal,* March 1996, 69–71

5. Cox, J. A., D. W. Schlueter, K. K. Moore, and D. Sullivan, "A Look Behind Corporate Doors: Examining the Interview Process from the Organization's Point of View," *Personnel Administrator,* March 1989, 56–59.

6. Steward, C. J., and W. B. Cash, Jr., *Interviewing Principles and Practices,* 2nd ed. (Dubuque, IA: Wm. C. Brown, 1978).

7. Enhorn, L. J., "An Inner View of the Job Interview: An Investigation of Successful Communicative Behaviors," *Communication Education* 30 (1981): 217–228.

8. Ugbah, S. D., and R. E. Majors, "Influential Communication Factors in Employment Interviews," *The Journal of Business Communication* 29 (1992): 145–159.

9. Enhorn.

10. Ibid.

11. Ibid.

12. Ugbah and Majors.

13. Cox, Schleuter, Moore, and Sullivan.

14. Ibid.

3 Listening and Feedback in Organizational Relationships

One might think, given the increase in communication technologies such as fax machines and e-mail, as well as such nontraditional forms of management as self-directed teams and total quality management, that the importance of interpersonal relationships in organizations would be in decline. In fact, quite the opposite is true. Rather than replacing person-to-person interaction, communication technology makes it easier to maintain instantaneous contact with people over vast distances. Similarly, the new management techniques make interpersonal interaction more important than ever.

We define **interpersonal communication** as an exchange of messages between two people who are either copresent (in the same room) or connected through a technological medium such as a telephone or computer. The bulk of the average employee's day is usually spent in various interpersonal communication activities. Interpersonal communication in organizations is different from nonwork relationships in two ways. First, unlike our nonwork relationships, most work relationships are **involuntary**.[1] We meet and interact with people because we must in order to accomplish a job. Although some of our work relationships may, over time, become voluntary, most do not start out this way. Second, most organizational relationships provide **instrumental rewards** rather than **expressive rewards.** Instrumental rewards are those benefits that are tied to the job. That is, interacting with others may eventually pay off in terms of raises, promotions, and prestige within the organization. Expressive rewards, however, are more personal. They include social and emotional support, confirmation, affection, trust, and consensual shared meaning that occurs when good friends come to think alike. Although expressive rewards can be derived from organizational relationships, they are not essential to them and we do not require all or even most of our relationship in the organization to provide these rewards. The largely involuntary and instrumental character of interpersonal communication within the organization makes them unique.

Listening is one of the most important interpersonal communication activities in organizational settings. In terms of amount, the vast majority of our communication time is spent listening. As such, poor listeners spend much of their communication time prone to costly errors. There is ample evidence that listening errors are abundant. Studies done by University of Minnesota professor of rhetoric Ralph Nichols suggest that the listening efficiency of the average college graduate is quite low. Nichols measured short-term listening efficiency (the ability to recall major details of a ten-minute presentation) at only 50 percent. Long-term listening efficiency (the ability to recall major details after several months) sank to 25 percent.[2] According to Lyman K. Steil, head of Communication Consultants Associated, 80 percent of people surveyed rated their listening ability as average or below average.[3] Poor listening causes appointments to be rescheduled, necessitates shipments to be rerouted, and hurts employee morale. Thus, there is ample evidence that, despite their importance, our listening skills are woefully inadequate given the demands of the modern business environment.

Make no mistake about it, listening is vital for both organizational and individual success. For example, a large engineering firm employed a team of twenty-four engineers and an expensive consultant on a military project. The team encountered a critical problem that threatened to delay the project and cost the firm heavily in penalties for lateness under its government contract. The project head phoned the consultant and assigned him to work out a solution. Later, the project head learned that the consultant had been working on a different phase of the problem than the one for which a solution was required. Although both men believed they understood one another, this listening error cost the company $150,000 in lost person hours and penalties paid to the government.[4] Effective listening is vital for shared meaning and may be one of the most straightforward, least expensive ways to increase organizational productivity.

Listening is also vital to personal success. A study of employees at a daily newspaper indicates that effective listening plays a pivotal role in how others evaluate your competence, and such perceptions play a large role in advancement within any organization.[5] A second study examined the relationship between communication skills and upward mobility in a large, East Coast insurance company and found that the ability to view the world through others' eyes, a view partly learned through listening to others, was centrally related to a person's chance for promotion within the organization.[6] These studies demonstrate that personal advancement depends, in part, on your ability to listen to peers, customers, superiors, and subordinates. In Chapter 1 we emphasized the importance of listening and feedback to achieving shared meaning. In this chapter we discuss methods of improving two forms of listening: recall listening and empathic listening.

Recall Listening

Recall listening involves a person's ability to correctly interpret and remember the content of another person's message. Recall listening includes four processes: receiving a message from another person, attending to that message, assigning meaning to the message, and remembering the message.[7] **Receiving** the message means that you hear and process the message that another communicates. **Attending** to the message involves a listener's ability to focus on the message and direct his or her attention toward it without distraction. If you have ever been to a noisy party, but still heard your name mentioned across the room, you know the difference between merely hearing a message and focusing your attention on it. The act of focusing brings the message clearly into conscious attention and forces background noise to fade from awareness. **Assigning meaning** to the message means assigning an interpretation to it. In most situations (excluding the need for ambiguity, discussed in Chapter 1), the ideal interpretation is similar to the meaning the sender had in mind when encoding the message. Finally, **remembering** is the ability to store and recall the major themes of a conversation for use in later decision making.

Recall that listening is not a genetically determined trait. As we suggested in Chapter 1, habitual behavior can be improved with appropriate training and practice. In other words, there is hope for all of us, but altering our listening behavior requires conscious attention. You must first identify your best and worst listening behaviors, then consciously practice better habits until those sink to a lower level of awareness.[8] Your new, effective listening behaviors will become habitual, and you will do them automatically. At the end of this chapter we present a variety of learning activities to help you identify your poor listening habits and guide you through the process of replacing bad habits with good ones. The following tips will help you improve recall listening.

Motivate Yourself to Listen

People who lack motivation to listen are ineffective because, from the outset, they regard the content as dull and listening appears unimportant.[9] Studies indicate that, when subjects are promised a reward for remembering the content of a presentation, their listening improves over those not promised any reward.[10]

To combat the motivation problem, listeners must develop their own reasons to listen. Good listeners admit that a subject may sound dry or that a presentation or group meeting may not be directly related to their job, but they then decide that, being trapped anyway, they will use this situation to their advantage. They develop motivation by listening for something that benefits them.[11] Good listeners search the messages for information that will provide insight into the speaker's background or psychological predisposition that could help in later interactions. They search for an idea that can be turned into a profitable product, or save the organization money. As you search the message for these qualities or ideas, your motivation increases, as does your focus and attention on the message. Practice motivating yourself the next time you are part of a captive audience learning about a dull topic.

Focus on Content Rather Than Delivery

In the visual age in which we live—one that is dominated by images on movie, television, and computer screens—we have come to expect that messages will include slick delivery. It is not surprising, then, that we are turned off by more traditional message forms.[12] Little wonder that most businesses have gone "Hollywood," making stockholders' meetings or product unveilings into multimedia events. If we spend our time judging and critiquing the delivery, however, we are not attending to the message, and recall listening is hindered.

Effective listeners are able to make a quick judgment about a speaker's delivery or the production qualities of a video, but they quickly return their attention to the message. Begin looking for something that will benefit you in some way. Search for ways you can use this information, and you will be better able to attend to the message.[13]

Defer Judgment

One of the most severe barriers to effective listening is the tendency to become emotionally excited when a speaker's views differ from our own, or when a speaker uses emotional language. In such cases, poor listeners become preoccupied by trying to calculate a response to the disagreeable argument or language. At such times, we are no longer focusing on the message but have turned our attention to methods of embarrassing or humiliating the speaker when he or she is finished.[14] Evaluating a message prior to understanding it seriously compromises the listener's ability to assign the appropriate meaning.[15]

To solve this problem, listeners should defer judgment. Creative thinking and problem solving require that listeners withhold evaluation of messages until they have heard and properly understood everything the speaker has to say. Deferring judgment is easier when the listener tries to empathize with the speaker. Try to see the speaker's point of view; search for reasons for believing as he or she believes. Maintain emotional control and get back to the task of listening.

Take Advantage of Thought Speed

Although studies show that humans can think at a speed of over 400 words per minute, most people, be they in groups or in public presentations, speak at approximately 125 words a minute.[16] This difference is problematic because the extra time often causes listeners to lose their focus on the message, drift into other thoughts, or engage in daydreaming. As a result, the listener's focus is no longer on the message, and recall listening is hurt.

Effective listeners constantly apply their spare thinking time to the message. Spend the extra thought time identifying developmental, organizational, and argument tactics used by the speaker. How are the speaker's ideas structured? What kinds of evidence are being brought to bear on the topic? How does the message fit together into a coherent unit (if it does cohere at all)? Review and summarize the speaker's points. What are the two or three main ideas? Can you paraphrase these when the speaker is done? Anticipate where the speaker is heading next. What seems to be the line of reasoning? Compare your predictions to the actual message that you then hear. Using thought speed appropriately will improve your recall listening.[17]

Listen for Meaning

Listeners are often too focused on the words that speakers are using. But the meaning of a message comes not only from the words, but from the nonverbal cues as well. Nonverbal cues such as vocal qualities, facial expressions, and gestures constitute a large portion of the meaning of any message. According to some estimates, between 60 to 90 percent of the meaning of a message is nonverbal in nature.[18] Nonverbal cues comment on and help us interpret the words in the message. Imagine seeing this sign in a restaurant:

People who think the waiters are rude should see the manager.[19]

The message takes on two meanings depending on how it is read (with what nonverbal cues). One interpretation suggests that anyone who has a problem should take it to the manager. A second interpretation suggests that the manager might be even more rude than the waiters. As you can see, nonverbal cues help us assign meaning to messages. A simple response to a statement about whether people have a problem with the new proposal may elicit a "no" reply that suggests there is no problem, or "no" may be said in such a way that it clearly indicates a problem. Paying attention to nonverbal cues helps you to interpret messages properly.

Take Notes

It is apparent to us that many managers do not like to take notes. Perhaps managers view notes as secretarial work or believe they are unimportant to the larger process of communication and decision making. However, taking notes shows concern for what others have to say. In addition, experiments indicate that the behavioral involvement required for note-taking increases our attention to the message. Note-takers are better able to recall information than those who do not take notes.[20]

Be flexible in note-taking during a meeting or presentation. Make brief notes that record main ideas and significant supporting detail. After the presentation or meeting, write a **précis** (pronounced "pray-see," from the French term meaning a concise synopsis) of each major point.[21] Use complete sentences to write a brief paragraph summarizing the idea, and repeat this process as necessary. For example, after listening for thirty minutes to the Community Advisory Panel discuss ideas for television shows, I wrote the following précis.

> The first show introduces the idea of a Community Advisory Panel to the TV audience, explains our purpose, and interviews members and industry representatives to get their views. The second show is on emergency management responses to fires and chemical spills at the plants. Each organization will detail their plans for handling emergencies, and CAP members will participate with industry representatives in a panel discussion after the presentations. The third show will be on corporate philanthropy. The companies will describe their priorities for donating money to the community and, in a panel discussion, CAP members will comment on these priorities.

Taking adequate notes helps assure that the final step in the recall listening process, remembering the message, is achieved.

By practicing these tips you will be able to improve your recall listening abilities. At the end of this chapter you will find exercises to help you identify your recall listening problems and unfreeze your worst listening habits and begin the process of developing new, effective habits.

Empathic Listening

Recall listening is not the only skill required in organizations. A survey of training managers at 106 Fortune 500 companies found that effective listening also includes active or empathic skills such as building rapport and providing feedback. According to business communication researchers, good "workplace listening is interrelated with other communication behaviors and includes a good deal of 'empathy' in addition to recall."[22]

Empathic listening provides important expressive rewards to any organizational relationship. Empathic listening involves attitudes such as open-mindedness, listening with enthusiasm, displaying concern for the speaker, appropriate turn-taking, exchanging ideas; it includes nonverbal behavior that indicates one is listening, such as head nods, eye contact, tone of voice, and verbal behavior such as asking questions, answering questions, praise, advice, and thanks.[23] As you can see from this list, some of the qualities of a good listener are attitudinal, and involve your mind-set prior to listening, and others are communication related, including verbal and nonverbal feedback. Thus, empathic listening involves an **attitude of acceptance** for what others have to say, especially responding positively to emotions, and **providing feedback** that makes people feel as if their concerns have been addressed. Each of these will be discussed below.

Develop an Attitude of Acceptance

Whenever we communicate with another person we are doing more than presenting **content information;** we are also presenting our individual **experiences** and **emotions.** These experiences are usually communicated nonverbally, with only minimal awareness by the sender. Messages such as these may communicate: "I am an excited person," "I am a serious person," "I am a self-disciplined person," "I am businesslike," and so forth. The next time you make a phone call to a business, notice the way the person responds. Some individuals answer the phone in an excited manner, suggesting they are interested in their job and care about your call. Others respond with vocal qualities that lack enthusiasm or suggest defensiveness. When we respond, we are responding not only to the content, but to the experience or emotion the other person is communicating.[24]

Unfortunately, many organization members, especially those trained in modern business schools, believe that business is a rational enterprise, and as such, it is no place for emotions. This attitude couldn't be more wrong. Emotion does not indicate the failure of communication, but is a normal part of living and is reflected in communication. Thus, it is vital to accept others' emotions and the experience that generates these emotions, when listening to fellow employees.

Notice the manager's response to the employee's experience in the following hypothetical conversation.

> **LARRY:** Melissa, can I talk with you for a moment?
>
> **MELISSA:** Certainly, come on in.
>
> **LARRY:** You've always said that your door was open for us if we had a problem. Well, for the first time I do have a concern I would like to discuss. First I was turned down for a promotion in favor of someone outside the company, and today I was informed that I've been moved off the Smith Brothers account, one of the largest accounts in this agency. I can't believe this! Who in the company has it in for me? I'm mad as hell about this and want an explanation.
>
> **MELISSA:** Larry, why are you still on this promotion thing? You know I favored you for the promotion, but sometimes we can't get everything we want.
>
> **LARRY:** I don't need clichés, I want an explanation.

MELISSA: This isn't getting us anyplace. I thought we agreed that we won't talk about the promotion. It's in the past. Don't get emotional about it. As far as the reassignment....

LARRY: (Very agitated) I didn't agree to do any such thing. I'm tired of slaving for this company and never receiving any recognition. First the promotion, now the Smith Brothers account—that's one of our biggest accounts. Moving me off it signals that you don't have confidence in my work. It means I'll never have another shot at promotion. What are you doing to me?

MELISSA: I don't like your tone. You are rushing to judgment. Let's take an objective look at the shift in accounts. If you can't do that, then come back when you are in control of yourself.

In this excerpt, Melissa refuses to acknowledge or accept the experiences Larry is communicating because she doesn't want to deal with distressing emotional content. Although Larry is obviously upset about the promotion, she dismisses it because "It's in the past." She also overrules his experience of frustration when she says they should take an "objective look" at the shift in accounts. It is doubtful from this excerpt that Larry will leave feeling his concerns have been heard. Indeed, Melissa ignores and pushes aside Larry's frustrations.

Developing an attitude of acceptance means learning to probe behind people's gut reactions. Melissa might have responded more positively if she had started by paraphrasing Larry's feelings, and asking questions to probe the source of the response. Melissa might have said the following after hearing Larry's concerns:

MELISSA: I thought after our last conversation about the promotion that you were over that, but apparently this is not the case. Am I right in sensing that you are still very frustrated that you didn't get the promotion?

LARRY: Well, I thought I was okay about it, but then this account shift came up and it brought my original feelings about the promotion back to the surface.

MELISSA: I see. Are you frustrated with me about the promotion? Do you feel that I could or should have done more to help secure it for you?

LARRY: No. But it would be nice to know if someone higher up prevented me from getting the promotion and if that same person is responsible for this account shift.

MELISSA: I don't know if someone higher up had anything against you personally, although I find that difficult to believe. As far as the account shift, that was my idea. May I explain my reasoning?

In this response, Melissa has paraphrased Larry's emotional response as frustration and asked questions to try to understand why this feeling has returned. She goes on to ask whether she is the source of Larry's frustrations, and in so doing, is helping Larry probe beneath his response for its source. Although we don't know how this conversation will end, Larry will feel more positive about the conclusion because he will feel as if his concerns were addressed rather than dismissed.

Of course, learning to accept the emotions of others does not mean that employees are free to respond in irrational or bizarre ways, behave intolerantly, or threaten people. In the next chapter we discuss the importance of emotional maturity to organizational success. However, far too many managers interpret the slightest waiver in a person's voice, or the smallest display of fear, concern, pity, anger, or frustration as inappropriate and attempt to prevent these natural reactions. The second part of empathic listening is the ability to provide appropriate feedback.

Provide Feedback

Empathic listening includes feedback that indicates acceptance of the other person involved. Listeners should provide responses that confirm or reject others, rather than disconfirm them. This section discusses these responses as a vital part of empathic listening.

Confirmation.   **Confirmation** is a response that does two things: It accepts the content level of the conversation and it accepts the experience or emotion the person presents.[25] When your first author, Jim, called a national rental company to complain about waiting for over an hour to rent and return a carpet steam cleaner, the customer service representative on the phone was very confirming. He agreed with the content of the complaint, that an hour is too long to wait to rent a small piece of equipment, and confirmed Jim's emotions by saying he understood why he was angry and that this was a perfectly legitimate response. The response is confirming because it agrees with the content of Jim's communication and the emotion behind it, the anger and frustration he felt. Confirmation contributes to a person's feelings of self-worth and morale. Thus, the simple act of confirming others is a vital management tool.

There is a variety of different confirming behaviors that indicate you are an empathic listener, and these are listed in Table 3.1. As you can see in the table, confirming messages offer **direct recognition** of the other person by looking at the other, making frequent eye contact, speaking directly to the other person, not interrupting the other person, and other nonverbal acknowledgment. **Agreeing with the content** means the listener offers verbal agreement with or praise for the speaker's content. Finally, **endorsing the emotions/experiences** of the speaker accepts the other person's feelings as reasonable and legitimate rather than blaming the other for feeling a certain way or suggesting that his or her feelings are inappropriate or illegitimate.[26] Confirming responses make others feel as if they are being listened to and indicate empathic acceptance of them and their experiences. However, you need not agree with another person to offer a positive, empathic response.

TABLE 3.1   Definitions and Examples of Confirmation

Direct Recognition	Nonverbal signals of interest including: looking straight, frequent eye contact, head nods, and other indications of attentive listening
Agreeing with Content	Verbal agreement with or praise for the content communicated. "Yes, I think your assessment is accurate. Proceed as you see fit."
Endorsing Emotions/Feelings	Accepting the other's feelings as reasonable and legitimate. "I would feel the same way in your position." "You have every right to feel the way you do."

Adapted from: Cissna, K. L. N., and E. Sieburg, "Patterns of Interactional Confirmation and Disconfirmation," in *Rigor & Imagination: Essays from the Legacy of Gregory Bateson*, ed. C. Wilder and J. H. Weakland (New York: Praeger, 1982), 253–282.

Rejection.   Despite its harsh-sounding label, **rejection** is a type of confirmation. In rejection, we validate another person's experience or emotional reactions, but disagree with the content of the message.[27] For example, Janice and Satia are nurses in a hospital, and Janice is concerned about the way a particular doctor treats her. The doctor is abrasive and says things that make Janice feel incompetent. In talking to her friend Satia, Janice says she plans to take her problem to the hospital administrator. Satia responds by agreeing that her feelings are legitimate:

SATIA: Yes, I agree. If he had done the same to me I would feel like this too.

In saying this, Satia confirms Janice's feelings and gives them legitimacy. This is important to empathic listening. However, she disagrees with the proposed action:

SATIA: However, taking this problem to the administrator without first talking to the doctor may make you look like you can't handle your own problems. In addition, the head nurse will look bad in the eyes of the administrator if you don't discuss this problem with her.

In this response, Satia disagrees with the content of the message—going to the hospital administrator to handle the problem. As such, rejection acknowledges the validity of the emotions expressed, but denies the content of the communication, perhaps disagreeing with an assertion or suggesting an alternative course of action.

As you can see in Table 3.2, rejection includes a three-part message process. First, **direct recognition** behaviors indicate active listening, **disagreement with content** signals disagreement with the message content, and **emotional/ experiential qualifiers** indicate acceptance of the other person's feelings.

TABLE 3.2   Definitions and Examples of Rejection Messages

Direct Recognition	Nonverbal signals of interest including: looking straight, frequent eye contact, head nods, and other indications of attentive listening.
Disagreement with Content	Verbal disagreement with the content communicated. "I think you are wrong about how that event unfolded."
Emotional/Experiential Qualifier	Verbal or nonverbal signals of understanding or acceptance for the feelings the other expresses. "You should feel proud, you earned that promotion."

There are numerous events within organizations that call for the careful use of rejection. Organizational trainers, quality inspectors, line managers, human resource officers, and people who conduct performance appraisal interviews are frequently called upon to teach, correct, and provide negative feedback to employees. Rejection represents one of the most beneficial methods of framing and communicating negative feedback. In our experience as teachers and corporate trainers, the best rejection messages—those that are most empathic—explicitly include all three elements cited in Table 3.2. For example, a teller trainer your first author knew at a bank had a knack of teaching complicated procedures with minimal hurt feelings among her trainees. If a trainee continued to teller-stamp all incoming checks and documents rather than the few that required the stamp, she might say:

> Carol (looking directly at the person, making eye contact), I understand your desire to be sure about everything you are doing by teller-stamping every incoming check and document. After all, you are new at this; you're responsible for more money than you've ever seen in your life and you're trying to be sure you're covered [an emotional/experiential qualifier]. But these two documents are the only ones that require a teller stamp [disagreement with content]. Anything more will only confuse people in the Proof Department.

Sensitive rejection responses that include all three elements allow people to teach and correct with maximum empathy for the experience and feelings of other employees. In addition, rejection messages should be specific rather than general. To be told that one is "dominating" is less useful than to be told:

> I understand that you felt rushed to make a decision, but just now you did not allow several members of the group to make comments. I feel as if you are pushing the group faster than we should move.

Second, rejection should be directed toward the behavior the receiver can do something about. Frustration is increased when a person is reminded of short-comings over which he or she has no control. Third, good rejection should be well timed. In general, rejection is most useful at the earliest opportunity after the given behavior or comment is made. However, this also depends on the person's readiness to hear negative feedback and the ability to correct the problem. For example, criticizing how a person handled a group decision in front of subordi-nates is not an appropriate place for rejection. Be sensitive in your timing of rejec-tion messages. Confirmation and rejection are an important foundation for effective empathic listening. Disconfirmation, on the other hand, should be avoided in all listening situations.

Disconfirmation.   Because it signals a lack of empathic listening, **disconfirma-tion** denies a person's experiences or feelings and, consequently, the other's feel-ings of self-worth. In effect, disconfirmation signals indifference to both the person and the person's individuality.[28] For example, suppose an employee in a welding shop approached his manager and said:

> **EMPLOYEE:** I'm having trouble with this new procedure we were told to do. Can I ask for some additional training before starting on this job?
>
> **MANAGER:** This procedure is nothing compared to the job we will be getting into in a few weeks. I thought you were qualified. (Walking away) I guess we're going to have to do a better job of screening future applicants.

Disconfirming responses deny individuals' rights to experience what they are experiencing and makes people feel as if their concerns have not been addressed. Disconfirmation is devastating to a person's view of self and destructive to pro-ductive relationships. In the example above, the employee's request was met with an accusation that he is unqualified. It is doubtful the employee will ever openly speak of his concerns to the manager again. Table 3.3 lists and exemplifies several kinds of disconfirming remarks. In Table 3.3 you can see that disconfirmation includes **avoiding involvement** through impersonal language and nonverbal distancing cues such as avoiding eye contact, walking away while talking, failing to face the person directly, shuffling papers, or performing other tasks while lis-tening. These make a person feel that what he or she has to say is not important. Note that in the welding shop example the manager distances himself when he begins to walk away in the middle of the conversation. Next, **tangential** or **irrel-evant remarks** are not clearly connected to what the first person said and indi-cate a failure to listen. In the example above, the manager's response is irrelevant to the request. Long monologues are another form of irrelevant remark. **Imper-viousness** indicates a lack of concern for or awareness of the other person's feel-ings. Impervious responses may discredit the other in the form of flat denial, reinterpret the feelings so they are more acceptable, or challenge the speaker's right to have a particular feeling. In the welding shop the manager demonstrates

TABLE 3.3   Definitions and Examples of Disconfirmation Messages

Avoiding Involvement	Verbal or nonverbal distancing tactics. Includes avoiding eye contact, turning away, walking away, impersonal language, etc.
Tangential/Irrelevant Remarks	Verbal comments that are disconnected from or only minimally connected to the first person's remarks. A: "Let's discuss the production figures." B: "The next agenda item is the conference."
Imperviousness	Discrediting others' feelings. "You don't feel that way." (Flat Denial) "You're not angry at the decision, you're just a little miffed because you weren't told." (Reinterpretation) "You can't possibly hold those feelings." (Challenge the Right to a Feeling)
Disqualification	Direct disparagement of a speaker. "That wasn't a smart thing to do."

Adapted from: Cissna, K. N. L., and E. Sieburg, "Patterns of Interactional Confirmation and Disconfirmation," in *Rigor & Imagination: Essays From the Legacy of Gregory Bateson,* ed. by C. Wilder and J. H. Weakland (New York: Praeger, 1982), 253–282.

imperviousness when he says, "This…is nothing compared to the job we will be getting into in a few weeks," denying the employee's right to feel troubled by the present job. Finally **disqualification** occurs when someone disparages a speaker or the speaker's feelings.[29] The shop manager's statement "I thought you were qualified" is clearly an accusation that the employee is not qualified.

The disconfirming behaviors, whether they are expressed alone or in combination, indicate a lack of empathic listening because they disagree with the content another person expresses and the person's emotional experience. To improve your empathic listening abilities, develop an attitude of acceptance for the experience and emotions of the speaker and practice confirmation and rejection. Eliminate disconfirming responses from your repertoire.

Improving your skills at empathic listening will make your interpersonal relationships at work more enjoyable and effective. Good listening involves both recall and empathic skills. Because many organizational members spend entire days shuttling between interviews, meetings, presentations, and conversations with people, the vast majority of their time is spent listening. Effective employees are effective listeners. Devote yourself to improving your listening skills. The payoff could be huge.

Summary

The growing use of information technology and nontraditional management techniques has increased the importance of interpersonal communication. Unlike our nonwork relationships, work relationships are involuntary and largely instrumental. Advancement in many organizations depends on proficient listening skills. Studies show that our short- and long-term listening efficiency is poor. To improve recall listening, employees should motivate themselves, focus on content rather than delivery, defer judgment, take advantage of thought speed, listen for meaning, and take notes.

Whenever we communicate, our messages include both content and emotional/experiential information. Employees must develop the ability to accept emotional message elements and probe behind people's outward feelings for their source.

Empathic listeners respond with confirmation or rejection, but avoid disconfirmation. Confirmation responses agree with the content of the message and accept the emotional content as well. Confirming responses include direct recognition, agreement, and endorsing the other person's feelings. Rejection is a type of confirmation in that it validates the person's feelings but disagrees with the message content. Rejection behaviors include direct recognition, disagreeing with the content, and an emotional/experiential qualifier. Finally, disconfirmation signals indifference to the speaker. Disconfirming behaviors include avoiding involvement, tangential or irrelevant remarks, imperviousness, and disqualification.

QUESTIONS FOR DISCUSSION

1. We opened this chapter by discussing the major differences between work- and nonwork-based interpersonal relationships. Can you think of other differences? How do individual goals and communication patterns differ for the two relationships? Are there important similarities in goals and communication rules across these two types of relationships? To help you focus on these issues, imagine an office party where two people who are friends outside the office are having a conversation. Nearby, two people who interact only in the office are talking. What differences and similarities will you observe in the conversation of the two dyads?

2. Consider the harms that inadequate recall listening can produce in an organization. Can you think of an incident in your work experience that was characterized by inadequate recall listening? What, if any, problems did this incident create? Which recall listening techniques could have solved this problem?

3. Can you think of additional techniques to improve recall listening? As a group or class, list the additional methods.

4. As a class or group, develop additional examples of confirming, rejecting, and disconfirming. Are there any message examples that do not fit into one of the three categories?

5. As a class or group, develop a list of five errors you or your colleagues have made during your first few days on a new job. Now, come up with a way to talk to the person who committed the error using rejection. Follow the guidelines in Table 3.2 to construct your messages. Learn to use rejection to instruct and correct.

ACTIVITIES AND EXERCISES

1. This exercise will help you inventory your best and worst recall listening habits. After completing the survey you will be able to describe your strongest and weakest recall listening habits. We will then help you develop a priority plan for improving your recall listening.

Individual Application Survey of Listening Skills

Instructions: Read the list and put a check mark next to the habit if you use that habit 50% to 100% of your listening time.

1. If a topic is uninteresting, I tune it out and cease careful listening.
2. I work to minimize distractions in my listening environment by putting my phone on phone mail, turning down the radio, or going to a quiet office for conversations.
3. I tend to respond emotionally to arguments with which I disagree or language I find objectionable.
4. I refuse to allow unexpected distractions to interfere with my concentration and focus my mind on the speaker and his/her content.
5. I evaluate and judge the wisdom of what I have heard before checking my interpretation with the speaker.
6. I work to ignore a speaker's mannerisms or delivery and focus my attention on the message.
7. I develop arguments to refute what a speaker is saying so I can answer quickly when he or she is done talking.
8. I accept the emotional sentiments expressed by the speaker and use these to help me understand the content of the message.
9. I am easily distracted by the annoying or affected elements of a speaker's delivery.
10. I try not to let emotional language or strong disagreement with a speaker's ideas interfere with my concentration on the message.
11. I don't write the gist of important conversations on paper for future reference.
12. I try to listen for something useful in even the most dull topics.
13. I am uncomfortable with emotional displays and try to ignore these elements of a message.
14. I look at a speaker's face, eyes, body posture, and movement, and pay attention to other nonverbal cues while listening.
15. I tend to drift into other topics and concerns while listening.
16. I use a speaker's pauses and the time he/she spends forming ideas to identify the structure of the ideas, summarize the content, or anticipate where the argument is headed.

17. I ask questions about what I've heard before letting the speaker know what I have heard and understood.
18. I take notes on the major themes covered in my conversations.
19. I think about other topics and concerns while listening.
20. It is easy for me to ignore the unusual mannerisms of a speaker and focus on the message.
21. I tend to drift into my own thoughts if the speaker speaks slowly or seems to take an unusual path to his/her points.
22. I often paraphrase or summarize what I have heard before making my own comments.

A Plan for Improvement

In this survey, the even-numbered questions represent effective recall listening habits. The odd-numbered questions represent ineffective recall listening habits. Thus, all of the even-numbered statements that you checked represent your most effective habits and all the odd-numbered statements that you checked represent your most ineffective listening habits. Look over your analysis and determine your three most ineffective listening habits. In the space below, write down those three habits.

1. _____

2. _____

3. _____

Now that you have identified your worst listening habits, develop a plan to change the single worst habit. Remember from Chapter 1 that changing ingrained habits requires conscious attention. Write down the situations during which you will work to change your worst habit. For example, you may wish to devote conscious attention to better listening during a class lecture, or during conversations at home with your spouse. Work during the next two weeks to enact this plan. Practice new listening behaviors as often as it takes for them to become habitual. To overcome the habit, I plan to do the following:

_____

_____

_____

Practice your new listening behaviors as often as it takes for them to become habitual. You may wish to select other habits to correct. Follow the same procedure for changing all of your ineffective recall listening habits.

2. This exercise will help you evaluate your feelings of being confirmed by specific partners in the work environment. The scale below is referred to as the Perceived Confirmation Scale. Although the scale is not designed to measure rejection, it can gauge whether you feel confirmed or disconfirmed in a particular relationship. While thinking about a particular relationship at work (e.g., your boss, coworker, secretary, etc.), circle the number on each scale item that most accurately reflects your attitude as it relates to that relational partner.

1. He/She is aware of me.

7	6	5	3	2	1
agree very strongly	agree strongly	agree	disagree	disagree strongly	disagree very strongly

2. He/She isn't at all interested in what I say.

7	6	5	3	2	1
agree very strongly	agree strongly	agree	disagree	disagree strongly	disagree very strongly

3. He/She accepts me.

7	6	5	3	2	1
agree very strongly	agree strongly	agree	disagree	disagree strongly	disagree very strongly

4. He/She has no respect for me at all.

7	6	5	3	2	1
agree very strongly	agree strongly	agree	disagree	disagree strongly	disagree very strongly

5. He/She dislikes me.

7	6	5	3	2	1
agree very strongly	agree strongly	agree	disagree	disagree strongly	disagree very strongly

6. He/She trusts me.

7	6	5	3	2	1
agree very strongly	agree strongly	agree	disagree	disagree strongly	disagree very strongly

From: Sieburg, E., "Interpersonal Confirmation: Conceptualization and Measurement." Paper presented at the annual meeting of the International Communication Association, Montreal, Canada, 1973. Reprinted with permission.

To score the survey form, add the scores for items 1, 3, and 6. For items 2, 4, and 5, you need to reverse your scores before adding. To reverse scores, write down the opposite number of your response. If you put a 7 down for items 2, 4, or 5, replace it with a 1, if you circled 6, replace it with a 2, if you circled 3, replace it with a 5, and so on. Add the reversed scores for items 2, 4, and 5. Add your two figures up and divide by 6. This score represents your perceptions of confirmation with respect to the particular employee you were thinking about. The highest possible score is 7 and the lowest is 1.

Is there a correlation between the people you enjoy working with and how confirmed they make you feel? Are there particular areas in your relationship where you feel confirmed or disconfirmed? Think about your behavior toward other people in your workplace. What particular confirming behaviors discussed in this chapter can you employ to make your coworkers feel more confirmed? The Perceived Confirmation Scale can help you understand why you are more comfortable with some coworkers and superiors than others. It can also help you think about your own workplace behaviors and modify those that are not confirming. There is nothing to stop you from practicing this very important listening skill.

NOTES

1. Rawlins, W. K., *Friendship Matters: Communication, Dialectics, and the Life Course* (New York: Aldine de Gruyter, 1992).

2. Nichols, R. G., "Do We Know How to Listen? Practical Helps in Modern Age," *The Speech Teacher* 10 (1961): 118–124.

3. "Secrets of Being a Better Listener," *U.S. News & World Report,* 26 May 1980, 65–66.

4. Steil, L. K., L. L. Barker, and K. W. Watson, *Effective Listening* (Reading, MA: Addison Wesley, 1983).

5. Haas, J. W., and C. L. Arnold, "An Examination of the Role of Listening in Judgments of Communication Competence in Co-Workers," *The Journal of Business Communication* 32 (1995): 123–139.

6. Sypher, B. D., and T. E. Zorn, "Communication-Related Abilities and Upward Mobility: A Longitudinal Investigation," *Human Communication Research* 12 (1986): 420–431.

7. Brownell, J., "Perceptions of Effective Listeners: A Management Study," *The Journal of Business Communication* 27 (1990): 401–415.

8. DiSanza, J. R., "The Role of Consciousness in Interpersonal Communication: Pedagogical Implications for the Introductory Course" (ERIC Document Reproduction Service No. ED 341 098), February 1991.

9. Golen, S., "A Factor Analysis of Barriers to Effective Listening," *The Journal of Business Communication* 27 (1990): 25–36.

10. Beatty, M. J., R. R. Behnke, and D. L. Froelich, "Effects of Achievement Incentive and Presentation Rate on Listening Comprehension," *The Quarterly Journal of Speech* 66 (1980): 193–200.

11. Nichols.

12. Floyd, J. J., *Listening: A Practical Approach* (Glenview, IL: Scott, Foresman and Company, 1985).

13. Nichols.

14. Ibid.

15. Floyd.

16. Wolven, A. D., and C. G. Coakley, *Listening* (Dubuque, IA: Wm. C. Brown, 1992).

17. Ibid.

18. Whalen, J. D., *I See What You Mean: Persuasive Business Communication* (Beverly Hills, CA: Sage, 1996).

19. Watzlawick, P., J. H. Beavin, and D. D. Jackson, *Pragmatics of Human Communication* (New York: W. W. Norton & Company, 1967), 53.

20. Wolven and Coakley.

21. Ibid.

22. Lewis, M. H., and N. L. Reinsch, Jr., "Listening in Organizational Environments," *The Journal of Business Communication* 25 (1988): 59.

23. Ibid.

24. Watzlawick, Beavin, and Jackson.

25. Ibid.

26. Cissna, K. N. L., and E. Sieburg, "Patterns of Interactional Confirmation and Disconfirmation," in *Rigor & Imagination: Essays from the Legacy of Gregory Bateson,* ed. C. Wilder and J. H. Weakland (New York: Praeger, 1982), 253–282.

27. Watzlawick, Beavin, and Jackson.

28. Cissna and Sieburg.

29. Ibid.

4 Interpersonal Politics: Power and Sexual Harassment in Organizations

As we stated in the last chapter, interpersonal relationships in organizations are different from nonwork relationships because work relationships are involuntary and instrumental. We interact with people at work because we must to achieve organizational goals. As a result, most work relationships take place within a hierarchy of unequal power and authority.

Whenever hierarchies of authority, responsibility, and power develop, they bring with them power imbalances and political maneuverings. Most people view power and politics as the least enjoyable aspect of the work experience. How many times have you heard people lament "It's not what you know but who you know"? Many say they want to work in organizations devoid of significant power imbalances and political game-playing. Unfortunately, the very nature of hierarchy guarantees that power will never be evenly distributed. When imbalances occur, political maneuvering is sure to follow. In this chapter, we familiarize readers with the most prevalent features of organizational life: power and politics. First, we explain the nature of organizational power and politics. Second, we discuss the experience of women and minorities as they struggle to attain their own powerful political connections within the organization. Finally, because sexual harassment represents a serious imbalance of power, we suggest strategies for managing it. We hope this chapter motivates students to gain power in their organizations and to engage in constructive political activity.

Interpersonal Power and Politics

People are often disconcerted to learn that all interpersonal relationships involve some form of hierarchy. We define **hierarchy** as the relative position—above, below, beside—that people occupy vis-à-vis one another. The positions of a hierarchy are determined by who controls valuable resources in the relationship and who has power or influence to define the nature of the relationship (what will or will not take place). Rhetorical critic Kenneth Burke says that one of the defining features of humanity is our predilection for creating hierarchies. We are never satisfied with disorder and constantly rank and organize things, events, and even people into categories of higher, equal, lower; better or worse; superior, subordinate, peer; or gold, silver, and bronze. We apply these distinctions to all parts of our existence, including our interpersonal relationships.

However, in voluntary interpersonal relationships such as friendship and marriage, the hierarchies of influence and control are fluid and change more freely than they do in involuntary organizational relationships. In organizations, everyone is acutely aware of the hierarchy and knows that changing it requires enormous effort and energy. The more bureaucratic the organization, the more important and less fluid the hierarchy. Compared with voluntary relationships, people in organization relationships must learn to cope with an environment characterized by power and politics.

Unfortunately, most of us have negative attitudes toward organizational power and politics. We think of both as drains on human potential that should be minimized or perhaps even eliminated from organizational life. However, in this section we hope to change these perceptions so that you come to see power and politics as an inevitable—and perhaps even positive—part of organizational life. We firmly believe that until the perfect human is created, a human devoid of self-interest and, therefore, of emotion and passion, power and politics will remain an important part of organizational life. Thus, this section covers three main issues: the nature of power in organizations, the nature of organizational politics, and methods of developing political power within a professional setting.

The Nature of Organizational Power

Our culture typically defines **power** negatively, as the ability to dominate and control others. The ancient Greek Sophists, the entrepreneurial traveling teachers of Greece (entrepreneurial because they were the first to be paid for the knowledge they taught, a concept your authors are grateful for), believed that power was the ability to mobilize people and resources to accomplish a goal. Thus, we define power as the ability to influence others. If you successfully influence tellers to handle customers more rapidly, or salespeople to sell more cars, you have exerted influence over those individuals; you have exerted power. As a result, it is impossible to exist in the modern organization without trying to influence others, and, therefore, exerting power.

However, to suggest that power is influence does not mean that power is a characteristic of individuals. Leaders have no influence—and, therefore, no power—if followers do not act on their suggestions. Except when physical violence is used to coerce people, power is always partly exerted, as when people try to influence others, and partly given, as when others choose to be influenced. The amount of power someone has in a relationship could be expressed in a simple formula:

$$P_{ab} = D_{ba}$$

(The power of a over b is equal to the dependence that b has on a).[1] The power (P) person "a" has over person "b" depends on the extent to which "b" is dependent on "a." If person "b" desires the rewards "a" controls, then "a" has power over "b." If, on the other hand, "b" cares little for "a's" rewards, then "a" has little influence over "b." For example, a bank we studied tried to convince tellers to sell more services to customers, and it offered financial rewards or the promise of full-time work in return. Because most of the tellers were satisfied with their hourly wage and didn't want full-time work, the bank's offer had little influence and sales did not increase.[2]

There are four different sources of power in interpersonal relationships: resource control, expertise power, communication skills, and interpersonal linkage power.[3] Empowering yourself involves identifying what's needed in your organization and developing those resources for later use.

First, when a person holds a position that provides control over promotions, pay, or valuable assignments, his or her power is based on **resource control.** The higher individuals advance in the organization, the more resources they control and the greater their power, assuming other members desire those resources. **Expertise power** comes from special skills or knowledge that someone else values. Unlike resource control, which usually depends on a formal position in the organizational hierarchy, expertise power can be acquired by any employee. For example, toolmakers create the factory machines that mass-produce everything from cars to canned peaches. Modern toolmaking involves computer-controlled equipment and an operator skilled in mathematics. Toolmakers that understand computers and advanced math will command higher salaries, faster raises, and more promotions than employees who don't have the same skills. If an understanding of basic accounting is valued in your organization, acquiring this knowledge will provide you with added power. Although self-learning is one way to improve expertise power, your local vocational school, community college, or university offers twenty-first-century skills to update your knowledge base. Powerlessness is certain for employees who fail to update their skills and knowledge.

Communication skills are the focus of this book. People who listen well, persuade others, argue in favor of their positions, or lead groups are valuable organizational members. As we emphasize throughout this book, corporations of the twenty-first century value members who have strong communication skills.

Interpersonal network power depends on a person's network of contacts, friends, and supporters. If you are good friends with the head of a small manufacturing firm and are able to get other friends interviews at this firm, your influence with those friends may increase. Interpersonal networks allow you to gain power through coalition formation. Trade unions are simply an institutionalized form of interpersonal linkage power within organizations. Less formal associations, cliques, and networks improve personal power in an organization.

A career means, in part, a never-ending commitment to the identifying of and adapting to the needs of your organization. In so doing, you improve organizational productivity and gain power in the process. And, power is essential to effectively handling a second ubiquitous feature of organizational life, politics.

The Nature of Organizational Politics

After interviewing over 100 executives from three large chemical firms, Robert Jackall, a business writer, argued that modern bureaucracy is a "moral maze" where slick talk, self-promotion, and sheer luck contribute more to success than effort or intelligence.[4] Further, most employees probably share the negative definition of politics put forward by Mayes and Allen:

> Politics is actions not officially sanctioned by an organization that [employees take] to influence others in order to meet [their] personal goals.[5]

In this view, politics consists of wheeling and dealing for personal rather than organizational gain.

However, the inventors of modern politics, the ancient Greeks, did not share this negative view. For the Greeks, any organized entity, be it a government or a business, is a conglomeration of divergent interests. Organizations need some way to reconcile interests through consultation and negotiation. For Aristotle, politics is a means of creating order out of diversity while avoiding forms of totalitarian rule. We agree with this point and define **politics** as the use of power to negotiate between and consolidate competing interests in an organization.

Our definition of politics clashes with modern preferences. Today, we criticize politicians and managers for failing to set aside personal interests and work only for the greater good of the nation or organization. We clamor to "throw the bums out" because they are more loyal to the party than to "the people." Such protests, however, ignore two important principles. First, whether we are talking about professional politicians or organizational politics, most of us believe that our interests coincide with the larger interests of "the people" or the organization. Thus, asking any one of us to sacrifice our interests for the organization doesn't make sense: Our interests are the organization's interests! Second, none of us would voluntarily sacrifice our individual interests for the sake of the organization. Ask yourself if you would voluntarily give up your job to help out the organization during an economic downturn. Given these two realities, it is unlikely that politics will ever disappear from the modern organization. Of course, this does not mean that all organization politics is ethical. See the Ethics Brief for an explanation of ethical principles to guide political activity.

Generally speaking, there are two dimensions to organizational politics, both of which are related to communication. **Overt politics** involves a variety of communications including threats, promises, negotiations, orders, coalition formation, and a host of other strategies to influence others and fulfill self- and/or organizational interests.[6] Any attempt to get a proposal accepted, sell an idea to other members, or convince a group that your interpretation is correct involves you in acts of overt politics. **Hidden politics** is the process by which employees decide which issues to raise in public, what arguments to present, which battles to fight, and how to fight them.[7] Let's look at two examples of politics in action.

Salt Lake City officials were devastated! In 1990, the International Olympic Committee selected Atlanta as the site of the 1996 summer Olympic Games, and the decision likely meant that another U.S. city would not be considered for host duties for some time. Salt Lake officials were trying to land the 2002 Winter Olympic Games, but things looked grim. According to a report in *The Wall Street Journal*, Salt Lake City officials turned to a member of the International Olympic Committee for help. That person, Anita DeFrantz, had become an influential member of the American contingent to the Committee. Salt Lake City officials held a banquet in Ms. DeFrantz's honor, gave her helicopter tours of the area, and taught her to ski. In return, Ms. DeFrantz helped the committee:

> She started tipping off the bid committee to the personal interests of each IOC member (upon learning from Ms. DeFrantz that one member was an avid gardener, the committee bought him a fancy book on horticulture). She talked Salt Lake boosters out of a planned statewide torch relay; locals thought the event would impress Olympic officials, but Ms. DeFrantz suspected they would consider it an inappropriate use of one of their most famous symbols.[8]

In this example we see both overt and hidden politics. Ms. DeFrantz is courted and asked to join a coalition of interests supporting the Salt Lake games. In addition, hidden politics is practiced as Ms. DeFrantz provides valuable advice designed to advance Salt Lake's bid. Of course, the world later learned that Salt Lake officials went well beyond small gifts to win the Games.

A more ethical example of overt and hidden politics is described below.

> James Johnson is the only African-American county manager in his southern state. He has been in his current position for six years, a remarkable achievement considering that the average tenure of county managers in his state is twenty-six

Ethics Brief

Carlos, the chief operating officer of a small antenna design and manufacturing firm, is in a quandary. He has two competing proposals for new products, but his company can only afford to pursue one of the ideas. The first proposal is from Jenny, who believes that the company's existing CB antenna line is badly in need of retooling to take advantage of the newest technology. She believes this retrofit is vital if the product, an important source of company revenue, is going to remain competitive. The second proposal comes from Marcus, who wants to develop an entirely new line of marine antennas and thinks that, with the proper investment, the company's product will outclass the competition. Jenny is a personal friend of Carlos, the CEO. The two came to the company at about the same time and formed a quick friendship. In order to push her proposal for a revamped CB antenna, Jenny spent more time than normal with Carlos, playing golf, having lunch, and so forth. Whenever she could work it into the conversation, she discussed the advantages of retooling the CB antenna.

Marcus, on the other hand, is uncomfortable around people. He believes proposals should be accepted or rejected based only on their technical merit. Despite the fact that he has been with the company longer than either Carlos or Jenny, he never formed a personal relationship with either and is not interested in taking time away from his family to "hang out" with people from work. He is concerned that Carlos's decision will be based on politics rather than the merits of the case. The whole situation reminds him how much he hates organizational politics.

What are the ethical implications of Jenny's political behavior? How should she proceed while still meeting some standards of decent, ethical conduct? In this brief we outline three standards for the ethical conduct of organizational politics. These guidelines may help you engage in political activity that is both ethical and beneficial to you and your organization.

First, employees should balance self- and organizational interests. According to Nancie Fimbel, a professor at San Jose State University, almost all political activity is designed to bring about benefits to the organization and benefits to the self. Using political power to make a proposal, complete a job, acquire resources, or steer a team to a final decision benefits the organization because work is accomplished. However, these activities also benefit the individual because the proposal or job brings increased credibility and esteem. As such, Fimbel suggests that ethical politics balances both organizational and individual interests. Unethical political activity benefits mainly the individual at the expense of the organization and its membership.* For example, junkets to distant manufacturing operations for inspections and a day of skiing, hiring consultants who are friends, or favoring a proposal mainly because it benefits your unit, are examples of politics where personal interests might outstrip organizational interests. As such, these activities should be carefully considered.

Because we aren't always aware of our own motives, you should carefully analyze your political activity to be sure that the organization and its members are receiving significant benefits from your activities. If these benefits are not apparent, then it may be necessary to reevaluate your goals. In other words, if Jenny truly believes that the retooled CB antenna is vital for organizational success, she can feel more comfortable politicking on its behalf.

Second, employees should maintain vigilant openness to change. Simply because it appears, in the early stages of a proposal, that your idea would benefit the organization doesn't mean that will always be true. Things change quickly in business. The ethical

(continued)

Continued

employee must be open to new information that might diminish the organizational value of his or her proposals. Jenny may, for example, learn that the CB antenna market is expected to decline in the coming years. As a result, the benefits of her proposal are diminished. If she disregards this new information and continues to push for her proposal, her actions are less ethical than before. The ethical employee seeks out counterarguments and tests the available evidence, remaining open to changing or withdrawing proposals that produce little or no organizational benefit.

Third, the ethical employee works to minimize harm to others. Despite attempts to politic for their ideas, employees must minimize the harm of their political activities throughout the organization. This can be done in several ways. (A) Attempt to maintain a positive, professional relationship with your rivals throughout the organization. Destroying collegial relationships is bad for morale. Besides, even if your proposal is accepted over others, you may need these people to make your ideas a reality. (B) Don't allow your success to be based purely on political maneuvering. If you also win the contest of ideas, your credibility will go up with both your superiors and your internal competitors. (See Chapter 10 for more information on making logical proposals.) (C) Be fair when

arguing privately for your proposal. Admit the limits of your arguments and evidence. Acknowledge the strengths of competing proposals. Focus on the benefits of your ideas rather than the weaknesses of other people's ideas. Focusing on weaknesses when project supporters are not present to speak for themselves is unethical. In private, build up your ideas, don't tear down others' ideas. (D) Spread the benefits of your success to other organizational members. Distribute politically won resources to newcomers and allow them to prove themselves. Compliment opponents for the quality of their ideas and for forcing you to focus and sharpen your thinking. Publicly thank subordinates and other team members who had input into the ideas you presented. Be generous in your praise of other contributors.

Because almost all organizations are characterized by uncertainty and scarce resources, organizational politics is a fact of life. Remembering these three guidelines will help you practice politics in an ethical manner.

*Fimbel, N., "Communicating Realistically: Taking Account of Politics in Internal Business Communications," *The Journal of Business Communication* 31 (1994): 7–26.

---

months. He attributes his longevity to his ability to understand and adapt to organizational and local politics and still accomplish a great deal for the county's residents. Fortunately, he is also committed to teaching these skills to others. Two years ago he hired a bright young accountant. After completing an audit of all the county's operations, she came to him with a proposal to reallocate a substantial part of the budget.

She had discovered that use of the county's workshop for disturbed youth (which I will label AT) had dropped steadily during the past five years, resulting in a costly and inefficient operation. Furthermore, the ratio of clinicians (psychiatrists, psychologists, and social workers) to clients was almost three times the state-required level. She also discovered that the Retired Citizens' Rehabilitation Center (labeled RCRC) had become seriously overloaded and understaffed. Since the population projections that she had obtained from the state indicated that the shift would continue at least through the year 2000, she devised a plan to shift resources from the first program to the second. She developed a twelve-point presentation, complete with slide and videotape aids, to support her arguments that (1) the overall needs of the county's residents would best be served by the shift, (2) the county could save a great deal of money because the licensed psychologists and lawyers on retainer as consultants for the AT could be dismissed, and (3) the funds could be used more efficiently because the success rate of the RCRC was almost four times as great as that of the AT. Before going to the county board of commissioners with the proposal, however, she wanted Johnson to sit in on a rehearsal of her presentation.

After the rehearsal he congratulated her for the quality of the presentation, but suggested that there were some details about which she might not be aware: (1) one of the board members had two children in the AT program and had saved thousands of dollars in psychotherapy expenses because it was available, (2) another commissioner's spouse was a consultant for the AT program, (3) two other commissioners had been reelected primarily because they claimed to have done a great deal for the county's retired citizens (and almost certainly would be embarrassed by the funding comparison included in the slide presentation), and (4) in the past the commission had voted in favor of money-saving recommendations only in odd-numbered years, when a majority of them were up for reelection.

The young accountant was perceptive enough to understand that these were invaluable hints. She revised her presentation, making three major changes. First, instead of arguing that the county was inadequately meeting its obligations to retired citizens, she argued that the growth in the use-rate of the RCRC demonstrated how effective the existing programs had been under the leadership of the current board and suggested that their programs warranted continuation and expansion. Second, she argued that the plummeting use-rate of the AT program demonstrated the success of professionally designed and led treatment, and she proposed that the staff be professionalized further in two steps. As nonsupervisory personnel resigned (which happens quite often in programs with assaultive adolescents), their salaries would be frozen until a sufficiently large sum was available to hire the most senior consulting psychologist (who coincidentally was the commissioner's spouse) on a full-time basis. Because the AT staff's professional skills would be increased by the completion of step 1, the remaining consulting contracts could be shifted to the RCRC and the remaining nonsupervisory personnel could be transferred to that agency.

Finally, the accountant arranged to have Johnson present the proposal at the next commission meeting, which she would attend in order to provide "technical support." Thus, she was able to adapt to the existing power relationships, and to do so without the knowledge of anyone except her supportive, and quite satisfied, supervisor. (A postscript: While revising her presentation, she found two filed-away proposals much like her original one. Evidently, she was not the only accountant to notice this misallocation of funds. But the others had either chosen not to speak out or did so ineffectively).*

---

*Excerpt from *Strategic Organizational Communication,* Third Edition by Charles Conrad, copyright, 1993 by Holt, Rinehart and Winston, reprinted by permission of the publisher.

As you can see, Mr. Johnson engages in overt politics by forming coalitions with his young staff. These exchanges work to the benefit of both parties, but especially for the young staff members, who acquire a valuable source of information. In addition, Mr. Johnson's advice represents hidden politics; Mr. Johnson helps his accountant decide on the most effective persuasive appeals for the county commission.

However, it's difficult to succeed in organizational politics without an adequate base of power. Resource, expertise, communication, and interpersonal linkage power are vital for effective political participation. In the next section we focus on building one of the four power sources, interpersonal linkage power. We cannot provide more specific advice on gaining resource and expertise power, and because this entire book is based on communication skills, we won't spend more time on this power source. Instead, we will explain how to use interpersonal linkages to build a base of political support in an organization.

Creating a Power Base for Political Action: A Focus on Interpersonal Networks

As we have seen in the last two extended examples, interpersonal linkages can be the source of enormous political power. Increasing your interpersonal network power involves two abilities: impression management and aligning oneself with powerful others. Each of these is discussed below.

Impression Management.   **Impression management** means displaying traits that are rewarded by the organization. It involves conforming to organizational norms for dress and appearance, as well as such deeper norms as the organization's core values and decision premises. At the U.S. Forest Service, for example, natural resource conservation is a deeply help premise, forming the core of the organization's mission. Employees must reflect conservation values in their daily work if they hope to make a favorable impression on others. We group impression management skills into three categories: emotional maturity, showing competence, and expressing confidence.

According to Joseph M. Fox, chairman of Software A&E, and Donald G. Zauderer, at The American University in Washington D.C., many talented professionals find it difficult to advance within their organizations because they fail to demonstrate **emotional maturity.**[9] Although people are rarely praised for being emotionally mature, immature behavior stands out and reduces peoples' perceptions of your competence. Even a single inappropriate outburst could destroy your credibility.

Emotionally mature people, on the other hand, have a sense of perspective—the ability to tolerate and accept life's many setbacks without becoming overly frustrated or resentful.[10] One colleague we knew would express anger over the smallest perceived inequity. This person would explode with anger when she found out, for example, that the department wouldn't pay for faculty business cards. Such annoyances are part of life and mature people handle them without complaint. Emotionally mature people talk out their stress with friends, peers, and acquaintances to relieve work-related anxiety. Such talks can help solve problems or merely serve as an opportunity to vent feelings. Finally, emotionally mature people accept responsibility for their actions. They don't blame others for their personal or professional problems. We have known employees who blame their fellow employees for every problem in their lives. The failure to get a promotion or to succeed on an important assignment, even failures in their personal lives, are all due to actions others performed or failed to perform. Such is not the mark of maturity.

According to Nancie Fimbel at San Jose State University, **showing competence** means having the technical knowledge needed to efficiently solve routine problems. Competent people can handle their routine work without running to a superior to ask questions about every hiccup. However, they also know when the problems in a routine assignment have become so great that help is required.[11]

Expressing confidence is another way to cultivate a favorable impression. According to Fimbel, managers expect a sender to display the confidence warranted by their competence. "Sentences that state facts but that secondarily congratulate the message sender herself, as in 'I have completed the task,' sound confident. Phrases such as 'of course,' and 'clearly' add certainty to the content of the message by presenting assumptions as indubitable fact; 'as we decided' and 'as you know' assume the audience's agreement."[12] Nonverbally, confidence is communicated with high-immediacy behaviors such as voice modulation to express appropriate affect and suitable variation in pitch, rate, and volume, rather than monotone speech. Steady, sustained, substantial eye contact, and affirmative body cues such as head nodding and hand gestures communicate high energy and a sense of confidence.[13] Confident people derive self-esteem from their own accomplishments and don't need constant reinforcement from others. Some of the most frustrating employees view the smallest correction as a death blow to their self-esteem. Although modern managers must work to build the confidence of their employees, they are too busy to make this their life's task.

Finally, confident people do not focus on failure. It isn't uncommon to think about the consequences of failure when working on a large or important project. When your first author was selected to facilitate a community advisory panel structured by two of our town's largest employer's, Jim experienced both joy at having been selected but also fear that the success of the project rested mainly on his shoulders. When early meetings were poorly attended and the group seemed to be drifting apart, his fear of failure became more acute and he started to bring these fears up with management at both organizations. Fortunately, Nancy reminded him that effective managers don't spend time thinking or talking about failure because it reduces people's confidence in their leadership. Instead, effective managers refocus their fears to analyzing and correcting problems. Talking about failure prevents you from focusing on the problem and may actually create the failure you fear. Instead, talk fears out with family members and friends. At work, display an attitude of confidence to increase the confidence others have in you.

In summary, impression management involves emotional maturity, showing competence, and expressing confidence. Good impressions mean that others are eager to associate with you which improves your interpersonal linkage power.

Aligning Oneself with Powerful Others.   Finally, developing interpersonal linkages means forming coalitions with others to gain power and influence. For employees who are new to an organization, this is best accomplished by seeking out a **mentor,** "an individual with some tenure in the organization who is willing to serve as advisor, friend, observer, giver of feedback, helper, teacher, and sounding board, to a newer member."[14] The **mentee** or **protégé** is someone willing to be guided by the knowledge accumulated by the mentor. Mentors provide both instrumental and expressive benefits to the protégé. Instrumental benefits include information, expertise, professional advice, political access, exposure to upper management, help in getting important assignments, and advocacy for promotion. Expressive benefits include friendship, social support, and enjoyment. In the extended example presented earlier, Mr. Jackson serves as a mentor to his new employees. Although some organizations have formal mentoring programs in which a newcomer is assigned to learn from a more experienced employee, the newcomer is usually left on his or her own in such matters.

Developing a mentor involves several steps. First, the new employee must scout appropriate mentor possibilities in the organization. Research shows that both mentors and protégés choose partners who are of like identities, sharing similar interests and world views. This can become a problem for women and minorities in the organization because similar people are often underrepresented in the higher reaches of management. We will discuss this problem in the next section of this chapter. Generally, you should search for someone who is somewhat similar to you in attitudes and interests, someone who is politically well connected in the organization, and someone who will serve as a mentor. Once you have selected several mentor possibilities, initiate a relationship with these people. Make an appointment to talk about your present assignment. Ask their advice about a decision you face. Seek their input about the organization's culture. Remember, it is the mentor, not the protégé, who decides whether a relationship is possible. If one person isn't very open to your inquiries, back off, reassess the situation, and continue to check out other people in the organization. If a person responds positively, take his or her advice and make it clear that you have acted on suggestions provided. Offer praise for his or her ideas and thanks for the help given. Share some of the credit if the mentor provided helpful advice on a successful assignment. Such comments increase your potential mentor's visibility in the organization and give him or her a reason to develop a closer working relationship with you. Offer to handle some of your mentor's workload or accept some of your mentor's less appealing tasks. All of these provide the potential mentor with incentive for building a stronger relationship. Unfortunately, building interpersonal networks can be a problem for women and minorities. The following section of this chapter addresses the difficulty women and minorities have networking in large organizations.

Building Interpersonal Networks:
The Experience of Women and Minorities

As we have explained throughout the previous section, building interpersonal networks in organizations is vital for personal success and productivity. However, despite the growing presence of women and minorities in organizations, research shows that these employees are sometimes excluded from informal interpersonal networks. As a result, these employees suffer from restricted knowledge of the organization, have difficulty forming coalitions for political gain, have trouble finding powerful mentors, and, as a result, are less likely to move up the organizational hierarchy. The mobility limit is often referred to as the **"glass ceiling,"** an invisible barrier that prevents women and minorities from reaching the highest levels of management. Here, we address the reasons that women and minorities have difficulty gaining access to the informal communication network in organizations and suggest ways to overcome these obstacles.

Barriers to the Informal Network

Although outright prejudice and exclusion was common fifteen years ago, many of these problems have diminished since the enactment of the civil rights legislation in the 1960s and through changing perceptions of women and minorities. For example, fair hiring guidelines assure that applicant pools are open to women and minorities. Title VII of the Civil Rights Act forbids discrimination in compensation, terms, conditions, or privileges of employment. The barriers to advancement of women and minorities in the '90s are much less overt, and more difficult to alter through new laws. Knowing about these subtle barriers can help women and minorities overcome them and help nonminority managers advance the careers of their talented minority employees.

The first, and arguably most important, barrier to women and minorities in forming organizational networks and mentorship relationships is a universal **preference for similarity** in our organizational relationships. Similar gender, ethnic, and racial identities provide people with a shared set of communication symbols, interests, and experiences that contribute to attraction and shared meaning. A recent study shows that the race of the mentor is the best predictor of the mentoring relationship.[15] As a result, white mentors tend to guide white employees and African American mentors tend to guide African American employees. The problem is that there is a much smaller pool of politically well-connected minority managers in most organizations to adequately mentor the much larger pool of minority protégés. Because both protégés and mentors prefer similar others, women and minorities may remain outside of important organizational networks.

In addition to the preference for similarity, a second obstacle to minority advancement is the **stereotype** that some white male managers may hold. Despite their advances into management ranks in the last fifteen years, negative

stereotypes of women and minorities persist in some organizations and industries. In some organizations, the presence of token female and minority employees leads some white male managers to exaggerate the differences between
themselves and minority employees. They may inappropriately ascribe lower
status and competence to all members of different gender, racial, or ethnic
groups. Such perceptions lead some managers to view women and minorities as
having fewer resources and less potential for advancement, making a mentor
relationship less advantageous to them.[16] Women and minorities who cannot
find similar others to network with may therefore be excluded from cross-gender
and cross-racial relationships.

Finally, even if minority employees do accomplish cross-sex or cross-racial
network relationships, these are likely to be weaker than same-sex, same-race
contacts. Relationships based on similar gender and racial ties provide greater personal attraction, social support, and identification for both members than do relationships based on differences.[17] Cross-race or cross-gender ties require more
effort to maintain and may not allow women or minority employees the same
access into political networks, the same visibility to decision makers, and the
same expressive benefits, emotional support, confirmation, or social support as do
ties based on similarity. As you can see, even organizations that attempt to
become more diverse can still present problems for minority employees. There
are, however, solutions to these problems.

Overcoming Informal Network Barriers

The problems just discussed leave women and minorities with a choice. First,
they can pursue close, stable network contacts with similar individuals. Because
these contacts are based on similarity, they are likely to provide enormous expressive benefits, but these ties may not provide visibility or political connection. On
the other hand, women and minorities can forsake the expressive benefits of sim-
ilarity-based ties and seek to network with different people. While expressive
benefits may not be met in these networks, instrumental benefits are more likely.
Faced with these choices, most women and minorities attempt to steer a middle
course, maintaining two separate networks—one a network of like-minded individuals of similar gender and race that provides expressive benefits, and one a
network of politically connected acquaintances and mentors who are committed
to advancing minorities and provide access to organizational resources and information.[18] Properly managed, steering the middle course is a viable option for
upwardly mobile women and minorities.

The following suggestions are made to help women, minorities, and any
other employee who wants diverse contact with politically connected senior
organizational members. Because of the limited number of women and minorities in the highest reaches of many organizations, finding similar mentors
requires **reaching across the organization** in terms of both hierarchy and
geography.[19] For example, African American managers have more extradepart-
mental relationships and broader support networks than do white managers

because of their relationships with other African Americans outside their department.[20] Creating a broader network, although time-consuming, ends up being an advantage. Broader contacts are information-rich because they are better connected to the larger organization. Also, the advent of such new communication technologies as fax machines and e-mail make keeping in touch with geographically or functionally dispersed contacts easier than in the past. You should work to turn a disadvantage into an advantage by seeking contacts across the organization's functional and geographical boundaries.

A second piece of advice is to **seek out nonminority managers** who demonstrate a desire to advance women and minorities. Although barriers and stereotypes remain, many managers acknowledge the benefits of a diverse labor force. They actively seek minority protégés, help build their resumes, and advance them in the corporation.

Third, minority employees must counter the stereotypes about their competence and desire to advance through company ranks. To counter unwarranted assumptions, women and minorities should constantly **express and demonstrate the desire for advancement.** For example, taking on high-profile assignments will bring you to the attention of higher-ups. Successful completion of those assignments increases others' perceptions of your competence. Express confidence in yourself, your work, and your eventual promotion. Seek constant evaluation and feedback from your superior and mentors. Ask them to rate your performance against the top employees at your level and work to make the improvements they suggest. Finally, advancing in any organization requires taking risks to stand out and get noticed.

Fourth, almost all supervisors are forced to distinguish between those subordinates that demonstrate higher commitment, trustworthiness, and competence than subordinates that, while not incompetent or untrustworthy, are less distinguished than the others. The **in-group** of employees may be a select association of protégés or a clique of the superior's most trusted employees. The in-group is given inside information, influence in decision making, attractive tasks, personal latitude, support, and attention from the superior in return for their commitment. According to researchers George Graen and Terri Scandura, the negotiation of in-group or **out-group** status usually takes place during a newcomer's first few weeks in the new organization. In stage one, the leader tests the subordinate with requests or assignments and evaluates the subordinate's response for possible in-group membership. The superior is watching for greater-than-required expenditures of time and energy, the assumption of greater responsibility and commitment. This can be accomplished by staying after hours to complete a project, working hard to provide higher quality work, and completing the task in less than prescribed time limits.[21] In stage two, the superior may propose a more collaborative relationship by offering resources in return for desired behaviors from the subordinate. The newcomer may respond positively, signaling an intention of becoming an in-group member.[22]

Finally, women and minorities will find it easier to acquire entry into the informal network if they acquire the expertise needed in their organizations. As we suggested earlier in our discussion of personal empowerment, acquiring expertise needed in the organization is an excellent way for any employee to plug into the informal communication network. Although we have talked about organizational power and politics in positive terms, there are times when power imbalances lead to oppressive behavior, such as sexual harassment. The final section of this chapter defines sexual harassment and presents formal and informal solutions to this abuse of power.

Sexual Harassment: A Gross Imbalance of Power

Since the 1991 Hill-Thomas hearings, workplace sexual harassment has received enormous attention. As a result, reports of sexual harassment have increased, and one of the professional world's dirtiest secrets has been forced into the light. Other prominent examples of sexual harassment include the diaries of Oregon Senator Robert Packwood, the Navy Tailhook court-martials, the accusations of sexual harassment at the Mitsubishi plant in Normal, Illinois, and, most recently, the accusations of sexual harassment and rape at the Army's Aberdeen Proving Ground in Maryland.

Except in cases of physical manhandling or assault, sexual harassment is based on communication. Lewd remarks, sexual jokes, or negotiations for sexual favors all involve some form of verbal and nonverbal communication. In addition, the methods of controlling and eliminating sexual harassment, such as formal grievances and lawsuits, or individual solutions such as attempting to convince the harasser to cease and desist, are all based on communication.

We opened this chapter explaining that hierarchies create power imbalances in interpersonal relationships. Under normal circumstances such imbalances are not a problem. Sexual harassment, however, represents the abuse of organizational power. In this section we define sexual harassment and describe a variety of interpersonal communication solutions to the problem. Although sexual harassment has a variety of costs associated with it, including psychological and physical costs to the victims and direct and indirect costs to the organization, our position is that sexual harassment is discrimination against a particular gender, usually women, and represents a gross abuse of power.[23]

The term "sexual harassment" was introduced into the English language by feminists to refer to behaviors whereby men humiliate women and treat them as "objects."[24] **Sexual harassment** was defined legally in 1980 when the Equal Employment Opportunity Commission (EEOC) established guidelines to interpret sexual harassment. The guidelines were established under Title VII of the 1964 Civil Rights Act. Sexual harassment includes:

> Unwelcome sexual advances, requests for sexual favors, and other verbal or physical conduct of a sexual nature that takes place under any of the following circumstances.

1. When submission to the sexual advance is a condition of keeping or getting a job, whether expressed in implicit or explicit terms.
2. When a supervisor or boss makes personal decisions based on an employee's submission to or rejection of sexual advances.
3. When conduct unreasonably interferes with a person's work performance or creates an intimidating, hostile, or offensive work environment.[25]

In practice, "sexual harassment has been characterized as an expression of **gender discrimination** coupled with the **abuse of organizational power.**"[26] Most often, sexual harassment involves a range of unsolicited and unwelcome male attention that serves to emphasize a woman's sex role over her work skills and abilities. Although reports indicate that sexual harassment of women against men does occur, it is relatively infrequent (at most, in surveys 15 percent of men report being sexually harassed),[27] and because the nature of sexual harassment directed at men is significantly different from that directed at women,[28] this chapter focuses on the problem of sexual harassment as it is perpetrated against women.

Practically speaking, sexual harassment may include several general categories of behavior. **Verbal commentaries** such as sexual jokes, lewd comments, and excessive comments about bodily appearance are forms of harassment. For example, an anonymous communication professor reported the following incident of verbal commentary:

> I was in class lecturing when I was writing something on the board and as I turned around a male voice from the back of the class said: "She's got nice looking tits." This was said loudly enough for the entire class to hear. I was so stunned and shocked that I said nothing. But when I told my mentor, who was then the dean of a law school what had happened, he chuckled and said: "Well, you do have nice tits."[29]

Verbal negotiation includes propositions for sex, especially those that involve the promise of reward or threat of punishment if the woman does not comply. **Physical manhandling** is unwanted groping, or inappropriate touching, and **physical assault** is the use of physical force.[30]

There are a variety of solutions that individuals and groups can take to the problems of sexual harassment. **Formal solutions** include creating policies against sexual harassment, communicating those policies throughout the organization, training employees to recognize and intercede to stop harassment, and enforcing the rules so that perpetrators are punished. Formal solutions also include filing grievances or lawsuits to get the harasser to stop. **Informal solutions** involve face-to-face communication with the harasser.[31]

According to Shereen G. Bingham, a communication researcher at the University of Nebraska at Omaha, whatever strategy one selects to stop harassment must address three goals: first, to **get the harassment stopped,** second, it must **maintain employment,** and third, it must help the victim **manage her own psychological and emotional well-being.** The primary obstacle to achieving these goals is the power imbalance that usually exists between the harasser (the high-power person) and the victim (usually a person of low power).[32] Because this imbalance makes it very difficult for a woman to achieve all three interpersonal goals, responses should be made with appropriate thought to increase the likelihood of success.

Formal Strategies for Managing Sexual Harassment

Formal strategies for managing sexual harassment involve filing a formal grievance or a lawsuit. The precise steps to filing a formal grievance—or larger still, a lawsuit—depend on the particular harassment situation, the organization's rules about sexual harassment, and its formal grievance procedures. Thus, it is difficult to make specific recommendations. We can, however, offer several pieces of advice. First, whether we like it or not, our system of justice is based on the belief that a person (even a harasser) is innocent until proven guilty. The burden of proof in any harassment complaint rests with the victim of harassment. Unfortunately, the circumstances of harassment make this particularly difficult. Most harassers commit their misdeeds in private, when only the perpetrator and the victim are present, and it is difficult to corroborate harassment incidents. This disadvantage can be mitigated by following two rules.

First, many organizations encourage the victim to clearly say no to the harasser. This reduces the harasser's ability to claim his actions were all in fun or that the victim really wanted this kind of relationship. Of course, such direct rejection may put the victim's job and career at risk.

Second, victims should document the incidents by keeping written records, which protects the woman from fallible memory and makes any case more convincing. Record exact words and language and try to describe the feelings produced by the harassment. Date the record and save it for future action. Without documentation, a victim's chances of redress are severely diminished.

Informal Strategies for Managing Sexual Harassment

Despite the considerable evidence suggesting that direct, informal confrontations between victim and harassed are successful only half of the time, there are other benefits to be gained from confrontation, including personal empowerment. By taking matters into her own hands, a woman may develop a stronger sense of personal power and control over her life.[33] As such, we have culled the following strategies from a larger list complied by Shereen G. Bingham. We selected the strategies in Table 4.1 because research demonstrates these have the highest probability of success.

The first strategy in Table 4.1 is the **nonassertive message,** which represents avoidance. Nonassertive behaviors entail remaining silent, avoiding the harasser,

TABLE 4.1 Communication Strategies for Responding to Sexual Harassment

Nonassertive Message
 a. *Description.* Hide or deny one's thoughts, feelings, beliefs, or wants.
 b. *Example.* Silence

Messages with a Face-Saving Component
Assertive Message
 a. *Description.* Express thoughts, feelings, beliefs, and wants in direct, honest, and appropriate ways.
 b. *Example.* "I don't like it when you make sexual comments about my body and I want you to stop doing it. This is a workplace; sexual jokes and comments are not appropriate."
Assertive-Empathic Message
 a. *Description.* Express thoughts, feelings, beliefs, and wants in direct, honest, and appropriate ways and express special concern for the harasser's feelings and perspective.
 b. *Example.* "I don't mean to hurt your feelings but it bothers me when you make comments about my body. I enjoy working with you but I'd appreciate it if you would stop making sexual jokes and comments."
Rhetorical Multifunctional Message
 a. *Description.* Redefine the situation in a way that precludes continuation of the sexual harassment, while also deflecting the implication that the harasser has a negative identity or that the harassing behavior has harmed the working relationship.
 b. *Example.* "I appreciate the fair treatment you've always given me on this job because I have something on my mind that relates to how well we work together. When you make sexual comments to me I know you're just teasing, but deep down I end up feeling insulted anyway and if we don't get this straightened out I'm afraid it might start to affect our work. I know you would never want to put me down or interfere with my job performance and I would never want to do that to you. So I think the best solution here is for us to stop the sexual jokes and comments altogether. Sound fair to you?"

Messages that Include Little or No Face-Saving Element
Threat
 a. *Description.* Express intent to inflict injury or punishment on the harasser if the harassment does not stop.
 b. *Example.* "If you don't stop making sexual jokes about my body, I will file a complaint with your supervisor."
Aggressive Message
 a. *Description.* Express thoughts, feelings, beliefs, and wants directly and honestly in a way that coerces or attacks the harasser.
 b. *Example.* "You stepped over the line with that last comment, wise guy. Shut your big mouth and get away from my desk. I don't take abuse from you or anyone else."

(continued)

TABLE 4.1   Continued

Overt Manipulation
   a. *Description.* Provide information in a manner that influences the harasser to stop the harassment, reveals to the harasser that the influence was intended, but prevents the harasser from admitting awareness of the influence process (due to potential shame, embarrassment, or other negative consequences).
   b. *Example.* "I couldn't hear your last remark. Could you please repeat that comment a bit louder? Where did you say you want to touch me?" (said loudly in front of other workers)

From: Bingham, S. "Communication Strategies for Managing Sexual Harassment in Organizations: Understanding Message Options and Their Effects." *Journal of Applied Communication Research,* 19 (1991): 88–115. Used by permission of the National Communication Association.

*Bingham's original scheme was divided into three categories: Assertiveness Literature, Intra-Organizational Influence Literature, and Interpersonal Message Design Literature, and included seven additional strategies not listed here.

or tolerating the harassment if it is minimal. This strategy is also useful if the victim views the harasser's motives as innocent or ignorant of the nature of the behavior and the damage it is doing. Finally, the nonassertive message is useful if the risk to job or career is so high that the safest course of action is avoidance. Nonassertiveness may also serve as a temporary strategy while collecting information prior to a formal complaint. Bingham notes, however, that if the nonassertive strategy is used too long it increases feelings of insecurity, powerlessness, and self-loathing.[34]

After the nonassertiveness, the remaining strategies are divided into two categories: strategies that help the perpetrator save face, and strategies that include no such face-saving measure for the perpetrator. The concept of **face** represents the desire of a person to present a positive and approved image to others.[35] One of the most important face needs is to have one's abilities respected and sense of competence preserved. Message strategies that preserve a person's face refuse the sexual harassment of the offender, but do so in a way that minimizes damage to the person's image of self. Face-saving messages may minimize the harasser's desire to retaliate against the victim.

The first face-saving strategy is the simple **assertiveness message,** which allows the victim to stand up for personal rights in a clear and direct way without violating another person's rights.[36] As such, the assertive message may be the best way to say "No" to the harasser in a way that would be approved of by other decision makers in the hierarchy. However, the downside to the assertiveness message is that it rejects the harasser, who may then choose to retaliate against the woman's career.

According to Bingham, the **assertive-empathic message** attempts to "reconcile being assertive with being liked and maintaining rapport."[37] The message is assertive but includes an empathy component that may reduce the desire of the harasser to retaliate. The **rhetorical multifunctional message** includes features that protect the image of the harasser and expresses liking for the job or the present relationship, while refusing to accept harassment. These strategies aim at achieving all three goals for interpersonal messages.

The first nonface-saving strategy is a **threat,** which tells the harasser to cease the activity and states that the victim will proceed with a formal grievance if the harasser doesn't stop. Because the threat does nothing to protect the face of the harasser, it invites retaliation. However, with some harassers, a threat is the only form of persuasion that will be effective. It is unwise to use threats as bluffs. If the bluff is called and the victim does not carry out the threat, the victim will look even weaker in the eyes of the perpetrator, inviting further harassment. Therefore, issue threats with forcefulness and clarity so they will be believed; if the harasser refuses to stop, follow through on the threat.

The second strategy is the **aggressive message**—a coercive message that ridicules or intimidates the harasser. Unfortunately, this message is so blatant that it greatly increases the chances of retaliation. However, Bingham notes that some harassers may not take a woman's objections seriously unless they are addressed in an aggressive fashion.[38] **Overt manipulation** turns the tables on the harasser in public, within earshot of his wife, family, or coworkers, thereby embarrassing the harasser.

To decide on the appropriate strategy, it is necessary to evaluate the seriousness of the harassment, the organization you are in and its attitude toward this kind of abuse, the support you are receiving from colleagues, friends, and other organizational higher-ups, the likelihood that the harasser will retaliate, your relative power in the organization, the harasser's relative power in the organization, the likelihood of your submitting a formal complaint, and several other factors related to personal preference for conflict versus tolerance of the offending behavior. Sexual harassment represents a terrible paradox to any woman. The choice is one of maintaining an important career and putting food on the table versus trying to stop a behavior that makes a normal work life impossible. The larger solution to the problem lies in our organizations and our society. Only when we adopt zero tolerance for this behavior will we be able to eliminate its damaging personal and organizational costs. This kind of change can come about only when everyone in organizations, women and men alike, stand up together and say they will not tolerate this behavior.

Summary

Politics is a central facet of communication within hierarchical organizations. Although our attitudes about power and politics are generally negative, this need not be the case. We define power as the ability to influence or persuade. The four sources of organizational power are resource control, expertise power, communication skills, and interpersonal network power. Organizational politics has two dimensions: Overt politics involves threats, promises, negotiations, coalitions, and a host of other strategies to influence organizational members. Hidden politics involves deciding what issues to raise and how to present them for greatest effect.

One way to succeed politically is to create an adequate base of support through interpersonal networks. Increasing this source of power involves impression management and aligning oneself with powerful others.

Building interpersonal networks can be problematic for women and minorities. Preferences for similarity, subtle stereotyping, and the difficulty of creating strong ties across gender and racial boundaries limit networking possibilities for women and minorities. To overcome these barriers, women and minorities should reach across organizational boundaries for contacts, seek out nonminority mentors, demonstrate their desire for advancement, become a member of the supervisor's in-group, and acquire technical expertise needed in the organization.

Because of recent revelations from the military, government, and large organizations, the subject of sexual harassment is finally out in the open. Sexual harassment is the result of gender discrimination and the abuse of organizational power. Most often, sexual harassment involves a range of unsolicited and unwelcome male attention that serves to emphasize a woman's sex role over her work skills and abilities. Sexual harassment can involve verbal commentary, verbal negotiation, physical manhandling, or physical assault. Surveys indicate that approximately 40 percent of American working women report at least one incident of sexual harassment.

Formal solutions to sexual harassment focus on creating, communicating, and enforcing policies against this abuse of power, filing formal grievances, or taking legal action. Informal solutions should accomplish three goals: stopping the harassment, maintaining employment, and managing psychological and emotional well-being. The primary obstacle to achieving these goals is the power imbalance that exists between perpetrator (usually the person with the power) and the victim. Victims are encouraged to say "No" and document harassment episodes prior to filing a formal complaint.

Informal strategies fall into two categories: those that preserve the face needs of the harasser and those that do not preserve the harasser's face (see Table 4.1). Those that preserve the harasser's face reduce the possibility of retaliation, but may not be strong enough to stop the harassment. Victims should carefully weigh the advantages and disadvantages of each strategy before confronting a harasser.

QUESTIONS FOR DISCUSSION

1. Describe your opinion about organizational politics before you read this chapter. What was the source of this opinion? Has reading this chapter changed your opinion about organizational politics in any way? Why or why not?

2. Early in the chapter we suggested that the "glass ceiling" that blocks women and minorities from advancement in organizations is partly a result of poor access to

important political networks. Can you think of other barriers to advancement for women and minorities? What can be done to remove these barriers and create more equal opportunity for all organizational members?

3. Why does human nature make organizational politics inevitable? What kinds of preferences and abilities would people need to make organizational politics a thing of the past? Would you want to live in a world where organizational politics no longer exists?

4. Discuss the advantages and disadvantages of the sexual harassment reduction strategies we discussed in this chapter. In what circumstances would you select formal over informal strategies? In what circumstances would you select informal over formal strategies? How might the strategies be combined for greatest effect?

ACTIVITIES AND EXERCISES

1. Review the story of James Johnson cited early in this chapter. Identify all the examples of overt and hidden politics in the story. Can you distinguish between the two kinds of organizational politics? Are there any political actions that do not fit into either category?

2. Apply the ethical standards outlined in the Ethics Brief to the story of James Johnson. Does the accountant in the story work to balance organizational and individual interests? What does she do to remain vigilant and open to change? What, if anything, does she do to minimize harm to others? In your opinion, is this an example of ethical or unethical political activity? Why?

3. Work with classmates to develop an example of sexual harassment in the workplace. Then, develop responses to the harassment that are assertive, assertive-empathic, and rhetorical multifunctional. Make your responses as clear and precise as possible. Discuss probable success or failure of these messages with your group or class.

4. Work with classmates to develop another example of sexual harassment in the workplace. Then, develop responses to the harassment that are threatening, aggressive, or overtly manipulative. Make your responses as clear and precise as possible. Discuss the probable success or failure of these messages with your group or class.

NOTES

1. Emerson, R. M., "Power-Dependence Relations," *American Sociological Review* 27 (1962): 31–41.

2. DiSanza, J. R., "Shared Meaning as a Sales Inducement Strategy: Bank Teller Responses to Frames, Reinforcements, and Quotas," *The Journal of Business Communication* 30 (1993): 133–160.

3. Hocker, J. L., and W. W. Wilmot, *Interpersonal Conflict* (Dubuque, IA: Wm. C. Brown, 1995).

4. Jackall, R., "Moral Mazes: Bureaucracy and Managerial Work," *Harvard Business Review,* September–October 1983, 118–130.

5. Mayes, B. T., and R. W. Allen, "Toward a Definition of Organizational Politics," *Academy of Management Review* 2 (1977): 420.

6. Conrad, C., *Strategic Organizational Communication* (Fort Worth: Harcourt Brace, 1994).

7. Ibid.

8. Thomas, E., Jr., "Former U.S. Medalist Emerges as Quiet Force in the Olympic Arena," *The Wall Street Journal,* 28 June 1996, A1.

9. Fox, J. M., and D. G. Zauderer, "Emotional Maturity—An Important Executive Quality," *Management Solutions,* September 1987, 41–45.

10. Blai, B., Jr., "Emotional Maturity at Work: Tips for the HR Executive," *Personnel,* December 1987, 56–58.

11. Fimbel, N., "Communicating Realistically: Taking Account of Politics in Internal Business Communications," *The Journal of Business Communication* 31 (1994): 7–26.

12. Ibid., 13.

13. Leathers, D. G., *Successful Nonverbal Communication: Principles and Applications* (New York: MacMillan, 1986).

14. Pepper, G. L., *Communicating in Organizations: A Cultural Approach* (New York: McGraw-Hill, 1995), 131.

15. Kalbfleisch, P. J., and A. B. Davies, "Minorities and Mentoring: Managing the Multicultural Institution," *Communication Education* 40 (1991): 266–271.

16. Ibarra, H., "Personal Networks of Women and Minorities in Management: A Conceptual Framework," *Academy of Management Review* 18 (1993): 56–87.

17. Ibid.

18. Ibid.

19. Ibid.

20. Thomas, D. A., "The Impact of Race on Managers' Experience of Developmental Relationships (Mentoring and Sponsorship): An Intra-Organizational Study," *Journal of Organizational Behavior* 2 (1990): 479–492.

21. Dansereau, F. Jr., G. Graen, and W. J. Haga, "A Vertical Dyad Linkage Approach to Leadership within Formal Organizations," *Organizational Behavior and Human Performance* 13 (1975): 46–78.

22. Graen, G. B., and T. A. Scandura, "Toward a Psychology of Dyadic Organizing," in *Research in Organizational Behavior 9,* ed. L. L. Cummings and B. M. Staw (Greenwich, CT: JAI Press, 1987), 175–208.

23. Albrecht, T. L., and B. W. Bach, *Communication in Complex Organizations* (Fort Worth: Harcourt Brace, 1997).

24. Bingham, S. G., "Communication Strategies for Managing Sexual Harassment in Organizations: Understanding Message Options and Their Effects," *Journal of Applied Communication Research* 19 (1991): 88–115.

25. Sheffey, S., and R. S. Tindale, "Perceptions of Sexual Harassment in the Workplace," *Journal of Applied Social Psychology* 22 (1992): 1502–1520.

26. Albrecht and Bach, 251.

27. Ibid.

28. Bingham.

29. "'Our Stories': Communication Professionals' Narratives of Sexual Harassment," *Journal of Applied Communication Research* 20 (1992): 378.

30. Loy, P. H., and L. P. Stewart, "The Extent and Effects of the Sexual Harassment of Working Women," *Sociological Focus* 17 (1984): 31–43.

31. Bingham.

32. Ibid.

33. Ibid.

34. Ibid.

35. Folger, J. P., M. S. Poole, and R. K. Stutman, *Working Through Conflict* (New York: Longman, 1997).

36. Bingham.

37. Ibid., 100

38. Ibid.

Communicating in Organizational Groups and Teams

Despite the portrayal of the organization as the home of rugged individualism, professional work is often done in groups and teams. Developing, marketing, and selling any product or service in a global market involves the coordinated efforts of many people. The concept of rugged individualism in organizations is a media-inspired myth.

A **group** is a collection of three or more individuals who perceive themselves as a group, possess a common fate, and communicate with one another over time to accomplish both personal and group goals.[1] Therefore, people waiting in line for a ride at an amusement park are not a group, but several students who decide to study together do represent a group. Groups can take many forms, including the senior management group, regional sales groups, accounting groups, or engineering groups.

In the past ten years, however, the term "group" has gone out of favor, replaced by one of the newest management innovations, the **self-directed team.** Teams emerged as an explicit attempt to do more with less in an era of global competition and shrinking resources.[2] The self-directed team eliminates the job of supervisory managers on a production line, for instance, and places all authority for coordination, manufacturing, and delivering the product in the hands of the team. The team also hires, fires, and disciplines its own members, sets its own work goals, and completes jobs on its own with little or no supervision.[3] Because decisions are in the hands of a small number of teams, the company can react quickly to changing markets, producing a leaner, more flexible organization.

Teams differ from groups in several important ways. First, teams have more decision-making authority than do groups. Second, because of that authority, teams are more interdependent and communicate more frequently with other members than do groups. Teams often meet several times a day to coordinate activity, avoid duplication, and make necessary decisions. Finally, teams emphasize constant training and assessment of progress toward clearly articulated performance goals.[4]

Despite their popularity, the implementation of teams has a spotty record in industry. As early as 1993, such companies as Ford, Procter & Gamble, Honda, and GM's Saturn plant retreated from teams, finding that they slowed decisions and shielded people from taking responsibility.[5] Levi Strauss's attempt to introduce teams into piece-work factory settings created morale and productivity problems.[6] It is difficult to determine if the team concept is the wave of the future or a management fad destined to disappear in a few years. Nevertheless, the term, at least, is here to stay. Although most of the concepts we discuss in this chapter apply equally to teams and groups, we will focus on team-building throughout the chapter. We begin with a discussion of the roles that team members play. We then cover the most frequently practiced team activity, the meeting, and close the chapter with a discussion of conflict management.

Team Membership Roles

Team members operate by taking a variety of roles. A **role** is an expectation about individual behavior patterns. Just as members of a family perform behaviors that distinguish them as parents, grandparents, and children, people in teams take on a limited set of repetitive behaviors that distinguish their membership roles. "Leader" is a term used to describe particular behaviors. Taken together, these behaviors are called a role.[7] The leadership role and various followership roles are crucial to team performance.

The Leadership Role

Leadership is a complex and complicated phenomena that is sometimes confused with management. **Managers** guide members by explaining job requirements, setting performance criteria, and monitoring output; they provide compensation for successful work and punish failure. The authority to set goals and deliver rewards is conferred by the organization, and employees comply with the requirements to the degree that they desire the manager's rewards and want to avoid punishments. Referring to Chapter 1, management represents a contractual agreement whereby each person gives up something he or she would rather not part with or do in order to get something valuable from the other person. By and large, these contractual arrangements are adequate for directing most small groups. Supervisors in fast-food chains, retail stores, and other service industries usually function as managers rather than leaders. Because of the part-time nature of employment, high turnover, and unskilled work, the simple employment contract provides adequate motivation for group members.

Self-directed teams, however, require more member commitment than managers can create using simple employment contracts. The increased authority and independence of the self-directed team requires that members be motivated and work hard without the benefit of direct supervision. Leadership provides a way to address these needs.

Leaders are able to specify issues of importance to members, raise subordinates' awareness of these issues, define how they should be interpreted or perceived, and then motivate members to transcend individual self-interest for the sake of the team.[8] Unlike simple management, where the authority is granted by the organization, the leader's authority comes from the members themselves, who voluntarily give up part of their right to specify goals and define issues to the leader. Members follow the leader not for rewards, but because they buy into the leader's vision. In Chapter 1 we referred to this kind of agreement as consensual shared meaning, where people agree about basic objectives and values. Steven Jobs, cofounder of Apple Computers, is the classic example of a leader; a person who can drive individuals to innovate, create, and sacrifice for the company—not for financial rewards, but because the leader's vision is so compelling.

Although some managers do emerge as team leaders, it is equally likely that management and leadership roles are concentrated in different people. Whereas Jerry is the manager of his work group, he doesn't spend much time on the shop floor and doesn't know much about manufacturing details. He tries to hire good employees and protect the department's budget from cuts. Juan is the senior operator, and Jerry gives him wide latitude in deciding manufacturing priorities. Juan has no control over resources, but employees follow his lead because they like him and believe he knows what's best for the department.

What kind of person is likely to emerge as a team leader? Research indicates that emergent leaders are more communicatively flexible than nonleaders. In other words, leaders emerge by adapting their behavior to individual members of the group, to different tasks, and to different group priorities, depending on the circumstances.[9]

A study of several decision-making teams exemplifies leaders' adaptive behavior. In one meeting, the leader needed an open-ended, creative discussion of an agenda item. To facilitate this he made few procedural comments, such as calling for votes, limiting discussion, making critical evaluations, or seeking critical evaluation. Instead, he encouraged people to talk and be creative, and used group identity comments to emphasize the creative and nonbureaucratic nature of this team. In a later meeting the same leader needed to reach resolution on three agenda items. His procedural comments increased from the first meeting, and his identity comments about the group's special role and creativity diminished. This leader adapted his performance to meet the different needs of the team in two different meetings.[10] Team leaders are audience centered; they can assess member needs in context of the larger goal and enact behaviors that move the team forward. Despite the importance of flexibility, it is possible to describe two important categories of leader behavior: Leaders organize team efforts and define the team's context.

Leaders Organize the Team's Work.   Team activity is usually disorganized and messy, characterized by circular discussions, dead-end ideas, and conflicting solutions. Leaders use their communication skills to bring order to chaotic processes. Professors John F. Cragan and David W. Wright divide leadership communication behaviors into three categories: task, procedural, and interpersonal (see Figure 5.1). **Task communication** skills focus on accomplishing the team's performance goals. Therefore, **contributing ideas** and solutions is an important leadership function. If other members are hesitant to express their ideas, the leader can ease fears by laying out her own ideas. If members are still reluctant to contribute their ideas, it is up to the leaders to **seek ideas** through direct questions such as: "Kim, do you have any ideas on this problem?" or "Gabrielle, we haven't heard from you for a

---

FIGURE 5.1   Leadership Communication Behaviors

Task Leadership Communication Behaviors
    Contributing Ideas
    Seeking Ideas
    Evaluating Ideas
    Seeking Idea Evaluation
    Stimulating Creativity

Procedural Leadership Communication Behaviors
    Goal-Setting
    Agenda Making
    Clarifying
    Summarizing
    Verbalizing Consensus

Interpersonal Leadership Communication Behaviors
    Regulating Participation
    Climate Making
    Resolving Conflict

Adapted from: Cragan, J. F., and D. W. Wright, *Communication in Small Groups: Theory, Process, Skills* (Minneapolis/St. Paul: West Publishing, 1995). © Wadsworth Publishing Co. Reprinted by Permission.

while. What's your opinion?" It is up to the team leader to seek contributions from all group members.

Effective teams must not only develop ideas, they must cull poor ideas so only the strongest solutions remain. The leader must **evaluate ideas** in such a way that members do not feel attacked. This means rejecting other peoples' ideas without disconfirming their experience or emotional reactions (see Chapter 3). The leader must also **seek idea evaluation** from other group members through such direct questions as: "What do you think of our first solution?" "Are there ways to improve this concept, or should we set it aside for now?" Finally, under task communication behaviors, the group leader must **stimulate creativity,** allowing members to propose wild and offbeat ideas without criticism. This can be accomplished through various discussion techniques including brainstorming, nominal group technique, and group decision support software.

Leadership in the **procedural area** sets the agenda for the team's process. **Goal-setting** behaviors establish short and long-range objectives. Leaders are also responsible for **agenda making** to keep meetings on track. Leaders must ask members to **clarify** their abstract ideas. This can be accomplished through specific questions such as, "What do you mean by that?" "Can you provide an example of how this idea would work in practice?" and "How will this help us reduce our costs?" When asked in a nonthreatening manner, these questions can encourage members to think more deeply about their ideas. Clarification is required if abstract ideas are to become workable solutions.

Good leaders also keep the team on track by **summarizing** the group's progress. Consistent summary statements help members understand where the group is going: "So, what I hear is that we have not one, but two problems. We don't deal adequately with members of the environmental community and we are terrible with the press." Consistently summarizing members' ideas brings order to disorderly discussions. **Verbalizing consensus** involves finding the areas on which members agree. Such comments as: "I believe we agree that in the future the press will not be invited to attend our meetings," made through-out the meeting (rather than at the end of a meeting), increase the chances of eventual agreement.[11]

Finally, **interpersonal communication** skills create a productive environment for members. First, the leader must **regulate participation.** Dominant members must be held in check and less active members must be encouraged to participate. For instance, a comment such as, "Larry, I know you're very concerned about this issue, but let's take the time to hear from people who haven't spoken," can open a meeting up to other opinions. **Climate making** means creating a nonthreatening atmosphere so members feel comfortable contributing even their "crazy" ideas. Censuring members who make personal attacks and focusing criticism on ideas rather than individuals helps create a positive climate. Last, team work creates conflict, and good leaders are able to **resolve conflicts** and move the group forward. The last section of this chapter discusses a variety of conflict-management skills. In addition to organizing group activity, good leaders must define important issues for members and motivate them to transcend individual self-interest.

Leaders Define the Team's Focus.   According to professors Carl E. Larson and Frank M. J. LaFasto, effective teams adopt elevating goals that inspire lofty and sincere aspirations.[12] "Charisma" is the word we use to describe leaders who can focus members' attention and devotion to a goal, and charismatic leadership is the effective use of symbols. As we said in Chapter 1, events do not have any particular meaning; we use symbols to give meanings to events. Charismatic leaders are exceptional at communicating their interpretations of an event, their vision or goals, in such a way that followers accept the interpretation as correct.

For example, in the early 1980s, Dale Daniels took over Lockheed's L1011 jumbo jet plant in Antelope Valley, California. Aircraft production at the plant was behind schedule and over budget. The previous management's fear tactics turned individuals and teams against one another. Daniels wanted to change the plant's culture to a more cooperative one. One of his first acts was to fire a supervisor from the previous management team who would not or could not stop using the fear tactics Daniels deplored. He also explained repeatedly that the firing was not "retaliation" but was a first step to creating a more "cooperative spirit" at the plant.[13] Daniels's explanations helped reinforce his vision for the plant and employees. Group leaders use a variety of strategies to communicate and gain commitment to their vision.

Labels are catchy symbols that categorize or describe a thing or event. A good label can help employees grasp the vision the leader wants to communicate. In their book, *In Search of Excellence,* Peters and Waterman tell the story of a navy man named Bud Zumwalt who attempted to improve the crew's morale by changing the ship's voice call sign. He stated his case in a letter to superiors:

> Since recently assuming command of Isabell, this commanding officer has been concerned over the anemic connotation of the present voice radio call. When in company with such stalwarts as fireball, viper and others, it is somewhat embarrassing and completely out of keeping with the quality of the sailormen aboard to be identified by the relatively ignominious title Sapworth.[14]

After much effort, a new call sign was eventually approved.

> The voice Hellcat proved immensely popular. Arnold J. Isabell's officers and men proudly wore sleeve patches and baseball cap patches showing a black cat with a forked tail stepping out the flames of hell and breaking a submarine with its paws. The impact on morale was remarkable.[15]

While the label "Sapworth" might lead sailors to perceive their ship and crewmates as weak and ineffective, "Hellcat" implies competence, power, and fearlessness. The label changed the crew's interpretation of their experience.

As CEO of Maytag Corporation, Leonard A. Hadley inherited a company that was notoriously conservative when it came to investment in new products and technology. "For decades Maytag had a policy not to be the first to market with new technology, saying it would 'rather be right than be first.'"[16] In 1993

Mr. Hadley created the "Galaxy Initiative," a series of new products each named after a planet in the solar system. The label was, no doubt, created to evoke feelings of cutting-edge technology and expansiveness, encouraging employees to think more innovatively than before.

Labels influence how we think about things, and leaders can focus and define member attention through catchy words or phrases that communicate their vision. If the leader repeats the phrase often and behaves in ways consistent with the spirit of the label (as Dale Daniels did), members may eventually come to accept the leader's definition.

Leaders can also communicate their vision by elevating **heroes** who exemplify that vision. Although it may be difficult for people to become attached or connected to abstract visions expressed in such words as "competitiveness," "quality," or "customer service," it is easy to emulate someone who personifies an abstract vision. Heroes become symbols that stand for the leader's vision. By their recognition, heroes can set a high standard of performance that the leader wants from the team. The hero must, however, not be so superior that members view the standard as unattainable. Rather, the hero must set an achievable standard for other group members.[17]

A **ritual** is an event of passage that takes place when a milestone is achieved. Rituals include initiation ceremonies for new employees or parties celebrating individual accomplishment. Rituals often focus on praising heroes for important accomplishments. An officially sanctioned event at a publishing company is the annual meeting of the Ten Year Club, otherwise known as the "Screw In-Ceremony." During the event, new members of the Ten Year Club are initiated into the realm of long-term employees. A plaque with each new member's name is screwed into the mantel above the fireplace in the company's library. Newly "screwed-in" members are roasted, toasted, and presented gifts by other members. The event reinforces the importance of longevity in a company that encourages employees to become a part of the corporation, just as their names become a part of the building in which they are working.[18]

Leaders can specify important group values by encouraging rituals that reinforce those values. Rather than try to create new rituals from scratch, wise leaders capitalize on events the group has already developed, adjusting them to reinforce appropriate visions.

Identification occurs when members' interest and goals overlap.[19] Employees who identify with their team experience feelings of commitment, membership, and similarity with the group.[20] Members who identify with the team are devoted to its tasks and committed to success. Leaders can encourage team members to identify in a number of ways. The first method is **praise for the team's accomplishments,** which raises members' esteem and reminds them of the team's importance within the larger organization.[21] Another method of creating identification is by **espousing shared values.** For example, during a meeting the team leader emphasizes, "We all believe that customer service is our number one priority." In essence, members are told that they all share the same interests and priorities.[22]

Constant references to a **presumed "we"** often go unnoticed, but reinforce a taken-for-granted common bond among members. Statements such as "We must work together to solve this problem," or "We are going to improve quality in the next year" subtly suggest that all team members are committed to the same mission.[23]

Finally, nothing unites a group like a **common enemy.** Companies often emphasize threats from "outsiders" as a way to stress togetherness and identification among employees.[24] Portrayals of powerful enemies bent on destroying the team can lead to an increased sense of unity, and stronger collective acceptance of group values. Enemies should be chosen with care, however. Making an enemy of another unit in the company can poison relations between teams and prevent cooperation on important projects. A less destructive approach is to create a healthy sense of competition between teams to spur members to increased performance. Outside the company, portraying competitors as enemies creates a sense of commitment to team goals. The methods of encouraging identification with a team are summarized in Figure 5.2. Although leadership is vital, without committed followers, leaders can't accomplish much.

Membership Roles in Groups and Teams

A taxonomy of membership roles was created by Kenneth D. Benne and Paul Sheats, and includes three general categories: task roles, relationship roles, and self-centered or self-interested roles (see Figure 5.3). Members fulfilling roles in

---

FIGURE 5.2   Methods of Creating Identification

Praise for a Group's Accomplishments: Raises members' esteem for the team.

> "I want to congratulate the entire team on its efforts over the past six weeks. You've worked harder and accomplished more than any team I have ever led. Your efforts will play an important role in the coming product roll-out."

Espousing Shared Values: Explicitly state that the team members share the same values.

> "I know none of you would have come to this agency if community service were not your primary goal."

The Presumed "We": Subtly suggest that all members are committed to the same mission.

> "*We* are going to move forward with this project despite the setback because *we* know how important it is to *our* company's future."

The Common Enemy: Portray outside interests that are trying to destroy the team.

> "This is not a level playing field because competitors in other countries have the benefit of government subsidies and low wages operating in their favor. To combat these unfair practices we must become as efficient as possible in our own operation."

FIGURE 5.3   Team Membership Roles

Team Task Roles	*Team Relationship Roles*
Initiator-Contributor	Encourager
Information Seeker	Mediator
Information Giver	Tension Releaser
Opinion Seeker	Feeling Expressor
Opinion Giver	Silent Observer
Clarifier	*Self-Centered Roles*
Elaborator	Blocker
Coordinator	Aggressor
Evaluator-Critic	Deserter
Energizer	Clown
Recorder	Special-Interest Pleader

From Benne, K. D., and P. Sheats, "Functional Roles of Group Members," *Journal of Social Issues* 4 (1948): 41–49. Reprinted by permission of Blackwell Publishers.

the first two categories help the team accomplish its goals; the self-centered roles interfere with or restrain the team from goal accomplishment.

According to Benne and Sheats, certain role behaviors help the team accomplish its task, whether that is deciding on budget cuts or devising new product packaging. At least one person needs to fill each of these roles for successful task completion. Since there are more roles here than there are people on most teams, the average member must consistently fill two or more roles.

Referring to Figure 5.3, the following **task roles** are vital for effective performance. The **initiator-contributor** proposes definitions, provides information, or suggests solutions. This person is often creative and capable of looking at problems from a variety of angles. The **information seeker** tests ideas by asking for evidence. An information seeker may, for example, ask, "Do you have the figures on what that kind of packaging will cost per unit?" The **information giver** provides relevant facts, statistics, and evidence to the discussion. This role is usually shared by a number of members. These people generally have excellent research skills, analytical abilities, and knowledge about the particular problem. The **opinion seeker** asks others for their perceptions or beliefs about important issues. For example, "If you had to make a guess about whether this market is on its way up or down, what would that guess be?" The **opinion giver** is another role shared on most teams. For instance, an opinion giver might say, "I really think that 10Com, although it is a small company, can meet our specifications. We should give them this contract."

The **clarifier** provides examples or analogies to explain and define complex ideas. In addition, clarifiers offer a rationale for suggestions the group is about to agree on: "So, what I hear is that the group is going to support the second applicant because her education is more in keeping with our needs." The **elaborator** is able to envision how an idea will work in practice: "What this means is that for every book we publish we will ask the author to send a chapter through a pre-production process to work out any glitches prior to actual publication." The **coordinator** clarifies the relationship between ideas and pulls thoughts together into a coherent whole: "What I hear you saying is two things: You don't want to close the meetings to outsiders, but you do want procedures for regulating their input when they do attend." The **evaluator-critic** is a vital role because this person tests ideas and decisions against a set of standards. The person who fills this role is practiced in the various forms of reasoning discussed in Chapter 10 on proposal presentations.

The **energizer** stimulates and encourages the group to greater productivity by providing enthusiasm and interest in the project. An energizer might say, "I think this project will have a lasting effect on the entire organization and help change the way things are done." Finally, the **recorder** performs the function of record-keeping. Although unglamorous, the recorder's role is vital for team progress. It is hard to stay on track if the goal is not clearly recorded and past decisions are forgotten. The recorder keeps track of where the group has been and where it is going.

Relationship roles focus on building and maintaining positive interpersonal bonds between members. Teams with strong interpersonal bonds tend to be more cohesive, and cohesive groups tend to be more productive than noncohesive teams.[25] The **encourager** offers recognition, solidarity, praise, agreement, and warmth. For example, "That's a good suggestion, let's pursue this for a few moments," is an encouraging comment. The **mediator** manages conflict and is skilled in the conflict-management techniques we discuss at the end of this chapter. The **tension releaser** can relax the group, which is important during conflict. This person can use self-deprecating humor or crack the right joke at the right time. Humor at the expense of other group members, however, almost always increases rather than decreases tension. The **feeling expressor** monitors and comments on the team's emotional tone. For example, "Well, I can see that nobody agrees about this issue and that emotions are quite strong; maybe we should take a break before returning." Often, the **silent observer** is not an expert on a topic and prefers to follow the team's will. However, in productive teams, members will not adopt this as their sole role.[26]

Finally, when members adopt role behaviors that satisfy individual rather than team needs they are filling **self-centered roles.** The **blocker** is an evaluator-critic who goes too far. The blocker prevents progress toward the goal by refusing to agree to the team's ideas without offering logical reasons. The **aggressor** elevates his or her status by putting others down through derogatory humor, insults, and interruptions. The **deserter** withdraws from the group's deliberations and forces other members to pick up the slack.

The person whose humor is too continuous or ill-timed becomes the **clown.** The clown is cynical or engages in distracting horseplay. The **special-interest pleader** claims he or she is speaking for other audiences, using them to cloak or hide a personal ideology. "I know that Bob at Rayon Knit can provide us this at lower cost. We're foolish for not considering this option."

Although the self-centered roles interfere with task accomplishment, members should fill as many of the task and relationship roles as possible. The flexible team member is able to fill roles that other members have left open. Because teams are responsible for so much decision making, they spend an enormous amount of time in meetings.

Decision Making in Group and Team Meetings

According to a recent issue of *USA Today,* meetings have become the bane of American workers and an impediment to corporate productivity. Although people have complained for years about the number of meetings they attend, the advent of self-directed work teams and new technologies means that more meetings are called than at any time in the past. Roger Mosvick, a communication professor at Macalester College in St. Paul, Minnesota, found that the number of meetings between 1981 and 1995 had jumped from 7 to 10 a week. Many meetings, Mosvick says, are mind-numbing in their mundane content. Business professionals spend 25 to 60 percent of their time in meetings, and as much as half of that time is unproductive.[27] In this section we suggest ways to increase the productivity of meetings.

Preparing and Conducting Meetings

The **agenda** is the map or guidebook for the meeting and, if it is thrown together thoughtlessly or not created at all, the meeting is very likely to spin off in unproductive directions.

Developing the agenda starts by soliciting topics from members. Team leaders should avoid scheduling oral reports during meetings. Reports are interesting

An effective team meeting requires extensive thought and preparation. Credit: Caryn Elliot

only to a small subset of attending members and are better handled electronically. John E. Tropman, author and organizational consultant, recommends that each item for inclusion be sorted into one of three categories depending on the kind of activity it represents: announcements, discussion, or decision.[28] **Announcements** are brief information items (not reports) that the entire group needs to hear. **Discussions** allow members to share information or examine a problem from a variety of different angles. **Decision** items require the group to vote or reach consensus on a topic. A sample agenda appears below.

Agenda
The Portneuf Valley Community Advisory Panel
Thursday May 13, 1999

1. Jeri Taylor from AGP will briefly explain why the company postponed plans for the liquefied gas plant in Wyoming (Announcement).
2. Teresa Martinez from the state Division of Environmental Quality will discuss the new proposals for hazardous waste clean-up (Discussion).
3. Phillip Wilson wants the group to choose a date for the upcoming open house (Decide).

Notice also that this agenda is appropriately detailed. Many agendas do not include enough detail for members to know what is happening. Examine the sample agenda below:

Agenda
The Portneuf Valley Community Advisory Panel
Thursday May 13th, 1999

1. AGP on the postponement.
2. The clean-up plan.
3. Open house.

This agenda is not detailed enough to let members know what will happen at the meeting.

When arranging the agenda items, Tropman recommends that announcements be placed early and controversial decision items be placed during the latter two-thirds of the meeting. Late arrivers are not harmed by missing the announcements, but will arrive in time for important decision making. Early leavers will not have left prior to controversial decisions. Because controversy creates conflict, saving easier decisions for the last part of the meeting provides time to express support and reach agreement before adjourning.[29] After the agenda is created and sent, a brief reminder on members' message machines may be appropriate.

Start the meeting on time; do not wait for late arrivers. Waiting gives the impression that lateness is fine and encourages future lateness from others. Do not admit any new business during the meeting. Although members are usually unprepared to discuss new agenda items, this doesn't stop people from talking.[30]

At the end of a community advisory meeting in Pocatello, a panel member brought up rumors that one of the two companies sponsoring the group was using the panel's name on legal documents, to give the impression the panel endorsed the company. A 15-minute discussion ensued. Later investigation showed the rumor was false, but it wasted 15 minutes better spent elsewhere.

After the meeting, the team leader creates a record, usually in the form of minutes. However, normal minutes are too cursory to let outsiders know what happened. For example:

Minutes
Staff Sales Meeting

1. Members discussed falling sales in the western region.

    Moved: Meet with advertising at the next opportunity and discuss changing ad agencies.

    Approved by 6 to 2 vote.

This review is too brief to fully explain the content of the meeting. On the other hand, transcribing the entire content of the meeting is not a viable option. Instead, team leaders should create **content minutes.** Each heading in the agenda should have a corresponding heading in the minutes. The recorder writes a summary of the discussion in one or two paragraphs and highlights the team's decision, if any, in bold or italics.[31] Take a look at the following example.

Minutes
Portneuf Valley Community Advisory Panel
September 10, 1999

1. The group reviewed its early planning for a PM-10 study.

    Several people discussed concerns they had about the study, including the time it would take, the number of respondents that would have to be involved, and the kind of help needed to conduct it properly. The number one problem, of course, is money. Sue Wong reported that she might be able to come up with $15,000 to $18,000 to fund the project. The agency has some money set aside for such things. The only condition is that the study methods be approved by the agency prior to disbursement of the funds.

Decisions: The group formed a subcommittee of Bill, Jean, and Bob to contact both the university and the agency in order to set up the study and procure the funds.

Content minutes are superior to regular minutes because the summaries include relevant details and decisions are highlighted.

Finally, leaders must follow through on the team's decisions. Remind the team about the implementation of previous decisions in the announcement phase. Members are more likely to see meetings as productive when decisions are carried out and assessed for effectiveness.

Decision-Making Agendas

Although the research is somewhat mixed, there is support for the notion that rational decision-making schemes produce more reasonable and intelligent results than teams that follow no particular procedure.[32] Most writers on decision making acknowledge the seminal influence of the philosopher John Dewey, who identified a set of mental operations for decision making referred to as the "Reflective Thinking Sequence." The basic steps of the Reflective Thinking Sequence are:

I.   Define the Problem: A concise statement of the problem, its type, nature, and causes.
   A. What is the harm? What are the symptoms of the problem?
   B. How serious is the harm? Does the problem warrant a solution?
   C. Is there any way to look at the problem as a benefit?
   D. Who is affected by the harm?
   E. How widespread is the harm?
   F. What are the root causes of the harm?
   G. What, if any, obstacles are there to developing a solution?

II. Develop Criteria: A set of standards against which to evaluate the worth of various solutions.
   A. What are the important standards that a solution must meet?
   B. Rank-order criteria in terms of importance.

III. List Solutions: A list of possible solutions.

IV. Select a Single Solution: The solution that best meets the established criteria.
   A. Eliminate solutions that obviously fail to meet the criteria.
   B. What solution or combination of remaining solutions will solve the problem?
   C. Does the solution adequately meet the criteria previously elaborated?

V.   Implement the Solution: The steps necessary to implement the solution.
   A. What must be done and who will be responsible for implementing the solution?
   B. How will we know if the solution has been effective?

Unfortunately, defining the problem is the most misunderstood step in the process. The American character in management emphasizes action over analysis. As a result, most teams rush past the problem on their way to solutions, leading to ineffective decisions. Imagine, for example, that you manage a large state recreation area. You want to address a recent drop in attendance at picnic and campground sites along the river. Several rangers believe the drop-off is the result of recent fee hikes at the park. An overzealous team will inappropriately define the problem as "visitor decline caused by increased user fees." By asking questions under "defining the problem," the team can develop a more thorough understanding of the decline. For example, by inquiring about the harm and seriousness of the drop-off the team can understand whether the problem is truly serious. Perhaps a decline might help the local environment recover. As such, the fact of fewer visitors becomes a benefit and the problem is how to capitalize on the decline to help the environment recover. It is also important to ask who is affected by the harm. If the state allocates money based on usage, then the reduction signifies less money for future improvements at the facility. This might be serious enough to warrant action. The group must also understand root causes: Are the fee hikes really the cause of this problem? Or, is the new state-of-the-art swimming facility in town the real source of the decline? Finally, it is important to inquire about the obstacles to developing a solution. If, for example, the state legislature sets fees for all state facilities, then reducing the fees is not an option.

The definition of the problem greatly influences the team's solution. As you can see in Figure 5.4, the solution depends on how the team defines the problem. If the team decides the decline is caused by the new pool, then one solution is better advertising to encourage customers to come to the park on weekends, the most crowded time at the pool. If, however, the group defines the problem as a benefit to the environment, the solution is to invest in environmental recovery. Finally, if the group decides the problem is really related to fees, then one solution is to add amenities to the facility, making the fee increase seem less burdensome. As you can see, a thorough understanding of the problem is necessary for creative problem-solving.

The next step is to develop criteria against which to evaluate solutions. Criteria must be specific and detailed, rather than general. When hiring a new employee, it is not enough to say "We want the best candidate." The team needs

FIGURE 5.4   Defining the Problem

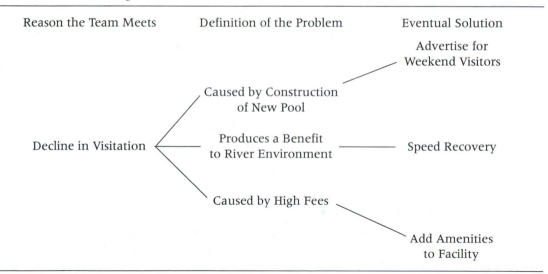

to decide what standards they will use to determine the "best" candidate. The best candidate may have to meet the following criteria: A degree from a top-ten school according to industry rankings, a GPA above 3.2 in computer programming classes, and strong letters of recommendation. The park rangers developed the following criteria for their decision concerning the state recreation area:

> The solution cannot be to adjust fees because these are set by the legislature.
>
> The solution can cost no more than the $90,000 allocated for improvements to this area for the year.
>
> It is preferable that the money be spent on capital improvements at the site rather than on noncapital expenses.
>
> The solution should not increase environmental degradation to the recreation area.

Those criteria are rank-ordered from the most important to least important.

Following the development of criteria, the team generates a list of possible solutions and then culls unworkable plans. Techniques such as brainstorming, nominal group discussion, or computer decision support systems are useful methods for generating solutions.

The team selects a plan by eliminating plans that are obviously unworkable or fail to meet the specified criteria. For example, solutions that adjust fee structures are eliminated because they fail to meet the first criteria. Other ideas that cost more than $90,000 can also be dismissed. The remaining list represents solutions that are at least minimally appropriate. If one solution clearly meets all the criteria, then this is the appropriate choice. If, however, there are several competing solutions, each of which meets some, but not all, of the criteria, use the rank ordering to help make the decision. For the park rangers, two competing solutions were evaluated: creating an advertising and education program to encourage attendance, or adding improved playground and parking facilities to make the fee increase less onerous to patrons. Although both solutions meet the first two criteria, the advertising campaign does not meet the third criterion, that money should be spent on capital improvements. The team, therefore, decided to add playground and parking facilities to the sites. Finally, the team should spend time deciding who will implement the solution, and the team should meet again to evaluate the solution after its implementation. Although the procedural order presented here is not the only one available, it is serviceable for many kinds of decisions.

Discussion Techniques

Over the years, consultants and researchers have developed a variety of techniques to facilitate group discussion and problem-solving. We will explain the goal of each technique and discuss how to use it in the discussion process.

Brainstorming.   In his famous book on creative thinking, Alex Osborn invented the technique of brainstorming. Because **brainstorming** emphasizes creativity and innovation, it is useful when unconventional solutions are required. Brainstorming includes the following steps:

I. Instruct members in the procedures and warm-up
II. Brainstorm
III. Clarify ideas and eliminate redundancy
IV. Evaluate ideas and select the best solution[33]

In step I, inform members of the rules and engage in a warm-up session that brainstorms ideas to a nonsense problem (e.g., "Think of all the different ways to use an empty Coke can"). The warm-up helps members get into the spontaneous, freewheeling frame of mind necessary to develop creative ideas. In step II, lead the group in an actual brainstorming session while recording ideas on a flip chart, overhead, or blackboard. The rules for the brainstorming session are as follows. First, all evaluation or criticism of ideas is forbidden. The leader must interrupt criticism and discipline members to refocus their energies on generating ideas. Because putting limits on ideas dampens the creative process, wild and offbeat ideas are encouraged. Third, encourage members to make connections between ideas.

In step III, eliminate or combine redundant ideas. In step IV, evaluate and dismiss clearly unworkable solutions. After this, the team discusses and decides on the best solution(s) to the problem. Brainstorming is a frequently used and effective means of developing creative solutions to team problems.

Nominal Group Technique.   Sometimes organizations use ad hoc groups whose members do not know each other, do not meet regularly, but come together on a one-time basis to solve a problem. The **nominal group technique** equalizes participation among ad hoc group members who don't know each other and may be reluctant to speak.[34]

Most versions of the nominal group technique follow four steps:

I. Silent generation of ideas
II. Round-robin recording of those ideas
III. Clarification of ideas through discussion
IV. Preliminary vote or ranking of ideas

Your first author facilitated a meeting for the U.S. Forest Service that used the nominal group technique. The agency wanted to protect migrating elk from off-road vehicles. After a presentation from Forest Service officials about elk habitat, the twenty citizens were arranged into five groups and asked to silently generate solutions to the problem. In step two, each group facilitator recorded member ideas on a flip chart. The facilitator moved around the group recording ideas until all the solutions were represented on the chart.

In step three, members briefly clarify and discuss each idea. Members clarify their own ideas, and statements of agreement or disagreement are allowed, but this must not degenerate into open argumentation. Finally, in step four each group ranked their solutions. In the case of the Forest Service, each group's ranked solutions were given to the Forest Supervisor, who made a final decision in consultation with his management team. In other cases, the entire assembly can come back together to discuss each group's ideas and craft a single solution. Nominal group procedures save time and ensure equal participation among members who have no history together.

Delphi Technique.   Delphi was the Greek oracle who foretold the future. The **Delphi technique** allows group forecasting and decision making without face-to-face interaction. Although originally conceived of as a method of forecasting organizational needs through the mail, fax machines and e-mail make the Delphi technique useful for everyday group discussion and decision making.

The Delphi technique includes the following steps:

   I. Submit a question for discussion, input, or decision.
  II. Collect participants' ideas.
 III. Integrate various ideas submitted by participants.
 IV. Submit the final list for rank ordering by members.

In the first step a question or problem is submitted to the group via e-mail or fax. After members return their solutions, the leader eliminates redundant ideas and submits the remaining ones for rank ordering. The leader can make a final decisions from the rank-ordered list or submit the first two or three solutions for a final vote. The Delphi technique is an inexpensive and efficient way to make decisions in geographically dispersed organizations.

Teleconferencing.   **Teleconferencing** is another solution to the problems of time and distance in the global marketplace. The teleconference is an electronically mediated gathering that allows people from a variety of locations to "meet" and converse together as a group. Teleconferenceing can be limited to audio or it can include both audio and video. At Lord Corporation, an international manufacturer of parts for the aerospace industry, the teleconference room is booked almost every hour of every working day for business meetings.

The following guidelines apply to both audio and video teleconferencing. Choose a moderator or gatekeeper to facilitate the meeting. The facilitator should have the clout to enforce simple rules and remind participants about the limits of the technology. Because nonverbal cues cannot be seen or heard as easily in a teleconference, participants must remember to make all their input verbally. In addition, some teleconference setups require participants to push a microphone button when they wish to talk. Because it severely disrupts the flow of the meeting, the facilitator must prevent members from interrupting one another. Finally, participants should identify themselves before they speak so that others will know who is talking. This is especially important in an audio teleconference where there is no visual help in identifying speakers. The use of teleconferencing is likely to increase because it cuts travel costs while maintaining the advantages of group decision making.

Group Decision Support Systems.   Group decision support systems (GDSS) combine communication, computers, and discussion techniques to aid group or team decision making.[35] At Idaho State University, the Simplot Decision Center is typical of GDSS arrangements. As you can see in Figure 5.5, the Simplot center includes twenty individual computer terminals for group members around a crescent-shaped semicircle.

The terminals provide public and private message capabilities with other group members. A screen at the front of the room is controlled by a facilitator and displays information such as vote tallies and brainstorming lists. The software provides access to a variety of group functions including analyzing and defining problems, brainstorming, and nominal group technique. Companies from around the country rent time at the Simplot Center for strategic decision making. However, as network computing increases in popularity and decreases in cost, it is possible that more companies will invest in GDSS facilities and software.

A variety of advantages are claimed for GDSS decisions. First, since comments can be made simultaneously and are posted on everyone's screen as soon as they are made, "conversation" is not linear, making GDSS decisions faster than those made in normal groups. GDSS decisions are also designed to resolve problems of bias and authority. Because ideas and comments are posted anonymously, powerful members of the group cannot exert undue influence, and decisions will be based more on the merits of arguments rather than on who stated the points. Finally, because member comments are anonymous, reticent members will be encouraged to express themselves, thus, participation is equalized and the entire group benefits.

Research on the effectiveness of GDSS decisions is mixed. Some research supports the benefits of GDSS cited above. Other research, however, is less positive. For example, a study by Susan G. Straus found that computer support systems do partially equalize participation, but this benefit was accompanied by a number of problems. For example, the lack of context cues and status markers prevented members from recognizing task-relevant experience from experts. In other words, the computer reduced the influence of the most knowledgeable members, which could lead to disaster in a real decision. Strauss also noted that computer groups were less satisfied with the process than face-to-face groups.[36] Craig R. Scott, communication professor at the University of Texas, speculates that the repeated use of GDSS would reduce the benefit of equal participation and influence as members learn to recognize one another by identifying individual response habits.[37]

To make matters worse, a study by Marshall Scott Poole and his associates at the University of Minnesota found that control groups exceeded the GDSS groups

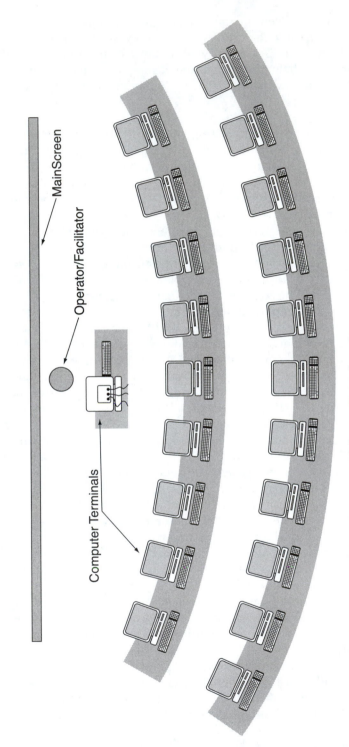

MainScreen

Operator/Facilitator

Computer Terminals

FIGURE 5.5   The Simplot Decision Center at Idaho State University

on a variety of critical and analytical thinking measures. Specifically, control groups showed more criteria definition statements, more solution statements, and more evaluation statements than GDSS groups. Overall, GDSS groups showed a lower level of critical discussion than normal groups.[38] Straus concludes:

> Results of this and other studies discussed earlier paint a rather dismal picture of the use of [GDSS] for problem-solving tasks; performance outcomes are no better, or worse, than outcomes produced by [face-to-face] groups, satisfaction in [GDSS] groups is consistently lower, and [GDSS] groups invariably require more time to complete tasks.[39]

Despite these initial findings, researchers will continue to examine the costs and benefits of group decision support systems and business will continue to experiment with the technology.

Conflict in Groups and Teams

Conflict is an unavoidable part of human relationships. This is especially true in teams, where contrary opinions are common. Conflict is defined as the interaction of interdependent people who perceive incompatible goals and interference from each other in achieving those goals.[40] The parties to a conflict are interdependent in that the actions of any member affect the entire team. Although managers often attribute conflicts to differing personalities or faulty communication, the vast majority of conflicts would not exist without a real difference of interests or opinions. While some members of a team, for example, may want to hold firm on their salary demands, others may want to make concessions. The different goals create the conflict, not personality or miscommunication. Finally, each party to the conflict interferes with the other as they attempt to achieve their goals. The part of the team that wants to make concessions encounters interference from the side that does not, and vice versa. Despite the fact that most people prefer to avoid conflict, too little conflict can be as bad for a team as too much conflict.

Too Little Conflict

Conflict is absolutely necessary for team performance. A healthy dose of conflict keeps a team from becoming complacent and forces members to constantly analyze and evaluate their decisions. In contrast, too little conflict leads to a phenomenon called groupthink.

Groupthink occurs in teams that are so cohesive and lacking in conflict that members cease critical thinking, often leading to disastrous results. Irving Janis, the social psychologist who developed the groupthink hypothesis, believes several important U.S. policy failures, such as the Bay of Pigs in Cuba (1961), the Nixon Watergate scandal (1972), the destruction of the U.S. Pacific fleet at Pearl

Harbor (1941), and the explosion of the space shuttle *Challenger* (1983) were the result of groupthink.

Some of the symptoms of groupthink include the **illusion of invulnerability,** whereby members believe nothing bad can happen to the team and that its decisions will always work out for the best. This illusion, especially common in highly successful groups, can lead to decisions that are not carefully evaluated. A second symptom is closed-mindedness, characterized by **rationalizations** to discount critics of any proposal. Group members also tend to **stereotype** outside critics as enemies who don't merit attention; thus, their opinion is ignored. Within the group, members work to enforce conformity to emerging decisions by putting **direct pressure** on dissenters ("You can't possibly believe that criticism is accurate") and using self-appointed **mind guards** to protect the group from contrary opinions.[41]

Leaders who want to avoid groupthink should assign every person the role of critical evaluator, encouraging every member to analyze and critique proposals. Leaders must also evaluate ideas if other members fail in this role and seek idea evaluation to ensure adequate decision making. Leaders should also insist on using the Reflective Thinking Sequence described earlier in this chapter. Despite the importance of conflict to decision making, it is possible to have too much conflict. In such cases, the conflict must be managed or resolved.

Too Much Conflict

Although too little conflict can lead to groupthink, too much conflict tears at the fabric of group cooperativeness and hinders task accomplishment. It may surprise you to learn that people adopt certain strategies for handling conflict at the expense of other strategies. For example, Kim comes from a traditional Asian family that emphasizes deference to authority and resolving differences individually rather than in public. As such, he deemphasizes direct confrontation in favor of resolving issues in a one-on-one setting. Anthony comes from a loving but boisterous family who is not hesitant about "having-it-out" when differences of opinion are apparent. Based on their different backgrounds, these two people developed different conflict styles. A **conflict style** is a person's orientation to conflict, which emphasizes certain strategies and tactics and ignores others. People have characteristic conflict styles that they use repeatedly, regardless of the situation.

Five traditional conflict styles are distinguished along two different dimensions: assertiveness and cooperativeness (see Figure 5.6).[42]

Assertiveness is the degree to which the participant attempts to satisfy personal needs in the conflict. **Cooperativeness** is the degree to which the person attempts to satisfy the other's concerns. Each style inside the matrix represents a different combination of assertiveness and cooperativeness.

In the top left corner the **competitive style** is marked by high assertiveness and minimal cooperativeness. Forcing, threatening, and toughness are common tactics in the competitive conflict style. Although it may appear to be negative,

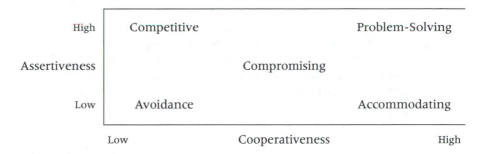

FIGURE 5.6 Conflict Styles

the competitive style is useful when the issues involved are extremely important, time is short, you don't trust the other party, and you aren't interested in maintaining a long-term relationship with the other person.

At the bottom left corner is the **avoidance style,** marked by low assertiveness and low cooperativeness. Avoiders are apathetic and refuse to engage in conflict. This style is useful if preserving the relationship with the team member is more important than the issue. The **accommodation style** is characterized by high cooperativeness and low assertiveness. The accommodating person will engage in conflict but quickly caves in to the other person's demands. Accommodation is useful when the other person is more powerful, and you will lose any competition.[43] It is also useful if preserving the relationship is more important than the issue.

In the middle of the figure is a style that emphasizes moderate levels of assertiveness and cooperativeness. The **compromising style** means that participants are willing to give in on some demands in return for concessions from the other. Trade-offs and tit-for-tat bargaining are common tactics for the compromiser. Compromising is superior to withdrawing or accommodating when both the issues and the relationship are important. If, however, the other person refuses to concede anything, the compromiser may feel betrayed. Even if the other party compromises, both sides often leave feeling they gave too much to the other person, which is why some people view compromising as a lose-lose proposition.

In the upper right corner of the matrix is the **problem-solving style,** characterized by high assertiveness and high cooperativeness. In problem-solving the team member works to create solutions that meet the important interests of both parties. An example of this kind of solution is found in the 1978 negotiations between Egypt and Israel over the Sinai Desert. The Sinai was Egyptian land before Israel won it during the Six Day War. Egypt's main interest was in the return of their ancestral lands without dividing them with Israel. Israel wanted to keep the Sinai as a buffer to give the country time to respond should Egypt ever mount an armed offensive. "Time and again, people drew maps showing possible boundary lines that would divide the Sinai between Egypt and Israel. Compromising in this way was wholly unacceptable to Egypt."[44] A solution was developed that forced neither side to compromise. Although the entire Sinai was given back to Egypt, they were not allowed to station any military forces near Israel. A problem-solving approach met the needs of both parties.

Which strategy is the most effective? It depends on the circumstance. Competing is best when there is one best solution and when conflicting values make the issue unresolvable through compromise. Problem-solving is more effective when parties have to work together in the future, they are open-minded, they show a willingness to ignore power differences and work together as equals, and problem-solving tactics are initiated before the conflict escalates.[45] Problem-solving is also a useful first approach in a conflict, whereas competing and compromising serve as useful backups. In general, competing, compromising, and problem-solving are superior to avoiding or accommodating because they encourage open discussion rather than deny the conflict. To help members resolve conflicts, we present a four-phase process that emphasizes problem-solving and compromising (see Figure 5.7).

The process in Figure 5.7 can be used to resolve conflicts between or within teams. In the **introduction phase** the team leader or mediator opens with a brief review of the agenda for resolving conflict. The leader should remain neutral and emphasize the importance of understanding the source of the conflict before proceeding to solutions. In the **explanation phase,** each side of the conflict discusses the source of its disagreement. The leader can open by asking, "What is the problem we are confronting?" or "What is creating the discord in the team?" Each person should be allowed to speak his or her mind and explain concerns. The leader should use all the listening skills mentioned in Chapter 3 to understand each person's concerns. Don't interrupt or let others interrupt the speaker. Remind all participants that they, too, will have a turn to express themselves.

During the explanation session, the team leader should listen for both the positions people express as well as the interests behind those positions. A **position** defines what one person wants. For example, a property owner may want $200.00 per square foot for office space in her building, although property in that market usually rents for $175.00 a square foot. The rental price is the landlord's position. The landlord's **interests** are the needs, desires, fears, and concerns that motivate her to select the rental price.[46] Although that price may be high for the area, the landlord wants it so she can, for example, upgrade the phone wiring for faster Internet access. Rewiring the building is one of the interests that motivates

FIGURE 5.7   A Four-Phase Model of Conflict Resolution

Introduction	Brief statement reviewing procedures for conflict resolution.
Explanation	Every party to the conflict discusses the source of the difficulty.
Clarifying	Develop a better understanding of all relevant positions and interests.
Problem-Solving	Brainstorm solutions, eliminate solutions, settle on a final solution.

the price demand. It is easy to reach an impasse when parties negotiate over positions. Reconciling interests is much easier and more likely to lead to successful conflict resolution. Learn to listen for the motivations that drive people to adopt positions.

During the **clarifying phase** the leader or mediator develops a better understanding of each person's positions and interests. Open questions that begin with such words as "how," "what," or "why" encourage people to clarify their interests. The leader can keep track of the issues by keeping a list of the positions of each party on a two-column sheet of paper. For each position, list the interests down the column. In the example in Figure 5.8, the landlord's position is $200.00 a square foot. She needs this for phone line upgrades, electrical rewiring, and to meet new fire and earthquake codes. The potential tenant is the head of an engineering firm whose position is $175.00 per square foot, which he claims is the market rate in that area of town. His interests are in keeping the cost of the services provided by his company as low as possible. To try to negotiate on the positions is very difficult. The best that could be hoped for is a compromise between $175 and $200. The interests, however, will prove useful in the resolution stage.

In the **problem-solving stage,** parties to the conflict develop a list of possible solutions using the brainstorming technique described above. Solutions that obviously do not meet the interests of either party are eliminated. Once the list is narrowed, take the remaining solutions and craft problem-solving ideas that meet the interests of both parties. For example, our hypothetical engineering team overcame their impasse by suggesting that the landlord drop the price to $175 a square foot and in return the firm would draft the designs for the building improvements free of charge. The landlord said this was acceptable if the rent was set at $185. The minor increase was acceptable to the head of the engineering firm. If a solution that meets all party's needs cannot be developed, the leader or facilitator will have to suggest compromises that force each party to make concessions. The four-phase model is an efficient way to resolve many conflicts within and between groups.

FIGURE 5.8   Sample List of Positions and Interests

Landlord	Potential Tenant
$200.00 a square foot	*No more than $175.00 a square foot*
Need the extra money to upgrade phone lines for the Internet.	Can't add costs to services and still compete.
Need money to upgrade electrical wiring.	
Need money to meet new fire and earthquake codes.	

Summary

Much work of organizations is done in groups and teams. A group is a collection of three or more individuals who perceive themselves as a group, possess a common fate, and communicate with one another over time to accomplish personal and group goals. A self-directed team has full authority for coordination, manufacturing, and delivering a product or service.

Group and team members operate by taking on a variety of roles. A role is an expectation about individual patterns of behavior. The management role guides group activity by explaining job requirements, setting performance standards, and monitoring output. Leaders, on the other hand, specify issues of importance, raise subordinates' awareness of these issues, define how they should be interpreted, and motivate employees to transcend individual self-interests for the sake of the team. Adaptable communicators are more likely to emerge as group leaders than inflexible members. Leaders organize the group activity through their communication behaviors in the task, procedural, and interpersonal areas summarized in Figure 5.1. Leaders are also responsible for defining the team's focus through labels, recognizing heroes, enacting rituals, and encouraging identification.

Group members fill the task, relationship, and self-centered roles that are summarized in Figure 5.3. Prior to team meetings, the leader should prepare an agenda of announcement, discussion, and decision items. After the meeting, the leader should create content minutes that summarize the group's discussion and highlight its decisions. The Reflective Thinking Sequence includes five basic steps: define the problem, develop criteria, list solutions, select a single solution, and implement the solution. Several discussion techniques aid decision making including: brainstorming, nominal group technique, Delphi technique, teleconferencing, and group decision support systems.

Conflict is a part of every group or team. Too little conflict creates groupthink, which leads to poor critical thinking and ineffective decisions. The illusion of invulnerability, rationalizations, stereotypes, direct pressure, and mind guards are all symptoms of groupthink. Leaders of a group suffering from groupthink should assign every member the role of critical evaluator and use the Reflective Thinking Sequence.

People adopt preferred styles for handling conflict regardless of the situation. The competitive style is characterized by high assertiveness and low cooperativeness. The avoidance style is marked by low assertiveness and low cooperativeness. The person so characterized refuses to engage in conflict. Low assertiveness and high cooperativeness characterize the accommodating style, wherein the person engages in conflict but caves in quickly to the other person's demands. Compromising means the person has moderate assertiveness and cooperativeness. The goal in the problem-solving style is to find solutions that meet the needs of both parties.

The four-phase model of conflict resolution emphasizes problem-solving and compromising. The first step is the introduction phase, where ground rules are set and explained. In the explanation phase, each party to the conflict explains his or her positions. In the clarifying phase the mediator or leader attempts to understand the interests behind everyone's positions. Brainstorming is used to develop solutions in the resolution stage.

QUESTIONS FOR DISCUSSION

1. Recall several uncooperative people you have encountered in classroom or work groups in the past. Which self-centered role did each person play and what were the effects of this role on the group's performance?

2. What can leaders do to minimize or eliminate the harm that self-centered role performances have on a group or team?

3. Think of a supervisor you have worked for in the past. Was this person's supervision oriented toward leadership or management? What behavior did you see that supports your assessment?

4. Have any of your supervisors used the symbolic behaviors of leadership described in this chapter? Which strategies did they employ? How effective were these strategies and why?

5. What is your preferred conflict style? What experiences have you had that produced this habitual orientation toward conflict?

ACTIVITIES AND EXERCISES

1. Write an agenda for one of your classes with enough detail that someone who did not attend can understand what happened. Show your agenda to someone who did not attend the class. Can this person understand the basic outline of that class period? If not, rewrite the agenda in the appropriate detail.

2. There are several instruments available to measure your conflict style. Your instructor may give you one of these instruments to assess your style preferences. Fill out the instrument and determine your preferred conflict style.

3. Your instructor may provide you with a group discussion problem. Follow the Reflective Thinking Sequence to resolve the problem. In what ways did the Sequence influence your creative thinking? What was the most difficult part of following the agenda? What problems cropped up in the use of the Sequence? Are there any ways to modify the the Reflective Thinking Sequence to make it easier to use?

4. Your instructor may divide the class into groups of three students then provide an overview of a conflict between two parties. Two people in the group will play the roles of the conflicting parties, and the third person will mediate the conflict using the four-phase model of conflict resolution explained in this chapter. Was the facilitator able to resolve the conflict between the two parties? What was the most difficult part of resolving the conflict? Did seeking the interests behind the positions

help resolve the conflict? Of what use was brainstorming in resolving the conflict? Are there any modifications you would make to the phase model of conflict resolution?

5. List a conflict you have had with a classmate or coworker in the past month. List the positions people took. List the interests that motivated your positions. Put yourself in the shoes of the other person and attempt to list the major interests for each position he or she took. Compare the two lists of interests. Can you see any problem-solving solutions that meet the interests of both parties? If not, what compromises could be worked out to resolve this conflict?

NOTES

1. Baird, J., *The Dynamics of Organizational Communication* (New York: Harper & Row, 1977).

2. Eisenberg, E. M., and H. L. Goodall, Jr., *Organizational Communication: Balancing Creativity and Constraint* (New York: St. Martin's Press, 1993).

3. Barker, J. R., C. W. Melville, and M. E. Pacanowsky, "Self-Directed Teams at Xel: Changes in Communication Practices During a Program of Cultural Transformation," *Journal of Applied Communication Research* 21 (1993): 297–312.

4. Gribas, J., informal conversation, Pocatello, ID, 9 July 1998.

5. Eisenberg and Goodall.

6. King, R. T., Jr., "Levi's Factory Workers Are Assigned to Teams, and Morale Takes a Hit," *The Wall Street Journal*, 20 June 1998, A1 & A6.

7. Wilson, G. L., and M. S. Hanna, *Groups in Context: Leadership and Participation in Small Groups* (New York: McGraw-Hill Inc., 1993).

8. Bass, B. M., *Leadership and Performance Beyond Expectations* (New York: The Free Press, 1985).

9. Fisher, B. A., "Leadership: When Does the Difference Make a Difference?" in *Communication and Group Decision-Making*, ed. R. Y. Hirokawa and M. S. Poole (Beverly Hills, CA: Sage, 1986), 197–215.

10. Wood, J. T., "Leading in Purposive Discussions: A Study of Adaptive Behavior," *Communication Monographs* 44 (1977): 152–165.

11. Gouran, D. S., "Variables Related to Consensus in Group Discussions of Questions of Policy," *Speech Monographs* 36 (1969): 387–391.

12. Larson, C. E., and F. M. J. LaFasto, *Teamwork: What Must Go Right/What Can Go Wrong* (Beverly Hills, CA: Sage, 1989).

13. Snyder, R. C., "New Frames For Old: Changing the Managerial Culture of an Aircraft Factory," in *Inside Organizations: Understanding the Human Dimension*, ed. M. O. Jones, M. D. Moore, and R. C. Snyder (Beverly Hills, CA: Sage, 1988), 191–208.

14. Peters, T. J., and R. H. Waterman, Jr., *In Search of Excellence: Lessons from America's Best-Run Companies* (New York: Harper & Row, Publishers, 1982), 261.

15. Ibid.

16. Quintanilla, C., "Maytag's Top Officer, Expected to Do Little, Surprises His Board," *The Wall Street Journal*, 23 June 1998, A8.

17. DiSanza, J. R., "Shared Meaning as a Sales Inducement Strategy: Bank Teller Responses to Frames, Reinforcements, and Quotas," *The Journal of Business Communication* 30 (1993): 133–160.

18. DiSanza, J. R., "The Wadsworth Publishing Company: An Ethnographic Analysis of Cultural Values," (master's thesis, San Francisco State University, 1985).

19. Cheney, G., "The Rhetoric of Identification and the Study of Organizational Communication," *Quarterly Journal of Speech* 69 (1983): 143–158.

20. DiSanza, J. R., and C. Bullis, "'Everybody Identifies with Smokey the Bear': Employee Responses to Newsletter Identification Inducements at the U.S. Forest Service," *Management Communication Quarterly* 12 (1999), 347–399.

21. Ibid.

22. Cheney.

23. Ibid.

24. Ibid.

25. Shaw, M. E., *Group Dynamics: The Psychology of Small Group Behavior* (New York: McGraw Hill, 1981).

26. Wilson and Hanna, 165.

27. Armour, S., "Business' black hole: Spiraling number of meetings consume time and productivity," *USA Today,* 8 December 1997, A1 & A2.

28. Tropman, J. E., *Making Meetings Work: Achieving High Quality Group Decisions* (Beverly Hills, CA: Sage, 1996).

29. Ibid.

30. Ibid.

31. Ibid.

32. Gouran, D. S., "Rational Approaches to Decision-Making and Problem-Solving Discussion," *Quarterly Journal of Speech* 77 (1991): 343–384.

33. Osborn, A. F., *Applied Imagination: Principles and Procedures of Creative Thinking* (New York: Scribner's, 1959).

34. Delbecq, A. L., A. H. Van De Ven, and D. H. Gustafson, *Group Techniques for Program Planning: A Guide to Nominal Group Techniques and Delphi Process* (Glenview, IL: Scott, Foresman, 1975).

35. Poole, M. S., M. Holmes, R. Watson, and G. DeSanctis, "Group Decision Support Systems and Group Communication: A Comparison of Decision Making in Computer-Supported and Nonsupported Groups," *Communication Research* 20 (1993): 176–213.

36. Straus, S. G., "Getting A Clue: The Effects of Communication Media and Information Distribution on Participation and Performance in Computer-Mediated and Face-to-Face Groups," *Small Group Research* 27 (1996): 115–142.

37. Scott, C. R., "A Rationale for Declining Benefits Associated with Repeated Usage of Group Decision Support Systems for Organizational Decision Making" (paper presented at the annual meeting of the Western States Communication Association, San Jose, CA, February 1994).

38. Poole, Holmes, Watson, and DeSanctis.

39. Straus, 138.

40. Hocker, J. L., and W. W. Wilmot, *Interpersonal Conflict* (New York: McGraw Hill, 1998).

41. Janis, I. L., *Victims of Groupthink* (Boston: Houghton Mifflin, 1972).

42. Ruble, T. L., and K. W. Thomas, "Support for a Two-Dimensional Model of Conflict Behavior," *Organizational Behavior and Human Performance* 16 (1976): 143–155.

43. Folger, J. P., M. S. Poole, and R. K. Stutman, *Working Through Conflict: Strategies for Relationships, Groups, and Organizations* (New York: Longman, 1997).

44. Fisher, R., and W. Ury, *Getting to Yes: Negotiating Agreement Without Giving In* (New York: Penguin Books, 1983), 42.

45. Phillips, E., and R. Cheston, "Conflict Resolution: What Works?" *California Management Review* 21 (1979): 76–83.

46. Fisher and Ury.

6 Considering Audience Feedback

Analyze the Situation
Occasion
Size
Organizational Culture
Physical Environment
Time

Analyze Listener Characteristics
Demographics
Captivity
Predisposition toward the Speaker
Predisposition toward the Topic
Knowledge of the Topic

Meaning for the Topic
Favorable Audience
Apathetic Audience
Neutral Audience
Active Audience
Hostile Audience
Mixed Audience

Techniques for Analyzing the Audience

Summary

Miguel and Jim had high hopes. The two sell advertising for an NBC affiliate, a station that is number one in overall ratings. They hoped their presentation to the largest home repair center in town would initiate a long and lucrative advertising campaign. They emphasized overall ratings, hit programming, and solid local news numbers. The center's managers listened attentively, but they only bought some spot ads during weekend sporting events. They made a much larger advertising deal with the local ABC affiliate.

What had Miguel and Jim done wrong? They spoke with their supervisor who, on learning the content of their presentation, was quick to find the flaw. "Who was your presentation designed for?" she asked. The two looked blankly. "It sounded like your presentation was a simple rehash of our ratings. You didn't consider the center's concerns about the construction of the new Home Depot and that mid-week traffic had dropped-off. You didn't create an advertising package to solve these problems. The two of you didn't think about your audience. A presentation is a two-way street."

Chapter 1 emphasized that effective communication is audience centered. Audience-centered communicators adapt message and mode to meet the needs of diverse audiences. In dyadic and group encounters we adapt to audiences by paying attention to immediate feedback or through role-taking. Feedback is information about how our message was received. In role-taking, we imagine how others will react to our message. As we explained in several prior chapters, astute interviewees anticipate organizational needs and highlight the experiences they have that meet those needs. Successful organizational politics involves the ability to imagine what arguments will be most successful with decision makers. We explained that outstanding leaders monitor their group's progress and enact behaviors needed to move the group forward. Role-taking and feedback are relatively efficient ways to adapt to interpersonal and group situations because feedback is immediate, audiences are small, and messages are less prepared and more spontaneous.

It is possible to adapt spontaneously to feedback in public presentations, the same as in dyadic or group encounters. A smart presenter, seeing quizzical looks, might slow down, stop and review a complicated point, or ask for questions. We know of salespeople who, seeing their prepared presentation draw negative reactions, ignore the text and develop a more interactive discussion of problems and solutions. Jim and Miguel could have done this had they noticed that their discussion of ratings was not impressing the audience. Of course, adaptation "on-the-fly" requires enormous self-confidence, extensive speaking experience, vast knowledge of the topic, and, even then, represents a significant gamble.

For public presentations, something more formal is required to fully account for and adapt to audience views. **Audience analysis** is a formal method of role-taking that is useful for larger audiences. Through audience analysis, speakers can adjust the topic, presentation mode, and persuasive appeals prior to the presentation, eliminating or minimizing the need for adjustments on-the-fly. A careful audience analysis would have helped Jim and Miguel land the home center account. Although some people reject the entire notion of audience adaptation as a form of pandering, we maintain that it is the single most important key to effective communication. The Ethics Brief in this section defines the difference between legitimate audience adaptation and unethical pandering.

This chapter develops and highlights key issues about the audience that need to be considered when preparing a presentation. Specifically, the chapter describes how to conduct a situational analysis and a listener characteristics analysis. We explain how to adapt to informed and uninformed audiences. We relate five different kinds of audiences and suggest content, structure, and delivery choices appropriate for each. We provide the Audience Adaptation Checklist as a tool for analyzing the situational and listener characteristics prior to the presentation. This chapter will help you create presentations that meet or exceed their potential.

Ethics Brief

One of the oldest raps against teaching communication or persuasion is that students are trained to pander to audiences. Some argue that by teaching students to adapt to audiences, communication professors are telling students to change their message so it caters to the audience's tastes and desires. As a result, communication classes teach an unethical form of flattery, rather than a real academic discipline. We agree that pandering is unethical. However, like most communication professionals, we also believe that it is possible to adapt to an audience without capitulating to it. While we admit that the line between appropriate adaptation and inappropriate pandering can be difficult to draw, we can offer some advice in this regard.

First, most communication experts make a clear distinction between changing the means of presenting an idea to an audience so that the idea is easily understood or more acceptable, and changing one's ideas to fit the audience. In the former, the speaker finds visual aids that can make a complicated concept clear or arguments that are persuasive to an audience. In the latter, the speaker changes his or her opinions to flatter the audience. Adapting to the audience does not force a speaker to develop inconsistent goals or philosophy. Rather, the outstanding communicator has a consistent philosophy, but is inconsistent in how this philosophy is expressed. We are advocating inconsistency not in people's goals, but in the strategies they use to explain those goals, and the motivational strategies they use to encourage others to adopt those goals.* Such inconsistency is needed in today's diverse work environment where no two individuals or groups respond similarly. If you find yourself changing your goals and philosophy frequently, you may have gone beyond simple adaptation and moved toward pandering. If, however, your goals are consistent, but your means of achieving them are flexible, then you are probably operating in the legitimate realm of audience adaptation. It is useful to talk with close friends in the organization, family members, or friends outside the organization if you are concerned about crossing the line between adapting and pandering. These individuals may be able to provide healthy perspective to your decisions.

*Hart, R. P., and D. M. Burks, "Rhetorical Sensitivity and Social Interaction," *Speech Monographs* 39 (1972): 75–91.

Analyze The Situation

A first step in audience analysis involves **situational variables** including occasion, audience size, organizational culture, environment, and time considerations.

Occasion

Speeches are given on various occasions. The **occasion** is the purpose and context of the presentation. Occasions include an evening presentation to let the public know about a local Superfund site or a meeting of the city council to fund a community youth center.

To understand the occasion, the speaker must first consider the **purpose** for the presentation, and adapt the message to fit that goal. A speaker who doesn't consider audience expectations about the purpose is likely to fail. For example, a person running for union president who uses an informative presentation on retirement planning to stump for election could well lose, rather than gain, votes. An engineer is likely to be upset to hear sales presentations from environmental consulting firms in a conference panel describing new waste treatment techniques. As listeners we learn to expect certain activities at particular events and are disturbed if these expectations are violated. A speaker must, therefore, understand the reason for the presentation in order to meet audience expectations about the purpose. Mention the purpose of your presentation in the introduction, because this clarifies your goal and allows you to fulfill audience expectations.

Context is another important part of the occasion. **Context** involves what happens before and after your presentation. Are other presentations scheduled? If so, what will these speakers talk about? Is your topic related or not? Is there a common theme? If so, where does your speech fit? Will you be expected to acknowledge other speakers or the common theme? Generally, it is a good idea to make connections between your speech and the other speakers, the occasion, the theme, and the audience. This can be done by explicitly mentioning other speakers by name, referring to their topic, or explaining how your content fits into the larger theme. Specific methods for accomplishing these goals are covered in the next chapter.

Size

Imagine walking into a large auditorium for a presentation to 150 people only to discover seven people sitting in the auditorium. Or, consider the opposite situation: You expect to speak before ten people and you find that a hundred have come to hear you. It is vital to know the approximate size of the audience so you can present with the appropriate **formality.** The general rule of thumb is that as the size of the audience increases, so should the formality. It's easy to be conversational and make specific references to individual listeners when a few people are sitting around a table, but the same interaction is difficult for large audiences.

There are a variety of ways to adjust the formality of a presentation. For example, formal attire denotes a more formal presentation. Extemporaneous delivery from notes emphasizes moderate to low formality. Reading from a manuscript increases formality. Holding questions until after the presentation is finished denotes more formality than handling questions throughout the presentation. Delivering an entire presentation from behind the podium creates psychological distance from the audience and suggests greater formality than delivering from beside the podium. Speaking from in front of the podium or moving among the audience reduces formality. Adapt the formality of the presentation to the size of the audience. Visual aids should also be adapted to the audience size. Although it may be possible to pass a model around a small group, the same is not advisable for an audience of a hundred. Whatever visual aids you select should be easy to manipulate during the presentation and large enough for the entire audience to see. Chapter 8 presents guidelines for creating visual aids.

Organizational Culture

When speaking in an organization that is not your own it is important to have some information about its **culture.** Most organizations have implicit rules or conventions that are vital to the group's basic function.[1] Breaking the implied rules may damage the speaker's credibility and effectiveness. Consider the bank supervisor who spoke at a luncheon for part-time tellers. The organizational culture for part-time tellers was different than for full-time tellers because of their peripheral involvement and inability to move up the corporate ladder. In her speech, the supervisor emphasized the importance of commitment to the organization, using arguments that were appropriate for full-time employees, but wholly inappropriate for these part-timers. After the lunch, the tellers dismissed the supervisor's speech as irrelevant because she failed to recognize their unique circumstances.[2]

Understanding the organization's culture requires knowing the conventions or norms for the specific group to whom you will speak. What status differences are there among audience members? Do those differences influence the way the people look at issues? Do the managers reserve decision making for themselves, do they consult with employees, or are decisions made by consensus? Will decision makers be present for your presentation? If not, should you arrange to meet them separately? Are you part of a regularly scheduled meeting? Can you visit the meeting of decision makers prior to the presentation? How long do presentations typically last? How are questions handled? Answers to these questions are vital because it is difficult to recover from violating organizational norms.

Physical Environment

The **physical environment** also plays a critical role in successful presentations. Determine the seating arrangement, the availability of microphones, and audiovisual equipment. If possible, visit the site ahead of time. Is there anything in the room that might confine movement during the speech? Will you be tied to a microphone and podium? Consider the noise that may interrupt the presentation. Many meeting rooms in hotels are adjacent to other rooms and noise from other meetings can be distracting. Will caterers enter with dessert, ice water, or the like? Although it is impossible to anticipate all the environmental issues that could disrupt the presentation, the more prepared you are the less likely such distractions will fluster you. Often, it is best to make light of obvious distractions because the audience has already taken note of them. If possible, pause until the distraction fades.

Time

A final variable to consider when conducting a situational analysis is the amount of time allotted. A speaker is never told to "talk until you're done"; everyone is expected to speak for a given time limit. Whether you are a classroom teacher, a workshop leader, or the CEO of a company, if you run long past the allotted time, audiences will "tell" you (in various ways) that the time is up and their obligation to listen has ceased. Speaker credibility diminishes rapidly when a speech runs over time. Rest assured that if you insist on speaking beyond the time limit you will lose the audience and lose credibility.

Teresa had 30 minutes to discuss retirement plans and investment options for new employees at her public accounting firm. Teresa was the fourth speaker during an afternoon meeting scheduled from 3:00 to 5:00 P.M. The three people scheduled before her spoke for 40 minutes each, leaving Teresa with less than 15 minutes. Rather than giving her prepared 30 minute presentation and forcing the new hires to stay late, she condensed the presentation, disseminated handouts, and encouraged employees to visit her individually to discuss the details. Teresa's presentation was more effective than the others because she adapted to the time constraints. Whereas the other speakers droned on "until they were done," the audience listened intently while Teresa spoke and then thanked her for her consideration at the end.

The situational factors of occasion, size, organizational culture, physical environment, and time are important issues to consider before you prepare to speak. Adapting to each of these situational constraints can play an important role in a successful presentation. In addition to considering elements of the situation, the speaker must consider various listener characteristics.

Analyze Listener Characteristics

Before preparing the presentation it is vital to understand various **listener characteristics.** These characteristics include relatively stable features, for example, demographics and captivity, and mutable interpretations, such as predisposition toward the speaker and topic.

Demographics

An audience can be described according to its basic demographic characteristics. **Demographics** are the qualities over which an audience has relatively little control, such as age, gender, economic status, education, religion, sexual orientation, ethnic background, or cultural heritage.

Sometimes demographic information can help speakers tailor their message to specific audience interests. For example, if you were to speak at a monthly meeting of the AARP (Association for the Advancement of Retired People), it is relatively safe to assume that most of the audience are older Americans. A topic such as changes in the tax code should be adapted to the interests of AARP members by discussing the effects of these changes on retirement benefits, health care, and social security.

Demographic information can also help those who speak in foreign countries. Asian conceptions of decision making, for example, are different from those in North America, where individual responsibility is idealized. Asian cultures tend to avoid individual decision making in favor of consensus.[3] When traveling to Latin America it is useful to know that people there prefer less interpersonal distance than people in North America. There are many similar recommendations that researchers and consulting firms can offer to international business travelers.

On the other hand, adapting to demographic characteristics, especially religious, cultural, and ethnic distinctions, can be deadly to a speaker in North America, Europe, or other diverse, capitalist societies. For example, while working for a firm in San Francisco, a consultant, seeing many "Asian faces," decides to apply her knowledge of Asian decision making. But, because the members of this audience were born and raised in America and share American approaches to decision making, they interpret the consultant's comments as patronizing and take offense. Diverse, capitalistic democracies tend to make group stereotyping based on appearance impossible. Will all Americans of Latin descent prefer closer interpersonal distance than non-Latino North Americans? Perhaps, but living in a diverse society tends to wash out many of these differences. Do Swedes who have lived in Canada for ten years still focus on the importance of correct job titles?[4] Will cultural generalizations still apply to the worker in Singapore who has traveled widely as a Nike employee for the past ten years? For presentations in diverse capitalist societies, focus on the varied perspectives your audience has toward the topic, not superficial characteristics that indicate racial and ethnic make-up. Adapt to group differences only if you are absolutely sure that the members of your group share the relevant interpretations and meanings applicable to your topic.

Captivity

After demographics, it's important to consider why the audience is at the speech. A **voluntary audience** is one that attends a presentation of its own free will. A **captive audience,** on the other hand, is required to attend.

Lively material will help hold the interest of captive audiences. Let the audience know you understand their situation. Acknowledge their required attendance and provide some additional motivation. For example, Gina Marcelini, a human resources specialist, spoke to a group of new employees about the company's benefits package. In the beginning of the presentation she acknowledged that her audience was captive, but offered additional incentive for them to pay attention.

> I know that the only reason you're here today is because you have to be and that you have sat through long sessions that cover the employee manual, job rules, etc. Everyone knows you have to attend this workshop before you can begin your job. But let me assure you that the information I have is critical to your future. If you listen closely I can help you save money by choosing the right benefits package.

Speakers are sometimes tempted to think of voluntary audiences as favorably predisposed to the speaker and topic because they want to attend, whereas a captive audience is negatively predisposed to the speaker and topic. However, just because an audience is voluntary does not mean it is favorable. For example, some people voluntarily attend a presentation on a political topic to offer a contrasting point of view, others might attend to heckle. Similarly, a captive audience is not necessarily unfavorable. Captive audiences can become interested in the speaker and topic despite their captivity. The only way to know about the audience's predisposition toward the speaker and topic is to ask the audience or their representatives. We will explain how to do this momentarily.

When you do not know if the audience is captive or voluntary, or cannot generalize about members' varied reasons for attending, it is best to assume that the audience is captive and provide motivation for listeners to pay attention. A volunteer audience can hear reminders about the importance and relevance of your topic without its negatively affecting their perceptions of the speech.

Predisposition toward the Speaker

The audience's **predisposition toward the speaker** is a vital element of listener analysis. A speaker's ability to inform or persuade is largely based on how **credible** the person is to the audience. Typically, listeners will have a negative attitude if they believe the speaker is not a qualified expert on the subject or if they believe the speaker doesn't have their best interest in mind.

If the audience doesn't know much about the speaker and his or her credentials, it's important to do something to build credibility. If, on the other hand, the audience believes the speaker is credible, further credibility-building efforts may be unnecessary. In the worst case, the audience sees the speaker as inexperienced or unqualified on the topic, and in such situations it is vital to build credibility by touting qualifications or trustworthiness.

A good way to overcome skepticism about your qualifications is to have someone introduce the presentation and state your credentials, expertise, and experience on the subject. If this is impossible, you should establish credibility yourself in the speech introduction. We will discuss when and how to do this in the next chapter. Decisions about the speech introduction can be made more easily when you know the audience's predisposition toward you as the source.

Predisposition toward the Topic

Listeners' perceptions about the topic are based on two general issues: what they know about the topic and their meaning for the topic.

Knowledge of the Topic. Determine what the audience already knows about the subject. Think of **knowledge of the topic** as a continuum: At one end listeners are unaware of the topic and at the other end listeners are experts on the topic. It is vital to know where listeners are on the continuum to avoid speaking over people's heads or being condescending. Sometimes speakers make the mistake of confusing an intelligent audience for a knowledgeable one. Confusing intelligence with knowledge has lead many a speaker to rush through complex material or use technical language with listeners who, although bright, know little about the specific topic. Speakers must assess members' actual knowledge of the subject, not their IQ. In order to determine what your audience knows, you need to ask members what they know about the topic. This information can make the difference between a powerful presentation and a boring one.

Understanding audience knowledge is vital for informative presentations, whereas persuasive presentations must also consider audience interpretation of the topic. Use the guidelines in Figure 6.1 to adapt informative presentations to audience knowledge. The left-hand column of Figure 6.1 provides tips for adapting to audiences with minimal or no knowledge of a topic and the right column includes strategies for audiences with extensive knowledge. Audiences with minimal knowledge require a justification in the introduction. The justification step clarifies why the topic is important or relevant to the audience. It makes a connection between the topic and listeners' concerns. Without this, listeners may not make the effort to pay attention. Members with extensive knowledge, on the other hand, are often interested in the topic and, thus, don't require justification. Of course, audiences with minimal knowledge also require extensive background information, and speakers should start the audience out at the most basic level. For knowledgeable audiences, extensive background may be interpreted as patronizing.

Referring again to Figure 6.1, speakers must remember to define every unfamiliar term and concept for uninitiated listeners. Don't assume that because you know what a concept means that your listeners will as well. The knowledge-

FIGURE 6.1   Strategies for Adapting to Differential Audience Knowledge

Minimal or No Knowledge	Extensive Knowledge
• Solid justification step required to tie topic to the audience's experience and concerns.	• Justification step may or may not be necessary.
• Provide extensive background material on the topic.	• Extensive background material is unnecessary.
• Define all relevant concepts and terms	• Define only those terms for which conflicting definitions exist.
• Avoid jargon in favor of simple, everyday language.	• Use of jargon may be appropriate, depending on organizational norms.
• Use visual aids to picture difficult structures or processes.	• Visual aids may be unnecessary.
• Thoroughly explain all major parts of the visual aid.	• Explanations of visual aids, while still necessary, can be less thorough.

able audience needs definitions only for those terms with conflicting or ambiguous meanings.

When presenting to uninformed audiences, avoid scientific or technical jargon in favor of simple language. For knowledgeable audiences, the use of jargon depends on the prevailing norms of the organization. As we mentioned in the chapter on interpersonal politics, employees need to adapt their language use to local organizational norms. In addition, visual aids are vital to help uninformed audiences understand difficult structures or processes. Referring to the communication model in Chapter 1, visual aids provide a second channel through which information can travel to listeners. Because visual aids add interest and variety to the presentation they are also useful for informed listeners. Finally, it is crucial that every aspect of the visual aid be explained to the uninformed audience. Explanations can be significantly less thorough for the informed audience.

Some of the most challenging audiences include a mix of informed and uninformed listeners. Making the presentation too basic may bore informed members, but pitching the information at a higher level may confuse the uninformed. In these situations, publicly acknowledge the mixed nature of the audience:

> As many of you know, we have a difficult situation here because several of you are already experts on this topic, but the rest of you are just starting out.

The acknowledgment makes the audience aware of the difficulty you face and makes them more likely to overlook periods of boredom (the informed listener) or confusion (the uninformed listener). The content for a mixed audience should err on the side of basic information so that few are left behind. Do this even at the risk of alienating more expert listeners. Those experts will be more forgiving if you have mentioned the difficulties inherent in the audience. The exception to the rules for mixed audiences is if the less informed members do not have decision-making authority. In this case, aiming the content at knowledgeable members might be most appropriate.

Meaning for the Topic. Persuasive speakers must not only understand the audience's knowledge level, they must also know the meaning the audience assigns to the topic. An audience's **meaning for the topic** is their interpretation, positive, negative, or neutral, and the reason they hold this interpretation. For example, after the dissolution of Robert's partnership in a firm that made antennas, he decided to start his own antenna company. He sought out old customers from the previous partnership and proposed that they purchase products from his new firm. Although they liked Robert personally, they expressed concern about contracting with Robert's fledgling company. When pressed for reasons, company representatives said they were concerned about whether Robert could deliver the desired specifications in the given time period. The representatives' concerns and the reasons for them are the meaning they assign to Robert's proposal. Robert must make these negative interpretations into positive ones if he is to get the contracts.

Once you know about the audience's interpretation of the topic, it is possible to choose specific adaptation strategies. Figure 6.2, The Matrix of Audiences, categorizes audiences based on interpretation of the topic (positive or negative) and knowledge about the topic (minimal or extensive). Categorizing the audience aids in the selection of adaptation strategies for content, structure, and delivery. Each of the five audiences is discussed below.

Favorable Audience.   As shown in Figure 6.2, a **favorable audience** has a positive attitude toward the topic, yet has little specific knowledge. The speaker's task is to reinforce and strengthen favorable attitudes while supplying specific information the audience lacks. The content, structure, and delivery suggestions for favorable audiences can be found in Table 6.1.

Because favorable audiences lack knowledge, the speaker should avoid confusing concepts and use common language whenever possible. Whenever new terms are introduced, include clear definitions and examples. Make the content relevant with examples that connect the topic to the audience's experience. Because favorable audiences will be predisposed to acting on persuasive appeals, encourage listeners to act on their beliefs.[5] For example, while speaking to a favorable audience about starting a charter school in his community, Terrell didn't simply end the speech with a general appeal for action. Because he knew the audience was already in favor of a charter school, he decided to create three committees to start the school. He circulated sign-up sheets at the end of his presentation, encouraging members to support the school by signing up for committee duties. In this way, Terrell helped the group act on their positive interpretations.

In terms of structure, any of the patterns we discuss in Chapter 7 is appropriate. However, because the audience doesn't know much about this topic, the speech will require extensive use of the connective devices discussed in Chapter 7.

Just because the audience is favorable does not mean that members should be taken for granted. Delivery for a favorable audience should include sustained eye contact, varied vocal pace and rate, and—most important—colorful, intense language. Maintain eye contact with the audience, vary your delivery style to

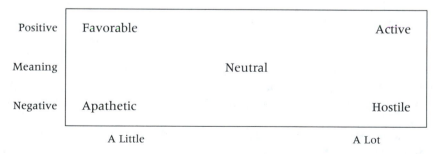

FIGURE 6.2   The Matrix of Audiences

TABLE 6.1   Strategies for Adapting to Specific Audiences

Audience Type	Content	Structure	Delivery
Favorable	• Avoid abstract concepts • Use everyday language • Include visual aids to clarify content • Make content relevant with clear definitions and examples • Secure commitments through specific appeals to action • Be creative	• Most patterns work well • Employ frequent connectives	• Maintain eye contact • Vary pace, rate, & pitch • Use colorful, intense language
Apathetic	• Use powerful attention-getters in the introduction • State your personal interest in the topic in the introduction • Introduce a little information at a time and support it with vivid illustrations and examples • Keep language simple and clear • Use frequent, clear definitions • Focus on informative rather than persuasive content • Action steps should be incremental and simple	• Use a pattern that is familiar: cause-effect, problem-solution • Include clear connectives • Encourage audience participation and feedback	• Enthusiastic, energetic, interactive delivery • Vary pace, rate, & pitch • Move around the room • Use colorful and interesting visual aids • Avoid handouts
Neutral	• Explicitly state credibility • Emphasize the urgency and relevance of topic to audience • Develop examples that indicate the relevance of topic to the audience • Demonstrate fairness to both sides of the issue • Support arguments with vivid examples and illustrations	• Include counterarguments and refutations • Initiate a question and answer session • Close the speech by emphasizing the "pro" arguments	• Be enthusiastic and energetic
Active	• Focus on concrete actions the audience can take	• Use a structure that emphasizes action • Use a structure that covers refutations strategies	• Use a conversational, interactive style • Interactively work with audience to develop refutations
Hostile	• Establish common ground • Don't alienate the audience with credentials • Cite the sources of statistics and testimony • Use sources the audience considers fair and credible • Use reluctant testimony	• Move from areas of agreement to areas of disagreement • Use the balance structure • If possible, omit the question and answer session, if not, insist on a moderator	• Exhibit calm confidence • Avoid overt enthusiasm for your position • Maintain eye contact

keep their attention, and use humor and personal examples to make learning fun. Because a favorable audience already supports the topic, speakers are free to experiment by trying new ideas, and urging specific action.[6]

Apathetic Audience.   Picture an audience that is uninformed and listless about listening to your presentation. Perhaps one of the toughest is the **apathetic audience**— a group that has little knowledge and a negative interpretation of the subject (Figure 6.2). Presentations for apathetic listeners need to inform and motivate favorable meanings. Thus, the task is to grab the audience early and develop the speech in an interesting fashion to maintain interest.

Open the speech with strong attention devices to overcome apathy.[7] When clarifying your credibility in the introduction, explain your interest in this topic. Revealing personal interests will help garner attention. In the speech body, emphasize clear explanations. Develop ideas slowly, provide a little information at a time, and support this information with vivid illustrations, examples, and stories to capture the audience's imagination and aid learning. Keep language simple and make definitions frequent and clear. If at all possible, focus on informative rather than persuasive angles.[8] An audience is less likely to react negatively to straightforward information. If you must persuade an apathetic audience, focus on small, but specific action steps that clearly explain what is needed, when it is needed, and where it is needed. Because apathetic audiences are likely to balk at action that is difficult, make the action as simple and easy to take as possible. For example, if you want your audience to make their feelings known to a state senator, create a petition for members to sign. If you want the audience to purchase a product, fill out order forms in advance so members don't have to do it themselves. Finally, arrange for future contacts with audience members in order to follow up on your appeal to prevent backsliding.

Apathetic groups require familiar structures such as the cause-effect or problem-solution patterns. Familiar patterns make information easy to understand and reduce the tendency to tune out. Include clear connectives to help the audience learn new information. Motivate the apathetic audience by encouraging participation in a question and answer session after the presentation.

Delivery is the key to overcoming listener apathy. When speakers are energetic and demonstrate commitment to ideas, audiences are more likely to listen. In essence, effective delivery encourages audience members to say, "What's got her so excited?" Enthusiasm, if genuine, can be contagious. Vary your vocal pace, rate, and pitch. Move around the room to display energy. Use colorful and interesting visual aids to improve understanding and interest. Avoid handouts, because they are an easy way for the audience to ignore you while they read (or stare at) your literature. Do not give the audience an excuse to tune out!

Neutral Audience.   A group that has a moderate amount of knowledge and is neither favorable nor unfavorable toward the topic is classified as a **neutral audience.** A speech before a neutral group should open with a statement of your credibility and experience on the topic. The audience must know that the speaker is qualified if they are to become more favorable. Neutral audiences can be won over by emphasizing the urgency and relevance of the topic. Convince listeners that both the topic and their views of the topic are important. Develop a variety of specific examples to capture audience interest and help listeners see the various ways they are affected by the issue.

Demonstrating fairness is also critical. Neutral audiences are unlikely to be moved to more favorable positions if the speaker demonstrates one-sided, ideologically biased arguments. Neutral people are often turned off by such attacks. Instead, speakers should demonstrate fairness to both sides of the issue, but end by emphasizing that after all the data are weighed, the speaker's position is the strongest. Use examples and illustrations to emphasize why your view of the topic is both fair and correct. Because this is time-consuming, avoid packing too much information into one presentation.

When devising an organization strategy for the neutral audience, use a structure that addresses and refutes opposing points of view. Refutation is an argument that counters an objection to your proposal. For example, an audience may object to a sales pitch because they believe the product is too costly. Refutation rejects the objection by, for example, saying that the price is competitive to similar products on the market, or by claiming that the price is a little higher but the quality makes the extra investment worthwhile. (Refutations are covered in Chapter 10.) Consider including a session that allows the audience to ask questions about the topic and your position. Once the question-answer period has concluded, offer a closing statement that summarizes the strengths of your position.

Delivery for a neutral audience should exhibit energy and enthusiasm. Communicate the interest you have for the topic. Enthusiasm can move listeners to make a commitment.

Active Audience. An **active audience** is an informed audience that is favorable toward speaker and subject. Active audiences are enjoyable because the speaker fulfills a "pep talk" function that reinforces audience beliefs and actions. As with favorable audiences, there is little risk to speaking with the active audience. The key is to capitalize on listeners' favorable interpretations by encouraging specific action. Your second author was asked to speak to a student rally on campus about a state initiative to cut property taxes. Students were generally against the initiative because the resulting budget cuts would force fee increases. Nancy knew this was an active audience, so she emphasized two specific actions: First, she encouraged students to vote against the initiative, and second, she asked every member of the audience to convince a friend or family member to vote against the initiative. Nancy's action step specified what her audience needed to do to act on their beliefs.

The structure for an active audience should emphasize specific action. These structures are covered in Chapter 10. It is also useful to provide the audience with refutations (counterarguments) that they can use against objections they might hear from others. When listeners use these refutations in other situations it further reinforces their own commitment.[9]

Presentation style should reflect more interactive approaches than with previous audiences. Be conversational with the active audience. Build refutation strategies with them in the question and answer session. Provide written materials that reinforce belief or action.

Hostile Audience.   In contrast to the active audience, the **hostile audience** is knowledgeable about the topic but members disagree with the specific viewpoint the speaker advocates. The audience's knowledge about the topic makes them difficult to persuade.

The first task in dealing with a hostile audience is to establish goodwill.[10] The introduction should establish common ground with them. Remind them that you share basic values or that everyone shares a desire to resolve the problem. Common ground helps the audience view you more favorably. However, don't make the mistake of creating contrived or artificial commonalties with the audience. Instead, emphasize whatever similarities exist between you. Be especially careful in the introduction not to highlight credentials that might alienate the audience. For example, a member of the Sierra Club speaking to a community where jobs are threatened by environmental regulations should not focus on her Sierra Club attachments. She should, instead, emphasize the importance of both a healthy economy and environment. Focus on the similarities with the audience without sounding condescending or patronizing.

As you develop your position, cite the sources of your statistics and testimony at every turn. Use sources that the audience considers fair and credible. Reluctant testimony—evidence that speaks against the self-interest of the source—is especially powerful to hostile audiences. In the case of the Sierra Club speaker, testimony from labor leaders who support environmental proposals is the strongest kind of evidence available.

The organizational structure should emphasize common ground and build from similarities before articulating differences. If possible, make your speech a two-step process: Build rapport and goodwill in the first part and address the specific differences in the second step. The balance structure, covered in Chapter 10, in which the speaker eliminates possible solutions, ending with his or her solution, can be persuasive for hostile audiences. Be sure to acknowledge the downside of your solution, but suggest that it is the best alternative given the constraints. Depending on audience hostility, a question and answer session may be inadvisable. Avoid it if you fear ideologically motivated attacks. If it can't be avoided, insist on a neutral moderator to ensure that the discussion is respectful. Andrew was making a presentation to a local religious group against the statewide antigay rights initiative. He expected harsh comments from a few members of the audience and asked for a moderator to lead the question and answer session. The moderator cooled hot tempers by directing the discussion to Andrew's argument that support of the initiative would hurt the tourist industry.

Delivery to a hostile audience should exude calm and confidence. Avoid overt enthusiasm for your position because it may alienate those who believe you're wrong. Rather, exhibit confidence in your viewpoint. Don't be afraid to look directly at the audience. Eye contact communicates confidence and conviction.

Mixed Audience. Many speaking situations include various combinations of the five audiences just discussed. The problem, of course, is that any approach is bound to alienate some members of a **mixed audience.** One researcher suggests that "the way to deal with a mixed audience is with delivery, not content."[11] Specifically, prepare the content of the speech as if the audience were impartial and stick to the prepared text and supporting material throughout, adding nothing, but cutting material if it appears that the audience does not need or want elaboration, and/or if they appear bored. Then, adapt your delivery as the speech progresses. Begin with a tone of voice that is controlled and calm.[12] Monitor audience feedback and adjust the nonverbal language and delivery style according to audience response. For instance, if listeners "nod, smile, lean forward and watch you—typical signs of interest—shift to a more energetic and involved delivery."[13] But, if the response seems somewhat hostile, tone down the delivery to reflect a more neutral style. If the audience seems bored, pump up your enthusiasm. Tailor the style to the specific audience reaction but do not change your content. It is more difficult to make impromptu changes in what you are saying than in how you are saying it. Furthermore, it is difficult to rethink an entire position "on-the-spot" without introducing contradictions.

Knowing all the adaptation strategies we have presented, the key question is: How do I determine what kind of audience I am facing? This question is answered in the next section.

Techniques For Analyzing The Audience

It is probably clear by now that audience analysis is time-consuming. However, Figure 6.3 presents the Audience Analysis Checklist, a list of useful questions for analyzing situational and listener characteristics. These questions can be used in a variety of ways to better understand the audience prior to the presentation.

One way to use the Checklist is to take it whole and find answers to each and every question. In other cases, it is best to select the questions that are most relevant to your specific presentation. For example, when speaking to people from a variety of organizations, the questions about organizational culture become irrelevant and can be eliminated. If your presentation has an informative goal, as in a technical presentation, there is no need to go beyond the questions about audience knowledge. If, however, the presentation is persuasive, the speaker should include meaning questions and go on to use the matrix in Figure 6.2 to determine the type of audience he or she is facing. Choose the appropriate questions for your specific presentation.

Once you have developed a list of specific questions, it is time to get answers. Some questions can be answered by the speaker, using his or her prior knowledge. For example, if you have seen presentations in the same room, you

FIGURE 6.3   The Audience Analysis Checklist

(Use this list to stimulate appropriate questions for audience members or their representatives.)

SITUATION ANALYSIS

Occasion

Why has the audience gathered to hear this speech? What expectations does the audience have? What level of formality is expected?

Are other speakers making presentations that must be acknowledged? Is there a common theme to the presentation? Should you connect your presentation to previous speakers or a common theme?

Organizational Culture

Are there any informal conventions or norms for speakers in this organization?

How will questions be handled?

Who makes decisions? Will decision makers be present at the presentation? If not, should a separate meeting be scheduled?

Environment

How large is the room? What is the layout of the room? What visual aids can be used in this room? How many people will be in the audience? What is the potential for noise and distraction?

Time

How long should the speech last?

LISTENER ANALYSIS

Demographics

Are there any relevant demographic features you need to adapt to?

Captivity

Is the audience voluntary or captive?

Predisposition toward the Speaker

Is your credibility high, low, or neutral? Does the audience believe the speaker is trustworthy? Does the audience believe the speaker displays goodwill?

Predisposition toward the Topic

Knowledge

Have you heard about this topic before? On a scale of one to ten, how much information do you have about this topic? If you had to rate your knowledge of this topic, how much would you say you have, a little, a moderate amount, a lot of information? Briefly describe what you know about this topic.

Describe any previous experience with this topic. On a scale of one to ten, what level describes your interest in this topic? Would you take time out to watch a television show about this topic? Would you volunteer to hear a speech about this topic? On a scale of one to ten, how concerned are you about this topic?

Meaning

Describe your basic attitude toward this topic. Do you agree with the following claim? What is your opinion of this topic and why? On a scale from one to ten, with one being strongly against and ten being strongly in favor, rate your support for this claim. In what, if any, ways do you support this claim? In what, if any, ways do you not support this claim? Describe your objections to the following argument. Write the top three reasons you have for supporting this proposal. Write the top three objections you have to this proposal. If you have had experience with a similar proposal, was that experience positive or negative? Why?

Based on answers to a series of predisposition questions, decide whether your audience is favorable, apathetic, neutral, active, hostile, or mixed.

are well aware of its size, layout, visual aid possibilities, and potential for noise and distractions. Briefly write answers to these questions. The answers to other questions, however, aren't within the speaker's experience and must be obtained from the audience. For example, questions about the occasion, the audience's captivity, and predisposition toward the speaker and the topic cannot be answered unless you speak to audience members. Interview audience members to get answers to the most pressing questions on your list. If it's impossible to interview audience members, contact the representatives of the audience and speak with them. Representatives are usually the people who lead the group or set up the speaking schedule. As such, they are usually in a good position to answer questions about situational and listener characteristics.

If representatives of the audience are not available, try to interview people who are similar to the audience in most critical traits. These people may provide useful information about audience characteristics. It is also possible to get information about the audience by reading audience materials such as newsletters, or newspaper or magazine articles, or finding the group's page on the World Wide Web. These materials may reveal implicit group norms and provide insight into audience predispositions toward a variety of topics. If none of these options is available, the speaker must make educated guesses about the audience characteristics and hope these are adequate. Write the answers to the questions from the Checklist and save them for speech preparation, which is the subject of the next chapter.

Summary

This chapter provides information about audience analysis and feedback. The most effective way to adapt to an audience is through a formal audience analysis. Audience analysis allows the speaker to adjust topic, presentation mode, and persuasive appeals prior to the presentation, eliminating or minimizing the need for spontaneous adaptations.

Audience analysis begins with situational variables. Speakers should match their speech goals with audience expectations about the occasion and purpose. Context involves what happens before and after the presentation. Some contexts require speakers to make connnections between their speech and the other speakers, the occasion, the theme, and the audience. Speakers should also adapt the formality and visual aids to the anticipated size of the audience.

Organizational culture includes implicit rules or conventions that guide group functioning. In terms of physical environment, speakers should determine the seating arrangement, the availability of microphones and audiovisual equipment, and whether anything in the room might confine movement. Finally, speakers should remain within the prescribed time limits.

Audience analysis also includes analyzing listener characteristics. Demographic features are the qualities over which the audience has little control, including age, gender, education, ethnic, or cultural heritage. In diverse, capitalistic democracies, group stereotyping based on appearance is risky and should be avoided.

Speakers should, however, learn whether the audience is voluntary or captive. For captive audiences, acknowledge the attendance requirement and provide additional motivation for listening. Audiences will be more favorably predisposed to the speaker if they believe the speaker is knowledgeable and has the listener's best interests at heart. To overcome skepticism about qualifications, have someone state your credentials and expertise, or do it yourself in the introduction.

For most informative presentations, audience analysis can cease once the speaker understands what the audience knows about the topic. Audiences with minimal knowledge require solid justifications, extensive background material, clear definitions, simple language, and clear visual aids. For knowledgeable audiences, justifications and extensive background material may be unnecessary. Definitions should cover contested concepts.

Persuasive presentations require that the speaker understand the audience's interpretation of the topic. These meanings may be positive, neutral, or negative. Audiences can be classified into one of five categories. A favorable audience has a positive interpretation of the topic, yet has little specific information. The apathetic audience has little knowledge and a negative interpretation of the topic. The neutral audience is neither favorable nor unfavorable and has moderate knowledge about the topic. An active audience is informed and favorably predisposed to the topic. The hostile audience is knowledgeable about the topic and has a negative interpretation.

To acquire information about the audience, employ the questions in the Audience Analysis Checklist. Select questions that are relevant to your presentation. To answer the questions, use prior knowledge or ask members of the audience or their representatives for information.

DISCUSSION QUESTIONS

1. When conducting a situational analysis, which of the four factors discussed is most critical: the occasion, the organizational culture, the environment, or the time allotted?

2. Why is knowing the size of the audience important for the speaker? Specify what a speaker can do if, instead of speaking before a group of thirty, there are 130 people to address. Or, what should one do if there are ten, rather than the projected thirty-five, audience members?

3. When can a demographic analysis be revealing and helpful for adapting a speech to an audience?

4. The text identifies several types of audiences and adaptation strategies for each. Can you think of an audience type that is not identified? What specific strategies might be most appropriate for that audience?

5. Bruce Evans was a political candidate running for Congress in the Pacific Northwest. He believed that the needs of the environment must be balanced with

economic and job issues. Bruce's opponent, Patti James, was a staunch environmentalist. She believed that the long-term environmental issues should not be compromised at all, especially when it came to short-term issues like job loss. The two candidates were set to square off in a series of three debates. One debate was in front of a general audience sponsored by the League of Women Voters, held in a local high school auditorium. A second debate was for business leaders and employees of the largest factory in the region, sponsored by the Chamber of Commerce. The third debate was in front of environmental activists in the community, sponsored by the Sierra Club.

Both speakers must consider the varied audiences and how to best present their messages to fit audience interests. What strategies might each speaker use for the debates? Since Bruce Evans believes in "balancing" the varied interests, would it be acceptable for him to deliver a "pro-economic" message to the Chamber of Commerce meeting and a "pro-environmental" message to the Sierra Club? Why or why not? What is the difference between adapting to the audience and pandering to an audience? When, if ever, is it acceptable to do the latter?

ACTIVITIES AND EXERCISES

1. Before your next presentation, develop an individualized version of the Audience Analysis Checklist in Figure 6.3. Develop a list of questions that are appropriate for your topic. Administer that questionnaire to as many members of your classroom audience as you can. Summarize the answers to the questions and write this information out separately for use when preparing your presentation.

2. For an advertisement in a magazine, identify the target audience. Identify the specific strategies that are used in the advertisement to adapt to the target audience.

NOTES

1. Pepper, G. L., *Communicating in Organizations: A Cultural Approach* (New York: McGraw Hill, 1995).
2. DiSanza, J. R., "Superior-Subordinate Communication: A Case Study of Persuasion Strategies and Responses" (paper presented at the annual meeting of the Western States Communication Association, Pasadena, California, February 1996).
3. Victor, D. A., *International Business Communication* (New York: HarperCollins Publishers, 1992).
4. Ibid.
5. Simons, H. W., *Persuasion: Understanding, Practice, and Analysis* (New York: Random House, 1986).
6. Elsea, J. G., "Strategies for Effective Presentations," *Personnel Journal*, September 1985, 31–33.
7. Simons.
8. Ibid.
9. Ibid.
10. Ibid.
11. Elsea, 33.
12. Ibid.
13. Ibid., 33.

CHAPTER

7 Preparing and Delivering Presentations

According to William K. Rawlins, a communication professor at Purdue University, the fastest route to professional success is to accept every possible opportunity to speak in public. Presentations allow the audience to associate your ideas with your face, personality, and style.[1] Successful people stand out; and making presentations is one of the best ways to stand out in any organization. This chapter focuses on the steps involved in preparing and delivering professional presentations, including phrasing goals, researching the topic, structuring, outlining, introductions, conclusions, and delivery.

Unfortunately, many people believe delivery is the most important factor when preparing to speak. Nothing could be further from the truth. The needs of most professions emphasize command of subject, thorough research, and clear organization, rather than delivery. Decision makers rely on the quantity and quality of the information they are presented. If forced to make a choice, most professionals prefer a well-researched, well-organized speech, with plodding delivery, over thin content in a flashy package. Of course, the ideal presentation includes both excellent content and delivery. Creating an ideal presentation starts with the general purpose.

Decide on the General Purpose

There are two **general purposes** common to speaking in business and professional situations: to **inform** and to **persuade.** Informative speeches teach, demonstrate, or instruct an audience on some topic or process. Persuasive speeches, on the other hand, induce an audience to accept a belief or action. Although some speeches include a bit of both, it is usually possible to settle on one overriding purpose.

The general purpose in professional settings is often determined for the speaker in advance. Everyone knows that sales presentations are persuasive and that corporate training seminars focus on instruction. However, there are situations in which it is up to the speaker to determine the purpose. For example, should a speech to the sales staff merely review performance or attempt to stimulate improvements? In these cases, it's up to the speaker to decide on an appropriate general purpose by combining personal goals with knowledge of what the audience expects. In later chapters we will cover specific kinds of informative and persuasive presentations. Whereas technical presentations are primarily informative, proposal presentations, sales presentations, and crisis briefings are largely persuasive. Risk communication, which is covered in Chapter 12, can be either informative or persuasive, depending on the situation. Whatever the topic, the presenter must know whether the primary goal is informative or persuasive.

Select a Topic

Many—perhaps even most—business or professional **topics** are determined by superiors, the organization, or the expectations of the audience. If you are selling office supplies to local business owners, then the topic is the product you sell. If you are addressing an organizational crisis, then the organization's response is the topic.

On other occasions, speakers are afforded the opportunity to develop their own topics. Addressing employees at a rally or giving a talk to the local Rotary Club are two such occasions. Topic ideas for such speeches are limitless but may include:

Conducting Market Segmentation
Clean Water
Rain Forest Destruction

Opening Markets in Asia
Diversifying Our Local Economic Base
Attracting New Retailers to Town
Funding Local Business Expansion
Juvenile Crime
Local Superfund Sites

When selecting a topic for a presentation, speakers should consider **personal experience** and **interests.** It is difficult to create interest in an audience if you are bored by the topic or lack the necessary experience to address it. **Audience interests** are also crucial. Is the audience interested in the subject? At a minimum, can an interest be developed? Audiences are usually interested in novel, timely, or useful topics. If audience interest can't be generated, the topic should be reconsidered.

Finally, as we mentioned in the previous chapter, the speaker should consider the **audience's expectations about the occasion.** If the presentation is part of a serious discussion of an agency's problems, a light-hearted informative presentation is clearly inappropriate. If the audience expects a brief review of last year's sales figures, an extensive persuasive appeal is also wrong. Consider the audience's expectations about the occasion before selecting a topic.

Develop the Specific Purpose Statement

Once a speaker has a topic, the real work of creating the presentation begins. The next step in the process is the **specific purpose statement,** which focuses the speech on one aspect of a larger topic. According to Dorothy Leeds, president of New York City–based Organizational Technologies Inc., the specific purpose statement does not specify what the speaker intends to say in the body of the speech.[2] Instead it states the **audience outcome** that the speaker desires. The outcome is related to the general purpose of the speech and may include understanding (if the general purpose is to inform) or belief or action (if the general purpose is to persuade).

For example, consider the general topic El Niño, the cyclic warming of waters off the coast of South America that produces worldwide climate changes. For this general topic, a host of specific purpose statements could be developed:

I want my audience to understand the effects of El Niño on the local weather.

I want the audience to know the causes of the El Niño event.

I want the audience to understand the probable impact of El Niño on the local farm economy.

I want the audience to understand how improved computer modeling has increased the predictability of El Niño's climate changes.

> I want to persuade the audience to take precautions to protect their businesses against losses from El Niño.

> I want to convince the audience that they need not fear climate changes from El Niño.

As these examples demonstrate, the specific purpose statement helps the speaker narrow a broad topic to a manageable subject. Notice also the phrasing of the statements, each of which focuses on a single audience outcome for the presentation. The first four purpose statements focus on informative outcomes, and the last two on persuasive outcomes. When phrased as an outcome, the specific purpose statement provides a clear criterion against which to measure success or failure, which is vital in professional settings. Other specific purpose statements include:

> I want my audience to understand the basics of product liability laws.

> I want to persuade my audience that Cre-Act School's arts-oriented curriculum is the best alternative to the public schools in our area.

> I want to convince my audience to purchase ad time at my radio station.

The following guidelines should be used to formulate a clear specific purpose statement. First, purpose statements should be written as full infinitive sentences, not as phrases or questions.[3] For example, this specific purpose only announces the speaker's topic.

> *Specific Purpose:* Nuclear waste.

This purpose doesn't refer to the audience and doesn't specify the speaker's objective. The next example is stronger.

> *Specific Purpose:* I want my audience to understand the four different categories of nuclear waste.

This statement narrows the topic to an informative one and clearly states the objective, learning about the different categories of nuclear waste.

Limit your specific purpose statements to one distinct idea. The following example is not limited to a single idea.

> *Specific Purpose:* I want my audience to understand how the global positioning system works and the history of its development.

A better purpose statement focuses on a single, distinct idea.

> *Specific Purpose:* I want my audience to understand how the global positioning system of earth-orbiting satellites operates to locate people on the ground.

Specific Purpose: I want to convince my audience that synthetic carpet is superior to wool.

Finally, specific purpose statements should be worded so they are sharp and precise. The purpose statement below is too vague.

Specific Purpose: I want my audience to understand pollution.

The most important term in the statement, "pollution," is vague. What kind of pollution will the speech cover—surface water, groundwater, soil, subsurface soil, or air pollution? A better example appears below:

Specific Purpose: I want my audience to understand the sources of groundwater pollution in our town.

This purpose is precise because it narrows the subject to local sources of groundwater pollution.

Develop the Main Idea Statement

After the specific purpose has been clarified, it is time to consider the main ideas. The **main idea statement** is a precise statement of the two to five main ideas in the speech body.

Main Idea: In this speech I will cover the five categories of nuclear waste including: high-level, low-level, transuranic, mill tailings, and mixed waste.

Main Idea: In this speech I will define "tort" law and then explain the major categories of tort law.

Often, the main idea statement emerges only after extensive research on the subject. The main idea statement serves as a guide for outlining the body of the speech. With minor word changes, the main idea statement can be used as the preview of main ideas in the introduction. The main idea should be stated precisely in a declarative sentence, not a question. For example, the following main idea is not precise.

Main Idea: For this speech I will cover theories about why the body ages, including: random damage and hormonal influences, as well as genetic programs.

The wording of this statement is unclear for several reasons. How many theories are there? Do hormonal influences and random damage constitute one or two theories? An improved version appears below.

Main Idea: For this speech I will cover three theories that explain why the body ages: random damage, hormonal influences, and genetic programs.

This statement clarifies the three theories by distinctly stating each one. Enumeration can improve the clarity of a main idea statement.

Main Idea: In this speech I will cover three theories about why the human body ages: first, random damage; second, hormonal influences; and third, genetic programs.

Gather Supporting Material

As you develop and refine the main idea statement, it is appropriate to collect **supporting material.** A few main ideas are hardly enough for an effective presentation. Just as the framework of a house requires electrical wiring, plumbing, walls, and a roof before it is habitable, main ideas need examples, statistical support, and quotations from experts for clarity and proof. This section will define and explain the use of supporting material.

Examples

Examples are specific instances that illustrate a larger point. An example can be factual, meaning that the instance really happened, or hypothetical, meaning that the instance is a composite of real incidents or the speaker's guess about a future event. When discussing the fire risk at a chemical plant, the speaker may decide to use a factual example:

> The major risks in area five involve the large compressors. As many of you recall, five years ago a malfunction in one of the large compressors caused it to begin belching smoke. When an employee entered the building to investigate, the compressor exploded, causing second-degree burns to 20 percent of the employee's body and a fire in the building that shut the plant down for two days.

This example dramatically illustrates the fire risk in the compressor room. If a factual example cannot be found, a hypothetical illustration can be employed.

> What would have happened if you had invested $5,000 in a mutual fund last year and over that year the fund had risen from a value of $21 a share to a value of $32? That equals more than a 52 percent increase in the value of your stock. A 52 percent increase on $5,000 equals $2,600.

Hypothetical examples are more useful for illustration than persuasion because they do not prove anything. If you have a choice, use factual rather than hypothetical examples.

Statistics

Statistics are a collection of individual examples delivered as raw numbers or averages. While giving a classroom speech against the killing of buffalo outside Yellowstone National Park, Shawn Anderson provided raw numbers:

> Buffalo levels in [Yellowstone] Park have been decimated to only 1,700 animals, the lowest levels experienced since the mid '70s.

In other cases, raw numbers are averaged in some manner:

> Of the 50 percent of the bison that have antibodies to the disease brucellosis, a much smaller amount of the population is actually infectious.

The typical method of averaging raw numbers is by calculating the mean; the mathematical average of a list of figures. Speakers should avoid confusing listeners with too much statistical information. If your speech includes many statistics, use visual aids to make the data concrete (see Chapter 8).

Statistics are more meaningful when combined with **comparisons.** For example, in a news story about the Snake River Plain Aquifer in Idaho, various statistics were used to indicate its approximate size. The aquifer is 5,500 feet deep, 100 miles long, and provides water for 130,000 Idahoans. Although interesting, these figures don't help an audience visualize the enormous size of the aquifer. The story added that if it were completely drained, the water in the aquifer would fill Lake Erie.[4] Bud Mandeville, the assistant plant manager at a potato processor in Idaho, uses a statistical comparison to describe his plant's processing capabilities. Every day, three million pounds of potatoes are turned into French fries. This is equivalent to two and one-half semi-truck trailers full of potatoes every hour.[5] Look for comparisons that make statistical information more meaningful.

Testimony

Testimony is a direct quotation or paraphrase of witnesses, experts, or other informed people. Quotations can make ideas memorable or add credibility to your persuasive appeal. Tari Jensen, speaking in favor of contractor licensing in the state of Idaho, argued that licensing is needed because home buyers risk a lot of money:

> These statements lead me to a passage in the magazine, *Modern Real Estate Practice*, which says, "Buying a home is usually the biggest financial transaction of a person's life. The home buyer pays out more cash, undertakes more debt, and has a deeper personal interest in this transaction than in any other purchase made during his or her lifetime" (p. xvii).

The quote clearly supports Tari's contention that home buying involves enormous financial risk. Build your credibility by selecting testimony from sources your audience considers expert. Briefly cite the source of your testimony, as Tari did, so the audience can evaluate its strength. Developing supporting material requires an understanding of basic research techniques.

Research the Topic

Research involves collecting supporting material for the specific purpose and main idea statements. Typical research tools for professional presentations are the library, the Internet, and the interview.

Using the Library

For reasons that we will discuss in a few moments, the **library** is still the hands-down winner in the information technology battle. Despite the vast growth of the Internet, it still pales in comparison with the library for quality sources, ease of use, and availability of research material.

Your library's **computerized catalogue** can run book searches by title, author, or subject. More advanced systems at most libraries allow combined searches such as a subject and title search, or a subject and author search. Check with the librarian about the most efficient means of locating books on your topic.

An effective search of any on-line catalogue depends on developing a list of **key terms** or **phrases** from your specific purpose statement. For example, for a speech on PM-10 (particulate matter smaller than 10 microns in size) pollution, different terms will assist a catalogue search. Such terms as "PM-10" or "PM-10 pollution" might be a good start. Similar phrases might also be useful, including "particulate pollution" or "particulate." Popular terms such as "air pollution" or "smog" might also lead to important sources. In any search, it is vital that you become familiar with the key words or phrases used to describe your topic.

In addition to the on-line catalogue of books, most libraries include various periodical indexes or abstracts. **Periodical indexes** and **abstracts** are paper or electronic databases that list and/or abstract (summarize) articles in popular and academic periodicals. There are numerous indexing and abstract databases that libraries subscribe to, most of which are now available in electronic form. For example, *The Reader's Guide to Periodical Literature* indexes articles in a variety of popular magazines including *Time* and *Newsweek*. More specialized periodicals are indexed by *General Science,* covering the physical sciences, the *Political Science Index,* or the *Social Science Index.* Searches for most professional speech topics should probably start at a general index such as *The Reader's Guide* and then seek out at least one other specialized index. For specific business research, the *ABI/Inform* business index and the *Wilson Business Abstracts* cover numerous popular and scholarly journals. We used both extensively while researching this book. A useful list of specialized periodical databases appears in Figure 7.1. Ask your librarian about a specialized index for your specific speech purpose. Like all searches, periodical indexes and abstracts rely on key terms and phrases to summarize the topic.

FIGURE 7.1   A List of Subject-Specific Periodical Indexes

Biological & Agricultural Index
Bioethicsline (ethical research in medicine, biotechnology, etc.)
CINAHL (Cumulative Index to Nursing & Allied Health Literature)
General Science (journals and articles for nonscientists)
HealthSTAR (journals and articles targeted to medical professionals)
Index to Legal Periodicals
ComAbstracts (communication, speech)
Essay & General Literature Index (humanities journals)
Psychological Abstracts
Public Affairs Information Service (PAIS, journals and articles about world politics and economics)
Social Science Citation Abstracts
Social Sciences Abstracts
ABI/Inform (business journals)
Wilson Business Abstracts

Experiment with a variety of phrases and terms to find information for your speech.

Some topics require a search of newspaper articles. Any of the indexes listed in Figure 7.2 can locate newspaper articles for your speech. Although a library's systems of data storage and retrieval may seem complicated at first, they only take a few hours' practice to learn. The information storage, indexing, and retrieval systems are time tested, unlike the incomplete systems on the Internet. As such, library research has yet to be replaced by the Internet.

Using the Internet

The **Internet** is a set of linked computer networks that began as a federally funded project to maintain military communication during a nuclear war. The Internet is not run by anyone, but exists as a few committees who establish the languages by which computers interact with one another. As such, the Internet is "a bit like the old Wild West—anything and everything goes, and there's no sheriff to keep law and order."[6]

FIGURE 7.2   Newspaper Indexing Services

The Newspaper Index	Wall Street Journal Index
Christian Science Monitor	Washington Post Index
Los Angeles Times Index	

Unfortunately, the Internet has become the defacto research tool for many students and business professionals alike. This is unfortunate because the limits of the Internet are numerous, and any search is likely to miss more than it finds by many orders of magnitude. Although many of the Internet's limitations will, no doubt, be corrected in coming years, it is important that you understand the limitations of such research.

First, finding books and articles through the Internet is difficult. Unless someone with a Web page, for example, has taken the time to cite a particular book or research article, it will not show up in any search. The haphazard citation of books and articles makes systematic research almost impossible. This problem can be solved by connecting your computer to a major university research library or the Library of Congress. Of course, all this does is allow you to use the library at a distance. Assuming you are able to find citations for important books and articles on the Internet, actually getting that source requires a trip to the library. Few research books and periodicals are available on-line, which means you cannot download them to your computer.

And this leads to a second problem with Internet research: The quality of the content that is available for downloading is generally poor. The best authors do not publish their material on the Internet because they don't want their intellectual property downloaded without receiving a royalty. What's left on the Internet is the dross that couldn't make it into print. Clifford Stoll, author of *Silicon Snake Oil,* asks:

> Which of [the files on the Internet] are well written? Which are worth your time to read? In short, which have any value? You don't know until you download, decompress, and read 'em. Without reviews, simple ways to skim information, and a Dewey decimal system to direct your attention, you will waste gobs of time.[7]

So what's the Internet good for? We believe the Internet is a valuable addition to, rather than a substitute for, effective library research. First, the Internet is excellent for finding recent articles in newspapers and popular magazines. Because many news organizations such as the *Washington Post* and *USA Today* put their material on the Internet, it is easy to search for recent articles.

In addition, the Internet is excellent for finding up-to-date information about particular organizations, local happenings, and government agencies. If you need information about an organization you are going to interview with, search for that organization's page on the World Wide Web. Want to find out how the Targhee National Forest in Idaho handled recent land closures? See if an update is included on their Web page. If this fails, search for the forest supervisor's e-mail address and ask your questions directly. The Internet is an excellent place to find the latest information on local happenings or public information about companies and government agencies—information that doesn't get into print because it is too limited, too local, or too ephemeral. In other cases, accurate information is made available on the Internet by universities, nonprofit organizations, and government agencies as part of their public service mission. Although we believe this work is the exception rather than the rule, it can be found with appropriate patience.

The most useful part of the Internet is the **World Wide Web,** a series of Internet linkages used by millions of people around the globe. Navigating the Web requires a Web browser program. A **browser** is a series of operating instructions that allows your personal computer to interact with the documents stored on the Web. The two most popular Web browsers are Netscape, by Netscape Corporation, and Microsoft's Internet Explorer.

Browsing allows a person to access **Web documents,** which are sites on the World Wide Web created by universities, publishers, companies, and individuals. Because the Internet is unregulated, anyone can create a Web document. Each contains links to another place in that same document or to other, related documents. The document's author decides on these links, which are indicated by underlined or colored words or images. Clicking on these words or images automatically downloads the new document for viewing. Once you find a site that contains useful information you can follow the links to other relevant sites.

Each site on the Web has a **uniform resource locator,** or **URL,** which starts with the letters (http://). The URL is similar to a post office box address. For example, the URL address for CNN's Wall Street Update page is (http://www.cnnfn.com/markets/us_markets.html). When entered, the URL provides instant access to a variety of market indicators such as the Dow Jones Industrial Average.

Browsing, however, is not an efficient way to do research because there are literally millions of documents stored on various computers around the world. The solution to this problem is a search engine. **Search engines** are programs that look through a giant index of Web pages—an index created by robot programs that roam the Web collecting information.[8] Two popular search engines are Yahoo (http://www.yahoo.com) and Alta Vista (http://altavista.digital.com). Because Yahoo organizes sites according to general categories, it is an appropriate engine for researching such a general topic as "affirmative action." Alta Vista, on the other hand, organizes Web sites by indexing the contents of each Web document. Alta Vista is the best search engine if you are looking for something very specific, for example, supreme court decisions on affirmative action.

Let's run a search using each of the two engines. First, we enter the URL for the Yahoo search engine or click the "Search" button on the tool bar in Netscape or Internet Explorer. Click on the "Yahoo" search engine. Let's imagine that we want to create a corporate training program in risk communication. Risk communication is any communication about uncertain physical or environmental hazards.[9] The Yahoo search engine provides two means of finding information. The researcher can type in the general topic in the search box or click on any of the menu items below the search box. The menu organizes Web documents into a variety of broad categories such as "Arts," "Business and Economy," "Government," "Recreation and Sports," "Science," "Social Science," and "Society and Culture." Because risk communication is considered a social science, click on this category. This brings a list of social science options that include "African American Studies," "Canadian Studies," "Employment," "History," "Humanities," and so forth. There is nothing in the list under the specific topic of risk communication, but there is a category for "Communication." Clicking on that brings up a variety of features including "Courses," "Conferences," "Forensics," "Rhetoric," "Institutions," and "Organizations." Nothing here seems obviously relevant to risk communication, but a click on the "Institutions" category reveals useful results.

Among the list of communication institutions is a group called "Research for Communication and Public Involvement." This is close to the idea of risk communication and worth a closer look. Indeed, the group's mission is risk communication, and the home page links to an annotated library of twenty sources on risk communication. Among these sources are two that are extremely promising:

Chipman, H., P. Kendall, M. Slater, and G. Auld. "Audience Responses to a Risk Communication Message in Four Media Formats." *Journal of Nutrition Education* 28 (1996): 133–139.
Duffy, R., and L. Craven. "Disarming NIMBY with the facts." Strategic communications (On-line case study). Available (http://www/wwmedia.com/stratCom/ffpwork/caseintr.htm), (1996, May 3).

The first study is easily found in any university library. The second is an examination of a Florida public awareness program for a hazardous waste treatment facility. To examine this document, click on the URL or enter it on the "Location" line of your toolbar. Yahoo searches are quick and easy when one is looking for information in a general subject.

Alta Vista, on the other hand, is useful when searching for more specific information. For example, imagine that we want information about risk communication in the nuclear industry. Using Alta Vista, enter the key word or phrase for the topic (in this case, "risk communication") and click the search cue. The computer responds with a list of Web documents that include either the word "risk" or the word "communication." In this case, approximately 144,522 citations were produced, obviously too many for any researcher to handle. Narrow the search by putting quotation marks around "risk communication." The program will now search only those documents that use the two words together. This yields approximately 1,765 citations. To narrow the search further, we entered the following (+nuclear+"risk communication"). The + signs before "nuclear" and before "risk communication" restrict the search to items that contain both sets of key words. This produces 169 documents, which is now manageable. Figure 7.3 includes a list of useful search engines.

There are high quality Web sites that have been around for years and are unlikely to disappear prior to this book's publication. These sites, listed in Figure 7.4, may be helpful to researchers in business and the professions.

FIGURE 7.3   Internet Search Engines

Yahoo	LookSmart	Go To
Excite	Netscape	MSN Web Search
Lycos	Infoseek	

FIGURE 7.4   Web Sites for Research in Business and the Professions

Kind of Information	Source	URL Address
Information and addresses for all major U.S. government Web sites	U.S. government	(http://www.law.vill.edu/Fed-Agency/fedwebloc.html)
World statistical, geographical, and political information	CIA	(http://www.odci.gov/cia/cia-home.html)
Statistical information	U.S. government	(http://www.censu.gov/statab/www)
Various news outlets: CNN, Time, CBS, ABC Radio, NPR, MSNBC, etc.	Total News	(http://www/tpta;mews/com/)
Daily news	USA Today	(http://www.usatoday.com)
Region- or country-specific international business information	Michigan State University	(http://ciber.bus.msu.edu/busres.htm)
Business research, economic indicators, consumer price index, etc.	University of Nebraska-Lincoln	(http://www.bbr.unl.edu/NatCond.html)
Business strategy, management, & communication	*Strategy & Business* magazine	(http://www.strategy-business.com/)

Because Web documents can be created by anyone with a computer, the Web can include both experts with something to say as well as "Charlatans, extremists, and malcontents."[10] Careful scrutiny of your research content is vital for any business presentation. Figure 7.5 offers a series of questions to test the credibility of Internet Web pages. The questions focus on the qualifications and relative bias of the author and institution and the recency of the Web page.

Conducting Interviews

Interviews are face-to-face, telephone, or Internet conversations with experts. In general, they should wait until the end of the research process so you have thorough knowledge of the topic prior to taking someone's time with an interview.

You should clearly define the purpose of the interview prior to contacting potential interviewees. The purpose should relate closely to the specific purpose statement or one of the main ideas in the body of the presentation. Develop ques-

FIGURE 7.5   Assessing the Credibility of Internet Sources

Authority

Who authored the Web page?
Are the author's credentials included on the Web page?
Is the author qualified to publish a page on this topic?
What, if any, institution supports the Web page?
Is the institution qualified to support a Web page on this topic?

Objectivity

What are the goals or objectives of the Web page?
Are these goals likely to lead the author or institution to slant information?
Given what you know about the author or institution, are they relatively free
    of bias?

Recency

When was the Web page produced?
How recent is the Web page?
When was the Web page last updated?

tions prior to the interview so you have something to show if the interviewee wants to see the questions in advance. The questions will also keep the interview on track and prevent wasted time. Avoid yes and no questions because these answers can be found in other sources.

To save time, many interviews can be conducted over the phone. An even better source of interview information is e-mail. After receiving permission to conduct the interview, the researcher can e-mail her questions and the respondent is free to reply at his convenience. A final e-mail may be necessary to probe for details and ask follow-up questions. A written thank-you note is a vital courtesy following any interview.

Apply the Information Learned from the Audience Analysis

After the initial research, it is time to consider audience feedback. The previous chapter demonstrated how to analyze audience features relevant to professional presentations. The questions on the Audience Analysis Checklist provide a set of guidelines for asking relevant questions about audience needs and expectations. To apply that knowledge, speakers should use the Speech Adaptation Checklist in Figure 7.6. The questions in the Speech Adaptation Checklist will help you adjust the content and delivery of your presentation to your specific audience. To answer the questions, use your knowledge of the audience from the Audience

FIGURE 7.6   Speech Adaptation Checklist

Adapting to the Situation

Occasion

Does your specific purpose statement match audience expectations?
(This is a classroom speech in Business and Professional Communication. The audience expects a business-related topic. I will use examples and stories throughout the speech that emphasize how tort laws affect business people.)

Does your central idea statement match audience expectations?
(Because this is a classroom speech, there are not many expectations here.)

Will your delivery create the appropriate level of formality for the audience and the situation?
(Little formality expected. Emphasize conversational style and eye contact.)

If it is expected, have you connected your specific purpose to the theme the audience expects to hear about?
(N/A)

If expected, have you made an effort to refer to other speakers and their content in your speech?
(N/A)

Organizational Culture

Have you adapted your content and delivery to local conventions and norms?
(N/A)

Have you adapted to the organization's mode of asking questions?
(N/A)

Will you be talking to the ultimate decision maker?
(N/A. No decision required for classroom speech.)

Environment

Have you prepared your delivery for the size of the room and the number of people expected?
(Yes. Minimal formality for a night class of business professionals.)

Can your visual aids be seen in all parts of the room?
(N/A. No visual aids in this speech.)

Have you prepared for any unusual limitations in the room?
(N/A)

Have you prepared for any noise or other distractions possible in this room?
(N/A)

FIGURE 7.6   Continued

Time

Will the speech fit within the given time limit?
(Yes)

Adapting to Audience Traits

Demographics

Have you adapted to relevant audience demographic features?
(N/A)

Captivity

Is this audience captive or voluntary? If they are captive, have you adapted to their needs?
(Captive. I want to open with an interesting, business-related story. I will try to provide some hypothetical examples that are common enough to happen to anyone in the audience. Perhaps I can also refer to the O. J. Simpson criminal and civil trials, since they are in the news every day. I will use "you" and "we" pronouns to remind them that tort laws apply to everyone. I will keep the delivery lively.)

Predisposition toward the Speaker

Have you arranged to provide credibility information for the audience?
(I will mention my business law class to build my credibility.)

Have you built proof of your goodwill into the presentation?
(I will mention that I want to protect them from lawsuits.)

Predisposition toward the Topic

What, if any, interest does this audience have in the topic?
(Very little. I need to remind the audience that everyone in business needs to know this information.)

What if any knowledge does the audience have about this topic?
(Almost none. Most audience members haven't had business law. I will start out by making a distinction between civil and criminal law. I will clearly define all terms including: tort, civil law, and criminal law. I will provide numerous examples. I must carefully define each category of tort.)

What kind of audience are you facing: favorable, active, neutral, apathetic, hostile, or mixed?
(N/A)

Have you incorporated the specific content and delivery suggestions for each kind of audience in the previous chapter?
(N/A)

Analysis Checklist as a guide. Be specific in your answers. Try to think of specific examples, structures, persuasive appeals, and delivery styles that will be most interesting or convincing to the particular audience. Figure 7.6 demonstrates how to answer the questions for the sample speech on tort law that appears later in this chapter.

Structure the Main Ideas in the Body of the Speech

Research shows that people will understand and remember data if they are clearly structured, rather than presented chaotically. According to Dorothy Leeds, structure is equivalent to leadership. Speakers lead by taking command of the audience and guiding listeners to conclusions. "However, nothing diminishes your leadership potential faster than disorganization. If your listeners can't follow you, you lose their respect and attention."[11]

Speeches are divided into three major parts, the introduction, the body, and the conclusion. The **introduction** should gain attention, justify the topic, clarify the speaker's credibility, and preview the main points in the body of the speech. The main ideas reside in the speech **body.** Finally, the **conclusion** reviews main ideas and emphasizes the specific purpose statement. We will cover introductions and conclusions later in this chapter. Here we address structuring the main points in the speech body.

Because most business audiences demand detailed information, speakers rarely have time to cover more than two to five **main ideas.** These should be stated in full sentences rather than phrases or key words. For example, in a classroom speech on bacteria-contaminated food, Jacob M. Lewis started with the following main ideas.

> *Specific Purpose Statement:* I want my audience to understand how bacteria-contaminated food makes people sick.
>
> *Main Idea:* Bacteria contaminate and propagate in food in different ways.
> *Main Idea:* Bacteria can produce enzymes that make people sick.
> *Main Idea:* Bacteria can produce exotoxins that make people sick.
> *Main Idea:* Bacteria can produce endotoxins that make people sick.
> *Main Idea:* Government regulations are designed to protect people from contamination.
> *Main Idea:* The following are examples of companies that had serious contamination problems.

Developing main ideas should be a freewheeling exercise similar to brainstorming. Record every idea no matter how silly it may appear; then eliminate main

An effective presentation is more than just good delivery. It involves clear structure and a detailed outline. Credit: Kevin C. Wellard

ideas that are unrelated to the specific purpose statement. Some points can be subsumed under other main ideas as supporting material. Because the main idea above on government regulation isn't related to the way bacteria make people sick, it can be eliminated. Because the last main point is a series of examples, it is better used as supporting material for other points.

Once the main ideas have been narrowed they must be structured. There are five patterns for structuring speech content.

Chronological Structure

The **chronological structure** follows a time pattern that moves from earliest to latest, or first to last.

> *Specific Purpose:* To inform the audience about how the El Niño phenomenon affects winter weather in the Northwest United States.
>
> I. Water temperature in the Pacific Ocean off of Peru warms.
> II. This warming creates high pressure in the Pacific off the West Coast.
> III. The ridge prevents storms from entering the region by splitting the jet stream.

The chronological structure is used in historical speeches that narrate events or in process speeches that demonstrate how something is done.

Spatial Structure

The **spatial structure** follows a geographic or directional pattern when someone covers something from top to bottom or right to left. For example, one could describe the major tribal groups in Idaho by moving from North to South.

> *Specific Purpose:* To inform the audience about the major Native American tribes in Idaho.
>
>   I. Northern Idaho includes the Nez Pierce and the Coeur d'Alene tribes.
> II. Southern Idaho includes the Shoshone and Bannock Tribes.

A speech to convince a sporting goods store to carry your company's tennis racket can be organized spatially.

> *Specific Purpose:* To convince the sporting goods retailer to carry our racket.
>
>   I. The grip on the racket is superior to our competitors' grips.
> II. The frame of the racket is made of graphite for superior durability and power.
> III. The head of the racket has a specially designed shape for more ball control.

Cause-Effect and Effect-Cause Structures

The **cause-effect** structure describes how one event leads to another. This structure is especially useful in technical presentations.

> *Specific Purpose:* I want my audience to understand how bacteria-contaminated food can make people sick.
>
>   I. Improper processing or storage can induce bacteria growth in food.
> II. Once on the food, bacteria produce three toxins that result in illness.

Some topics warrant placing the effect first and the cause second.

> *Specific Purpose:* To help our marketing people understand why the manufacturing process is introducing flaws into some of our tennis rackets.
>
>   I. Customers have noticed three flaws in our rackets.
> II. The cause of these flaws is the way materials are extruded during manufacturing.

As the examples above illustrate, a cause-effect structure should be limited to two main ideas, one dealing with the cause and the other covering the effect. If there are several causes or effects, these should be grouped as subpoints under the main idea.

Problem-Solution Structure

The **problem-solution** structure defines a difficulty and suggests a remedy. Extremely popular in proposal and sales presentations, the problem-solution structure can also be employed in technical and risk communication. As with the cause-effect structure, problem-solution structures should include two and only two main ideas.

> *Specific Purpose:* I want to persuade my audience that a perpetual inventory system is superior to a periodic system.
>
> I. There are three major problems with a periodic inventory system.
> II. The solution to these problems is a computerized perpetual inventory system.

Topical Structure

When the speaker divides a topic into logical categories, she is using a **topical structure.** Each topical category becomes a main point in the speech. For example, a speech detailing the nutrition content of fast food could divide the topic into different kinds of food, including chicken restaurants, hamburger restaurants, and taco restaurants. A speech on nuclear waste can also be organized topically.

> *Specific Purpose:* I want my audience to understand the different kinds of nuclear waste.
>
> I. Low-level nuclear wastes emit relatively small amounts of radioactivity.
> II. High-level nuclear wastes emit high amounts of radioactivity.
> III. Transuranic wastes are materials such as tools and clothing that become contaminated with man-made radioactive particles chemically heavier than the element uranium.
> IV. Finally, mill tailings are soils left over after radioactive elements have been mined.

The speech on contaminated food can be organized topically.

> *Specific Purpose:* I want my audience to understand how bacteria-contaminated foods can make people sick.
>
> I. Bacteria produce enzymes that make people sick.
> II. Bacteria produce exotoxins that make people sick.
> III. Bacteria produce endotoxins that make people sick.

A clear structure organizes information logically so the speaker can lead the audience to the desired conclusion.

Outline the Speech

Creating any kind of presentation involves two somewhat contradictory challenges. First, professional audiences demand well-structured presentations. This requires a thorough, full-sentence outline of all the main and subideas in the presentation. A full-sentence outline compels the speaker to examine the underlying structure and logic of the speech. On the other hand, audiences also demand enthusiasm and a sense of spontaneity that can rarely be produced by reading from a full-sentence outline. We therefore recommend using two outlines: one for preparing the speech and a second for delivering the speech.

The Preparation Outline

The **preparation outline** is a full-sentence outline of virtually everything the speaker intends to say. It allows the speaker to test the structure, the logic, and the persuasive appeals in the speech. Use the following guidelines for creating the preparation outline. These guidelines are exemplified in the sample speech outline on tort law in Figure 7.7.

The preparation outline should include the general purpose, the topic, the specific purpose, and the main idea statements. Next, label the parts of the speech—Introduction, Body, and Conclusion—and start with a new set of Roman numerals in each of the three parts of the speech. Develop a consistent pattern of symbolization for main and subpoints. The traditional pattern of symbolization is as follows:

- Main headings are designated with Roman numerals
- First-level subheads are indicated by capital letters
- The following subheads are in Arabic numerals and lower-case letters in that order

    I. First main heading
      A. Clarification or proof of I
        1. Clarification or proof of A
          a. Clarification or proof of 1
            (1) Clarification or proof of a
              (a) Clarification or proof of (1)
              (b) Further clarification or proof of (1)
            (2) Further clarification or proof of a
          b. Further clarification or proof of 1
        2. Further clarification of A
      B. Further clarification or proof of I
    II. Second main heading (etc.)

FIGURE 7.7   Sample Speech Outline

Tort Law

By Lori Braase

Topic:	Tort Law
General Purpose:	To inform
Specific Purpose:	To inform the audience about tort law.
Main Ideas:	First, I will define what tort law is, and then I will explain the major categories of tort law.

INTRODUCTION

 I. A six-year-old boy lights his shirt on fire with a Bic lighter and suffers severe burns. His mother sues the Bic Corporation for damages and wins. An 81-year-old woman orders coffee from a McDonald's drive-through and accidentally spills it in her lap, causing severe burns. She sues the McDonald's Corporation and wins $640,000 in damages.

 II. It is hard to pick up a newspaper today without reading about liability lawsuits that involve millions of dollars in awards.
   A. Tort law is the part of the legal code of this country that addresses issues of liability.
   B. Everyone needs a basic understanding of tort law to understand the reasoning behind the judgments you read about in the paper.
   C. As future business people, you will need a knowledge of torts to protect yourself and your company from lawsuits.
   D. Today I will inform you about some of the basic concepts of tort law.

 III. My name is Lori Braase and I am currently enrolled in a business law class that focuses, in part, on tort law.

 IV. Tonight I will be defining the concept of a tort, and then explain the major categories of tort law.

(Transition: Let's start by defining a tort.)

BODY

 I. "Tort" is a French word for wrong, and it has to do with wrongful conduct by one person that causes injury to another.
   A. Tort law is an area of civil law, not criminal law.
     1. Criminal law is concerned with wrongs or crimes against society as a whole.
       a. The state prosecutes a person who commits a criminal act.
       b. If convicted, those who commit criminal acts are punished by the state.
         (1) Robbery is a criminal offense.
         (2) The same is true of murder.

(continued)

FIGURE 7.7   Continued

2. On the other hand, torts are an area of civil law, which is concerned with the responsibilities that exist between people or between citizens and their government.
   a. In the case of torts, victims, not the state, initiate the lawsuit.
   b. Those who are found guilty of civil violations usually compensate the victim financially.
      (1) If, for example, you slip in the grocery store and break your leg you could sue the grocery store to recover your medical bills.
      (2) Although O. J. Simpson was found not guilty of criminal acts, the families of the victims sued him in civil court and won that verdict.
   B. As you can see, a tort is an area of civil rather than criminal law.

(Transition: Now that you know the definition of a tort, let's get to the different kinds of torts.)

II. There are three broad categories of torts: intentional torts, negligence torts, and strict liability torts.
   A. First, intentional torts are concerned with the intent to commit an act that interferes with another person's rights, such as physical injury, physical security, trespassing, property damage, reputation, privacy, dignity, etc.
      1. For example: assault and battery is an intentional act that may cause physical injury.
         a. Assault occurs when George threatens to hit Mike with a baseball bat.
         b. Battery is the completion of the act that occurs when George hits Mike in the arm with the bat.
      2. Defamation of character is a tort that occurs when someone wrongfully hurts another's good reputation through libel or slander.
         a. You could be charged with a tort of slander if you orally defame another person by saying they have a loathsome communicable disease.
         b. You could be charged with a tort of libel if you publish an article in the local paper falsely describing an attorney's unethical behavior in a nightclub.
   B. The second category of torts involves negligence that can occur when the conduct of a person or business creates a risk of negative consequences.
      1. Negligence occurs when someone suffers injury because of another's failure to live up to a required duty of care or responsibility for our actions.
         a. Allowing a friend to leave your home too drunk to drive may be considered a breach of duty if she/he becomes involved in an auto accident.
         b. If someone slips and breaks his or her leg on your icy front steps, you may have committed a breach of duty and be sued under negligence tort.
      2. Both individuals and business are open to suits under the negligence tort.
   C. Finally, the third category of torts involves strict liability, sometimes referred to as liability without fault, and these involve business or manufacturing operations.
      1. Strict liability torts are governed by three assumptions.
         a. First, consumers should be protected against unsafe products.

FIGURE 7.7   Continued

 b. Second, manufacturers and distributors should not escape liability for faulty products.
 c. Third, manufacturers are in a better position to bear the costs associated with injuries caused by their products than are consumers.
 2. For example, the Bic Corporation was held liable for severe burns on the six-year-old boy who lit his shirt on fire.
 a. According to the jury, the Bic Corporation was in a better position to bear the costs of the boy's injuries than the family.
 b. As a result of the judgment, Bic modified its lighters to stop young children from using them.

(Transition: Understanding these three broad categories of torts provides you with the ability to understand an important portion of our legal code.)

CONCLUSION

 I. In conclusion, I have covered two major points about tort law; I have defined a tort, and explained the three major categories of torts.

 II. Now you can apply your own legal reasoning to understand more about the liability lawsuits you read, see, or hear about in the media.

(Bibliography)

Because phrases and questions are unclear, state main and subpoints in full declarative sentences. Consider the following example:

Specific Purpose: I want my audience to understand the damage free radicals do to the body.

 I. Free radicals.
 II. What's to be done?

What does the speaker intend to discuss in the first main idea? Is she defining free radicals, explaining the problem of free radicals, or describing the source of free radicals? The answer is unclear. Stated as a question, the second main idea is also unclear. Will the speaker inform the audience about a variety of solutions or present a single solution? The following example is stronger.

 I. Free radicals are electrically charged molecules that damage the cells in our body.
 II. Free radicals can be reduced by taking certain vitamins.

Use one symbol for each main or subidea. Can you spot the logical flaw in the outline below?

    I. There are several sources of PM-10 pollution.
       A. Smoke from combustion and fumes from chemical reactions are common sources.
       B. Dust is another source of PM-10.
       C. Mist from spraying or condensing water vapor is another PM-10 source.

Point A includes two ideas, combustion and fumes, under a single symbol, which makes the sources of PM-10 difficult to follow.

Once the major features of the outline are solidified, it is time to insert appropriate connectives throughout the body of the speech. **Connectives** are linguistic devices that link ideas. Connectives serve as maps; they let the audience know where they have been and where they are going. Five kinds of connectives are common in business presentations. **Transitions** are full-sentence statements that are inserted in parentheses between the introduction and the body, between the body and the conclusion, and between all main ideas in the body of the speech. The appropriate locations are show below:

INTRODUCTION
    I.
   II.
  III.
  IV.
(Transition)

BODY
    I.
(Transition)
   II.
(Transition)
  III.
(Transition)

CONCLUSION
    I.
   II.

Generally, transitions state both the idea that the speaker is leaving and the upcoming idea. A speech on nuclear waste should include several transitions.

Specific Purpose: I want my audience to understand the different kinds of nuclear waste.

INTRODUCTION
  I.
  II.
  III.
  IV.
(Trans. Let's begin by examining low-level waste.)

BODY
  I. Low-level nuclear wastes are materials that emit relatively small amounts of radioactivity.
(Trans. Whereas low-level wastes emit small amounts of radioactivity, high-level wastes are quite different).
  II. As the name suggests, high-level wastes emit high amounts of radioactivity.
(Trans. The third category of waste, transuranic waste, is different from high-level wastes.)
  III. Transuranic wastes are materials such as tools and clothing that become contaminated with man-made radioactive particles chemically heavier than the element uranium.
(Trans. The fourth category of waste, mill tailings, is the result of mining.)
  IV. Mill tailings are materials of the Earth left over after radioactive elements have been mined.
(Trans. Now that you understand the four varieties of waste, let me finish with a few points.)

CONCLUSION
  I.
  II.

A second form of connective is **forecasting,** where a speaker develops main ideas such that they preview subpoints. Although not necessary for all main ideas, forecasting is a valuable source of clarity for listeners. For example,

Specific Purpose: I want my audience to understand what particulate pollution is and why it is a concern.

BODY
  I. In the first part of the speech I will define particulate pollution by explaining what it is and where it comes from.
    A. First, air pollution exists as solid matter, liquid droplets, or gas.
    B. Second, particulate pollution can come from a variety of sources that are both natural and human.
(Transition: Knowing what particulate pollution is, you can now begin to understand why it is a problem.)

II. To understand why particulates are an air pollution problem, you must understand how small this kind of pollution really is and how it is classified by scientists.
  A. First, particulate pollution is so small that it is measured in terms of microns.
  B. Second, based on the size of the particles, particulate pollution is classified into one of two categories: coarse and fine.

Both the main points in this example clearly forecast the subpoints.

Parallel order is an organizational device that should be used throughout the speech. If, for example, a speaker forecasts two subpoints in the first main idea, then those subpoints should appear in that same order. **Parallel language** means that the same words or phrases are repeated in previews, main ideas, and subpoints. In the above example, the speaker uses parallel language in the first main idea when he says he will cover where particulate pollution "comes from," and that same phrase is used below in the second subpoint. In the second main idea the terms "small" and "classified" are used to forecast the subpoints, and these terms are employed again in the subpoints themselves.

Finally, **transition phrases** indicate the relationship between subpoints. Some transition phrases illustrate such relationships as comparison and contrast: "in comparison," "similarly," "instead," "in contrast," and "nevertheless." Other transitional phrases list things in sequence: "first," "second," "after," "before," "during," and "finally." Physical description is another form of transition phrase: "above," "below," "on the left," "on the right," and "alongside." Finally, transition phrases can indicate cause and effect: "as a result of," "because of," "cause," "effect," "leads to," "If...then," and "as a consequence of." Insert transitional phrases at various points throughout the body of the speech. See the sample speech in Figure 7.7 for its use of transition phrases.

The Delivery Outline

The **delivery outline** is an abbreviated version of the preparation outline. Its brevity forces the speaker to select words and phrases on the spot, enabling a more spontaneous presentation than if the speaker read from the preparation outline.

Apply the following suggestions to your delivery outline. First, the delivery outline should use the same outline framework as the preparation outline. Thus, if the preparation outline includes three main ideas and two subpoints under the first main idea, so should the delivery outline.

Second, write the delivery outline legibly or use a computer-printed version. Scribbled notes are difficult to read, especially with the stress associated with public speaking. Many speakers prefer an extensive delivery outline, but this is a mistake. Speaking from an extensive outline is the same as reading from a manuscript. Delivery suffers and the presentation becomes boring. Keep the delivery outline brief.

Finally, write important **speaking directions** in brightly colored ink. Speaking directions include underlines for points that require emphasis, two lines (//) for important pauses, or words in the corner that correct common delivery errors such as going too slowly, too rapidly, or filling dead space with such vocalized pauses as "um…" and "ah…" A sample delivery outline can be found in Figure 7.8.

Develop the Introduction and Conclusion

Many speakers become stalled trying to develop the introduction and conclusion prior to the body. This can be avoided by saving the introduction and conclusion until last.

The Introduction

The basic introduction should accomplish four purposes:

    I. Gain the audience's attention.
   II. Justify the importance of the topic to the particular audience.
  III. Build the speaker's credibility or authority on the subject.
  IV. Preview the main points in the body of the speech.

It is not necessary to gain attention or justify the topic if the audience is already familiar with and interested in the subject. If the audience believes the speaker is knowledgeable and trustworthy, a credibility step isn't necessary.

Gain Attention. In many presentations it is important to **gain the audience's attention.** This can be done by opening with a **rhetorical question,** one that does not require a verbal answer, or a **real question,** one that requests a response from the audience. Questions encourage the audience to consider issues relevant to the presentation. In some cases, a series of questions will focus the audience on the subject. In a speech on juvenile crime, a local judge opened her speech with a series of questions:

    I. How many of you have ever been victims of juvenile crime? How many of you have ever visited one of our local high schools? How many of you have children who are now or will be attending one of our local high schools?

Because more audience members can respond affirmatively to each successive question, they become progressively more involved in the topic.

    Another way to gain attention is to make a **startling statement.** For example, in a classroom speech to persuade people to buy credit life and credit disability insurance when purchasing a car, Cade Rindfleisch said:

    I. Last year, more than one million Americans declared bankruptcy, a 29 percent increase over the previous year.

FIGURE 7.8   Sample Delivery Outline

INTRO

  I. Six-year-old boy lights shirt Bic. An 81-year-old woman orders coffee McDonalds, $640,000.

 II. Difficult see newspaper w/o reading liability lawsuits involve millions in damages.
   A. Tort law is part of legal code address liability.
   B. Everyone needs basics to understand decisions.
   C. As future business people, need avoid lawsuits.
   D. Today inform you tort law.

III. Name, BLE class focuses on tort.

 IV. Tonight define concept of tort, explain the major categories tort law.

(Trans: Start with definition tort.)

BODY

  I. "Tort" French wrong and with wrongful conduct one person cause injury another.
   A. Civil not criminal.
     1. Criminal with wrongs against society.
       a. State prosecutes criminal acts.
       b. If convicted, punished by state.
         (1) Robbery
         (2) Murder
     2. On the other hand, tort is civil law, which concerns responsibility btw. people or btw. citizens and gov.
       a. In the case of torts, victims, not state, lawsuit.
       b. Guilty usually compensate victim $.
         (1) Grocery store
         (2) O. J. won criminal, lost civil.
   B. As you can see, civil not criminal.

(Trans: Now that definition, different kinds.)

 II. Three categories: intentional, negligence, strict liability.
   A. First, intentional are intent commit an act interferes with another person's rights: physical injury, trespassing, property damage, reputation, privacy, dignity.
     1. Assault and battery is intentional act of physical injury.
       a. Assault is George threatens.
       b. Battery is completion.
     2. Defamation character offers hurt reputation: libel or slander.
       a. Loathsome communicable disease.
       b. Publish article unethical.
   B. The second category is negligence, conduct creates risk negative consequences.
     1. Negligence is suffer injury b/c failure live up to duty, care, or responsibility.
       a. Friend drive drunk.
       b. Slips on steps.
     2. Both individuals and business open to this.

FIGURE 7.8 Continued

C. Finally, the third category is strict liability, liability without fault, usually business or manufacturing.
   1. Governed three assumptions:
      a. Consumers protected.
      b. Manufacturers/distributors not escape liability.
      c. Third manufacturers in better position pay.
   2. For example, Bic held liable burns on boy.
      a. Jury said Bic in better position to pay.
      b. As a result, Bic modified lighters.

(Trans: Know three categories provides ability understand legal code.)

CONCLUSION

I. In conclusion, covered two major points: define tort law, and explained three major categories.

II. Now can apply legal reasoning to stories in paper.

Opening with a **quotation** can draw an audience into the speech. For example, a speech critiquing the findings of quantitative social science could open with a quote from the anthropologist and communication theorist Gregory Bateson:

> I. Of attempts to measure human behavior with numbers, the anthropologist and communication theorist Gregory Bateson said, "If it's not worth doing, it's worth doing well."

Make quotations short and directly relevant to the topic.

Stories are examples that almost always draw an audience into a speech. Stories have protagonists, antagonists, and a problem to be resolved. The story may be hypothetical or real, but if the former choice is made the audience must be informed that the tale isn't real. A speech persuading people to check their homes for carbon monoxide opened with this story:

> I. Last year, while renting a basement apartment in town, I noticed that I spent most of the winter tired, nauseous, and sick with colds and flus. After moving out, I spoke with my former landlord who told me that he had the furnace replaced because it was leaking carbon monoxide into the air. I quickly realized that I had been suffering from a mild form of carbon monoxide poisoning. Had the furnace been in worse shape I might have died.

Keep stories brief and to the point. Make careful language choices so the story creates the appropriate emotional response.

Justify the Topic.   In some business and professional presentations it is necessary to **justify the topic** by informing the audience why the issue is important or relevant. The justification step relates the topic to the audience by explaining how it affects their interests. In the speech persuading new car buyers to purchase credit life and credit disability insurance, Cade continued his introduction with the following justification.

> **II.** According to *USA Today,* the typical filer for bankruptcy is a white, married homeowner, working full-time.
>   **A.** As such, this growing problem can affect each of us sitting in this room.
>   **B.** We don't anticipate bankruptcy; it slowly creeps up, suddenly strikes, and by then it is too late to do anything about it.

Cade used several techniques to justify the topic. First, the *USA Today* testimony reminded his mostly white, married audience that they are not immune from bankruptcy. He made a direct appeal to the audience, stating that any of us could go bankrupt. He made use of "us" and "we" pronouns that remind the audience the topic is vital to our interests. Of course, in many business settings, a justification step is not required because the audience is either naturally interested or must know the topic as part of their job.

Somewhere in the attention or justification steps the speaker should clarify the specific purpose. People want to know why you are speaking and what you want them to understand, believe, or do at the end of the speech.

> **I.** Last year, more than one million Americans declared bankruptcy, a 29 percent increase over the previous year.
> **II.** According to *USA Today,* the typical filer for bankruptcy is a white, married homeowner, working full-time.
>   **A.** As such this growing problem can affect each of us sitting in this room.
>   **B.** We don't anticipate bankruptcy; it slowly creeps up, suddenly strikes, and by then it is too late to do anything about it.
>   **C.** Today I want to convince you to purchase credit life and credit disability insurance when you buy your next new car so you can avoid becoming another bankruptcy statistic.

In this example, subpoint C clarifies the speech goal. In most cases you can modify the specific purpose statement for use in the attention or justification step. In cases where an attention and justification step are not required, the speaker can open the speech with the specific purpose statement.

Establish Credibility.   The third objective of the introduction is to establish credibility. **Source credibility** is the audience's perception of the speaker's expertise, trustworthiness, and dynamism. If the audience is unfamiliar with the speaker's expertise, or worse yet, if the audience has a negative view of the speaker's competence, then a credibility step is a vital part of the speech introduction. As such, the speaker's source of expertise on the topic should be cited in the credibility step. For example, in a speech to persuade state lawmakers to create contractor licensing requirements, Tari Jensen made the following credibility statement:

> **III.** My name is Tari Jensen. I have been involved in the construction industry for over twenty years.
>   **A.** Our company is named Jensen Bros. Builders. We build ten to twenty residential homes per year and have gross sales of $1,500,000 to $2,000,000 per year.
>   **B.** I have been president of the Building Contractors Association for Southeast Idaho and received the state association's Builder of the Year Award for 1995.
>   **C.** To prepare this speech, I interviewed Dave LeRoy, the past attorney general of Idaho, Dave Wilson, the national representative for the Building Contractors Association for the state of Idaho, Evan Frasure, our district senator, and Jack Robinson, a local real estate attorney; I read and reviewed many articles and books from the ISU library, the Marshall Public Library, and trade magazines.

This statement makes numerous references that support Tari's source credibility.

Of course, some professional presentations are made among people who know and have a high opinion of the speaker. As such, a credibility step may not be necessary. It would, for example, be redundant for a team leader to include a credibility statement in every presentation to his team. It is up to the speaker to judge the audience, the topic, and the situation to determine whether a credibility step is warranted.

Preview the Main Ideas. The fourth goal of the introduction is to **preview** the main ideas in the body of the speech. Like connectives, previews provide a helpful mapping function for listeners. The main idea statement can be modified to serve as the preview statement. In his classroom presentation about wool versus synthetic carpet fiber, Joseph Wilcox included the following preview:

> **IV.** I will cover these different carpet fibers in four main steps: First, I will acknowledge that many people think wool is the best carpet fiber. Second, I will discuss why people think wool is better. Third, I state that wool is not superior. And fourth, I will illustrate why synthetic fiber is superior to wool.

It is often useful to enumerate each point in the preview as Joseph did in his speech. The points in the body of the speech should be covered in parallel order and written in parallel language to those in the preview. Examine the sample speech outline in Figure 7.7 for a well-crafted introduction.

The Conclusion

The **conclusion** puts the speech back together by tying the end back to the beginning. It does this in two steps: The conclusion reviews the main ideas in the body of the speech and ends with a capstone statement.

Review the Main Ideas.   Like the preview, the **review** ties the speech together by summarizing the main ideas. For example, in Joseph Wilcox's speech on carpet fiber, he reviewed his main ideas as follows.

> **I.** To conclude, I have stated that most people think wool is the best fiber for carpets, and explained why people think wool is superior. I then rejected the idea that wool is superior to synthetics, and listed reasons why synthetic fiber is superior to wool.

Almost all business presentations should include a brief restatement of the main ideas in the body.

End with a Capstone Statement.   Close the speech with a **capstone statement** that reinforces the specific purpose. There are many ways to do this, including any one of the methods of gaining attention previously mentioned. To close his speech on bacteria, Jacob M. Lewis used a hypothetical story.

> **II.** So, the next time you feel queasy after eating week-old potato salad, you'll at least understand why you are rushing to the bathroom.

This humorous anecdote reminds the audience about Jacob's specific purpose: the way bacteria make people sick. Strong capstone statements can also employ questions, startling statements, or quotations.

Another effective way to tie the speech together is to refer listeners back to the introduction. In the introduction to her speech on contractor licensing, Tari Jensen described a family who lost their life savings at the hands of an inexperienced, unlicensed contractor. Her conclusion referred the audience back to the plight of that family.

> **II.** We should never allow the heartache, frustration, and years of suffering of our family in Pocatello to happen to anyone else in the state, ever again.

The capstone statement for a persuasive presentation should make an appeal to belief or action. An appeal to belief emphasizes the persuasive outcome in the specific purpose statement. In so doing, the speaker emphasizes the attitude or belief he or she wants the audience to adopt. In a speech protesting the killing of bison outside Yellowstone National Park, the capstone statement emphasizes the speaker's interpretation of events:

II. As I have made clear in this presentation, many of the bison in Yellowstone are not infectious, and the chances of disease transmission to cattle are almost nonexistent. There is therefore no legitimate reason to kill these animals.

The emotional tone of the clincher should be consistent with the content in the body of the speech.

A call to action is necessary in some persuasive speeches. State exactly the action you want the audience to take.

II. I encourage all of you who feel the way I do to make your voice heard by contacting the superintendent of Yellowstone National Park, Mike Finley.

Speakers must do more, however, than simply call for action. They should take steps to make the action easy for the audience. We will discuss methods of encouraging action in Chapter 10, on persuasive proposals. Examine the sample preparation outline in Figure 7.7 for its conclusion.

Rehearsal and Delivery Considerations

As we mentioned in Chapter 3, the verbal portion of the message accounts for as little as 10 percent of the total meaning of that message; nonverbal cues account for the rest.[12] As a consequence, delivery is a crucial component of any speech.

Despite its importance, delivery is very difficult to teach. The reason for this involves the limits of our conscious minds. Psychological studies show that the conscious mind can handle no more than seven discrete activities at one time. Most of our conscious processing capacity during a speech is taken up on the verbal portion of the message. We consciously read the delivery outline, select words, phrases, and sentences cued by that outline, manipulate visual aids, and watch the audience for feedback. Imagine for a moment that you also wanted to consciously control your eye contact so that you connect with every member of the audience at least twice; vary your facial expressions to reflect the proper emotional tone, alter vocal rate, pitch, and variety so you don't bore the audience; and emphasize certain gestures so they highlight appropriate points. Obviously, adding all these tasks to the verbal demands on our conscious attention would overwhelm any presenter. Many speakers try to solve this problem by memorizing facial expressions and gestures. Unfortunately, only great actors can manage this without looking contrived and stilted. Some other solution is necessary.

To improve your delivery, focus on rehearsal and attitude adjustment. First, delivery is always improved by thorough familiarity with the message. Mastering the message involves practicing the presentation at least twelve to fifteen times. The first few rehearsals will be halting and unsatisfactory. But, as rehearsal proceeds, your self-confidence with the delivery outline will grow. You will be able to stick to the outline enough to maintain logical consistency but also choose words and phrases on the spot, creating spontaneity. Rehearsal is one of the steps that many students ignore in their classroom speeches, and it clearly shows in the product. On the other hand, experienced speakers know that thorough rehearsal is the first key to solid delivery.

The second way to improve delivery is developing the proper attitude toward the topic and the audience. If you have enthusiasm for your topic and an intense desire to be understood by the audience, these emotions will be reflected in your nonverbal cues. According to Joel D. Whalen, a business professor at DePaul University, the most important emotion for business and professional presentations is enthusiasm:

> Of all the emotions that will move your audience to embrace your point of view, enthusiasm is the most important. It's the emotion that you should adopt as your primary tool in communication.[13]

Develop an intense enthusiasm for your topic and it will naturally show in the presentation. The audience, having no doubt listened to many dull presentations in the past, will be grateful for your effort and more interested in and persuaded by your ideas.

In addition to enthusiasm, develop a concern for audience comprehension. Too many speakers devote too little attention to helping the audience understand their ideas. Their main goal is to complete the presentation and sit down. When you really care about audience comprehension you can stop the speech in the middle and go over something again if you see quizzical expressions. You naturally highlight main ideas with your voice because you want the audience to understand, and you naturally exhibit appropriate nonverbal cues. Finally, learn to have fun. A sense of fun communicates competence and dynamism, two important elements of credibility. Let your nonverbal communication flow from the attitudes of enthusiasm, goodwill, and fun.

Summary

A good presentation involves solid preparation and enthusiastic delivery. Preparing a presentation begins by deciding whether the general purpose is to inform or persuade. Some topics for business and professional presentations are determined by superiors or by the organization, while others are up to the speaker to select. The specific purpose statement clarifies the primary outcome the speaker desires and should be stated in a single declarative sentence. The main idea statement clarifies the two to five main ideas in the body of the presentation.

There are three different kinds of supporting material, including examples, statistics, and testimony. Examples are specific instances. Statistics are a collection of specific instances that are delivered as raw numbers or averages. Testimony involves quotations or paraphrases from experts or other informed people. Research to collect supporting material involves using the library, the Internet, and interviews. To use the library, speakers must learn to use the computerized card catalogue and the computerized abstracts and indexes. To use the Internet, a search engine such as Yahoo or Alta Vista is necessary.

After library research, take the information from the Audience Analysis Checklist and apply it to the presentation. The Speech Adaptation Checklist provides a list of relevant questions that help speakers apply the results of their audience analysis.

Structure is vital to clear presentations. The speech body may be structured using one of the following patterns: chronological, spatial, cause-effect, problem-solution, or topical. The preparation outline helps the speaker flesh out the content of the speech. The preparation outline is a full-sentence outline of all the important ideas in the presentation. This outline should include a consistent pattern of symbolization, all ideas should be phrased in full sentences, and appropriate connectives should be inserted. Connectives are linguistic devices that link ideas. Transitions, forecasting, parallel order, parallel language, and transition phrases are five commonly used connectives. The delivery outline is an abbreviated version of the preparation outline for making the presentation.

The speech introduction should gain attention, justify the importance of the topic, build the speaker's credibility, and preview the main ideas in the presentation. Attention may be gained through the use of rhetorical or real questions, startling statements, quotations, and stories. The conclusion should review the main ideas in the body of the speech and finish with a capstone statement.

Delivery is important to an effective presentation. Delivery is improved through rehearsal and developing enthusiasm for the topic. Speakers are encouraged to have fun while making their presentations.

DISCUSSION QUESTIONS

1. Examine the sample preparation outline in this chapter. Was the introduction handled well? Label the main steps in the introduction. Are all four steps there? Is there anything you would have done to improve this introduction?

2. Look at the body of the speech in the sample preparation outline. What structure is used to organize the main ideas? Was this structure effective? Label the different kinds of supporting material in the body. Does the supporting material help clarify Lori's points? Is there anything you would have done differently to improve the use of supporting material? Label the different connectives in the presentation, including transitions, forecasting, parallel order, parallel language, and transition phrases. Were the connective devices easy to identify? Do they help the listener follow the presentation? Were there other places that needed connectives for clarity?

3. Examine the conclusion of the speech in the sample preparation outline. Was the conclusion handled well? How did the author draw the speech to a close? Was this effective?

A C T I V I T I E S   A N D   E X E R C I S E S

1. Bring in a professionally written editorial or opinion piece from a local or national newspaper. Read the article for the following features and discuss the questions in a group or with the entire class. What is the specific purpose of this article? Is it stated in the article or do readers have to reconstruct it for themselves? What kinds of supporting material are used to bolster the opinion? Is this material convincing? Why or why not? What are the article's main ideas? Are they structured according to one of the patterns discussed in this chapter? If so, what pattern is used? Would another pattern have made the information more clear or persuasive? How do the introduction and conclusion differ from the methods suggested in this chapter? To what do you attribute these differences? What changes would you make in the article to turn it into an effective speech?

2. Bring in a nonprofessionally (citizen-) written editorial or opinion piece from a local or national newspaper. Read the article for the following features and discuss the questions in a group or with the entire class. What is the specific purpose of the article? Did the author state it or do the readers have to reconstruct it for themselves? What kinds of supporting material are used to bolster the opinion? Is this material convincing? Why or why not? What are the article's main ideas? Are they structured according to one of the patterns discussed in this chapter? If so, what pattern is used? If not, has this affected your ability to understand the article? Would another pattern have made the information more clear or persuasive? How do the introduction and conclusion differ from the methods suggested in this chapter? To what do you attribute these differences? What changes would you make in the article to turn it into an effective speech?

3. In a small group or as a class, compare the two articles for the clarity of the specific purpose of each, the use of supporting material, the clarity and structure of the main ideas, and the introduction and conclusion. What, if any, differences do you see between the two? Do these differences affect your ability to understand and interpret the article?

4. Attend a speech, instructional workshop, sermon, or other public presentation and answer the questions on the following form.

Report on a Speech Heard in Public

What was the name, title, and/or position of the speaker?
What was the topic or title of the speech?
Identify the general purpose and the specific purpose.
> Did the speaker provide these or did you have to clarify these for yourself?
> Was the specific purpose appropriate for the audience and occasion? Why or why not?

What kinds of supporting materials were used in the presentation?
> Were examples well used?
> Did the statistics include comparisons for easier interpretation?
> Did the testimony come from sources you considered authoritative?
> Was the supporting material persuasive? Why or why not?

Did the speaker adapt the topic to the audience?
> Did the speaker adapt to the organizational culture?
> Did the speaker adapt to the environment, including room size, use of visual aids, etc.?
> Did the speaker adapt to relevant audience demographic characteristics?
> If the audience was captive, did the speaker adapt to this constraint?
> Did the speaker provide proof of credibility and goodwill?
> What kind of audience was this: favorable, active, neutral, apathetic, hostile, or mixed?
> Did the speaker adapt to that audience appropriately?

What, if any, structure did the speaker use for the main ideas in the body?
> Was that structure appropriate and easy to follow?
> Were appropriate connectives used? If so, which ones?

How was the introduction handled?
> Did the introduction include attention, justification, credibility, and preview steps?
> What, if anything, would you have changed to make the introduction more effective?

How was the conclusion handled?
> Did the speaker include review and capstone steps?
> What, if anything, would you have changed to make the conclusion more effective?

Was the speech well delivered?

NOTES

1. Rawlins, W. K., personal communication, October 1988.
2. Leeds, D., "No-fault selling," *Folio,* 1 December 1996.
3. Sprague, J., and D. Stuart, *The Speaker's Handbook* (Fort Worth: Harcourt Brace College Publishers, 1996), 127.
4. Robertson, R. G., "Layers of basalt hide water at Craters," *Idaho State Journal,* 10 May 1995.
5. Mandeville, C., phone conversation, January 1998.
6. Doyle, T. A., *Allyn & Bacon Quick Guide to the Internet* (Boston: Allyn and Bacon, 1998), 1.
7. Stoll, C., *Silicon Snake Oil: Second Thoughts on the Information Superhighway* (New York: Anchor Books, 1995), 40.
8. Doyle.
9. Renz, M. A., "Communicating About Environmental Risk: An Examination of a Minnesota County's Communication on Incineration," *Journal of Applied Communication Research* 20 (1992): 1–18.
10. Lucas, S. E., *The Art of Public Speaking* (Boston: McGraw Hill, 1998), 149.
11. Leeds, 75.
12. Whalen, J. D., *I See What You Mean: Persuasive Business Communication* (Beverly Hills, CA: Sage, 1996).
13. Ibid., 124.

CHAPTER

8 Creating and Using Visual Aids

We live in a visually oriented society! We derive most of our entertainment from television and film. Most Americans stay informed about current events through television and the Internet rather than newspapers. To compete, newspapers have "gone visual," offering color pictures as well as more charts and graphs than in the past. When more information becomes available over the Internet, people will take advantage of the visually pleasing information on the computer.

Our penchant for images is affecting all forms of communication, including business and professional presentations. Many organizations rely on their own video news releases rather than printed newsletters for internal communication. Yearly reports to stockholders have become multimedia events incorporating giant video screens, computer-generated graphics, and live video feeds from remote locations. The meeting rooms in most corporations include built-in VCRs and monitors, overhead projectors, and computers for displaying graphics. Effective business and professional presentations need to include informative, visually pleasing graphic aids.

The information in this chapter will help you create and use visual aids. We divided the chapter into three parts: First, we review the various types of visual aids available and explain guidelines for creating effective graphics. In section two we discuss guidelines for the effective use of visual aids during the presentation.

Finally, because computer-generated graphics are standard in many business and professional organizations, we devote the third section to the creation and use of this material.

When using visual aids it is important to remember one guiding principle: Professional presentations are a chance to exchange information and share ideas with an audience; therefore, visual aids should support rather than supplant speaker and content. Marya Holcombe and Judith K. Stein, authors of *Presentations for Decision Makers,* assert that a presentation "is not a picture show for which you provide the voice-over."[1] The purpose of any visual is to make the content more understandable or persuasive. Using a visual aid without any clear informative or persuasive purpose is, at best, distracting. Throughout this chapter we encourage the use of visual aids that support the speaker and the content.

Types of Visual Aids

A **visual aid** is any pictorial, textual, or graphic image that is presented visually rather than orally. Visual aids can add to the effectiveness of a presentation in three ways. First, visual aids increase the clarity of complicated pictorial, statistical, or conceptual material.[2] Imagine discussing the architectural features of a new building without showing pictures. Think about the difficulty of describing earnings trends over several years without the use of line graphs. When they are well constructed, visual aids communicate complicated information clearly and quickly.

Second, visual aids increase the persuasiveness of a message.[3] In a study conducted at the University of Minnesota, the use of computer-generated overhead transparencies increased a presenter's persuasiveness by 43 percent.[4] Other research showed that the addition of tables and pictures in a speech made the content more persuasive and increased the audience's perception of speaker credibility.[5]

Finally, visual aids make a presentation more dynamic, motivating the audience to pay attention.[6] There are, however, many different forms of visual material to choose from. What are the different types of visual aids and how can they be designed for the greatest effect? These questions are addressed below, where we explain the eight types of visual aids commonly used in business and professional presentations.

Objects

Bringing in an **object** is an excellent way to add interest and clarity to your ideas. For example, Jesse works for a tennis racket maker and needed to explain how a manufacturing problem created blemishes on the surface of many rackets. He brought in several rackets to show the audience the location and severity of the scarring. Objects are used in sales presentations when the speaker brings in the item for display or demonstration.

Objects might be the ideal visual aid, but for one problem—size. Many objects are too large to fit into a room or too small to be easily seen by the audience. For large objects, photographs or slides may serve as adequate visual representations. Photographs should, however, be made into transparencies for use with an overhead projector rather than passed around the audience. A scaled-down model is another means of displaying a large object.

If, on the other hand, the object is too small to be seen, resist the temptation to pass it around the room. The audience will not be listening to you as they manipulate and look at the object. Instead, use photographs or slides that can be projected onto a screen for easy viewing. Another solution is to create a larger model of the small object. If you must show the object by passing it around, temporarily suspend the presentation and give the group a chance to clearly examine the object and discuss its characteristics. Once this is completed you may reconvene and continue with the presentation.

Models

Models are scale, two-dimensional drawings or three-dimensional constructions that represent very large or very small objects. Models are an excellent substitute for objects that are too large or too small for easy viewing. For example, a model of the human heart is a useful way to show the placement and functions of a pacemaker. Models should be large enough for easy viewing by the entire audience. If you must pass the model around, follow the same guidelines previously stated for passing around objects.

Chalk Board/Marker Board/Flip Chart

The **chalk board,** or its more modern equivalent, the **magic marker board,** and the **flip chart** are staples of business and professional presentations. There are several reasons for the popularity of these aids. Information can be placed on a board or flip chart prior to the speech and referred to at the appropriate point in the presentation. Or, speakers can write down important statistics or verbal information during the presentation to reinforce note-taking and improve recall. In group settings, any of these devices allow a leader to keep track of ideas generated during brainstorming or extended discussion. Despite these advantages, the marker board and flip chart do have disadvantages. The aids are "low tech" and not very impressive. Also, unless they are done in advance, the time it takes to write things on the board or the flip chart interrupts the smooth flow of ideas in a presentation. Finally, if the chart is not flipped to a blank page or the board is not erased (both of which interrupt the speech), the information remains in view and distracts audience members long after it has been covered.

Given the limitations just described, we recommend the use of marker boards and flip charts in the following situations. Extended presentations (for example, lectures) often require boards or flip charts because ideas are developed and changed through interaction with the audience. Boards or flip charts are vital for group brainstorming sessions where ideas must be written down, narrowed, and solidified in front of the entire group. In both cases, audience input makes pre-

prepared visual aids impossible. Pre-prepared flip charts are useful in training sessions or informative presentations. Sales presenters in small groups sometimes find table-top flip charts useful. Make sure the chart is large enough for the entire audience to see. As a general rule, letters on a flip chart should be one to two inches high to be visible twenty-five feet away.[7] Leave a blank page between each visual so nothing distracts the audience when the chart isn't in use.

Handouts

Very common in college classrooms, **handouts** are also an indispensable part of business and professional presentations. Handouts can summarize information and provide a handy reference guide to audience members long after the presentation. Any visual aid shown to the entire audience can be reduced and included on handouts.

The disadvantage of handouts is the same as for passing objects or models around the room—they distract the audience. With handouts, audience members may move ahead of the speaker by considering information not yet covered, or miss important information by stopping to focus on one part of a handout. As a result, most business communicators recommend providing handouts after, rather than during, the presentation. If you must use handouts to explain complicated information, provide the handout only at the point in the speech when it's relevant, go over the handout thoroughly, and then move on with the rest of the presentation. Keeping the handouts until you are ready to review them prevents the audience from moving ahead of the presentation. With thorough handout explanation, the audience has little to linger over and draw their attention.

Photographs and Slides

Photographs and **slides** improve understanding and retention of complex information. As previously explained, they are an excellent substitute for objects that are too large or too small for the audience to see. The fact that slides are projected onto a screen makes them excellent aids for most presentations. The same, however, cannot be said for photographs. Normal-size photographs are too small to be seen without being passed around, distracting the audience from the message. As such, photographs must be enlarged for use in professional presentations. Most copy service companies can reproduce color photographs onto overhead projector transparencies. This same process can be used for maps and other graphic material. Once altered so they can be projected, photos are an excellent addition to any presentation. When using slides, include black-out slides or blanks in the tray for periods when no visual is required.

Charts and Graphs

Charts and **graphs** include any kind of two-dimensional visual aid that clarifies complicated statistical or relational information. As we said in the last chapter, statistics are a collection of individual examples delivered as raw numbers or averages. Relationships compare or contrast the performance of two or more variables.

Every chart or graph should include a title that communicates and emphasizes the meaning you want the audience to accept rather than merely what the chart represents.[8] For example, look at the titles of the two pie charts in Figure 8.1. While the title of the first chart merely describes it as the "Department Budget," the second title clearly explains the speaker's central meaning, that duplication has grown too large in comparison to the other budget items. Create titles that clearly state the interpretation you want the chart or graph to communicate.

Charts.   **Charts** are particularly useful for summarizing statistical information. The data in Figure 8.2 indicate the amount, in tons per year, of five different kinds of pollution emitted by various sources in a hypothetical town. The chart's numerous categories make it easy to compare the output of various sources.

Despite the usefulness of this chart to a decision maker in the privacy of her office, it is too extensive and too detailed for most presentations. Speakers should simplify charts so they clarify only the most important information. This means eliminating irrelevant data or grouping information into larger categories. For example, in a presentation about particulate emissions in her area, Sue Yang decided to simplify the chart by eliminating three of the sources of gaseous pollution, SO_2, NOX, and CO from the chart (see Figure 8.3).

As you can see, Sue created a simpler, cleaner chart, one that is easier for the audience to scan and comprehend. If Sue felt she needed to include all the pollutants, she could simplify the chart in other ways (see Figure 8.4). She knew

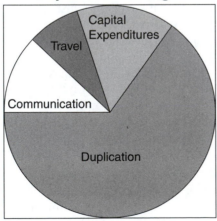

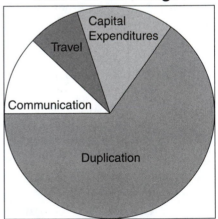

FIGURE 8.1

FIGURE 8.2   Sources for Five Pollutants
All figures are in tons/year

Source	PM-10	PM-2.5	SO$_2$	NOX	CO
Chemical Plant	950.00	1000.50	3090.79	300.67	145.23
Steel Plant	1367.00	2020.35	1945.50	700.67	303.00
Trucking Company	320.50	300.00	150.00	206.67	5760.00
Paving Company	250.50	50.00	5.30	10.65	467.00
Grain Elevator	15.00	250.56	00.00	00.00	00.00
Concrete Plant	660.50	45.80	75.98	956.50	00.00
Railroad	250.00	75.35	45.78	156.90	730.00
Agricultural Tilling	410.10	125.25	00.00	00.00	00.00
Windblown Dust	700.25	100.50	00.00	00.00	00.00
Paved Roads	350.00	21.34	00.00	00.00	00.00
Landfill Emissions	45.00	10.65	76.89	00.00	358.67
Residential Heating	310.00	150.00	176.98	00.00	43.78
Automobile Traffic	35.75	250.00	46.98	2567.90	12,678.15
Aircraft	50.60	100.56	10.78	200.67	500.50
Unpaved Roads	400.50	34.67	00.00	00.00	00.00
Total of All Sources	6106.70	4535.53	5624.98	5100.63	20,986.33

PM-10 = particulate matter smaller than 10 microns
PM-2.5 = particulate matter smaller than 2.5 microns
SO$_2$ = Sulfur Dioxide
NOX = Various Nitrogen Oxides
CO = Carbon Dioxide

her speech was mainly concerned with nonindustrial sources. As a result, she combined the industrial sources into a single row. The nonindustrial sources remained the same, but the chart was shorter and easier for the audience to comprehend. Simplify the layout and format of charts for easy assimilation.

Line Graph.   A **line graph** is a useful way to show changes in one or more variables over time. For example, the line graph in Figure 8.5 displays changes in the Dow Jones average of industrial stocks over a period of nineteen months.

An audience can easily see the general upward trend in the Dow Jones Industrial Average. The line graph also makes it easy to see smaller trends within the larger trend—for example, the sharp rise between mid-January and March 1996, or the slump in July 1996.

Figure 8.6 depicts a two-day measurement of particulate matter in a large city experiencing an air inversion. The vertical axis depicts the number of micrograms of particulate matter per cubic meter of air. The horizontal axis depicts the time of day in three-hour increments. The graph clearly shows a build-up of particulate

FIGURE 8.3   Sources of Two Pollutants
All figures are in tons/year

Source	PM-10	PM-2.5
Chemical Plant	950.00	1000.50
Steel Plant	1367.00	2020.35
Trucking Company	320.50	300.00
Paving Company	250.50	50.00
Grain Elevator	15.00	250.56
Concrete Plant	660.50	45.80
Railroad	250.00	75.35
Agricultural Tilling	410.10	125.25
Windblown Dust	700.25	100.50
Paved Roads	350.00	21.34
Landfill Emissions	45.00	10.65
Residential Heating	310.00	150.00
Automobile Traffic	35.75	250.00
Aircraft	50.60	100.56
Unpaved Roads	400.50	34.67
Total of All Sources	6106.70	4535.53

PM-10 = particulate matter smaller than 10 microns
PM-2.5 = particulate matter smaller than 2.5 microns

FIGURE 8.4   Sources of Particulate Pollution
All figures are in tons/year

Source	PM-10	PM-2.5	SO_2	NOX	CO
All Industrial Sources	3813.50	3742.56	5313.35	2062.06	7405.23
Agricultural Tilling	410.10	125.25	00.00	00.00	00.00
Windblown Dust	700.25	100.50	00.00	00.00	00.00
Paved Roads	350.00	21.34	00.00	00.00	00.00
Landfill Emissions	45.00	10.65	76.89	00.00	358.67
Residential Heating	310.00	150.00	176.98	00.00	43.78
Automobile Traffic	35.75	250.00	46.98	2567.90	12,678.15
Aircraft	50.60	100.56	10.78	200.67	500.50
Unpaved Roads	400.50	34.67	00.00	00.00	00.00
Total of All Sources	6106.70	4535.53	5624.98	5100.63	20,986.33

PM-10 = particulate matter smaller than 10 microns
PM-2.5 = particulate matter smaller than 2.5 microns
SO_2 = Sulfur Dioxide
NOX = Various Nitrogen Oxides
CO = Carbon Dioxide

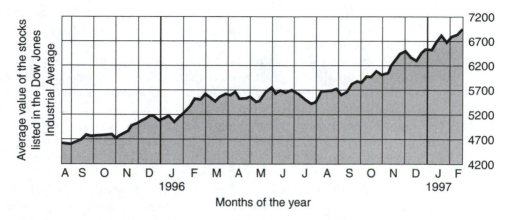

FIGURE 8.5   The Rising Dow Jones Industrial Average

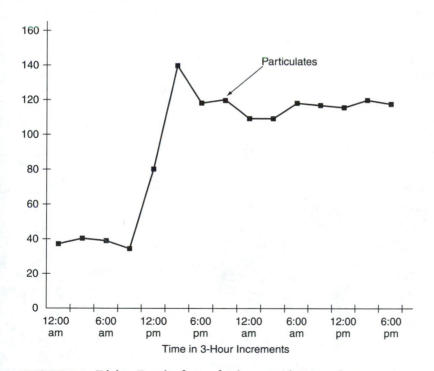

FIGURE 8.6   Rising Particulates during an Air Inversion

matter from 40 to more than 140 micrograms between 12:00 P.M. and 6:00 P.M. The levels drop off slightly during the next six hours, and then remain steady throughout the second day.

The rules for creating line graphs are similar to those for charts. Keep the information simple. Because too many lines cause confusion, limit the number of lines (each representing a different variable) to no more than three. When using more than one line, use different colors for each and clearly label which variable is represented by which color. Use the darkest, heaviest line for the most important variable. As with all visual aids, include only the information absolutely necessary to make your point.

Pie Charts.   The **pie chart** displays the relationship of various parts to a whole. For example, Figure 8.7 shows the relative contributions of various sources to total particulate pollution in a hypothetical town. The pie represents the particulate emitted into the air each year, and every wedge of the pie represents a significant particulate source. The pie chart provides a vivid way to explain the contributions of various polluters to the town's annual air quality.

When creating a pie chart, avoid slicing the pie into more than seven pieces. Small slices are difficult to label and confusing to the audience. Creating too many slices also sacrifices the impact of the chart, the ability of the viewer to quickly apprehend proportions of the whole. Finally, because audiences find it difficult to work between the pie chart and a legend, label pie pieces on or near the slice.

Bar Graphs.   Finally, the **bar graph** is an excellent way of making comparisons among magnitudes. In Figure 8.8 you can see a bar graph comparing the yearly earnings for a mutual fund. The bar graph makes it is easy to see the general earnings trend as well as anomalous years such as 1992. As with all visual aids, keep

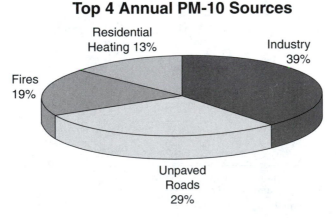

Top 4 Annual PM-10 Sources

FIGURE 8.7

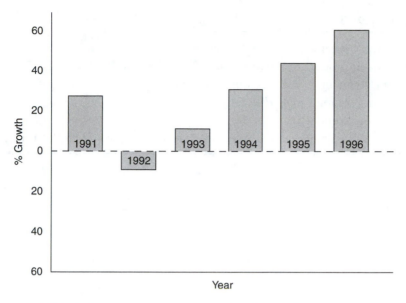

FIGURE 8.8   Strong Earnings Growth—1991–1996

the bar graph simple. Include no more than six bars and use different colors for different variables. Label the actual bars rather than creating a legend separate from the chart. Label the horizontal and vertical axes.

Videotape

Videotape can add dynamic impact to a presentation. For example, a speech reporting on the relative success of various television commercials should show those commercials. However, those commercials that are not directly relevant to the specific purpose are time-consuming and distracting. If you use videotape, cue the tape to the proper location and familiarize yourself with the VCR and TV monitors at the site prior to the presentation. We have seen many speeches disrupted by improperly linked VCRs and monitors. If you use video from a variety of sources, have the tape professionally edited so the cuts between excerpts are clean.

Text Visuals

Text visuals display the key features of the presentation in words, phrases, and sentences. Text visuals map the speech for the audience by previewing and reviewing main ideas (see Figure 8.9).[9] Always use action phrases, rather than full sentences or key words in text visuals. Full sentences are boring for the audience to read. Key words cannot clearly express full thoughts. Action-oriented

FIGURE 8.9   Text Visuals

Review the critical features of the new product
Compare our product to the competitors' product
Suggest two major markets for the new product
   • Young business people just starting out
   • College students
Block out sales pitches to encourage retail stores to carry and display the product

Preview
Product Overview
Competitors
Market
Sales

phrases express full thoughts concisely. Although the first visual aid in Figure 8.9 outlines the speech in action-oriented phrases, the key words in the second do not provide any detail about the main points. Text visuals should maintain parallel order with the information in the speech. People expect you to cover main ideas in the same order and with the same grammatical form as in the visual aid. Finally, do not provide a full-sentence outline of the speech, because this is boring. Highlight only the most important ideas in the text visual.

Whether you choose to use the object itself, a model, marker board, photographs, or some variety of graphs and charts, well-constructed visual aids can add to the clarity, persuasiveness, and dynamism of any professional presentation. Constructing the visual aid, however, is only half the process. The next section covers the effective use of visual aids during the presentation.

Presenting Visual Aids to the Audience

The following suggestions are essential for the effective use of any visual aid. The effort to create a visual aid is wasted if it is poorly presented. First, use visual aids only when they are justified; do not try to "jazz-up" a presentation with unnecessary ones. Empty vigor and verve distracts or annoys conservative, bottom-line-oriented professional audiences. An article in *The Wall Street Journal* described the danger of empty attempts to impress. John Weber, president of Vickers Inc., a Toledo, Ohio, manufacturer of hydraulic pumps, motors, and cylinders, needled one of his managers who used color slides in a presentation about the fat budget he must have. Although Weber meant the comment as a joke, he later learned that other managers stayed up all night converting their slides to black and white.[10] Visual aids are useful for clarifying information, but they are no substitute for solid research and accurate content.

Second, if you do decide to create visual aids, make sure they are large enough for the entire audience to see. It's annoying to listen to a presentation that has numerous, carefully prepared visual aids that cannot be seen from all locations in the room. A visual aid that cannot be seen cannot add to your clarity, persuasiveness, or dynamism.

Third, position yourself in such a way that the entire audience has a clear view of the visual aid. Never obscure or block the visual with your body. If you have to point to the visual, use a pointer so as not to obscure peoples' view. Laser pointers, which project a red dot, are an effective way of pointing to important items without getting in the audience's line of sight.

Next, display the visual aid only when you come to the relevant place in the speech and remove it from view before moving on to new information. Leaving the visual aid in sight distracts audience members who continue to examine it instead of listening to your next point. Fifth, visual aids need to be explained and interpreted for the audience. As we mentioned in Chapter 1, people do not automatically assign the same meaning as the speaker to a visual aid. The speaker's goal is to manage the meaning the audience assigns. This is done by explaining all major parts of the visual aid, pointing out the important statistical comparisons or graphic features. Leave nothing to chance; lead the audience to the interpretation you desire.

Sixth, when explaining the visual aid, use the same words from the VA's title and labels. Using different labels is a form of mixed message that can be confusing for the audience. Parallel language, in both order of coverage and grammatical form, is vital for complete understanding.

Finally, because the goal is communication with the audience, talk to them and not to the visual aid. Turn no more than one-third of your body toward the display. Figure 8.10 summarizes the guidelines for the effective use of visual aids. In the final section of this chapter we cover the special case of computer-generated graphics.

FIGURE 8.10   A Checklist of Guidelines for the Use of Visual Aids

1. Use visual aids only when they are justified.
2. Make sure your visual aids are large enough for everyone in the audience to see.
3. Never obscure or block the visual aid with your body.
4. Display the visual aid only at the relevant place during the speech, and remove it from view when you move on to new information.
5. Explain and interpret all important elements of the visual aid for the audience.
6. When talking about the visual aid, use the same words that are used in the title and labels of the visual aid.
7. Always talk to your audience, not to the visual aid.

Computer-Generated Graphics

Computer-generated graphics are created by software packages that make stunning overheads, 35 mm slides, or computer-controlled electronic slide shows. The software for these graphics is inexpensive, but sophisticated enough to provide high-quality graphic displays without the expense of graphic artists. As such, it is likely that organizations not using these programs now will do so in the near future. Figure 8.11 displays an example of a computer-generated slide. Although several companies sell graphics programs, including WordPerfect, Lotus, and Quatro Pro, the most popular program is Microsoft's PowerPoint. Because of its popularity we include brief instructions for creating PowerPoint graphics in the Activities and Exercises section of this chapter. The rest of this chapter provides guidelines for creating and displaying computer generated graphics, regardless of the particular program used to create them. First, we review various methods of integrating computer graphics into a presentation and then suggest rules for formatting slides.

Integrating Computer-Generated Graphics in the Presentation

Computer-generated graphics are, like any visual aid, excellent for augmenting and clarifying the content of technical, proposal, sales, risk, or crisis presentation.

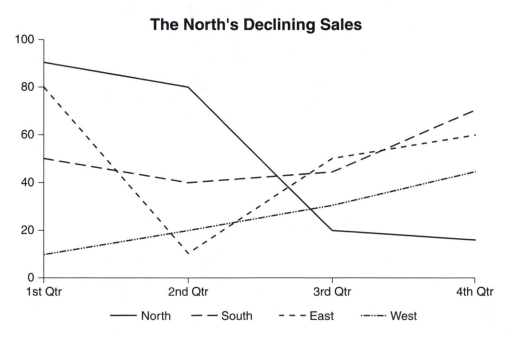

FIGURE 8.11

A problem develops when speakers, perhaps enticed by the technology, allow the graphics to become the focus for the entire presentation. We have seen people write speeches by first developing the visual aids and then developing the content. Unfortunately, the programs encourage this by providing content templates to flesh out the outline alongside the graphics. This is a classic example of putting the cart before the horse. Creating content through a graphics program shortchanges the speech in terms of detailed examples, logical reasoning, and clear evidence. Computer graphics have the greatest effect when the presenter deemphasizes the technology and emphasizes the human activities of sharing information and persuading others. As a result, the most important guideline for the use of computer graphics is to create them only after the introduction, body, and conclusion of the presentation have been thoroughly outlined. Write your outline and use the computer to visually augment important details.

There are two ways of incorporating computer graphics into a speech. The **traditional approach** uses computer-generated slides to clarify complex information in charts, graphs, photos, or text visuals. The visuals are on display only when they are called for, they are explained thoroughly, and a blank screen is used between visual aids. There are several advantages to the traditional method. The computer-generated slides look more professional than hand-drawn or photocopied slides. When controlled through the computer, slides can be changed with push-button ease. The traditional method deemphasizes the technology and prevents the speaker from fading into narrator status.

A second method of integrating computer-generated graphics is the **integrated approach,** wherein every portion of the presentation includes a slide and the speaker moves from slide to slide without any blank screens. The integrated approach is both entertaining and fast-paced. There are, however, several disadvantages to this method. The integrated presentation encourages the audience to focus on the screen, making the speaker almost invisible. In addition, most speeches include only a few graphs and charts, certainly not enough to fill an entire presentation. Speakers are then forced to create many text visuals covering the preview, review, transitions, main points, and subpoints of the speech. Others include extensive quotations or animated clip art and sound effects to fill the graphics void. However, writing the outline on the screen is unimaginative and encourages the audience to read the speech rather than focus on the speaker. The entertainment value of quotations, clip art, and cartoons also makes them distracting. In addition, even when the audience finishes reading the text or watching an animated clip, their eyes remain on the screen waiting for the next slide. It takes a very dynamic speaker to maintain full attention during an integrated presentation. Finally, the integrated presentation is very difficult to sustain using an overhead projector. On the overhead, each slide must be drawn from a stack, positioned on the projector, and removed by hand, which is time-consuming and distracting.

Since we aren't aware of any research on the differences in information retention, beliefs about speaker credibility, and persuasiveness between the traditional and integrated presentation, we must use common sense to suggest which is best. Based on the relative advantages and disadvantages just described, we recommend the traditional approach, where visual aids are used only to augment the speech. We believe this is best for speaker and audience in the conventional business presentation.

Formatting Computer-Generated Slides

This section offers recommendations for formatting computer-generated graphics. First, decide on a consistent style, font, and color scheme for the visuals throughout the presentation. When selecting a background design for the slides, the computer automatically selects colors for the text, charts, and graphs. The colors were selected for visibility and aesthetic qualities. Changing colors should be done with care to avoid slides that clash. Because the programs are fun to work with, it's tempting to experiment with everything available: switching style, choosing new colors, adding clip art and sound effects, for example. Some presenters use marbled backgrounds for slides that not only make words and graphics difficult to read, but do not reflect the conservative nature of business and professional audiences.[11] Ask yourself, do little smoke stacks instead of two-dimensional bars really add information to a bar graph? Do you need the sound of squealing tires when tables move into the slide? Don't allow technical sophistication to interfere with the basic message.

Instead of technology for the sake of entertainment, build a theme with the background, colors, and fonts and maintain that theme for every slide in the file. Changes should be made with a clear purpose in mind, such as changing the audience's mood during the speech. Consistency is the safer course. Indeed, most programs have subroutines to alert the user to both subtle and overt changes in slide format. Figure 8.12 displays a crowded, distracting version of the line graph displayed earlier in Figure 8.11. The addition of a third dimension in the line graph in Figure 8.12 makes the graph more difficult to read without adding any information. Because the data are not three-dimensional (there are only two variables, number of units sold and time in quarters), a three-dimensional graph is unnecessary. The graphic is difficult to read because the lines blend in with the background. Finally, although the title of the graph correctly emphasizes the North's poor performance, the line for the North's sales is in the background rather than the foreground and blends in with three of the other four lines. In short, the "fun" options offered by the program dominate the slide and the central message is obscured. Figure 8.11 displays a much more appropriate computer graphic that clearly emphasizes the North's declining sales. This graphic eschews three dimensions in favor of two, creates a background that does not distract from the message, and emphasizes the line for the North in the foreground, leaving all other lines in the background. Never let the variety of choices and options offered by the computer obscure your message.

In the past, controlling the slides through a computer for projection required dim lights, reducing the speaker's presence. This limitation is changing with improved technology. If the room is dark, however, you will have to compensate so you don't fade into the background. Also, use dark background and

The North's Declining Sales

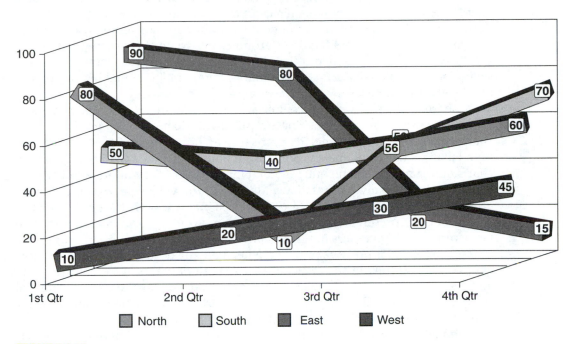

FIGURE 8.12

light text so the audience can read the screen even if the lights are up. If, on the other hand, you are printing graphics onto slides for use on an overhead projector, use a light background (to help light the room) with dark text.[12] This helps the audience see the text in the dark or semidarkened room.

Finally, for important presentations, prepare a backup set of slides for use on an overhead projector. Although this may be expensive, it's better than arriving at your speech only to find the computer you were counting on is under repair or incompatible. The cost of such a mistake could be significantly greater than the cost of backup overheads.

Summary

Visual aids should support rather than substitute for the speaker and content. A visual aid is any pictorial, textual, or graphic image that is displayed visually rather than presented orally. When used correctly, visual aids can increase the clarity and persuasiveness of a message, and increase perceptions of the speaker's credibility and dynamism.

Objects are an excellent way to add interest to the speech. Models are scale, two-dimensional drawings or three-dimensional constructions that represent a very large or small object. Objects and models should be easy for the entire audience to see. Avoid passing objects or models around the audience. The chalk board, the marker board, and the flip chart are excellent for keeping track of ideas during group brainstorming and discussion. Handouts can summarize information for the audience. Pass handouts around only when they are needed during the speech, and go over them thoroughly with the audience. Photographs and slides add dramatic impact to a presentation. Photographs should be copied onto overhead transparencies for easy viewing.

Charts and graphs clarify complicated statistical or relational information. Charts are useful for summarizing statistical information. Line graphs display changes in variables over time. Pie charts display proportions of a whole distribution. Finally, a bar graph makes comparisons among various magnitudes. Simplify charts and graphs by eliminating or combining unnecessary information. Videotape is useful in many presentations. Make sure the videotape machine is properly set and working prior to the presentation. Finally, text visuals display the key features of the presentation in words. Use action-oriented phrases rather than key words or full sentences in text visuals.

Use visual aids only when they are justified. Make sure visual aids are large enough for everyone in the audience to see. Position yourself so that the entire audience has an unobstructed view of the visual aid. Display the visual aid only at the relevant place in the speech, and remove it from view when you are finished. Explain and interpret all important elements of the visual aid for the audience. Use parallel language when explaining visual aids. Always talk to your audience, not the visual aid.

Computer-generated graphics are created by inexpensive software packages for use with computer-driven projectors, slide projectors, or overhead projectors. Thoroughly outline the speech prior to developing graphics. The traditional method displays computer graphics only when they are needed and leaves a blank screen when no visual aid is called for. This method deemphasizes the technology and focuses the audience on the speaker. The integrated method of using computer-generated graphics includes slides for every portion of the speech. This necessitates the use of many text visuals and encourages the audience to focus on the screen rather than the speaker. Choose consistent style, background, and fonts for all visuals. Change styles only when you have a clear purpose, such as altering the audience's mood during the speech. Make sure your work fits with the conservative culture of most professions.

QUESTIONS FOR DISCUSSION

1. Television has obviously contributed to our preference for visual information. In what specific ways has television influenced our preference for visual images? How do you think computers will contribute to this preference for visual material? Besides television and computers, are there other things that have contributed to our preference for visual information?

2. Are there other means of adapting to visually oriented audiences without becoming the narrator of a picture show? What can you do to keep the audience stimulated and interested despite the fact that your presentation does not contain "souped-up" visual aids? Develop ways to compensate for a presentation that is heavy on verbal information and light on visual aids.

3. What would you add to our guidelines for the effective use of visual aids? Can you think of any suggestions that we omitted?

4. In the chapter, we argued that the traditional rather than the integrated approach was the best way to use computer-generated graphics. In your opinion, which method is stronger? Can you think of other advantages and disadvantages of the integrated and traditional approaches? Have any of the additional advantages and disadvantages changed your opinion about the best way to integrate computer-generated graphics into a business presentation? Why or why not?

5. Many of the computer graphics programs include fancy special effects. For example, most programs allow words and charts to move on and off the slide, and sound effects such as gunshots or screeching tires can be added. What place do these special effects have in a presentation for business or professional leaders? Are there other places where these special effects might be relevant?

ACTIVITIES AND EXERCISES

1. Get several *USA Today* newspapers and examine the informative charts and graphs in the lower left side of the front page. What makes the graph clear or unclear? Which rules for developing charts and graphs are employed in the newspaper chart? What changes would you make in the chart to make it clear to the audience in a presentation?

2. Examine your local weathercaster's use of visual aids during the nightly newscast. Does the weathercaster use unnecessary visual aids? Is the weathercaster positioned in such a way that the visual aid is not obscured? Is each visual explained clearly, and of what quality is that explanation? What, if anything, does your local weathercaster do to lead you to the correct interpretation of each visual aid? What does your weathercaster do to avoid talking to the visual aid?

3. Investigate your college or university's computer network to see if Microsoft's PowerPoint program is on the system. This activity is designed to introduce you to the program and help you learn the basics of developing PowerPoint slides. Take these directions with you to the computer center.

   After you enter the program, a menu will appear offering three options: "AutoContent Wizard," "Template," and "Blank Presentation." The "Auto-Content Wizard" is useful for novices because it queries the user through the steps to build a presentation. However, this process is time-consuming and creates a series of constraints, depending on how the user answers the opening questions. The "Template" option prepares a series of slides based on the topic and purpose of the presentation, including: "Communicating Bad News," "Employee Orientations," and "Financial Reports." Again, the answers to initial questions will constrain later choices. The "Blank Presentation" is the best way to experiment with PowerPoint. Click on the "Blank Presentation" button and the "OK" button to begin.

The first screen will ask you to choose an "AutoLayout" for the first slide. Layouts include text slides, graph slides, or chart slides. To experiment with the program, click on one of the text slides and click the "OK" button. The screen will bring up a "text slide" with blank spaces for a title and text. Click on the title box and enter a title for your slide. The font and size of the title can be changed by highlighting the title with the mouse and clicking on the font or size buttons on the toolbar. Click on the content box and enter your content. Click outside the slide to close the text box and view the completed slide. To alter the slide, click on the box that you want to change.

The toolbar at the top of the screen includes several important buttons:

"Apply Design"—Allows the user to apply a colorful background to the slide.

"Slide Layout"—Places the information on the slide into a different layout.

"New Slide"—Asks the user to select a layout for the next slide.

"Insert Clip Art"—Lets the user insert picture, sound, or video clip into the slide.

"Insert Chart"—Inserts a bar graph into the highlighted box on the slide.

"Chart Type"—Lets the user select from a variety of line, bar, and pie charts.

To experiment with charts and graphs, click on the "New Slide" button, select a slide layout, and click on the "OK" button. Enter a title in the title box at the top of the slide. Double-click on the chart box, and the computer will add a bar graph to the slide. The screen brings up a predetermined bar graph complete with variables and values for each bar. Enter your own variables and values in the matrix that comes up with the bar graph. As your data are entered in the matrix, the computer will reformat the bar graph to the new specifications. To change from a bar chart to a pie chart or line graph, click the "Chart Type" button on the toolbar. Click on the kind of chart desired. Enter your own variables and magnitudes in the matrix, and the computer will reconfigure the pie chart or line graph to your specifications.

Finally, there are three buttons in the lower left toolbar:

"Slide Show"—This plays the slides in the order of their appearance, including any clip art or sound effects on the slide.

"Slide Sorter"—Displays a small version of every slide in the set.

"Slide View"—Returns to large view of a single slide.

Experiment with the PowerPoint program to create a chart, line graph, pie chart, and bar graph. Insert clip art into one or more of the visual aids. If you encounter difficulty, click on the "Help" button and let the computer lead you to a solution.

NOTES

1. Holcombe, M. W., and J. K. Stein, *Presentations for Decision Makers* (New York: Van Nostrand Reinhold, 1996), 95.

2. Grice, G. L., and J. F. Skinner, *Mastering Public Speaking* (Boston: Allyn and Bacon, 1995).

3. Ibid.

4. Antonoff, M., "Meetings Take Off with Graphics," *Personal Computing*, July 1990, 62.

5. Seiler, W. J., "The Effects of Visual Materials on Attitudes, Credibility, and Retention," *Speech Monographs* 38 (1971): 331–334.

6. Grice & Skinner.

7. Holcombe and Stein.

8. Ibid.

9. Ibid.

10. Helyar, J., "Solo Flight: A Jack Welch Disciple Finds the GE Mystique Only Takes You So Far," *The Wall Street Journal*, 10 August 1998, A1 & A9.

11. Schou, S., conversation with first author, Pocatello, ID, 24 January 1997.

12. Schou, C., conversation with first author, Pocatello, ID, 24 January 1997.

CHAPTER

9

Technical Presentations

Several trends in professional life make informative communication more difficult than in the past. Increasingly, the language and methodology of every discipline have developed along individual paths, making it virtually impossible for a single person to be an expert in more than one field. In hospitals, for instance, traditional radiology functions are combined with MRI (magnetic resonance imaging scanning) functions in the same unit, although different expertise is required to operate and interpret each diagnostic technique. Specialization makes it difficult for people to communicate with each other across disciplines. If this weren't bad enough, specialization has made communication with lay audiences all but impossible.

Although increased specialization has made communication difficult, the interconnected nature of society necessitates greater, rather than less, communication with nonexperts. Managers in private, public, and government organizations need information from technical experts to make decisions. In Pocatello, Idaho, for example, the city council needed to select a method of removing tricholoethelene (a solvent) from the city's wells, despite the fact that neither the council members nor the mayor has any expertise in hydrology. Managers in organizations make decisions that require technical knowledge from a variety of fields. But managers are not the only consumers of technical information.

Because communities are affected by layoffs, industrial accidents, and pollution, they demand more information and greater input into business decisions than in the past. As a result, organizations must provide technical information about their operations to the lay public. Technical communication is even more vital in government organizations. Whenever the Park Service, the Forest Service, or the Environmental Protection Agency propose changes in policy they are required to communicate the reasons for the change to interested publics. This requires condensing reams of information into something lay audiences can understand.

Two trends have conspired to create a communication problem. Just as increased specialization makes communication outside narrow disciplines more difficult, managerial needs and public demands have made communication more vital. Most professional positions require strong informative communication skills. And most informational presentations require communicating technical information to someone outside a particular field or to a lay audience. Many organizations no longer employ a staff of technical writers responsible for making information accessible to outsiders. Technical communication therefore is vital for people in engineering, pharmacy, public health, medical researchers, lawyers, health care providers, natural resource engineers, and any career track in which interacting with the public is important.

Technical communication is communication about scientific, engineering, technological, business, regulatory, legal, managerial, or social scientific information. A **technical presentation** is a prepared, formal presentation on one or more of these topics to a nonexpert audience. A variety of common presentations fit under the rubric of technical communication, including laboratory presentations, feasibility reports, progress/status reports, survey presentations, training lectures, and business reports. This chapter is devoted to improving your technical communication skills.

The two goals of technical communication are accuracy and shared meaning. First, technical communication must be **accurate.** This means that the information must be correct, complete, and detailed enough to fill the needs for the specific audience. The Ethics Brief reviews issues related to accuracy. Accuracy requires solid research, careful reading and note-taking, and constant verification of all facts.[1]

The second goal of technical communication is **shared meaning**—the ability to "present information in such a manner that the audience can draw one and only one meaning from the communication—the meaning intended by the communicator."[2] In other words, technical communicators seek a close correspondence between the speaker's understanding and the new understanding the audience achieves as a result of the message. The strategies we present in this chapter are designed to increase the likelihood of shared meaning. The chapter begins by reviewing audience factors relevant to the technical presentation. We then elaborate general guidelines for making technical information clear. In the third section we highlight two obstacles to shared meaning and explain strategies for overcoming these obstacles. The chapter closes with information on structuring the

Ethics Brief

In our "high-tech" society, those with the most technical knowledge are often the only ones empowered to make decisions. Democracy is endangered and the profit potential of business organizations is diminished when only a few participate in decision making. Technical communication empowers others to act because it spreads the knowledge required for decision making. We accept the following belief: no scientific or technical content is beyond explanation or understanding. If the presenter does an effective job of arranging and explaining the content, and the audience makes a commitment to understanding that content, then a shared understanding between speaker and listener is possible. The technical communicator commits herself to explaining even the most difficult content because it is people's right in a democracy to participate in decisions that affect their lives and because effective organizations take full advantage of their human resources. Although it's a task that requires logical thinking and careful attention to detail, technical communication serves a higher ideal: empowering people to participate in decision making.

Accuracy is the hallmark of ethical technical communication. Accuracy is the degree to which the information presented is correct and complete. Accuracy involves several processes and commitments. First, accurate communication requires excellent research skills. Skimping on research, relying on biased sources, or making up examples hurt the accuracy of a technical presentation. The best technical communicators are experts in their field, but more importantly, are diligent, thorough researchers whose goal is to bring the most up-to-date information to their audience. Research is the foundation for ethical technical communication.

Second, ethical communicators are willing to admit the weaknesses and limitations of their data. During a town meeting on the Environmental Protection Agency's propos-als to strengthen regulations on particulate emissions, an EPA epidemiologist presented data about the health consequences of particulate pollution. Although she clearly believed the data she presented, she also reminded the audiences that epidemiology studies can look only at association and correlation, not causation. As such, no study can prove that particulate pollution causes disease or death. Admitting limitations brings an added credibility advantage. The technical communicator who admits the limitations of her knowledge in some areas will command more trust from the audience when she does stand "four square" behind other data.

Third, even hard scientific disciplines are prone to conflicting data and disagreements among experts. When covering a topic that includes such conflicts and disagreements, the technical communicator doesn't gloss over opposition or contrary opinion; rather, he includes the full spectrum of opinion in the presentation. Documentaries or discussions of global warming should, for example, address both sides of the issue, at least until scientific opinion has reached consensus. To do otherwise is unethical.

Fourth, ethical communicators commit themselves to maintaining the integrity of the data. They refuse to "dumb down" the content through simplification and distortion. The strategies in this chapter are designed to help communicate complicated ideas without destroying the integrity of those ideas.

Fifth, ethical communication involves avoiding the use of jargon. Jargon is unnecessarily obscure terminology designed to prevent uninitiated members from participating in decision making. Jargon is often used to dazzle the audience, obscure meaning, or mystify the uninitiated, but is antithetical to technical communication's empowerment goal. We've even heard some adherents of jargon in the humanities claim that it is necessary because the concepts and processes described are complicated. This is no excuse! Jargon indicates a lack of commitment to empowerment and communication, and as such is both antidemocratic and lazy.

Finally, ethical communicators check their facts with other experts in the field. No person is infallible and no one person can know all there is to know in even a small technical field. Check your content with other experts to be sure there is nothing you have missed, and that your information is fair to competing positions and accurate based on the most recent knowledge. Ethical technical communicators commit themselves to the higher purpose and specific procedures outlined in this brief.

---

technical presentation. Although information in this chapter focuses on technical presentations, the advice is useful for any context wherein complicated information must be made clear.

Understanding the Audience for Technical Information

In Chapter 6 we discussed methods of analyzing the audience. The Audience Analysis Checklist presented questions to probe the situation and listener characteristics of the audience. Technical presentations require adapting to several listener traits including captivity, predisposition toward the speaker, and predisposition toward the topic.

As we have discussed, a voluntary audience attends a presentation of its own free will, whereas a captive audience is required to attend. The complicated content of technical presentations makes it difficult to hold the captive audience's attention. As mentioned in Chapter 6, speakers should acknowledge that the audience is required to attend and provide additional motivation to listen. In addition, colorful visual aids and interesting examples can hold the captive audience's attention. Above all, dynamic delivery is crucial to maintaining attention and interest.

The ability to communicate technical information is vital in our increasingly complex society. Credit: Kevin C. Wellard

The audience's predisposition toward the speaker is another critical variable for the technical presentation. It is unlikely that an audience will accept the validity of technical information if they don't think the speaker is a qualified expert on the topic. Follow the prescriptions in Chapter 6 to build speaker credibility prior to and during the presentation.

Finally, knowing the audience's predisposition toward the topic, especially their knowledge level, is important in technical communication. Audience knowledge exists on a continuum, with listeners who are unaware of the topic at one end and knowledgeable experts on the other. The most frequent problem in technical communication is overestimating audience knowledge. In so doing, speakers make reference to various facts, examples, and concepts that are clear to people in the specific field, but are not understood by lay audiences. For example, although a curie is a scale for measuring the amount of emitted radioactivity (calculated in the number of radioactive disintegrations per second), most audiences do not understand what this means without explanation. The effective technical communicator remembers that lay audiences are not experts and adapts the explanations, definitions, examples, analogies, and visual aids accordingly. The prescriptions in Figure 6.1 will help you adapt to differential audience knowledge.

Finally, for technical presentations it's also wise to consider the psychological meanings people derive from your major terms and concepts. In Chapter 1 we defined psychological meanings as the private associations individuals have for symbols. Some technical topics create reactions of fear (math), concern (pollution), or dread (cancer or radiation). A technical presentation about radiation dangers from a nuclear power plant must take into account the dread that people experience when they contemplate radiation. The audience's psychological meanings should influence how the speaker introduces and justifies the topic, builds credibility, and arranges the content in the speech body.

Becoming an audience-centered technical communicator means learning what your audience knows and how they will respond to a topic, and then adjusting what you have to say based on that understanding. Unfortunately, this is not easy for most technically minded people. Obviously, most experts are both knowledgeable and interested in their specialty, which makes it difficult to put themselves in the place of lay-audience members and adapt accordingly. However, this is exactly the role-taking skill required to communicate technical information. The effective technical speaker submerges his or her own knowledge sufficiently enough to be able to adopt, temporarily, the perspective of the listener and develop a presentation from that point of view. Use the Audience Analysis Checklist to improve role-taking skills and increase your ability to share technical information. In the next section, we discuss general techniques for making technical information clear.

General Guidelines For Communicating Technical Information

The following guidelines are applicable when communicating any kind of technical information. Observing the guidelines will increase the shared understanding between presenter and audience. Of course, the actual implementation of these guidelines depends on your understanding of the audience and the topic.

Make Appropriate Word Choices

Word choice can make technical information clear or muddle it beyond recognition. As a general rule, rely on short, two-syllable words as opposed to longer three- (or more) syllable words.[3] Don't add to listeners' struggle to learn complicated information with unnecessarily complicated words. Below are a series of complicated words and their shorter, clearer alternatives.

contiguous	connected
interface	talk
utilization	use
effectuation, enactment	operation
metamorphose, transfigure	change
retrofit	replace

Nothing is gained by using the more complicated words in the left column. Although it is sometimes necessary to use a technical term because there is no easier equivalent (e.g., photosynthesis), speakers should err on the side of short words.

It is impossible to make word choices in a technical presentation without considering the problem of jargon. You are aware that jargon is unnecessarily obscure terminology peculiar to a discipline.[4] Rather than making things clear, jargon obscures meaning and prevents uninitiated members from participating in decision making. In many cases, jargon is designed to obscure meanings and make something bad into something good. For example, one might make a battlefield retreat sound less disastrous by calling it a "tactical redeployment," or make an explosion at a manufacturing plant sound less violent by calling it an "energetic disassembly."[5] Because of its power to confuse, jargon should be avoided.

However, jargon is not the same as technical terms such as "alpha particle," "photosynthesis," "crystallization," "solubility," "catalyst," "millirem," "polymer," "anode," and "cathode." Technical terms are originated to have one and only one meaning.[6] A term with limited meanings helps scientists, doctors, and engineers communicate with greater accuracy than possible using a term that has more than one meaning. Technical terms improve the accuracy and precision of scientific communication and may be necessary in some technical presentations. If so, follow the guidelines for clarifying difficult concepts articulated later in this chapter.

Make Frequent Use of Examples and Analogies

As we mentioned in Chapter 7, an **example** is a specific instance that illustrates a larger point. A good example is not only more interesting than pages of dry description, but it can help an audience grasp abstract information. For instance, an example can explain the operation of latent viruses. Latent viruses are infections that retreat during recovery, but linger in the body for years, only to emerge later and cause disease. Chicken pox is a classic example of a latent virus.

> After initial infection, the virus becomes latent, lying low within the nerve cells of the vertebrae. In most people, the virus remains dormant for life. It can, however, reactivate, causing the painful back rash of a disease called shingles.[7]

Because most people are familiar with chicken pox, and may have parents or grandparents who have had shingles, the example provides a useful illustration of latent viruses.

Analogies are another powerful method of communicating technical information. An analogy is a comparison between two objects, events, instances, or people suggesting that what is true of one is also true of the other. The analogy explains a new idea by asserting that the unfamiliar concept is similar in some sense to the more familiar concept. To help his audience understand the amount of empty space in an atom, physicist John Gribbon used the following analogy:

> Imagine a pinhead, perhaps a millimeter across, at the center of St. Paul's cathedral, surrounded by a cloud of microscopic dust motes far out in the dome of the cathedral, say 100 meters away. The pinhead represents the atomic nucleus; the dust motes are its retinue of electrons. That is how much empty space there is in the atom—and all of the seemingly solid objects in the material world are made of these empty spaces.[8]

This analogy is not only clear but quite vivid. Frequent use of both examples and analogies will help an audience comprehend complicated information.

Translate Measurement Scales into Useful Analogies

The measurement scales used in scientific disciplines are difficult for lay audiences to understand. How big is a one-micron particle? What does it mean to say that there are 10^{28} atoms in the human body? Is the 10 millirems of radiation we receive from a dental X ray a lot or a little? Any measurement scale unfamiliar to the audience should include an explanation of that scale. For example, how many is 10^{28} atoms? A speaker could explain it by saying it is a one followed by twenty-eight zeros.

However, explanation alone isn't usually enough to help audiences understand the very large or very small scales common to many scientific fields. Saying that the Earth is five billion years old or the nearest star as five light-years away is fine, but the audience will not truly understand unless something is done to provide perspective to these figures. For example, the following translations help us comprehend the tremendous density of such astronomical objects as white dwarf and neutron stars.

> In white dwarf stars, where the atoms are compressed so closely together that the electrons in each atom may touch, the density is extremely high. White dwarf stars are so dense that "if a thimbleful of it were brought to Earth, it would weigh more than one million tons!" But white dwarfs are not as dense as neutron stars. The gravity of a neutron star has compressed the atoms so tightly that the elec-

trons have collapsed in on the nucleus of the atom. "A sugar cube of neutron star material would weigh 100 million tons; if dropped, it would fall through to the center of the Earth."[9]

Rather than simply describing density mathematically, the Earth-based measures of weight help explain density in a way that any educated person can understand.

Similarly, to help readers understand the Sun's enormous energy output, two authors made the following translations:

> Each second, the Sun converts nearly *5 billion tons* of mass into energy. The conversion of merely *one gram* of mass (one millionth of a ton) into energy can light a million light bulbs for an hour. An area of Sun the size of a single bed-mattress produces more than 100 million watts of power per second. And the Sun is not even a particularly hot star (italics in original).[10]

Although the authors could have stopped their explanation by saying the Sun converts five billion tons of mass into energy, they took the time to provide perspective to this incredible figure.

The same problem of perspective applies when communicating measurements on a microscopic, atomic, or subatomic level. For example, saying that a 10 micron particle is 1/25000 of an inch in diameter does not really help the audience picture the particles' size. However, saying the 10 micron particle is 10 times smaller than the diameter of a human hair translates the scale into something the audience can relate to. You will note also that translating measurement scales involves the use of analogy. In essence, you are comparing the measurement scales to something the audience can relate to more easily, for example, a thimble full of white dwarf star, the energy required to operate light bulbs, or the diameter of a human hair. Translating measurement scales requires the effective use of analogy.

Create Relevant Visual Aids

In Chapter 1 we argued that multichannel communication is more powerful than communication over a single channel. In Chapter 8 we reported research indicating that visual aids increase the clarity of complicated information. As such, visual aids are a must for most technical presentations. It's hard to imagine explaining a complicated process without a visual aid to communicate the essence of the event. Refer to the advice in Chapter 8 when creating visual aids for your technical presentation. In the next section we review obstacles to shared meaning and present solutions in order to overcome these barriers.

Overcoming Obstacles to Shared Meaning

As we stated in the beginning of this chapter, shared understanding is the goal of technical communication. One challenge of technical speaking is to analyze the principal obstacle that a topic presents and shape the speech to overcome that difficulty. Katherine Rowan, a communication professor at Purdue University, suggests two major obstacles to understanding informative content: difficult concepts and difficult structures or processes.

Difficult Concepts

Some technical information is difficult to understand because it involves **difficult concepts.**[11] People may have difficulty understanding the concept of flat versus graduated tax systems. The concept of PM-10 (particulate matter smaller than 10 microns) pollution is difficult to conceive because we don't usually think of smog as particles. Understanding nuclear waste storage is complicated because people don't know there are five different kinds of waste. In these cases, the audience's lack of familiarity with terms is an obstacle to shared understanding.

When people are attempting to understand the meaning of technical terms they are struggling to distinguish a concept's **essence,** features that are always present, from its **associated features,** features that are frequently but not necessarily present.[12] When trying, for example, to distinguish the difference between a flat and a graduated income tax, the listener needs to comprehend the essential features of a graduated income tax (people who make more money pay a larger percentage of that money in taxes) and the essential feature of a flat income tax (everyone pays the same percentage regardless of their income). Although many flat income tax proposals eliminate tax deductions for children, medical payments, and interest payments, this is not an essential feature of the flat income tax. A flat tax can include or exclude a variety of deductions without changing the essential nature of the tax, that everyone pays the same percentage regardless of income.

When trying to understand the difference between coarse and fine particulate pollution, listeners must understand that the size of the particle is the essential feature, not its composition. While coarse particulate matter is larger than 10 microns in size, fine particulate is 10 microns or smaller. PM-10 can be a particle, a liquid droplet, or any combination of the two; thus, the composition is an associated rather than an essential feature of particulate pollution. New concepts can be clarified by the inclusion of definitions, a typical example, varied examples and nonexamples, and transition phrases that indicate comparison and contrast.

Provide a Definition That Lists Essential Features.   Definitions clarify a concept's essential features. For example, when one is explaining product liability laws it is important for the audience to understand the definition of the term "tort," a French word for wrong, that has to do with the wrongful conduct by one person that causes injury to another. Several kinds of definitions are useful for communicating technical information.

Logical Definition.   The most important method of defining a concept is the **logical definition.** Logical definitions include two steps: Place the concept into a general category, then explain the characteristics that distinguish that concept from all other members of the category.[13] For example, a mutual fund can be logically defined as follows:

> Part 1: A mutual fund is a way to invest in the stock market.

> Part 2: Instead of buying individual stocks, the mutual fund investor turns his or her dollars over to the mutual fund manager who is responsible for overseeing the growth of the money by buying and selling individual stocks. Some mutual funds are organized to buy and sell stocks in a particular area of business, such as biotechnology or high technology companies.

Some technical speakers make the mistake of skipping step one. A speech on nuclear reactors defined nuclear fission as:

> Nuclear fission occurs when a large nucleus splits into two smaller nuclei.

This will not help the listener who does not have a context within which to understand the definition. The first step of the logical definition creates that context.

> Nuclear reactions are reactions that split or combine the nucleus of an atom. Whereas fusion combines two nuclei, nuclear fission splits a nucleus into two smaller nuclei.[14]

Be sure to include both steps in a logical definition. Logical definitions are the best way to help an audience understand the essence of a concept.

Operational Definition. **Operational definitions** explain how something functions. For example, in defining how the brain is divided into two hemispheres, the right and the left, a speaker could say that

> the right hemisphere is largely responsible for seeing holistic patterns, whereas the left hemisphere is responsible for linear, analytic thinking.

Many operational definitions explain the steps in a process.

> In any list of data, you can find the "mode" by identifying the number that occurs most frequently.

Operational definitions are almost as powerful as logical definitions for clarifying a concept's essence.

Definition by Etymology. Another common way to define a scientific concept is to explain how the word was derived from a historical event or another language. For example:

> The word *plastic* comes from the Greek *plastikos* meaning 'fit for molding' (italics in original).[15]

Although etymological definitions are interesting, they should be combined with other definitions for maximum clarity. Notice the following example.

> The term cybernetics is derived from the Greek term "Kubernetes," meaning steersman.[16]

Although the definition suggests that cybernetics has something to do with steering things, it doesn't say much else. Without knowing that cybernetics is an interdisciplinary science (larger category) concerned with communication and control (distinguishing it from other sciences), the audience won't have a complete understanding of the concept. Definitions help distinguish the essential features of a concept from its associated features.

Provide a Typical Example of the Concept or Idea.   A second way to clarify difficult concepts is to provide a **typical example.**[17] The typical example is representative of the whole group. A speech on investing in the stock market provided the following typical example of a mutual fund.

> A typical example of a mutual fund is the Seligman Communications and Information Fund. The manager of this fund is empowered to use investors' money to buy and sell stocks in various communication companies such as MCI or AT&T, and various information companies such as Intel and Microsoft. The goal is to buy stocks in these companies low and acquire value when and if the value of the stocks rise.

Provide a Series of Examples and Nonexamples.   Technical speakers should provide a series of examples and nonexamples to aid the audience's ability to distinguish between the concept and things that might be mistaken for the concept.[18] For example, a speech on PM-10 pollution included an overhead to distinguish between a variety of particulates, some of which are smaller than 10 microns, others of which are larger.

Size Comparison of Particulates

Viruses	.01 to .1 Microns
Insecticide dust	1 to 10 Microns
Bacteria	1 to 25 Microns
Pollen spores	10 to 100 Microns
Baking flour	25 to 50 Microns
Beach sand	100 to 500 Microns

Include Transition Phrases That Indicate Comparison or Contrast.   Because clarifying concepts is done, in part, through comparison (the use of examples) and contrast (the use of nonexamples), transition phrases guide listeners by indicating comparison and contrast. As you recall from Chapter 7, transition phrases indicate the relationship between ideas. Figure 9.1 shows transition phrases that

FIGURE 9.1 **Transition Phrases That Indicate Comparison and Contrast**

Comparison	Contrast
In comparison	Although
Similarly	But
Also	Conversely
Moreover	Nevertheless
Among	Instead
Additionally	In contrast
Like	However

indicate comparison and contrast. To describe PM-10 pollution, a speaker used several different transition phrases.

> *On the other hand,* human sources of PM-10 include....

> *In contrast* to coarse particulates that are larger than PM-10, fine particulates are equal to or smaller than PM-10.

Use a variety of transition phrases throughout the speech to clarify relationships. A second obstacle to shared meaning is difficult structures or processes.

Difficult Structures or Processes

Some technical information is difficult to understand because it involves **complicated structures** or **involved processes** that are hard for an audience to visualize.[19] How are laser beams created? How are microchips manufactured? How do viruses cause illness? How does the DNA molecule control human growth and development? In these topics, the obstacle to shared understanding is the complexity of key components or processes. The speaker helps the audience visualize the whole by providing an overall picture of the process, and providing an understanding of key parts, interrelations, or subprocesses of the larger process.

Provide a General Impression of the Structure or Process. Providing a **general impression** means letting the audience grasp the whole structure or process at once. There are two ways to accomplish this goal.

Provide a Graphic Model of the Process. One of the simplest ways to do this is to provide a **graphic model** of the process being described.[20] For example, the FMC elemental phosphorus plant in Pocatello, Idaho, encourages community members to tour its massive facility. Prior to touring the various manufacturing areas, visitors stop at a conference room that includes a huge poster displaying a flowchart of the entire process—from the entry of the raw ore into the plant, to the calciners that prepare the ore for burning, to the furnaces that heat the ore, to the place where the liquid phosphorus is loaded onto rail cars for the trip to eastern manufacturing facilities. While on the tour, representatives frequently refer back to the chart to remind us where we are in the manufacturing process. The graphic model provides a quick way to visualize the entire process. Use the suggestions in Chapter 8 to prepare and show your graphic model.

Use Organizing Analogies.   An **organizing analogy** communicates the general impression of a structure or process in a nutshell.[21] Read the organizing analogies below:

> The atom is like a small *solar system.*
>
> A laser is created when all the wavelengths of light are made to *line up.*
>
> To create liquid phosphorus we *cook* raw ore that contains phosphate and capture the *steam.*
>
> Viruses cause illness by *colonizing* cells.

An organizing analogy communicates the big picture in a way that is easy to grasp and lays the foundation for more detailed explanation.

Provide an Understanding of Subprocesses.

Once the audience has the big picture, it is necessary to communicate the connections and relationships between various subprocesses. This can be accomplished through various connectives, especially transition phrases. The following examples illustrate several kinds of connectives.

> Now that you understand the role electrons play in the atom, let's look at the nucleus. (transition)
>
> *The second step* in manufacturing phosphorus occurs when the ore is moved to the calciners. (transition phrase within a main idea)

In technical presentations, connectives link complicated subprocesses to the larger whole. Figure 9.2 includes a list of useful transition phrases that help clarify the relationship among variables or components in three general categories: sequence, physical description, and cause-effect.

Finally, good technical communication constantly links specific parts or processes back to the organizing analogy. For example, referring to the electrons of the atom that orbit the nucleus, the speaker refers back to the solar system analogy:

> As you can see, the electrons are to the nucleus of the atom what the planets are to the Sun.

Constantly referencing back to the organizing analogy clarifies how parts relate to the whole.

FIGURE 9.2   Transition Phrases That Indicate Sequential, Physical, and Cause–Effect Relationships

Sequence	Physical Description	Cause-Effect
First, Second, etc.	Above	As a result
After	Below	Because of
Soon	On the left	Consequently
Then	On the right	Cause
Before	Connected to	Effect
During	Further	Leads to
Earlier	Along the outside	Comes from
Finally	On the inside	If…then
Later	Beyond	As a consequence of
Following	Under	Thus
Next	Over	Therefore
		Forms
		Creates
		Results in
		Hence
		Due to

The primary obstacle to understanding technical content may be new concepts, difficult structures and processes, or both. For example, the main obstacle to understanding PM-10 pollution is new concepts. Thus, the author should focus on strategies for clarifying concepts. The main obstacle in other presentations is difficult structures or processes, which suggests an emphasis on graphic models and organizing analogies. A topic that includes both new language and difficult processes requires a combination of strategies for clarity. Analyze your topic for the obstacles it presents and adapt your content accordingly.

Structuring the Technical Presentation

Although there isn't a single best way to structure technical presentations, research indicates that clearly structured messages are understood and remembered better than unstructured messages.[22] Any of the structures discussed in Chapter 7 can be used in a technical presentation. For example, the PM-10 speech in Figure 9.3 includes three main ideas that are arranged topically.

This simple structure is entirely appropriate for a technical presentation. For presentations on complex structures and processes the cause-effect and problem-solution structures may be effective. Whatever structure you select, the technical presentation must be clearly organized for greatest effect.

FIGURE 9.3   Speech on PM-10 Pollution

Topic: Particulate Pollution

Specific Purpose: I want my audience to understand what particulate pollution is
                           and why it is a problem.

Main Idea: This speech will cover the issue of particulate pollution in three
                           main steps: first, I will define particulate pollution; second, I will
                           explain why the small size of this form of pollution is so
                           important; and third, I will explain why particulates are
                           hazardous to human health.

INTRODUCTION

I. Imagine that this tank represents the Portneuf Valley, Fort Hall area. The water is
   our air and the sides of the tank represent the hills that surround three sides of
   the valley. During an air inversion a cold air cap seals the tank, trapping pollution
   in the air. Imagine that this cup of milk is particulate pollution from industrial and
   individual sources. Under these conditions our air looks like this (pour milk in fish
   tank). This soup of gasses and particulates is the air we see and breathe until the
   inversion breaks.

II. Pollution is a concern to all of us in the valley, whether we live in Fort Hall,
    Chubbuck, or Pocatello.
    A. There are many forms of pollution that concern citizens and regulators:
       gaseous pollution like CO_2 (a greenhouse gas), or sulfur dioxides, lead from
       automobile exhaust (once a huge concern prior to the advent of unleaded
       gasoline), and ozone concentrations from various forms of combustion are all
       forms of pollution.
       1. However, in our valley one of the most important pollution concerns is PM-
          10 pollution—very fine particles of dust that come from a variety of natural
          and human sources.
          a. If you are at all concerned about pollution in the air you breathe (and
             who isn't concerned about such things?), then you must develop an
             understanding of PM-10 pollution.
          b. Because FMC and Simplot are significant sources of PM-10 pollution,
             the issue is a concern to the Portneuf Valley Community Advisory Panel,
             the group that sponsors these television shows.
       2. Although PM-10 is particularly noticeable during our winter air inversions
          when the pollution is trapped close to the valley floor, it is put into the air
          every day of the year.
    B. My goal today is to give you a better understanding of what particulate
       pollution is and why it is such a concern in our valley.

FIGURE 9.3 Continued

III. My name is Jim DiSanza and I teach in the Communication Department at Idaho State University. For the past three years I have served as the facilitator for the Portneuf Valley Community Advisory Panel, a group of volunteer citizens from Fort Hall, Chubbuck, and Pocatello who advise the FMC Corporation and the J. R. Simplot Company on a variety of issues, including air pollution.

    A. As facilitator of the PVCAP, I have spent three years working with the group on a variety of air pollution issues.

    B. I have heard presentations on particulate pollution from industry representatives, members of the Idaho Division of Environmental Quality, and the U.S. Environmental Protection Agency.

    C. For this speech I interviewed Audrey Cole, at the Pocatello office of the Division of Environmental Quality, and read several books on the subject from the ISU library.

    D. Information presented in this speech was checked for accuracy by members of the Idaho Division of Environmental Quality.

IV. I would like to cover the issue of particulate pollution in three steps: First, I will define particulate pollution; second, I will explain why the small size of these particles is important to pollution experts; and third, I will explain why particulates are hazardous to human health.

(Transition: So, let me start by defining the nature of particulate pollution.)

BODY

  I. In this first part of the speech I will define particulate pollution by explaining what particulate pollution is and where it comes from.

    A. First, air pollution exists as solid matter, liquid droplets, or gas (1, p. 30). (OH 1).*

      1. Substances such as carbon dioxide (thought to be a greenhouse gas) or sulfur dioxide are gasses, not particulates.

      2. Solid matter and liquid droplets, however, are referred to as particulates because they combine or chemically react to form particles. (1, p. 30)

        a. In such large communities as Los Angeles, the air is chock full of particulate pollution, which reduces visibility and causes human health problems.

        b. Here in the Portneuf Valley, particulate pollution, including both solid matter and liquid droplets, although always in the air to some extent, become pronounced during our winter air inversions, which trap particulate matter in the valley for several days at a stretch.

      3. Thus, particulate pollution includes particles of solid matter or liquid droplets that become suspended in the atmosphere.

    B. Second, particulate pollution can come from a variety of sources that are both natural and human (3, p. 23).

      1. Natural sources include particles from condensing water, wind-borne pollen, dead and living organic debris, various forms of fungi and mold, windblown

(continued)

*OH refers to Power Point overhead slides.

FIGURE 9.3   Continued

dust and rust, and particles from forest fires as well as natural volcanic and other geothermal sources (3, pp. 23–34).

2. On the other hand, human sources include:
   a. First, smoke from any form of combustion, including coal burning for heating or electricity, automobiles, railroad diesels, aircraft, trucks, heavy industry, and home heating.
   b. Second, fumes from chemical reactions such as smelting or refining.
   c. Third, dust from innumerable sources in our area include
      (1) Industrial sources such as phosphorous plants, the paving company, and the cement plant.
      (2) And nonindustrial sources such as agricultural tilling, paved and unpaved roads, even tire and brake wear on our cars.
   d. And, fourth, mist formed from spraying or condensing water vapor (1, pp. 31–33).

(Trans: Now that you know more about particulate pollution, let's examine why the size of these particles is so important.)

II. To understand why particulates are an air pollution problem, you must understand how small this kind of pollution really is as well as how it is classified by scientists.
   A. First, particulate pollution is so small that it is measured in terms of microns.
      1. (OH 2) A micron is equal to 1/1000 of a millimeter or 1/25,000 of an inch (1).
      2. A human hair is 10 times larger than a 10 micron particle (2).
         a. As you can see in the overhead, the diameter of a 10-micron particle is quite small.
         b. Only particles five times larger than 10 microns can be seen by the human eye.
      3. (OH 3) To get a comparison, examine the following overhead, which compares the size, in microns, of several kinds of particulates found in or near your household (3, p. 26).
   B. Second, based on the size of the particles, particulate pollution is classified into one of two categories: coarse and fine.
      1. Coarse particles are pollutants that are larger than 10 microns in diameter.
         a. These larger particles of pollution are, relatively speaking, heavy and if they get into the air either through combustion or are carried aloft by the wind they settle back to the ground quickly (1, p. 31).
            (1) This sand from a sandbox is approximately 100 microns in size.
            (2) Watch how quickly it falls to the ground as I throw it.
         b. As a result, particulate pollution larger than 10 microns is usually a problem only very near the source of the pollution (1, p. 31).
      2. Fine particles, on the other hand, are smaller than 10 microns in diameter.
         a. These particles are lighter than the coarse variety (1, p. 31).
            (1) If you remember from the last overhead, baking flour is about 25 to 50 microns in size.

FIGURE 9.3 Continued

        (2) I use it because I can't show you PM-10; it is microscopic.
        (3) Watch what happens when I throw this into the air.
        (4) See how it hangs in the air and remains there longer than the sand.
    b. Because of its small size and light weight, PM-10 hangs in the air for longer periods than coarse particles, and this is the basis of many pollution problems in the Portneuf Valley and throughout the country.
        (1) (OH 4) The thing to remember is that coarse particles are larger than 10 microns in size and are not a large pollution concern.
        (2) In contrast, PM-10 is particulate matter smaller than 10 microns and is a serious pollution concern—the 10-micron line is the important distinction.

(Trans: Now that you know why particulates smaller than 10 microns are a problem, let's examine the health consequences of this pollution.)

III. It is the small size of the particle that makes PM-10 dangerous to human health.
    A. The small size of the PM-10 particle makes it dangerous.
      1. First, when substances are broken down into smaller and smaller particles, more of the original particle becomes surface area that is exposed to the air.
        a. Under these circumstances, the particle becomes more attractive to other toxic substances.
        b. Toxins such as sulfur dioxide or oxides of nitrogen can coat the particle and hitch a free ride through the atmosphere (1, p. 33).
      2. If this weren't bad enough, the smaller the particle, the more easily it can become lodged deep in the lungs, toxic coating and all.
        a. Particles between 4 and 10 microns tend to get trapped in the mucus membrane of the nose and cannot then make their way deeply into the lungs.
        b. However, particles smaller than 4 microns pass through the mucus in the nose and lodge deeply in the lungs (4, p. 16).
          (1) These small particles enter the lungs, carrying various gasses such as sulfur dioxide and oxides of nitrogen.
          (2) Thus, the particle provides an avenue for other toxic gasses to be deposited in the lungs.
    B. As a result, breathing particulate matter that is smaller than 10 microns, especially matter below 4 microns, is linked to various forms of respiratory disease, both chronic and acute.
      1. Particulate matter has been linked to breathing problems in children and the elderly.
      2. It has been shown to cause lung tissue damage.
      3. And is linked to a variety of diseases from asthma to lung disease.

(Trans. To summarize, particulate pollution affects human health because the smaller particles stay in the air, they are the most chemically active particles, and they are the particles most likely to make it deep into our lungs.)

(continued)

FIGURE 9.3   Continued

CONCLUSION

I. To conclude this brief presentation, I have defined what particulate pollution is, described why the size of that particulate is so important, and discussed the human health effects of particulate pollution.

II. Remember that PM-10 pollution, particulate matter smaller than 10 microns, is a major pollution concern both here and nationwide.

III. The rest of this show is designed to provide you with more information about PM-10.
   A. First, Audrey Cole, of the Idaho Division of Environmental Quality, will discuss the various sources of PM-10 pollution in the Portneuf Valley.
   B. Then, Dean Hazen, an employee of the National Weather Service and a member of our Community Advisory Panel, will discuss how air inversions work to trap particulate matter.
   C. Finally, the CAP will hold a panel discussion with members of the FMC and J. R. Simplot companies to discuss particulate pollution in our valley.
   D. We hope the show is both informative and enjoyable.

Air Pollution		
Solid Matter	Liquid Droplets	Gases
	Particulate Pollution	

How Small is One Micron?

One Millimeter	One Inch
One Micron is 1/1000 of a Millimeter	**One Micron is 1/25,000 of an Inch**

Ten Microns

Human Hair

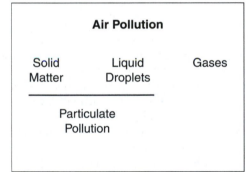

Size Comparison of Particulates

- Viruses   .01 to .1 Microns
- Insecticide Dust   1 to 10 Microns
- Bacteria   1 to 25 Microns
- Pollen Spores   10 to 100 Microns
- Baking Flour   25 to 50 Microns
- Beach Sand   100 to 500 Microns

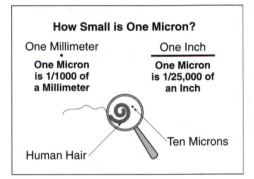

Size Comparison of Particulates

- Viruses   .01 to .1 Microns
- Insecticide Dust   1 to 10 Microns
- Bacteria   1 to 25 Microns
- Pollen Spores   10 to 100 Microns
- Baking Flour   25 to 50 Microns
- Beach Sand   100 to 500 Microns

10 μ

500 Microns

FIGURE 9.3 Continued

References

1. Natural Tuberculosis and Respiratory Disease Association, *Air Pollution Primer.* New York: 1969.
2. Idaho Department of Health and Welfare, Division of Environmental Quality (Informative Paper). "What is PM-10?"
3. Boubel, R. W., D. L. Fox, D. B. Turner, and A. C. Stern. *Fundamentals of Air Pollution.* San Diego: Academic Press, 1994.
4. Bates, D. W. *A Citizen's Guide to Air Pollution.* Montreal: McGill-Queen's University Press, 1972.

Summary

Specialization makes communicating scientific information to nonscientists exceedingly difficult. However, managerial needs and public demand have increased the need to communicate technical information with lay audiences. Technical communication is communication about scientific, engineering, technological, business, regulatory, legal, managerial, or social scientific information. A technical presentation is a prepared, formal presentation on one or more of these topics to nonexperts. Technical communicators should strive for accuracy and shared meaning. Accuracy is the correctness of the information. Shared meaning occurs when the meaning the speaker intends to communicate and the meaning the audience understands are similar.

Several audience factors are uniquely important for technical communicators. Speakers should provide additional motivation to listen, colorful visual aids, and dynamic delivery in order to maintain the interest of captive audiences. Audiences will not accept the validity of information if they do not think the speaker is a qualified expert. Build your credibility prior to and during a technical presentation. Consider the psychological meaning that audience members assign to such technical terms as radiation or cancer. Technically minded people must put themselves in the role of the lay audience member and develop the presentation from that point of view.

The following procedures can increase the chances of shared meaning with an audience. Rely on short words, avoid jargon, and clearly define all technical terms in the presentation. Make frequent use of examples and analogies. Analogies compare an unfamiliar concept or idea to one that is familiar to the audience and says that what is true of the familiar concept is also true of the unfamiliar concept. Communicators should also translate scientific measurement scales into useful analogies to provide a sense of perspective. Good technical speaking includes sound visual aids to help the audience grasp complicated ideas.

There are two common obstacles to understanding complex information: new concepts and difficult structures and processes. To teach new concepts, a speaker must help the audience distinguish between a concept's essence—features that are always present—and its associated features—features that are frequently, but not necessarily, present. Logical, operational, and etymological definitions help distinguish essential from associated features. Typical examples illustrate the essential nature of concepts. A series of examples and nonexamples distinguishes the concept from things that might be mistaken for the concept. Transition phrases that indicate comparison and contrast can clarify new concepts.

Some information is difficult to comprehend because it involves complicated structures and processes that are hard to visualize. Speakers can overcome these obstacles by providing a general impression through graphic models and organizing analogies. In addition, the audience can learn various subprocesses through connective devices and constant reference back to the organizing analogy. Research reminds us that clearly structured messages are understood and remembered better than unstructured messages. Speakers should select a structure that is both clear and fits the content.

Q U E S T I O N S   F O R   D I S C U S S I O N

1. Examine the sample technical presentation on PM-10 pollution in Figure 9.3. One of the primary obstacles to understanding technical content is difficult concepts. Does the speech use definitions, typical examples, and transition phrases to overcome the language obstacle? Label the places in the outline where these strategies are employed. Explain how the strategies create shared meaning. Was the speech effective or ineffective? What would you change to make the presentation more effective?

2. Below is a list of various technical topics. For each topic, identify the primary obstacle to audience understanding.

    How are messages sent on the Internet?
    How does aspirin relieve pain?
    How do bacteria come to contaminate meat products?
    How do scientists genetically engineer strains of insect-resistant plants?
    How does a television screen produce a picture?
    What is a laser beam?
    What is radiation?

A C T I V I T I E S   A N D   E X E R C I S E S

1. One of the best shows for communicating technical information to lay audiences is "The Magic School Bus," on PBS. In the show, the bus helps the children learn science by flying, floating, and shrinking so it can, for example, enter a person's throat to learn how bacteria cause infections. For this exercise, spend a half hour watching "The Magic School Bus" and note how the show uses definitions, exam-

ples, analogies, visual imagery, and language to make information clear to children. Compare the methods used in the show to the suggestions in this chapter. Does the show employ other techniques that are not covered here? How effective are these techniques? What changes do the producers have to make in order to communicate to children? Pay attention to how other informative documentaries communicate scientific information. What other techniques do these shows use to clarify information?

2. Create a technical presentation on a difficult topic. Decide whether the primary obstacle to understanding is difficult terms or difficult structures or processes. Use the prescriptions in this chapter to make the technical information clear to an audience. Examine carefully the sample speech in Figure 9.3 for guidance in structuring and outlining your presentation.

NOTES

1. Alvarez, J. A., *The Elements of Technical Writing* (New York: Harcourt Brace Jovanovich, Inc., 1980).

2. Barnette, G. A., and C. Hughes, "Communication Theory and Technical Communication," in *Research in Technical Communication,* ed. M. G. Moran and D. Journet. (Westport, CT: Greenwood Press, 1985), 40.

3. Alvarez.

4. Ibid.

5. Satchell, M., "Could you, er, say that again?" *U.S. News & World Report,* 20 April, 1987, 71.

6. Eisenberg, A., *Effective Technical Communication* (New York: McGraw Hill, 1982).

7. Zimmerman, B. E., and D. J. Zimmerman, *Why Nothing Can Travel Faster than Light…* (Chicago: Contemporary Books, 1993), 272.

8. Gribbin, J., *In Search of Schrödinger's Cat: Quantum Physics and Reality* (Toronto: Bantam Books, 1984), 31–32.

9. Zimmerman and Zimmerman, 76–77.

10. Ibid., 61.

11. Rowan, K. E., "A New Pedagogy for Explanatory Public Speaking: Why Arrangement Should Not Substitute For Invention," *Communication Education* 44 (1995): 236–250.

12. Merril, M. D., and R. D. Tennyson, *Teaching Concepts: An Instructional Design Guide* (Englewood Cliffs, NJ: Educational Technology Publications, 1977).

13. Sprague, J., and D. Stuart, *The Speaker's Handbook* (Fort Worth: Harcourt Brace, 1996).

14. Zimmerman and Zimmerman.

15. Ibid., 258.

16. Morgan, G., *Images of Organization,* (Beverly Hills, CA: Sage, 1986), 84.

17. Rowan.

18. Ibid.

19. Ibid.

20. Ibid.

21. Ibid.

22. Barnette and Hughes.

10 Proposal Presentations

Proposal presentations are a way of life for many professionals. Consider the following examples

- Mario owns a business that manufactures antennas. However, his products are more expensive than the competition's. He must persuade clients to spend more money for his antennas.
- Amartya thinks a coffee bar would do good business in her community. Now she needs to convince a bank to finance her endeavor.
- Ramon has identified a problem with the way travel authorizations work in his company. His solution involves a change in company policy.
- Anita is in charge of this year's United Way Campaign in her company. How will she encourage donations?
- Jeffrey's boss told him to "take care of the sales problem" with his tellers at the branch bank. How can he persuade the tellers to sell more services?
- Alexis must solicit community and corporate funds for new cardiology equipment at her hospital.

- Terry's committee will apply for a government grant to get new playground equipment at the local school.
- Tony proposes that the city council give his company, Environmental Solutions Inc., a contract to collect the city's residential trash.

To address each of these problems, the people involved must make effective **proposal presentations.** A business proposal should create shared meaning by persuading others that whatever you have to offer—an idea, a design, a program, new equipment, or a new procedure—is the best solution to their problem. Proposal presentations are a major part of day-to-day operations for many business and professional organizations. Research and development firms survive by presenting proposals to government agencies. For social service and arts organizations, proposals to foundations or government agencies mean the difference between continued operation and folding. In giant corporations, proposals for large government contracts may determine the company's future direction for up to five years. We made a proposal to the publisher outlining our ideas and the likely audience for this book before we were granted a contract. Charles E. Beck, of the University of Colorado, and Keith Wegner, President of Quantalex, Inc. claim, "proposals have become vital to organizational success" regardless of the type of business.[1]

This chapter covers proposals in several steps. After a discussion of audience concerns, we explain the use of various proposal structures. Because effective proposals are clearly argued, we discuss the construction and evaluation of logical arguments. We conclude with a discussion of speaker credibility and emotional appeals. Although the material in this chapter is, at times, technical, it's difficult for us to overstate its importance; the ideas form the core of both effective critical thinking and persuasive proposals. Given the importance of proposals in many organizations, it stands to reason that your ability to persuade others is vital to your professional success.

Audience Analysis for Persuasive Proposals

As always, the audience is the first consideration in a business proposal. Your understanding of the audience should guide your choice of structure, logical arguments, credibility, and emotional appeals. Bernard L. Rosenbaum, president of MOHR Development Inc., a training and development firm, contends that effective proposals focus on the issues that "are most important to the people present at the meeting. Too many presentations fail to do this."[2]

In Chapter 6, Figure 6.3, we introduced The Audience Analysis Checklist, a series of questions that guide audience analysis. For proposal presentations, the speaker must address all major categories under situation analysis (occasion, organizational culture, environment, and time) and listener analysis (demographics, captivity, predisposition toward the speaker, and predisposition toward the topic). Once you understand the audience's knowledge and meaning associated with the topic, you can plot the kind of audience you are facing: favorable, apathetic, neutral, active, or hostile. Then, follow the guidelines in Table 6.1 to adapt your content, structure, and delivery to the specific audience. Adapting to your audience is essential to the success of any proposal.

Proposal Structures

In Chapter 7, we equated structure with leadership. Speakers lead by taking command of the audience and guiding them to the preferred interpretation of an idea, product, or service. Gary Blake, a writing consultant, suggests that preparing a proposal without organizing one's thoughts is like a commercial pilot who takes off without a flight plan. Blake says, of all the "problems that plague businesspeople, none is more far-reaching or likely to cripple profits and profitability than lack of organization."[3] This section expands on the basic structures covered in Chapter 7 to include those uniquely suited to the proposal presentation.

Although we usually think of the content of a proposal as the main engine of persuasion, the structure itself can increase or decrease persuasiveness. This works in two ways: First, a rambling barrage of disconnected claims and facts cannot persuade because it cannot be interpreted. Second, because structures emphasize different elements of a proposal, matching the structure to audience concerns allows you to emphasize the elements of your proposal, order of presentation, and persuasive appeals that are most appropriate for a given audience. As such, the structure of a proposal is as important as the content. Table 6.1 in Chapter 6 suggests ways to adapt your structure to five different kinds of audiences.

In this section we explain four strategies for organizing persuasive ideas: the problem-solution structure, Monroe's Motivated Sequence, N-A-R structure, and the balance structure. Your choice of structures should be guided by your understanding of the audience and the topic.

The Problem-Solution Structure

The most common structure for proposals is also the most straightforward. In the **problem-solution structure,** the presenter articulates the problem the company has and provides a solution tailored to that company. Audience members who hear a proposal presentation, writes Richard J. Fulscher, head of the National Institute of Asset Management in Chicago, "want you to show your understanding of their problems, propose solutions, and demonstrate your capabilities" in carrying out the solution.[4]

When Ramon approached his colleagues about travel authorizations, his proposal followed the problem-solution structure. He indicated the problem: The company was losing $10,000 per month through incorrectly booked, reported, and processed travel authorizations. The solution: Employee travel will be booked through a single travel agent, and employees will turn in credit card receipts within three days of completed travel. If the audience is not aware of the need for your proposal, you should focus equally on the problem and the solution. Introduce the problem and its various effects. Demonstrate the problem through sound reasoning and evidence; then, provide a detailed explanation about how and why your solution can alleviate the problem. If the audience knows the problem, briefly review it and spend the bulk of the speech emphasizing the solution. Naturally, all claims in the problem and solution should be documented. The outline for a problem-solution structure should use the following format:

INTRODUCTION
   I. Gain Attention
  II. Justify the Topic
 III. Establish Credibility
  IV. Preview the Main Ideas
(Transition)
BODY
   I. Problem
(Transition)
  II. Solution
(Transition)
CONCLUSION
  I. Review
 II. Call to Action

Because of its no-nonsense focus this structure is recognized and well-liked by most business people.

Monroe's Motivated Sequence

Developed by Professor Alan H. Monroe, the **Motivated Sequence*** follows five steps that move an audience to adopt a specific solution. Although similar to the problem-solution structure, the Motivated Sequence adds several steps to get the audience involved (hence, the label "Motivated"), moving them to act on the proposal. If your audience is hesitant to act on your proposal, use the Motivated Sequence rather than the problem-solution structure.

The steps in the Motivated Sequence are attention, need, satisfaction, visualization, and action. Monroe knew that effective persuasion grabs the audience's attention. The techniques discussed in Chapter 7, including questions, rhetorical questions, startling statements, quotations, or stories, should be used in the **attention step** to hook the audience.

Like the problem step in the problem-solution structure, the **need step** in Monroe's Motivated Sequence identifies the audience's problem. Business speakers

---

*From *Principles and Types of Speech Communication,* 13th ed., by Bruce E. Gronbeck et al. Copyright © 1997 by Addison Wesley Educational Publishers Inc. Reprinted by permission.

should detail quantifiable problems such as missed deadlines, substandard quality, declining profitability, or customer service. The Motivated Sequence includes four steps to develop the problem: (1) **state** the specific problem, (2) **illustrate** the problem, (3) **reinforce** the need with additional examples and statistics, and (4) **"point"** the problem to the audience by showing how it relates to them. Bernard Rosenbaum, president of MOHR Development Inc., writes that too many presentations fail to fully develop the fourth step. The result is that people listening do not see how the need relates to them and they tune out.[5]

While convincing employees to give to the United Way, Anita developed her need step:

> I. The problem is that our community lacks programs for the elderly.
>   A. There is one program for elderly people on Saturday mornings at the Community Center.
>   1. That's it!
>   2. Each Saturday more than 50 seniors attend the Center, happy to have some place to socialize.
>   a. It's the high point of Sarah Johnson's week.
>   b. She said, "I'm so lonely during the week. And I hate being a burden to my family. I wish we had some other senior programs."
>   B. Although bad now, the problem is only going to get worse in the future.
>   1. Each year our community's senior population grows by 12 percent, or 120 seniors.
>   2. There will be more people with no place to go.
>   C. Our research indicates that next year more than half of our employees will be directly involved with this problem.
>   1. They have elderly parents who also feel lonely.
>   2. Some of you may even come to represent those statistics when you retire next year.

Notice that in this example the main idea states the problem, the first subpoint illustrates the problem, the second reinforces the problem, and the third points the problem to the audience.

The **satisfaction step** answers the question, "What can be done to solve the problem?" The satisfaction step is a two-stage process: (1) provide **support** for the claim that your plan will solve the problem, and (2) **address the objections** leveled against your plan. Anita's satisfaction step included supporting material from the United Way.

> I. The United Way has plans to solve the problem I just described.
>   A. Funds raised for this year's campaign are earmarked for a senior day-care center.

   1. The center will be a place for seniors to visit from 9:00 A.M. to 9:00 P.M. to do craft projects, join dance or exercise programs, and eat healthy meals.

   2. (Other supporting material.)

B. One major objection to a senior day-care center involves the costs of building the center.

   1. Well, in our case the solution is simple—the day-care center will be in an old elementary school, so the facility already exists.

   2. The United Way needs only $20,000 more to finish the renovations and furnishings.

C. The objection to additional costs for upkeep is easily addressed because the center will be self-supporting.

D. Last year our company contributed $17,825.00 to the United Way. All we need to do is each commit $10.00 more a month and we will have a new senior day-care center in our community.

Points B, C, and D address objections to the plan. We explain several strategies for refuting objections later in this chapter.

The fourth step in the Motivated Sequence is the **visualization step,** where the speaker paints a visual picture of the future if the plan is adopted. Use vivid verbal descriptions, visual pictures, charts, and graphs to clearly illustrate the effects of your plan. Anita's visualization step included projections about the kinds of productive things seniors could accomplish at the day-care center, as well as illustrations from people who would benefit from the center. Specific projections and concrete examples make the audience more willing to adopt the proposal.

The **action step** moves the audience to adopt the proposal. The appeal to action should be as direct and specific as possible. For example:

II. Each of you received your United Way donor card in your paycheck this morning.

A. If you need another card, please raise your hand and I will hand it to you now.

B. In the space marked "amount to contribute" consider writing $20.00 per month or a one-time donation of $240.00.

C. That's only $10.00 a month more than last year's average contribution.

D. Fill out the form and give it back to me by tomorrow. Let me know if I can answer any questions.

Notice that Anita helped her audience take immediate action by having the donor cards available and encouraged the audience to immediately fill them out. The outline for a Motivated Sequence proposal should follow this basic format.

INTRODUCTION
 I. Gain Attention
 II. Justify the Topic
 III. Establish Credibility
 IV. Preview the Main Ideas
(Transition)
BODY
 I. Need Step
(Transition)
 II. Satisfaction Step
(Transition)
 III. Visualization Step
(Transition)
CONCLUSION
 I. Review
 II. Action Step

The N-A-R Structure

The **N-A-R structure,** which was first developed in ancient Greece, is named for its three key components: narrative, argument, and refutation. Like other structures, the introduction to the N-A-R should gain attention and establish credibility. Unlike other structures, however, the introduction should not justify the topic or preview the main ideas. The preview ruins the effect of the pattern by eliminating the element of surprise. Thus, the introduction should gain attention and build the speaker's credibility.

After the introduction, the **narrative** tells a story that emphasizes the speaker's meaning associated with an issue, problem, or situation. Because stories depict protagonists, antagonists, and a plot line, audiences usually listen closely to them. As such, the story is constructed to reflect the speaker's interpretation of the event, an interpretation that supports the proposal. As long as the narrative is true to the facts, there is no harm in assigning labels or emphasizing events that put your proposal in the best light. Compare these two stories:

> (1) Children at an elementary school have no toys to play on. As a result, they occupy themselves in noneducational and sometimes dangerous games.

> (2) The "playground" is a big empty field. There are no toys to play on. Louisa stands ankle-deep in mud, using a stick to draw pictures. Joey throws mud at Mickey and Sam. Three children stand a few inches from the busy street; one waves at cars that pass while the other two push each other back and forth.

While the first narrative is accurate, it does little to communicate Terry's concern for what she saw. The second story is also accurate, but its detail better depicts the speaker's meaning. Use detailed description, vivid language, and forceful delivery to emphasize your meaning in the narrative. Because hypothetical narratives are easily dismissed, use real, documented stories.

The third step in the N-A-R structure is the argument section. An **argument** is a line of deductive or inductive reasoning. The next section illustrates how to develop and strengthen arguments. Fourth, after the arguments comes the refutation section. **Refutation** addresses the objections to your proposal and is covered later in this chapter.

In the conclusion, the suspense is over and there is no reason not to review the main ideas. In addition, the conclusion should make a call to action. An effective business proposal should close by inviting prospects to act immediately.

Because of its inclusion of a narrative, the N-A-R structure is appropriate for proposals that include dramatic testimonials or experiences. The emotional potential of the narrative makes it excellent for neutral audiences. Further, the argument and refutation sections allow speakers to both make their case and answer key objections. The outline for a proposal using the N-A-R structure should follow this format:

INTRODUCTION
  I. Gain Attention
  II. Establish Credibility
NARRATIVE
(Transition)
ARGUMENTS
  I. Argument One
(Transition)
  II. Argument Two
(Transition)
REFUTATION
  I. Refutation One
(Transition)
  II. Refutation Two
(Transition)
CONCLUSION
  I. Review
  II. Call to Action

The Balance Structure

Some proposals require you to address competing solutions and explain why your solution is superior. The audience for such proposals understands the nature of the problem but is undecided about solutions. For instance, a retail company may agree that the current antenna supplier is not working out, but disagree about whether it's best to find another supplier, manufacture the antennas internally, or eliminate the product line altogether.

The balance structure eliminates all the competing solutions until only the speaker's proposal is left.[6] The introduction to the balance structure should grab the audience's attention and justify the topic. A credibility statement may also be included, depending on the audience. Because it detracts from the structure's persuasive power, do not include a preview of main ideas in the introduction. In the body, the presenter develops each alternative or solution by first acknowledging its positive attributes, since there are, undoubtedly, merits to each choice. Acknowledging positive qualities demonstrates your objectivity (hence the label "balance") and goodwill toward individuals who prefer the solutions you are rejecting. But, after the positive qualities are cited, the majority of the time is devoted to demonstrating the plan's drawbacks. Provide reasons to reject the solution and then move on to the next alternative.

Once you have offered and indicted each alternative, it's time to develop your solution. Introduce your alternative by citing arguments in its favor. The audience will not know that this is your proposal. Next, mention some drawbacks to balance your presentation. Finally, state additional reasoning and evidence to support your proposal.

To be effective, the speaker must clearly refute all the reasonable alternatives. The structure's logic is not compelling if the audience believes one or more options are feasible or desirable. Thus, Mario's proposal to become the new supplier of cell phone and CB antennas for an electronics retail chain must explicitly address and dismiss all the chain's alternatives. In the introduction, Mario briefly restated the problem. "We all agree that your current supplier is inept: supplies are consistently back-ordered, the product is poorly manufactured, and returns are high." Mario then went on to discuss and eliminate alternatives.

BODY
I. One alternative is to discontinue this product line.
   A. This would obviously solve supply and return problems.
   B. However, it would do so at the cost of more than $300,000 of annual net profit.
   C. In addition, customers wanting this product would stop shopping in your outlets, possibly cutting into other sales as well.
(Trans. I have spoken with some people in your company who favor another solution.)
II. You could get a new, more dependable supplier overseas.
   A. This solution is workable, and given the currency crisis overseas, the product could be acquired more cheaply than from the present supplier.
   B. However, delivery from most overseas suppliers has been less— rather than more—reliable than from your present supplier.
   C. Quality control on products from the presently available list of overseas suppliers is no better than the current supplier.
(Trans. So, looking for overseas suppliers is not a viable alternative; what other solution is available.)

I. There is a new supplier available who is both dependable and high quality.
  A. I am a dependable supplier, as my current clients will attest.
  B. My products have superior quality engineering.
    1. We have patents on designs to increase antenna range.
    2. We have two patents on methods to allow adjustable tuning.
  C. Although my antennas cost a bit more, selling my antennas will actually increase your profits.
    1. The quality of the antenna is superior to any on the market.
    2. My dependable record ensures that you will always have what the customer wants in stock.

If the store's purchasing agent says, "Well, we've considered manufacturing the antennas ourselves," Mario's proposal could be in trouble. It's imperative to consider all the possible alternatives and indict each, leaving only the strongest proposal—yours—with the audience. The outline for the balance structure should follow the format below:

INTRODUCTION
  I. Gain Attention
 II. Justify the Topic
III. Establish Credibility
(Transition)
BODY
  I. Option A
(Transition)
 II. Option B
(Transition)
III. Option C
(Transition)
 IV. Option D
(Transition)
CONCLUSION
 I. Review
II. Call to Action

In the next section we move from covering the form of persuasive proposals to content considerations.

Developing Persuasive Arguments

If the audience is to share your interpretation of the proposal the members must hear adequate reasons and evidence. Imagine Amartya suggesting that a bank loan her $50,000 to open the coffee bar, "just because." Without reasons, no one will adopt your proposal. The best proposals use a variety of reasoned arguments, both deductive and inductive, to support each claim.

Deductive Arguments

A **claim** is a particular interpretation you want the audience to accept. Claims will not be accepted unless supported by some kind of reasoning. **Arguments** are lines of deductive or inductive reasoning that retrace your original thought process for the audience and answer the question, "Why should the audience accept my claim?"[7] **Deductive arguments** move from general principles to the application of those principles in specific cases.[8] If we know how two terms, concepts, events, or characteristics are related, we can discover other relationships that are logically implied.[9] We discuss three types of deductive reasoning below.

Causal Reasoning.   **Causal reasoning** connects two events and claims that the second event is produced by the first. Common causal arguments include:

> Interest rate increases lead to declining stock prices.
>
> Declining sales lead to decreased profits.
>
> Lower interest rates lead to increased consumer spending on large-ticket items such as homes and automobiles.

Causal reasoning should do more than state the linkage between events; it should also explain the way the causal connection operates. For example, the causal connection in the third example above is as follows:

> Declining interest rates reduce the cost of borrowing money, which makes people more likely to invest in products that require loans.

There are three tests to check the validity of causal arguments. Use these tests to critique and strengthen your reasoning prior to delivering your proposal presentation.

First, the speaker should ask: Does a causal relationship really exists? Just because one event precedes another does not mean that the first event caused the second. Thus, "I washed my car, so it rained" is invalid reasoning because car-washing cannot cause a rainstorm. Alexis, however, may legitimately claim that new cardiology equipment at her hospital is causally related to saving lives.

Second, the speaker should ask: Is the cause sufficient to bring about the effect? The relationship between the two events needs to be significant. Thus, the claim that "An increase in the price of potatoes for potato chips lead to nationally higher inflation" uses invalid reasoning. A rise in potato chip prices is insufficient to trigger a rise in the nation's inflation rate.

Third, the speaker should ask: Could the effect result from other intervening causes? While some events are related, there are often intervening causes that also account for the effect. Thus, claiming the lack of cardiology equipment led to a higher than average death rate from heart attacks in the community is partly true, but the higher rate could also be related to the community's diet and exercise habits, individual heredity, hypertension, or age. The deaths do not solely result from the lack of equipment because these other causes operate independently. Presenters strengthen their arguments when they demonstrate that the cause contributed significantly to the effect.

Argument from Sign.   **Argument from sign** is based on the idea that, when we see something, we infer that it represents or stands for the occurrence of something else. But, unlike causal arguments, reasoning from sign does not assume that the relationship between the two events is causal, only that they are related.[10] When a physician, for example, examines you and sees a red, irritated throat with white blotches, it is a sign of a bacterial infection. In some cases, physicians might verify their reasoning by administering a test for the bacteria. This causal verification is designed to check the accuracy of the physician's reasoning from sign. Look at the examples below:

> Mario may argue that late deliveries, poor communication, and higher customer returns are a sign that the current antenna supplier is not interested in servicing small accounts.

> When Amartya sees people driving 15 minutes downtown for coffee she infers that the area will support a new coffee bar.

> When Alexis sees patients drive two hours to the city hospital for cardiac treatment, she infers that physicians think that hospital is better equipped to help the patient than the local facility.

If signs always stood for something, then the connection between them would be certain. Unfortunately, this is not always the case. Simply because people drive downtown does not mean they will support a closer coffee bar. They may drive because the downtown bar is close to other work-related stops, or because they like to get away from the office. Use the following three tests to strengthen your arguments from sign.

First, is there another explanation that makes the relationship between events believable? It's possible Amartya jumped to a conclusion when she decided that driving downtown means people will support her establishment. If there are reasonable alternative explanations for the signs then the argument loses its strength.

Second, are sufficient signs presented? Signs come in clusters so that various signs must consistently signify a relationship between things or events. If only a few signs are present it may not signal the relationship. Seeing only a few antennas on the retail store's shelves may not signal problems with the supplier. It may signal a move to "just-in-time" delivery by the retailer. Such additional signs as poor service, inadequate supplies, and a high rate of return strengthen the conclusion about the supplier. Clearly, the more signs one has to draw on, the stronger the argument.

Third, are contradictory signs considered? Contradictory signs reduce the strength of the conclusion. For example, Mario may have failed to consider the popularity of the antenna and that no manufacturer could keep up with current demand. By considering and addressing contradictory signs, a speaker is better able to test the strength of the argument. The tests for causal argument, argument from sign, and syllogistic arguments are summarized in Figure 10.1.

Syllogistic Arguments.   Syllogistic arguments involve three statements that lead the audience from general categories to conclusions about specific instances.

FIGURE 10.1   Tests for Causal Argument, Argument from Sign, and Syllogistic Arguments

Tests for Causal Argument
1. Does a causal relationship really exist?
2. Is the cause sufficient to bring about the effect?
3. Could the effect result from other intervening causes?

Tests for Argument from Sign
1. Is there another explanation that makes the relationship between events believable?
2. Are sufficient signs present?
3. Are contradictory signs considered?

Tests for Deductive Syllogisms

Categorical Syllogisms
1. Three terms and only three terms may appear.
2. Each term must be used twice.
3. The middle term must be used in its universal or unqualified sense.
4. The middle term must be used for the second time in the minor premise.
5. At least one premise must be affirmative.
6. If one premise is negative, then the conclusion must be negative.
7. The major and minor premises must be accurate.

Hypothetical Syllogisms
1. The minor premise must either affirm the antecedent or deny the consequent.
2. If the minor premise denies the antecedent or if the minor premise affirms the consequent, no logical conclusion can be drawn from the syllogism.
3. The major and minor premises must be accurate.

Disjunctive Syllogisms
1. The major premise must include all reasonable alternatives.
2. The alternatives must be mutually exclusive.
3. The minor premise must eliminate all but one of the alternatives.
4. The major and minor premises must be accurate.

These statements are referred to as the major premise, the minor premise, and the conclusion.

> Major Premise: All managers need to develop time management skills.
> Minor Premise: Olivia is a manager.
> Conclusion: Olivia needs to develop time management skills.

The major premise is based on an assumption or general principle. The minor premise applies the general principle to a specific group, person, or event. The conclusion links the major and minor premises by saying that what is true of the general class is true of the specific instance. Taken together, the statements form a line of reasoning that is clear and compelling.

Lacking complete data, business leaders make decisions based on a variety of assumptions. These assumptions usually represent the major premise of a syllogism. The strength of the syllogism is based on the degree of certainty in its premises. If listeners accept the premises, they must accept the conclusion. The problem is that most business premises are far from absolute and may not be accepted by an audience. When they are built on probable rather than absolute certainties, syllogisms lose some—but not all—of their persuasive value. Speakers can compensate for some uncertainty by building on premises the audience shares. Thus, knowing your audience is important to persuasive reasoning. Learn the three kinds of syllogisms below to become a critical listener and persuasive speaker.

Categorical Syllogism. The major premise of a **categorical syllogism** classifies without qualification. Thus, the major premise is phrased with words such as, "all," "every," "none," or "no." Mario structured the following syllogism to sell his antennas:

> Major Premise: Any company that holds patents for its products demonstrates superior engineering.
>
> Minor Premise: 10Com has several patents on this antenna.
>
> Conclusion: 10Com's antenna demonstrates superior engineering.

To evaluate a categorical syllogism, it's crucial to identify the major term, minor term, and middle term. The **major term** is the predicate term (the term acted upon) in the major premise. It is usually the last term in the major premise (e.g., "demonstrates superior engineering"). The **minor term** is the subject of the minor premise (e.g., "10Com"). The **middle term** is the subject of the major premise (e.g., "Any company"). To test a categorical syllogism, apply the following standards:

1. Three terms and only three terms may appear.
2. Each term must be used twice.

3. The middle term must be used in its universal or unqualified sense.
4. The middle term must be used for the second time in the minor premise.
5. At least one premise must be affirmative.
6. If one premise is negative, then the conclusion must be negative.
7. The major and minor premises must be accurate.

Of these standards, number three causes the most confusion. Using a term in its universal sense means two things. First, the term must include all members of the class to which it is referring. A logical syllogism cannot be created from the following middle term:

Major Premise: Some businesspeople are unethical.
Minor Premise: John is a businessperson.

Does John fall into the category of ethical or unethical businesspeople? We don't know. Thus, the middle term must cover all the members of the class. Second, the middle term must accurately describe the individuals in that class:

Major Premise: All businesspeople are unethical.
Minor Premise: John is a businessperson.
Conclusion: John is unethical.

Although structured properly, the middle term does not accurately describe individuals who belong to the class "business people." The universal statement in the middle term must be accurate for the conclusion to be valid.

Learn to listen for the assumptions people use in their conclusions. Embedded are a series of assumptions that fit into a categorical syllogism. Learn to build more logical syllogisms for persuasive effect.

Hypothetical Syllogism.   The major premise of a **hypothetical syllogism** is concerned with uncertain or conditional instances and is phrased with words such as "if," "when," "assuming," or "in the event of." In Chapter 2 we emphasized the following hypothetical syllogism:

Major Premise: If you have grammatical and typographical mistakes on your resume, you probably won't be hired.

Minor Premise: Tom has grammatical and typographical mistakes on his resume.

Conclusion: Tom won't be hired.

Testing the hypothetical syllogism involves two terms. The **antecedent term** is the "before term," usually linked to the "If," "Assuming," "In the event of" statement (e.g., "If you have grammatical and typographical mistakes on your resume..."). The **consequent term** is the "after term," describing what will happen if the antecedent occurs (e.g., "you will not be hired"). To test the validity of a hypothetical syllogism, apply the following standards.

1. The minor premise must either affirm the antecedent or deny the consequent.
2. If the minor premise denies the antecedent or if the minor premise affirms the consequent, no logical conclusion can be drawn from the syllogism.
3. The major and minor premises must be accurate.

When either of the first two standards is violated, we encounter the problem of necessary, but not sufficient conditions for the conclusion. Examine the following syllogism:

> Major Premise: If you have grammatical and typographical mistakes on your resume then you probably won't get hired.
>
> Minor Premise: John has no mistakes on his resume.
>
> Conclusion: John will get hired.

The minor premise denies the antecedent because it says that there are no grammatical or typographical errors on the resume. But the conclusion does not follow from this reasoning. A clean resume is a necessary—but not a sufficient—condition for getting a job.

Disjunctive Syllogism. The major premise of the disjunctive syllogism presents alternatives, usually with terms such as "either...or," "neither...nor," or "but." Tony proposes that his company, Environmental Solutions Inc., be given the town's residential trash collection responsibilities, and includes this disjunctive syllogism:

> Major Premise: Either you use a private collection firm or you will continue to run a budget deficit.
>
> Minor Premise: Give my company the contract to collect residential trash.
>
> Conclusion: You will stop running a deficit.

Testing the strength of disjunctive syllogisms is easy with the following questions:

1. The major premise must include all reasonable alternatives.
2. The alternatives must be mutually exclusive.
3. The minor premise must eliminate all but one of the alternatives.
4. The major and minor premises must be accurate.

Examine the following disjunctive enthymeme:

> Major Premise: Either you get a college degree or end up a useless bum.
> Minor Premise: You have said you will not go to college.
> Conclusion: You will be a bum.

There are several problems with this syllogism. First, all the reasonable alternatives are not included since there are many life possibilities apart from going to college or becoming a bum. In addition, the alternatives are not mutually exclusive. Some people who go to college are still bums, and some who do not go to college are millionaires.

In organizations and interpersonal interactions, syllogisms usually appear as **practical syllogisms,** where one of the premises or the conclusion is not presented. Rather, the clarity of the reasoning is evident so that the audience supplies the missing information. Such arguments are very effective because they involve the listener in the reasoning process. For example, Mario might leave out the major premise of his syllogism, presuming the audience already shares this assumption:

> 10Com has several patents on this base station antenna. As such, our base station antenna demonstrates superior engineering.

The audience probably assumes that any company that holds patents has well-engineered products. Other syllogisms can be abbreviated in practical form:

- These cost-cutting strategies should be implemented because they save money.
- If you use my company for residential collections you will stop deficit spending.
- Because John has mistakes on his resume it's doubtful he will be hired.

However, if there is any doubt that the audience shares your assumptions, state all the premises in the syllogism and support each with appropriate evidence. In the next section we cover several forms of inductive reasoning.

Inductive Arguments

Inductive arguments move from particular observations to general conclusions. Thus, a report may cite the following finding:

> In an independent salary audit of 50 major corporations, male accountants were paid an average of 17 percent more than their female counterparts.

The speaker uses the statement to conclude that many corporations pay male workers more than their female workers. Inductive arguments make a leap beyond the evidence to draw a conclusion that is more or less probable. The goal is to collect enough specific instances to establish a pattern. We will discuss four types of inductive evidence.

Analogy.   **Analogies** are comparisons between two similar objects, events, instances, or people and suggests that what is true of one is also true of another. If the audience accepts the similarity, then it will accept the conclusion. A consultant suggests that Jeffrey, the bank manager, use peak-time tellers to sell bank products and services. He supports his suggestion with the following analogy:

First National Bank is similar to your bank in almost every way. They have branches in neighborhoods such as this one, they do similar volume, and their line of products and services is similar. They went to the peak-time process last year and have been very successful. The same process will work for you.

Use the following questions to test your analogic reasoning: First, are the compared cases essentially alike? It's important to ensure that the comparisons are alike in the most critical characteristics. In the analogy above, Jeffrey must consider whether the two banks are really alike. The consultant didn't mention an important area in which the two banks must be alike. If the part-time tellers at Jeffrey's bank are significantly less educated or motivated than the tellers at the other bank, it hurts the strength of the analogy and makes it difficult to determine if the plan will work.

Second, are the compared traits in the analogy accurate? If the products and services at Jeffrey's bank are really more complicated or less helpful to customers than at the other bank, it will be more difficult for the tellers to sell those products. The key traits of the analogy must be accurately described and compared. The tests for inductive arguments are summarized in Figure 10.2.

Example. **Examples** are specific instances that illustrate a larger point. Arguing from example uses a specific instance to draw conclusions about a larger event or class. A story in *The Wall Street Journal* used several examples to argue that American citizens are more interested in "high culture" now than in the past:

> More than 110 American symphonies—including the Louisiana Philharmonic in New Orleans and the Northwest Symphony near Seattle—have been founded since 1980.

FIGURE 10.2   Tests for Inductive Arguments

Tests for Analogy
1. Are the compared cases essentially alike?
2. Are the compared traits in the analogy accurate?

Tests for Examples
1. Are the examples typical?
2. Is the example relevant to the claim?
3. Are enough examples used to support the claim?

Tests for Testimony
1. Does the authority have expertise in the subject area?
2. Is the authority free from bias?

Statistics
1. Is the source of the statistic recent and valid?
2. Are the statistics based on an adequate sample?

Public radio stations, broadcasting a once exotic blend of classical music and introspective news, have more than tripled in number since 1980 to nearly 700.[11]

Use the following questions to strengthen your examples:

First, are the examples typical? Typical examples exhibit most of the traits of the larger class. Examples must not be extraordinary, but should reflect a general trend to qualify as typical and sufficient. The inclusion of raw statistical information in the two examples helps ensure that they are typical.

Second, is the example relevant to the claim? Examples must belong to the class about which the claim is made. Because sporting events are not considered "high culture," citing increased attendance at such events is not relevant to the claim that Americans are more cultured than in the past.

Third, are enough examples used to support the claim? To support its claim, *The Wall Street Journal* provided numerous additional examples, ranging from attendance at theatrical presentations to book sales.

Testimony. **Testimony** is a direct quotation by or paraphrase of witnesses, experts, or other informed sources. Arguing from testimony assumes that an idea is valid because it's supported by an authority on the subject. Tony used testimony to support his bid for residential trash collection:

> According to Brant Brown, Mayor of nearby Fairfield, "Since having our trash collected by Environmental Solutions Inc. our municipality has saved $25,000 over the projected savings.

Consider the following questions when testing arguments from testimony: First, does the authority have expertise in the subject area cited? To be valid, a source must have credentials related to the topic. Citing a mayor with no experience in sanitation or private collection is meaningless. Therefore, it is imperative to cite the source's credentials for the audience.

Second, is the authority free from bias? Consider the self-interest of the authority to determine the degree of bias. Positive comments from your company's CEO won't bolster a claim, because the CEO would not say anything to undermine her company. On the other hand, **reluctant testimony** defines the rare instance when a person does say something against his or her self-interest. Because of the negative impact on self-interest, reluctant testimony is very persuasive. Quoting sanitation officials in the city who agree that switching to Environmental Solutions Inc. will save money is strong because it works against self-interest.

Statistics. **Statistics** are a collection of individual examples delivered as raw numbers or averages. When arguing from statistics, we assume that what is true of the collected data can be extrapolated to similar circumstances where no data were collected. Tony should use statistics to quantify the savings the city can achieve by contracting with Environmental Solutions:

Based on my work in two similar communities, my proposal will save you 12 percent to 20 percent each year.

Contrary to the common axiom, "numbers speak for themselves," numbers cannot talk. As such, statistical information must be interpreted for the audience. Tony can translate his numbers into concrete terms to show the audience how large his projected savings really are:

That means that every person's bill would decrease an average of $12.50 per month, resulting in savings of $150 per household per year. I think you'll agree that this is significant.

Use the following questions to test the strength of your statistics: First, is the source of the statistic recent and valid? The business world moves quickly and statistics rapidly become outdated. Cite the source and date of your statistics and use recent information to avoid undermining your point.

Second, are the statistics based on adequate samples? Statistics are projections based on limited samples. Thus, it is important to know how the sample was gathered as well as its size. Tony cited his sample size—two cities—in his presentation.

Effective proposals support their claims. If you suggest that your proposal is the best because it increases profitability, reduces overhead, and promotes better employee relations, you must demonstrate the claims with good reasoning and evidence. Strong proposals also anticipate and refute audience objections.

Refutation Tactics

Three of the four persuasive structures carve out space for answering the audience's objections. **Refutation** is an argument that addresses and eliminates objections to the proposal. Use the questions under "Meaning" in the Audience Analysis Checklist (Chapter 6, Figure 6.3) to learn about the audience's objections.

Lead the audience into a refutation by stating the audience's objection in a phrase and then state your response in a phrase. For instance:

I. I know that many of you resist the city's proposal to go to automated garbage collection trucks because it's too expensive, but this perception is untrue.

II. I know that some are against the proposal to expand our operation because of the health risks to nearby communities, but I assure you that the risks are infinitesimal.

Although there are many ways to address objections we will introduce four of the most common strategies.

Denial counters an objection by saying it is not true. In his proposal to change travel authorization procedures, Ramon anticipated the key argument against his suggestion and stated, "Although some are concerned that this idea will require more paper work, this is untrue."

The **minimization** strategy suggests the counterargument is true, but its significance in relation to other issues is minimal. Amartya argues that, although the loan of $50,000 sounds significant, the amount is minimal in relation to the coffee bar's profit potential. Mario may refute the objection that his antennas cost more by demonstrating that quality and dependability outweigh the higher price.

A very powerful refutation technique is **exposing inconsistent statements,** beliefs, or actions by the opposition. Demonstrating inconsistency undermines the opposition's credibility, thereby bolstering your case. People believe that words and actions should be consistent. For instance, Anita may point out that although her coworkers pay lip service to supporting the community, declining donations reflect indifference. Truly caring people should contribute more to United Way.

Turning the tables suggests that while the objection is accurate, it actually supports rather than denies your proposal. "Indeed," the salesman said, "the Lexus or BMW is an expensive automobile, but that is what makes it distinctive." As such, the cost becomes part of the product's appeal.

Think of each refutation strategy as a label for a claim and, like any claim, it needs inductive and deductive reasoning for support. It is usually impossible to address all the objections to your proposal in a single presentation. Although easy to accomplish, refuting weak objections isn't persuasive because the audience will still have strong reasons for refusing your proposal. Therefore, select the two or three strongest objections and address those.

Outlining Your Points to Show Logical Relationships

Structuring your arguments can be challenging because there are many different ways to outline an argument. Sometimes your main idea is a single claim supported by a single line of reasoning. For example, examine the claim in the Motivated Sequence outline below:

I. You should stock 10Com's CB antennas because they demonstrate quality engineering.
   A. Any company that holds patents for products demonstrates superior engineering.
   B. 10Com has several patents for this CB antenna.
      1. Example of patent.
         a. Advantage of patent with syllogism or cause-effect reasoning.
         b. Advantage of patent with syllogism or cause-effect reasoning.
      2. Example of patent.
         a. Advantage of patent with syllogism or cause-effect reasoning.
         b. Advantage of patent with syllogism or cause-effect reasoning.
   C. 10Com's CB antenna demonstrates superior engineering.

In this example, the main idea makes a single claim and the three subpoints constitute a practical syllogism in support of the claim.

In other cases the main ideas make several claims and the subpoints support each claim.

> **II.** You should carry 10Com antennas because they demonstrate quality engineering, and excellent quality control, and we guarantee rapid, on-time delivery.
> **A.** 10Com CB antennas demonstrate quality engineering.
> **B.** 10Com exercises superior quality control for its CB antenna.
> **C.** At 10Com, we guarantee rapid and timely delivery.

In this example, the main idea makes three claims, and each subpoint supports each claim.

If the reasoning to support a claim requires extensive explanation, it's useful to use a main idea for each claim.

> **I.** 10Com's CB antennas demonstrate quality engineering.
> (Extensive supporting material)
> **II.** 10Com exercises superior quality control.
> (Extensive supporting material)
> **III.** 10Com guarantees rapid and timely delivery.
> (Extensive supporting material)

Finally, claims are usually stated before supporting reasons and evidence. Listeners may easily get lost as the steps of an argument unfold and evidence and reasoning are added. To avoid confusion, restate your claim as an internal summary at the end of a main point.[12]

> **II.** 10Com exercises superior quality control of its CB antennas.
> (Extensive deductive and inductive reasoning for support)
> {Internal Summary: For the reasons just mentioned, 10Com exercises superior quality control on its CB antennas.}

Logical organization helps lead the audience to "the correct" interpretation and increases the chances of shared meaning. Once the logic of an argument is understood and articulated, you need to consider speaker credibility.

Developing Effective Credibility Appeals

Audiences respond not only to the arguments people make, but also to the person making the arguments. If the audience doesn't believe you, then even the best arguments are irrelevant. **Credibility** is the audience's perception of the speaker's competence, trustworthiness, and dynamism. **Competence** is the audience's perception of the speaker's knowledge and expertise on the topic. If the audience is unaware of your competence, or worse yet, believes that your reputation is poor, steps must be taken prior to and during the presentation to improve these perceptions. Have someone introduce you who will tout your experience and expertise. Use the credibility step in the introduction to enhance your competence, and demonstrate your competence by knowing your subject and providing evidence of your research. Cite relevant research and the latest information to support your claims. When challenged about the effectiveness of his travel changes, Ramon included testimony from reputable accounting firms about the desirability of his proposal. The testimony beefed up audience perceptions of Ramon's competence. Cite only those sources the audience views as credible. Tari Jensen's sample speech in Figure 10.3 works to build audience perceptions of her competence on the subject.

Trustworthiness is the audience's perception of the speaker's honesty, objectivity, fairness, and concern for the audience. Perceptions of trustworthiness can be improved by establishing common ground with the audience. Let them know you share their values and understand their goals. Trustworthiness can also be increased by demonstrating objectivity. Focus on a variety of sources rather than a single source. Use unbiased authorities for your research and acknowledge the benefits of competing proposals.

Dynamism is the audience's perceptions of the speaker's energy, confidence, and enthusiasm. Although good listeners focus on speech content, it is difficult to follow a monotone presentation. Dynamic speakers are viewed by the audience as concerned, committed, and confident. It's easier to persuade an audience to commit to a proposal if you demonstrate your commitment with a dynamic presentation style.

Developing Effective Emotional Appeals

Effective proposals include emotional appeals. Emotional appeals encourage active listening and make listeners more willing to complete practical syllogisms. A persuasive proposal may wish to arouse a variety of emotions:

Envy	Pride
Fear	Dread
Compassion	Anger
Shame	Security
Commitment	Frustration

Decide on the emotional responses you want from the audience and use the following techniques to enhance these responses.

First, emotions can be aroused through **emotional examples.** Use vivid stories to help the audience identify with the topic. Alexis used the following

FIGURE 10.3   Sample Proposal Presentation

Consumer Protection and Contractor Licensing

By Tari Jensen

Topic:	Contractor Licensing
General Purpose:	To persuade
Specific Purpose:	To persuade the audience to support a contractor licensing law.
Main Idea:	I will persuade the audience that a public works license will protect consumers and that there are no legitimate objections to licensing.

INTRODUCTION

  I. In Idaho it is sometimes said that if you have a dog and a truck you are a contractor. Contractor licensing has been the subject of debate in the Idaho legislature for many years. Pocatello and Idaho Falls are the only cities that require a license. I propose that anyone involved in new construction or remodeling work be required to have a public works contractor's license. A public works contractor license will protect consumers and increase the respectability of the construction industry.

 II. My name is Tari Jensen, and I have been involved in the construction industry for over 20 years.
   A. Our company is named Jensen Bros. Builders.
    1. We build 10 to 20 residential homes per year.
    2. We have gross annual sales of $1,500,000 to $2,000,000 per year.
   B. I have been president of the Building Contractors for Southeast Idaho and received the state association's Builder of the Year Award for 1995.
   C. To prepare this speech, I interviewed Dave LeRoy, the past attorney general of Idaho, Dave Wilson, the national representative for the Building Contractor's Association for the State of Idaho, Evan Frasure, our district's Senator, and Jack Robinson, a local real estate attorney; I read and reviewed many articles and books from the ISU library, the Marshall Public Library, and trade magazines.

(Trans. Let me tell you a story about a local family that wanted to start a business in residential construction.)

NARRATIVE

This family decided to start a new business. All of their hopes and dreams of a better life were wrapped up in this goal. They wanted to become log home dealers. The log home dealership would set the logs and the family would finish the structure. This family sought a contractor who was willing and able to finish the homes.

(continued)

FIGURE 10.3   Continued

The gentleman they found started the foundation of the first home in May of 1995 and committed to finishing in October. On October 31, the home was not near completion. Cursory inspections of the incomplete home revealed numerous flaws. In the middle of December, the contractor left a note on the door saying he quit. The mother of the family told me that she felt as if she had been raped by the contractor.

This family borrowed more than $50,000 above their original bank loan on credit cards to finish the house. The general contractor declared bankruptcy.

Two years and thousands of dollars over budget, the family finally moved into their first log home. A public works contractor's license would have prevented this situation because their contractor would have been disqualified to bid on the log home job because he lacked the appropriate financial solvency. The license would have protected this contractor from getting in over his head and would have prevented the embarrassment and devastating losses this project cost. The family would not have hired the man and had their dreams butchered by someone lacking the proper skills, qualifications, and financial backing.

Definition: A public works license law was written many years ago to certify contractors who work for the state on publicly owned projects. The "Public Works Contractor's License Act" handbook states, "The Board believes the legislature in providing the License Act and subsequent amendments thereto, intended to afford some protection [for the state]…A 'Public Works Contractor' shall give to the investing public body some assurance of the contractor's reputation, ability, qualification, experience, and financial responsibility" (24).

(Trans. There are two main arguments in support of using the existing public works contractor's license law in residential construction.)

ARGUMENTS

I. A public works license would protect consumers by documenting a contractor's ability, qualification, experience, and financial responsibility.
   A. Licenses are granted to contractors based on their good reputation among peers, bankers, and the bonding company (Public 12).
   B. Licenses are granted on a graduated scale according to financial solvency, which protects the consumer by making sure the person hired can afford to pay damages.
      1. The amount you are allowed to bid on is determined by your financial statement.
      2. The law allows a maximum net worth of $300,000, and liquidity of $60,000, and a minimum net worth of $10,000 and liquidity of $2,000 (Public 27–28).
   C. The license requires an examination, which ensures that the contractors know the law and the penalties for violating the law.

FIGURE 10.3 Continued

II. A public works license will protect small contractors (i.e., the "Little Guys") entering the industry.

    A. Construction is a very complicated industry and a contractor needs vast knowledge to survive.

        1. Would we allow someone to calculate the trajectory of a spacecraft, which requires complicated trigonometry, before he or she has learned to add and subtract?

        2. In a complex industry, it is necessary to learn the business one step at a time, not by taking on all the steps at once.

    B. We must regulate by creating a graduated scale of qualifications, reputation, skills, and knowledge.

(Trans. So, if licensing will protect the consumer and help the "Little Guy" succeed, what could be wrong with this proposal?)

REFUTATION

  I. The first objection to licensing is that it increases government regulation, but this is inconsistent with the facts.

    A. The State of Idaho requires that before you do construction work for any publicly owned property you must have a public works license.

        1. If the state needs protection with licensing then citizens need protection with licensing.

        2. Residential construction should also require licensing.

    B. Professional money managers such as stock brokers, bankers, real estate agents, and insurance agents must be licensed.

        1. If construction workers handle a lot of money they should also be licensed.

        2. This leads me to a passage in *Modern Real Estate Practice,* which says, "Buying a home is usually the biggest financial transaction in a person's life. The home buyer pays out more cash, undertakes more debt, and has a deeper personal interest in this transaction than any other purchase made during his or her lifetime" (p. xvii).

        {As you can see, contractor licensing is consistent with licensing requirements for people who handle public money and for people who manage large amounts of other people's money.}

(Trans. Government regulation is one objection to licensing, but there are other objections.)

  II. Others say that this restriction prevents the "Little Guy" from entering the construction industry; I argue that these restrictions will actually help the "Little Guy."

    A. The public works license does restrict the "Little Guy" by limiting the jobs he can do according to his ability to pay for possible damages.

        1. But it also prevents him from getting in too deep too fast.

(continued)

FIGURE 10.3   Continued

---

     2. A law would create a loose apprenticeship by encouraging the "Little Guy" to start out where he can afford to pay for losses.

     3. As his solvency increases so could his license.

  B. Limiting competition to businesses that can afford to cover damage is not bad because it protects the "Little Guy" from judgments from which he could not recover.

(Trans. So, if we agree that licensing would protect the "Little Guy," we need to look at how much this process will cost.)

III. The third objection is the expense of creating a new agency and writing a new law, but costs can be cut by using already existing laws and agencies.

  A. Modifying the public works license law to fit residential builders would be easy and inexpensive.

  B. The Public Works Licensing Board already exists and could be modified to license residential builders.

     1. The board would require only additional secretarial help to handle the increased license volume.

         a. Gaylord Lake, at the Public Works Licensing Board, told me that he has tried to get this law amended and applied "statewide for years and would encourage [me] in this endeavor however he could."

     2. The city and county building departments already collect information for permits and would merely add a requirement to see proof of license when a builder bought a building permit.

(Trans. Since the costs to implement this law are minimal, let's look at the last objection.)

IV. Finally, some say that the industry is not in favor of licensing, but this is inaccurate.

  A. The Idaho Building Contractor's Association, which has well over 1,500 businesses as members, has written, sponsored, and lobbied for licensing for over ten years.

  B. The full-time, legitimate contractors in the industry see the problems created by unskilled, inexperienced, and under-funded part-timers and have begged for rules and legislation (Allen 3).

  C. When I interviewed Dave LeRoy, Dave Wilson, and Evan Frasure they said that the main objectors against licensing are the part-time contractors. These are the very people in need of protection and from whom consumers must be protected.

(Trans. If we review the objections against licensing we see that they are not persuasive and that modifying the public works license is an effective solution to the problem of fly-by-night contractors.)

CONCLUSION

  I. To create regulations for the single most expensive purchase consumers make in their lifetimes seem only sensible.

    A. The regulation will not prevent newcomers from entering the industry, but would force them to enter at a level they can afford and protect the consumer in the process.

FIGURE 10.3　Continued

 B. It is not expensive or difficult to implement this law.
 C. The full-time, qualified, knowledgeable, experienced, and financially solvent contractors are united in favor of this law.

II. We should never allow the heartache, frustration, and years of suffering that happened to our family in Pocatello happen to anyone else in the state of Idaho ever again.

DISJUNCTIVE SYLLOGISM

Major Premise:　We can either take the costly approach and develop a new agency to enforce the law or we can use an existing agency at low cost.

Minor Premise:　Creating a new agency is too expensive.

Conclusion:　We should use the existing agency.

CATEGORICAL SYLLOGISM

Major Premise:　We regulate people who work in complex jobs that control or manage a lot of money for individual citizens.

Minor Premise:　A contractor's job is complex and they control the largest investment most citizens ever make.

Conclusion:　Therefore, contractors should be regulated.

HYPOTHETICAL SYLLOGISM

Major Premise:　If the state feels the need to protect its own financial affairs from inexperienced and insolvent contractors, then citizens should also be protected.

Minor Premise:　The state has enacted laws to protect itself from inexperienced and insolvent contractors.

Conclusion:　Laws should be enacted to protect the citizen from inexperienced and insolvent contractors.

example to get her audience emotionally committed to giving money for new cardiology equipment.

Can one person really make a different in a community? Sue Finch did. Sue Finch represents what many of us would like to be—one who gave of herself to help others live better lives. She volunteered at the local homeless shelter, spoke as a child advocate in court proceedings, and belonged to the Optimist Club, where she was the driving force behind scholarships for entering college freshmen. Sue Finch celebrated her 44th birthday on August first. And on August fifth, Sue died tragically of a heart attack. The real tragedy is that Sue's death could have been prevented if our community had a heart catherization machine. But we don't have one and Sue died as many of us watched—helplessly. Sue's death was not an isolated one. Fully 75 people in our community die each year from similar heart failure. With your support, we could help reduce that significant number.

Alexis used emotional images of service and volunteerism to create a picture of an upstanding, ethical community member. She then used **vivid language** such as "tragedy" and "helplessly" to emphasize the sorrowful nature of the death. The **descriptive detail** of Sue Finch's contributions further raises emotional awareness and involves the audience in the tragedy. Finally, **effective delivery,** including commitment, enthusiasm, and nonverbal cues that reinforce the emotional interpretations you want from the audience, is crucial for raising emotions.

Summary

Persuasive proposals are crucial to the success of many business and government organizations. Persuasive proposals should create shared meaning by persuading others that whatever you have to offer is the best solution to their problems.

A speaker leads the audience to the preferred interpretation with well-structured proposals. The problem-solution structure articulates a problem or a need and provides a specific solution. Monroe's Motivated Sequence includes five steps. The speaker gains the audience's attention in the attention step. In the need step, the speaker states, illustrates, and reinforces the problem, and points it at the audience. In the satisfaction step, the speaker supports the solution and addresses objections. The visualization step paints a vivid verbal description of the effects of the plan. The action step makes a direct appeal asking the audience to adopt the proposal.

The N-A-R structure includes three major parts. The narrative tells a story that emphasizes the speaker's meaning for the issue, problem, or situation. The arguments include inductive and deductive support for the proposal. The refutation logically dismisses objections to the proposal. The balance structure eliminates competing solutions until the speaker's proposal is the only one left. All reasonable alternatives must be included and indicted in the balance structure.

Persuasive proposals use a variety of arguments to support their claims. A claim is any interpretation a speaker wants the audience to accept. Arguments are lines of deductive or inductive reasoning that retrace your original thought process for the audience. Deductive arguments move from general principles to an application of those principles in specific cases. Causal arguments connect two events and claim that the second event is produced by the first. When we infer that one thing or event stands for the occurrence of something else we are arguing from sign. Syllogistic arguments involve three statements that lead the audience from general categories to conclusions about specific instances. The categorical syllogism classifies without qualification. A hypothetical syllogism is concerned with uncertain or conditional instances. The disjunctive syllogism presents alternatives, all but one of which are logically eliminated.

In business organizations, syllogisms usually appear as practical syllogisms, where one of the premises or the conclusions is not stated. In these syllogisms, the clarity of the reasoning is self-evident and the audience supplies the missing information.

Inductive arguments move from particular observations to form general conclusions. Inductive argument makes a leap beyond the evidence to draw a conclusion. Analogies are comparisons between two similar objects, events, instances, or people and suggest that what is true of one is also true of the other. Examples are specific instances that illustrate a larger point. Testimony is a quotation by or paraphrase of a witness, expert, or other informed source. Statistics are a collection of individual examples delivered as raw numbers or averages. Refutation addresses and eliminates objections to the proposal. Four kinds of refutation are denial, minimization, exposing inconsistent statements, and turning the tables.

Credibility is the audience's perceptions of the speaker's competence, trustworthiness, and dynamism. Competence is the perception of the speaker's expertise and experience on the given topic. Trustworthiness is the audience's perception of the speaker's honesty, objectivity, fairness, and concern for the audience. Dynamism is the audience's perception of the speaker's energy and enthusiasm. Use examples, vivid language, descriptive detail, and effective delivery to raise emotional support for your proposal.

QUESTIONS FOR DISCUSSION

1. Which of the four structures identified here (problem-solution, Monroe's Motivated Sequence, N-A-R, and the balance structure) would you use for the proposal presentations described at the beginning of this chapter? Consider the topic, the audience, and the types of arguments for each presentation.

2. Describe the advantages of proposals that include only one kind of argument (e.g., argument from sign, causal argument). What are the disadvantages of reliance on a single line of argument?

3. Describe the advantages of deductive reasoning over inductive reasoning. Why are well-constructed deductive reasons more convincing than inductive reasons? What prevents speakers from relying exclusively on deductive reasoning for persuasion?

4. Many theorists, both ancient and modern, believe that credibility is the most important kind of persuasive appeal. Is this true in your opinion? Why or why not?

ACTIVITIES AND EXERCISES

1. Videotape an advertisement from a television show. Identify the structure the advertisement uses. Rewrite the ad using a different structure. Which structure works best, the original or your revision? Why?

2. Read a professional editorial from *USA Today, The Wall Street Journal,* or your local newspaper. Identify the deductive and inductive arguments used. Apply the relevant

tests to determine the strength of the arguments in the editorial. Is the editorial convincing? Why or why not?

3. Read each of the following practical syllogisms. For each statement: (a) structure the statement as a complete syllogism; (b) identify the type of syllogism it represents; and (c) apply the appropriate tests to determine its validity.

- Of course he supports lower taxes; he's a Republican.
- If you major in accounting you are assured a job when you graduate.
- Mary is a racist because she opposes affirmative action in corporate hiring decisions.
- If a company makes a poor product line it will go bankrupt, and Techware has poor products.
- The damage the hacker did to your computer system indicates its vulnerability.
- The movement of goods is the lifeblood of the economy. If the movement is cut off because of a trucker strike, the economy will collapse.
- Rather than fire the employee, I guess we'll provide the remedial training he needs to do the job.
- The governor is unethical because he actively deceives the public about policy initiatives.
- This oil improves gas mileage because it includes silicon additives.
- The ability to persuade others is vital to your career.

4. Look for the practical syllogisms in the sample speech in Figure 10.3. These can be found by scanning for assumptions (usually the major premise of a syllogism) or conclusions the author draws. Draw out the entire syllogism by writing the major premise, the minor premise, and the conclusion. Compare your syllogisms to the three the author drew out at the end of the speech. Did you find additional syllogisms? Apply the logical tests described in this chapter to the syllogisms. Are they logical and persuasive? Why or why not?

5. Examine the sample speech in Figure 10.3 for causal arguments, arguments from sign, and arguments from analogy, statistic, testimony, and example. Apply the tests to each argument. Is each argument persuasive? Why or why not? Overall, are you persuaded by the arguments in this presentation? Why or why not?

6. Examine the credibility appeals in the sample speech in Figure 10.3. How do the various credibility appeals affect your perceptions of the speaker's competence and trustworthiness? Do you see the speaker as credible? Why or why not?

7. Examine the refutation strategies used in the sample speech in Figure 10.3. Label each of the strategies the speakers uses to refute objections. How persuasive are these refutations? Why?

8. Think of your first day on a new job or your first day of class this semester. Think of someone who made a favorable impression on you. Which of the three elements of credibility—competence, trustworthiness, or dynamism—did this person demonstrate? What did the person do to convince you of his or her credibility? Conduct the same analysis for someone who did not make a positive impression. Compare the two lists. Is there a pattern of behaviors a person can exhibit that leads you to believe he or she is credible?

NOTES

1. Beck, C. E., and K. Wegner, "Toward a Rhetoric of Technical Proposals: Ethos and Audience Analysis," *Technical Communication* 39 (1992): 122.

2. Rosenbaum, B. L., "Making presentations: how to persuade others to accept your ideas," *Supervision,* May 1992, 9.

3. Blake, G., "It Is Recommended That You Write Clearly," *The Wall Street Journal,* 3 May 1995, A24.

4. Fulscher, R. J., "A No-Fail Recipe: Winning Business Proposals," *Journal of Property Management,* January/February 1996, 62.

5. Rosenbaum.

6. Ryan, H., *Classical Communication for the Contemporary Communicator* (Mountain View, CA: Mayfield Publishing Company, 1992).

7. Sprague, J., and D. Stuart, *The Speaker's Handbook* (Fort Worth, TX: Harcourt Brace College Publishers, 1996).

8. Ziegelmueller, G. W., and J. Kay, *Argumentation: Inquiry and Advocacy* (Boston: Allyn and Bacon, 1997).

9. Sprague and Stuart.

10. Ziegelmueller and Kay.

11. Blackmon, D. A., "Forget the Stereotype: America Is Becoming a Nation of Culture," *The Wall Street Journal,* 17 September 1998, A1.

12. Sprague and Stuart.

CHAPTER

11 Sales Presentations

Audience Analysis for Sales Presentations
   Asking Questions
   Listening for Metaphors

Visual Aids for Sales Presentations

Content Considerations for Sales Presentations

Delivering the Sales Presentation

Structuring the Sales Presentation

Summary

Without sales a business will eventually close its doors. Sales presentations can take many forms. Commercial advertising on radio, television, newspapers, and the Internet are all forms of the sales presentation. Retail selling, from small shoe stores to large automobile dealerships, requires sales presentation skills. Businesses make sales presentations to other businesses, when, for example, a laundry service acquires a contract to clean linens for a large hotel chain. In fact, if someone could enforce a ban on sales presentations nationwide, most corporations would go bankrupt and the U.S. economy would collapse.

Because commercial advertising is a specialized field, it is not considered in this book. Nor is retail selling, which represents informal, interpersonal communication. Instead, we focus on **sales presentations** between organizations, where a salesperson persuades a business to buy its products or services for use in the business or for eventual sale to retail customers. Such presentations may be given to a single person or to a group responsible for corporate purchasing. The salesperson's goal is to create shared meaning so that the receiver shares the sender's interpretation of the product or service.

On any given day, thousands of sales presentations are made by salespeople to a variety of industries. Large manufacturing outfits hear numerous presentations encouraging them to buy raw materials and equipment for manufacturing, office supplies for daily operation, contracting services to retool areas of the plant, and consulting services to the company's management. In other cases, salespeople try to convince wholesale and retail outlets to carry their products. Companies such as Hallmark and Radio Shack, to name just two, must purchase merchandise that they do not manufacture themselves. Small retailers in your town hear a variety of sales presentations from suppliers of business or retail goods and services. Even government agencies and social service organizations are becoming more "customer oriented."

Recent moves to privatize government will mean that agencies such as your city's water or sanitation department may soon be forced to bid for city services against for-profit businesses. In the city of Indianapolis, almost all city services except police and fire protection are put up for bid. If city departments want to continue providing services and employing their people, they must make competitive sales presentations.[1] Cities, counties, and states compete fiercely for new manufacturing plants or to persuade organizations to schedule conventions in their communities. For example, Marcy Roitman, the national sales manager for the Grapevine, Texas. Convention and Visitors Bureau, works to recruit convention business to Grapevine. A typical presentation is to the American Society of Law Enforcement Trainers to sell her small town as a convention and training site.[2] As such, sales presentations have become vitally important to local and state governments.

There are several elements to consider when putting together a sales presentation. In Chapter 1, we said that good communication requires the ability to adapt to audience needs and concerns, and nowhere is this more vital than in sales presentations. Effective selling means convincing customers that the particular product or service meets their individual needs. Next, the introduction of laptop computers and graphics software gives salespeople the ability to create appealing, interactive presentations that can be adapted to meet the needs of individual clients. The content of sales presentations must contain persuasive logical, credible, and emotional appeals. Finally, the chapter closes with a discussion of the delivery qualities required in selling and structures specific to the sales setting.

Audience Analysis for Sales Presentations

Conrad Levinson, author of the internationally acclaimed book, *Guerrilla Marketing*, advises salespeople to "Identify a need your prospect has and be certain you can fill it."[3] Michele Marchetti, writing for *Sales & Marketing Management*, says that the preparation to understand audience concerns will undoubtedly take more time than the actual presentation. However, failing to analyze the prospect for particular needs can result in presentations that are ill-suited for the client and often do not succeed.

> That was a mistake that Joan Mariani Andrew, vice president of sales and marketing for Chicago-based Bell & Howell Document Management Product Company, made for the first time and last time. Her first presentation—a "data dump" of everything she learned in sales school—consisted of samples, detailed flip charts, and an elaborate speech about the quality of the product. Although the prospects thanked her for a thorough sales presentation, she lost the sale because they could not see how the product fit the company's individual needs.[4]

A study of face-to-face selling in the construction industry indicates that salespeople who were able to adapt their presentations to the three client types served by this industry—government agencies, large private developers, and small one-time buyers—were more successful than salespeople who did not change their proposals for each client segment. As such, the authors conclude that:

> there appears no substitute for salespeople with adaptability skills. Adaptable salespeople are sensitive to different buying situations. They pick up cues from buyers and adjust their selling behavior. Less adaptable salespeople do not possess this sensitivity.[5]

Another study found that poor listening skills, failure to concentrate on customer priorities, and an inability to determine customer needs were three of the six most frequent reasons that salespeople fail.[6] As you can see, the ability to analyze and adapt to audience needs is a vital component in sales presentations.

In this section we present two means of assessing audience concerns for sales presentations. The first is a more obtrusive method that relies on direct questions. The second is unobtrusive because it involves paying attention to the language used by individuals in the prospect company. Used together, these methods provide powerful insight into the needs and interests of the audience.

Asking Questions

As we learned in Chapter 6 on audience feedback, asking questions is an effective means of understanding and adapting to your audience. The direct approach helps salespeople in two ways. First, direct questions help the salespeople find **qualified prospects**—potential clients who have the need, interest, and financial resources to purchase their product or service.[7] Although making calls on unqualified prospects is not necessarily a waste of time (altered business circumstances may change a prospect's needs), qualified prospects are the source of most sales. Asking questions requires the salesperson to make appropriate contacts in the prospective organization. Speakers should call in order to qualify the organization's purchasing agent prior to scheduling a presentation. Figure 11.1 provides a partial list of questions for screening prospects. The questions help the salesper-

---

FIGURE 11.1   Questions for Qualifying Sales Prospects

1. What are your needs or problems?
2. Is your organization considering the kind of product or service we offer?
3. Why are you considering or not considering this kind of product or service?
4. What criteria does the product or service have to meet?
5. What performance standards are required of this product or service?
6. What criteria tend to be most influential for decision makers?
7. Has anything changed since the last time we talked?

son understand the organization's perceptions of its present needs, the products or services it presently purchases, those it is considering, and the performance criteria that products and services must meet. If the salesperson learns that the prospect company is unaware of her product, then the persuasive task is to introduce it as a solution to a particular problem. If, on the other hand, the organization needs the product but can choose from several competing brands, the salesperson's task is to distinguish her product from the competition. Understanding the prospect's needs allows the salesperson to avoid "sales-dumps" and tailor each presentation to the particular organization.

Audience analysis does not end after prospects are screened. Sales presenters must analyze the situational features and listener predispositions toward the product. Use the Audience Analysis Checklist in Figure 6.3 to fit the presentation to audience needs.

Listening for Metaphors

While asking questions requires overt interaction with potential clients, **listening for metaphors** is a more subtle means of gaining insight into a prospect's thinking. **Metaphors** suggest that some object or event is to be understood as if it were another object or event. For example, "American Airlines is the on-time *machine.*" Although neither the people nor the physical, mechanical, and informational resources of American Airlines are a machine, the metaphor encourages us to think of the airline as if it were. Through the metaphor, the company wants us to associate American with the reliability and predictability of a machine. **Similes** are very much like metaphors but include "like" or "as" in the phrasing. "American Airlines is like an on-time *machine,*" is an example of a simile.[8]

Metaphors structure how people perceive themselves and their surroundings. For example, many people perceive arguments as war, where winners are victorious and the losers are vanquished. People often talk about argument using the following war-related metaphors:

> Your claims are *indefensible.*
> He *attacked every weak* point in my argument.
> His criticisms were *right on target*
> He *demolished* my argument.[9]

Others may think of arguments as dances ("We *moved around* the central point") or as a game ("I went for the *long bomb* on that argument"). Understanding a person's metaphors reveals the way he or she perceives the surroundings.

Marketing professors Robert W. Boozer, David C. Wyld, and James Grant claim that some business metaphors reflect the perceptions of competitiveness in that business or industry. For example, an industry can be thought of as war (we need to *capture* market share and gain back *lost territory*), a game (we need to get out of this *inning without losing* any more market share), a machine (a *breakdown* caused that delivery problem), an organism (we need to *grow* our marketing department), or a conduit (information *flow* is not sufficient in sales).[10] A second category of metaphors reflects one's personal experience working in the organization (we are a *family* here; this place *grinds* careers to chopped liver).

Listening for metaphors provides a basis for "talking the customer's language."[11] If the customer is at war then your product or service is a weapon. If the organization is an organism, then your product or service is nitrogen that is vital for growth. If the organization is a machine, then you can fix broken or damaged parts. By skillfully employing direct questions and paying attention to metaphors, salespeople can learn to qualify potential customers, learn about their needs and interests, and understand the perceptions under which they operate. Adapting to these needs and perceptions is the core of effective selling.

Visual Aids for Sales Presentations

The past few years have seen enormous growth in visual aid technology for presentations, some of which was detailed in Chapter 8. Nowhere has the growth of this technology been more evident than in sales presentations, where the use of high-technology visuals is almost mandatory. Without repeating what was covered in Chapter 8, we highlight several technologies commonly used in face-to-face or group sales presentations.

In 1993, Eastman Kodak Co. introduced the **Photo CD,** which allows 35mm slides or color negatives to be digitized and stored on compact disk for viewing on a television screen. The standard disk can store one hundred images, which can then be programmed to appear in a different order for each presentation.[12] This photo CD is less bulky than the traditional slide projector and eliminates the risk of spilling slides out of an unlocked tray. When using the Photo CD, follow the same guidelines for developing and presenting visual aids outlined in Chapter 8.

A **sales videotape** can demonstrate a product in a controlled manner that communicates precisely what the company wants to communicate.[13] The downside to these videos, however, is that watching TV is a passive rather than active experience. A video may also interfere with the dialogue the salesperson tries to establish with the client. As a result, sales videos should be less than five minutes in length. Because sales videos cannot be easily adapted to the needs of each client, they are best utilized as a "leave-behind" for the clients to examine at their leisure.[14]

New overhead projectors incorporate a liquid crystal panel that, when connected to a laptop computer, displays images from the computer directly onto a screen.[15] As the growth in computer-generated multimedia continues, the use of liquid crystal overheads will also increase. Follow the guidelines for the use of overhead projectors outlined in Chapter 8.

Finally, computerized multimedia sales presentations take the basic graphics programs we covered in Chapter 8 a step further by combining text, audio, graphics, motion, and spreadsheets, into a format controlled by a notebook-sized computer. The computer presentation can be used in a face-to-face presentation, with the salesperson sitting beside the client, or in larger presentations if the computer is linked to an LCD overhead. The computerized presentation can be customized to include background information about the product, competitive data, price lists, delivery schedules, product specifications, research statistics, spreadsheet performance data, and even "live" testimonials from satisfied customers.[16] Popular software includes "Harvard Graphics," by Software Publishing, "GEM Graph," by Digital Research, and "Chart," by Microsoft. These programs can be run on laptop computers that cost between $2000 and $7000 from such companies as Toshiba, IBM, Apple, Panasonic, and Texas Instruments.[17]

Like any technological innovation, computers have produced problems for some sales forces. Many companies give only minimal control of the content to the salesperson, preferring instead to have their own or an outside graphic arts department create the presentation. If the salesperson can't adapt the program to individual clients, the presentation becomes less effective. Other critics believe salespeople rely too heavily on the new technology, losing some of their important persuasive skills in the process. Betsy Wiesendanger, Senior Associate Editor at *Sales & Marketing Management*, says that electronic presentations have in some cases:

> become a cloak that hides poor selling skills or a straitjacket that constricts spontaneity. A whole new generation of salespeople is cropping up for which learning to fine-tune the video monitor is as important a skill as asking probing questions or overcoming objections...It means you need to stop thinking about your presentation as a series of visuals and start thinking about what you can say or do to meet a particular client's needs.[18]

Computer-generated visual aids and videotape demonstrations are no substitute for a solid relationship with the client, persuasive content, and responding to audience objections.

Jack Falvey, a contributing editor at *Sales & Marketing Management* recommends that salespeople ask themselves the following question before adding any visual aid to their presentation: "Does the visual contribute to (and not interfere with) the selling process?"[19] Once you have decided to include visual aids in your presentation, check each slide or visual against the three criteria in Figure 11.2. If an individual slide or visual cannot meet all three criteria, it should be removed from the list. Use visual aids carefully for greatest persuasive effect in sales presentations.

FIGURE 11.2   Criteria for Testing the Usefulness of Sales Visual Aids

1. Does the visual aid broaden experience by demonstrating a process or object that can't be demonstrated in any other way?
2. Does the visual aid improve client information retention?
3. Does the visual aid simplify complicated information?

Content Considerations for
Sales Presentations

Image is *not* everything! The content of a sales presentation is vital. Because selling is simply a specific kind of persuasion, the techniques covered in Chapter 10 are applicable to most sales presentations. In this section we review persuasive techniques that are especially relevant to selling.

Developing a clear specific purpose statement is vital for sales presentations. As you recall from Chapter 7, a specific purpose statement is not the subject of your presentation, it is what you want your listeners to remember or do as a result of the presentation. Many salespeople fail because they ignore this vital information and, rather than focusing on the objective, begin presentations with elaborate detail about company history or product development. James E. Lukaszewski, an organizational consultant, encourages people to "Always put your communications objective or message first. Then support the objective with an appropriate amount of additional information and detail."[20]

The meat of any sales presentation is in its arguments. Josh Gordon, president of Gordon & Associates, a publishers representative firm in New York, says the sales pitches that succeed are the ones that offer proof for their claims.[21] Proof, of course, involves solid inductive and deductive arguments as described in Chapter 10.

James E. Lukaszewski recommends that deductive arguments avoid merely listing features of the product or service. **Features,** he argues, are things that the salesperson or company that made the product care about. Arguments should be made about the **benefits** the product or service provides the customer.[22] Focusing on benefits helps the salesperson select deductive arguments appropriate for the prospective customer.

The testimony of satisfied customers provides significant persuasive impact to sales presentations. For example, a *Wall Street Journal* ad for the Deloitte & Touche Consulting Group asks, "Who goes the distance for MCI?" If a prestigious firm such as MCI appreciated Deloitte & Touche's consulting services, so too will other companies. An ad for Roadway Express trucking firm uses an extended example and testimony from a satisfied customer to advertise its Time-Critical Services. In multimedia presentations it is common to record such testimonials on videotape or CD-ROM.

Examples are also valuable inductive reasoning tools for selling. Relevant examples drawn from industries similar to the prospective client's are useful because they force the salesperson to talk in terms of benefits to the customer.[23] **Stories** are a valuable form of example in sales presentations. The psychological process of being caught up in a story resembles becoming engaged in a film or novel. The narrator includes good characters that arouse sympathy who are pitted against bad characters or circumstances that must be defeated. The conflict creates suspense because the outcome is in doubt.[24] To create an intense response, stories should be nontechnical and focus on the actions and emotions of people. The Roadway Express ad we cited describes a furniture warehouse manager who had to move an entire order to a trade show in Kansas City at the same time he needed an emergency appendectomy. In this case, time and the manager's health are portrayed as the enemy eventually conquered by Roadway's efficient customer service staff. A picture of the warehouse manager and the Roadway staff member are also included to create greater identification with the "good guys." In oral presentations, stories engage an audience and provide an opportunity for the salesperson's personality to shine through.

Metaphors can help communicate the intangible qualities of a product or service.[25] For example, the Roadway Express ad begins with the metaphor "Once again, Roadway beats the clock," and pictures a semi-truck in front of a stopwatch. The reader is encouraged to think of business as a race or sprint in which time is the sole measure of success. Roadway is fast enough to "beat the clock" and help customers win the race. In another ad, Gateway Computers claims, "You've got a friend in the business." Given the hesitancy with which some people approach computers, isn't it better to buy from a helpful, knowledgeable friend than a stranger? To be successful, metaphors must communicate pleasing and attractive associations to the customer.

Finally, the new multimedia computer programs now allow salespeople to tailor engineering, cost, and performance statistics for each customer. Spreadsheets allow customers to examine various operating scenarios and the results of each in productivity, power costs, energy savings, and pollution reductions. The adaptable nature of these tools is what makes them so persuasive.

Credibility is vital for effective sales presentations. Credit: Caryn Elliot

In addition to logic, credibility is an important form of proof in sales presentations. In Chapter 10 we discussed the importance of individual credibility; however, the credibility of your firm also influences buying decisions. In what communication theorists refer to as the **"halo effect,"** the relative credibility attached to the company covers the salesperson like a halo.[26] Of course, depending on the reputation of the company, this works to the benefit or detriment of the salesperson. To benefit from the halo effect, a salesperson must build the firm's credibility prior to and during the presentation. Have someone inside the client firm who knows you or your firm's work introduce you prior to the presentation. Use testimonials from other customers or mention (albeit briefly) your company's history and reputation as a leader and innovator. Building the firm's credibility can create an aura of positive credibility around the salesperson.

Despite misconceptions suggesting that business people are rational decision makers, emotion is a powerful persuasive force in sales communication. Almost all organizational decisions involve a host of emotions—from exhilaration, pride, satisfaction, and excitement to anxiety, worry, dread, and escape.

According to Joel D. Whalen, at DePaul University, the effective salesperson must diminish three common fears before the customer will purchase a product or service. People fear that they will not get what they were promised, they fear that they will pay too much, and they fear that other people in the organization will criticize them for buying your product or service.[27] Building a strong personal relationship with the client can reduce fears of being taken. Relating objective performance data or a list of satisfied customers can also build faith in your company. The refutation tactics in Chapter 10 can be used to ease a client's fear of paying too much for the product or service. To counter the fear of criticism, Whalen suggests "inoculating" the client against the arguments of others by stating counterarguments (objections) that the client is likely to hear and refuting these arguments.[28] The client will then have a series of arguments to make if criticized. As you can see, advances in sales technology have not lessened the need for strong content in the sales presentation.

Delivering the Sales Presentation

Enthusiastic delivery is vital for effective selling. In Chapter 7 we emphasized that great delivery depends on an attitude of respect for your listeners and enthusiasm for the topic. Dynamic delivery also contributes to audience perceptions of dynamism, which improves perceptions of credibility. There are several delivery issues that relate directly to sales presentations. Our delivery tips for sales presentation are listed in Figure 11.3. Good delivery means being **extemporaneous.** Working from notes rather than a script allows the presenter to immediately adapt to audience concerns. Extemporaneous delivery produces an informal quality that is difficult to duplicate with a script. No matter how many times the presentation is delivered, it must look as if it is being presented for the first time. A rehearsed performance will lead others to assume they are hearing a canned presentation. **Spontaneity** is more easily generated from an outline than from a script.

FIGURE 11.3   Delivery Tips for Sales Presentations

1. Use extemporaneous delivery from notes rather than reading from a manuscript.
2. Create a sense of spontaneity so that clients believe this is the first time you are giving the presentation.
3. Pace yourself appropriately and speak every sentence with its appropriate meaning.
4. Eliminate vocalized pauses from your speech.
5. Use humor in appropriate places.
6. Cite common experiences to establish common ground with the audience.
7. Be direct; don't hide your persuasive intent.

Communication specialists Joan Sered Smith and Patricia Haddock recommend that sales speakers learn to pace themselves appropriately. Presenters who speak too quickly give the impression of being hurried or lacking confidence. Slow down and speak every sentence in such a way that it carries the appropriate meaning.[29] Smith and Haddock also recommend removing all vocalized pauses from one's speech patterns, such as "um," "ahhh," and the like. Vocalized pauses are annoying to listen to and indicate hesitation and a lack of confidence.[30] Practice removing vocalized pauses from daily conversation, which usually translates into similar reductions during formal presentations.

Michele Marchetti, a writer for *Sales & Marketing Management*, recommends using humor in sales presentations.[31] Using humor does not mean telling jokes, which are hard for noncomedians to deliver effectively. It means letting humor flow by recognizing and taking advantage of humorous situations during the presentation. If someone makes a humorous remark, laugh with the audience. Laugh at yourself if you bungle part of the presentation. Self-deprecating humor makes an audience more friendly as long as it does not go so far that it damages credibility. Marchetti also recommends using common experiences to establish a common bond with the audience.[32] Remind people that you have the same goals that they do and that your lives are not that different. Express sincere admiration for the people and products of the company. Finally, don't hide your intention to sell a product or service; make it clear what you want at the beginning and the end of the speech. Ask for the order when you close a sales presentation.

Structuring the Sales Presentation

Many consultants argue that the most persuasive sales presentations first arouse awareness of a problem, describe a need, or present a unsatisfactory situation, followed by a step that (through the use of the salesperson's product or service) resolves the problem, satisfies a need, or corrects an unsatisfactory situation. As you recall, this two-step process of creating and fulfilling a need is the basis of several patterns including the problem-solution structure and Monroe's Motivated Sequence. As such, these are ideal structures for many sales presentations. Of course, other structures can be equally useful in sales presentations. The N-A-R structure works by providing an engaging narrative at the beginning of the presentation and the refutations to inoculate clients against objections. The balance structure is useful for audiences who know the full history of the problem.

Another structure developed by your second author is the Make-a-Claim-and-Prove-It pattern. As the label suggests, each main idea in the sales presentation is a claim about the benefits of the product, and the claim is supported with inductive and deductive reasoning. For example:

I. Vuarnet sunglasses protect your eyes from the sun's radiation better than any other pair of glasses on the market.
   A. The sun emits large amounts of short wavelength or ultraviolet radiation.
   B. Ultraviolet rays damage the eyes faster than any other kind of light
      1. Exposure to ultraviolet light can cause temporary loss of vision, cataracts, and blindness.
      2. According to Richard Young, professor of anatomy at the University of California Medical School, we should, "choose glasses with the most ultraviolet protection."
      3. To protect our eyes against ultraviolet rays, the lenses of our sunglasses should cut off 380 nanometers of ultraviolet rays.
   C. Vuarnet sunglasses ranked higher than any other glasses in the amount of ultraviolet rays eliminated from the eyes.
      1. Researchers found that the Vuarnet eliminated up to 470 nanometers of ultraviolet light.
      2. This was 60 nanometers higher than the second best pair of glasses.
   {Internal Summary: As these independent assessments verify, Vuarnet glasses protect your eyes far better than any other pair of glasses on the market}

Notice how the main point of this example makes a bold statement about the product's superiority. The subpoints then demonstrate that superiority through extensive reasoning. The complete body of Make-a-Claim-and-Prove-It structure could look like this:

Introduction
Body
   I. First assertion about the product
      A. Support
      B. Support
   II. Second assertion about the product
      A. Support
      B. Support
   III. Third assertion about the product
      A. Support
      B. Support
Conclusion

To conclude, structure is a vital part of any sales presentation. Good structure is equated with the ability to lead an audience to the conclusion you desire.

Summary

Sales presentations are vital for many businesses and government agencies. To cultivate qualified prospects, ask questions prior to scheduling the presentation. Metaphors are a less overt means of adapting to prospects' needs. A metaphor is a figure of speech suggesting that one thing should be understood as if it were another thing. Metaphors provide insight into client perceptions, helping the salesperson tailor the product to those perceptions.

New visual aid technologies such as photo CD players, videotape, and overhead projectors are commonly used in sales presentations. Computerized multimedia aids are also common and may include background information on the product, competitive data, price lists, delivery schedules, product specifications, research statistics, spreadsheet data, and "live" testimonials from satisfied clients. Every visual aid should demonstrate the process or object in a unique way, improve information retention, and simplify complicated information.

Good visual aids do not lessen the need for strong content. Clear specific purpose statements are vital in selling contexts. Presentations should focus on the benefits of the product or service to the customer. Testimony from satisfied customers adds impact to a presentation. Stories are dramatic examples that arouse interest and sympathy in the audience. Metaphors can help the salesperson communicate the intangible elements of a product or service. Computers can tailor statistical data for each customer.

Building your organization's credibility creates a halo effect that engulfs the presenter. Salespeople need to reduce three common fears among clients: the fear that they will not get what they promised, the fear that they will pay too much, and the fear that others will criticize them for buying the product. Building credibility helps reduce the first fear. Solid refutation skills can overcome the second. Inoculating clients against objections helps reduce the third fear.

Enthusiastic delivery is vital for sales presentations. Good delivery is spontaneous in that it sounds as if the presentation is being given for the first time. Presenters should pace themselves properly and remove vocalized pauses from their speech patterns. Let humor flow by taking advantage of humorous situations or self-deprecating humor rather than telling jokes. The Make-a-Claim-and-Prove-It structure makes a series of claims and supports each with persuasive reasoning.

QUESTIONS FOR DISCUSSION

1. Whether it was an appeal to buy a car, take home a new washer and dryer, purchase the latest pair of Nikes, or buy something over the phone, everyone has heard sales presentations. Discuss with your class some of the sales pitches you have heard recently. Did you purchase or refuse to purchase the product or service? What was

the source of this purchasing decision? Were the visual aids and the delivery appropriate and persuasive? Did the salesperson effectively employ appeals to logic, credibility, and emotion? What would you have done to make the sales presentation stronger?

2. Think of the last time you heard a sales presentation and refused to buy the product or service. Could anything the salesperson said have induced you to buy this product or service? Were you a qualified candidate? Describe the specific things that make a prospect qualified. When is it best to cease sales attempts to unqualified prospects?

3. Think of a product or service that could be sold to members of your class. As a group, develop several objections to purchasing this product or service. Brainstorm possible refutation strategies to each of the objections. Which strategies will be the strongest for each objection? Why?

ACTIVITIES AND EXERCISES

1. Because advertising in the *The Wall Street Journal, Business Week,* and similar publications is targeted specifically for people in business, the appeals used are very similar to those in face-to-face or group sales presentations. Select three ads from a business publication that employ some form of metaphorical appeal. What perception is the company encouraging with the metaphor? Is this metaphor pleasing or attractive? Is the metaphor persuasive?

2. Review a business publication for advertising that employs appeals to logic, credibility, or emotion. Analyze the appeals to logic in the ad. What kind of inductive or deductive reasoning is used? Is it logical and persuasive? Does the ad make appeals based on credibility? If so, are these effective? Does the ad do anything to reduce the three fears of buying? What would you do to improve the persuasive appeals made in the ad?

3. Think about a product or service you can sell to fellow students in your class. The product can be as simple as a detergent or as elaborate as an automobile. Interview two other classmates using the need questions in Figure 11.1. Are your two prospects qualified to purchase this product or service? If the prospects are not qualified, are they close enough to justify continued sales attempts? Write your reasons for either pursuing or ceasing to pursue sales to these two prospects. When is it best to try and qualify prospects and when is it best to cut your losses and cease the sales attempt?

4. Conduct research, using consumer magazines and the Internet, on a product or service that you can sell. The product can be anything from a soft drink to a lawn mower as long as a large portion of your audience is qualified to purchase the product or service. Become familiar with the strengths and weaknesses of the product. Create a sales presentation that is clear, uses visual aids, and includes strong content, delivery, and structure.

5. Develop five objections to purchasing the product you decided to sell in question four (too expensive, don't have a need for it, more features than desired, etc.). Then, using information you acquired from consumer magazines and the Internet, develop refutations for each objection. Use the four techniques of denial, minimization, revealing inconsistencies, and turning the tables to refute the objections.

NOTES

1. Jeter, J., "Indianapolis May Have Found a Way to Turn Lead Into Gold," *The Washington Post,* 29 September 1997, National Weekly Edition.

2. Yarbrough, J. F., "Toughing It Out," *Sales & Marketing Management,* June 1996, 81–84.

3. Levinson, J. C., "Show Time: Creating Presentations That Pay Off." *Entrepreneur,* February 1997, 90.

4. Marchetti, M., "That's the Craziest Thing I Ever Heard," *Sales & Marketing Management,* November 1995, 77–78

5. Withey, J. J., and E. Panitz, "Face-to-Face Selling: Making It More Effective," *Industrial Marketing Management* 24 (1995): 245.

6. Ingram, T. N., C. H. Schwepker, Jr., and D. Hutson, "Why Salespeople Fail," *Industrial Marketing Management* 21 (1992): 225–230.

7. Kennedy, D., "Screen Test," *Entrepreneur,* August 1996, 84–87.

8. Boozer, R. W., D. C. Wyld, and J. Grant, "Using Metaphor to Create More Effective Sales Messages," *The Journal of Consumer Marketing* 8 (1991): 59–67.

9. Lakoff, G., and M. Johnson, *Metaphors We Live By* (Chicago: The University of Chicago Press, 1980), 4.

10. Koch, S., and S. Deetz, "Metaphor Analysis of Social Reality in Organizations," *Journal of Applied Communication Research* 9 (1981): 1–13.

11. Boozer, Wyld, and Grant, 62.

12. Mullich, J., "Polishing your 'image,'" *Business Marketing,* January 1993, 49, 52, & 54.

13. King, A., and K. Fischer, "Sales Videos Put You in Control," *Business Marketing,* August 1991, T10–T11.

14. Falvey, J., "Does Your Company Need First Aid for Its Visual Aids?" *Sales & Marketing Management,* July 1990, 97–99.

15. Mullich.

16. Trumfio, G., "The Future Is Now," *Sales & Marketing Management,* November 1994, 74–80.

17. Ibid.

18. Wiesendanger, B. "Are Your Salespeople A-V Junkies?" *Sales & Marketing Management,* August 1991, 58.

19. Falvey, 99.

20. Lukaszewski, J. E., "Bridging the Communication Gap," *Sales & Marketing Management,* August 1991, 62.

21. Gordon, J., "Making a Sales Presentation Work," *Sales & Marketing Management,* March 1992, 91–93.

22. Lukaszewski.

23. Ibid.

24. Bormann, E. G., "Symbolic Convergence: Organizational Communication and Culture," in *Communication and Organizations: An Interpretive Approach,* ed. L. L. Putnam and M. E. Pacanowsky (Beverly Hills, CA: Sage, 1983), 99–122.

25. Boozer, Wyld, and Grant.

26. Whalen, D. J., *I See What You Mean: Persuasive Business Communication* (Beverly Hills, CA: Sage, 1996).

27. Ibid.

28. Ibid.

29. Smith, J. S., and P. Haddock, "To Be More Authoritative—Hold Your Breath," *Sales & Marketing Management,* February 1990, 90–91.

30. Ibid.

31. Marchetti.

32. Ibid.

12 Risk Communication

According to William D. Ruckelshaus, former head of the U.S. Environmental Protection Agency, the American public and its elected representatives must eventually "abandon the impossible goal of perfect security and accept the responsibility for making difficult and painful choices."[1] In our increasingly complex society, the goal of perfect safety is impossible. Eating meat, sitting in front of a computer screen, living near a large manufacturing operation, rock climbing, driving, nuclear power, pollution, and the like, all entail a certain degree of risk.

In a society filled with risks, the science of risk assessment has developed to quantify the various tradeoffs people are forced to consider. To communicate the results of risk assessment studies, the field of risk communication has developed as a relatively new communication specialty in the larger fields of communication, public relations, and public administration. **Risk communication** is any communication about uncertain physical or environmental hazards.[2] As such, risk communication is practiced by people employed in large business firms, by regulators such as the Environmental Protection Agency (EPA), and by government agencies at all levels. For example, in a southeastern Minnesota city the development of a waste-to-energy incinerator was preceded by an extensive risk communication program.[3] In Los Angeles, the construction of an aeration tower to strip contaminates from the groundwater entailed public involvement to explain the risks and benefits of the proposal.[4] Even our small town, Pocatello,

Idaho, has recently experienced several examples of risk communication. Pollutants in the city's wells necessitated discussions about consequent health risks and possible solutions. Two manufacturing facilities in town held public meetings to explain the risks posed by the local Superfund site. Risk communication is a burgeoning new field, with many opportunities for people skilled in presenting complex technical information and in effectively leading small groups. Although it is impossible for a single chapter to make anyone an expert in the complexities of risk communication, this chapter provides an important foundation for future learning and practice. The best way to learn about risk communication is to participate as an interested member of the public. We therefore encourage you to involve yourself in risk communication in your community.

This chapter opens with an overview of the importance of risk communication in business and government. We then briefly explain the process of risk analysis, with an emphasis on its benefits and weaknesses. Third, we examine what leads audiences to fear some risks and ignore others. The fourth section covers the many credibility challenges that risk communicators must overcome during a risk campaign. Finally, we cover risk messages by defining the goals of risk communication and discussing specific strategies for successful informative and persuasive risk communication.

The Significance of Risk Communication in Business and Government

According to M. Granger Morgan, at Carnegie Mellon University, "Americans live longer and healthier lives today than at any time in their history. Yet they seem preoccupied with risks to health, safety and the environment."[5] Many industry and elected representatives believe the public suffers from a poor sense of perspective, forcing industry and government to spend billions to reduce minuscule hazards. We believe quite the opposite, that most peoples' concerns about risks are legitimate.

First, we are troubled about risks because many of the diseases we face are more frightening than ever. Dying from AIDS or cancer is neither painless nor pretty, and few have been able to avoid losing a family member or friend to one or the other disease. Even worse, medical science is often unaware of the exact cause of many dread diseases. Did a cancer death in your family stem from smoking, poor diet, pollution, radon gas, or a genetic predisposition for the disease? Not knowing precise causes only increases our fear.

Second, our fear of a hazard is amplified by the interconnection we all share as residents of this planet. Interdependence means that the actions taken in one time and place can have consequences to others at distant times and places. Thus, our risks are often increased or decreased without ever knowing about or having a voice in the decision, and this increases our concern.

Finally, the complex nature of technology isolates decision making among a small group of technically proficient people, closing the lay public out of choices that affect their lives. We fear that which we do not understand and resent technical elites who make decisions without our consent. All these factors, and many more, legitimately increase our fears.

The federal government recognizes these concerns and has tried to make itself more accountable to the public. For example, the "Community Right to Know" provision of Title III of the Superfund Amendments and Reauthorization Act of 1986 mandates increased communication among all parties affected by environmental risks. Congress continues to consider legislation that will change how risks are communicated to the public.[6] Risk communication efforts are almost never limited to the highest level of decision makers, but involve a variety of people at all levels, including public relations experts, health and safety engineers, environmental engineers, employee groups, technical writers, community advisory groups, and media producers. It is likely that, as professionals in industry and government, you will be involved in some form of risk communication during your career.

Although the definition of risk communication presented previously sounds simple, three factors make any communication about uncertain physical or environmental hazards very complicated. First, despite its foundation in the scientific discipline of risk assessment, risk communication is inherently value laden. A sophisticated risk analysis may be able to provide accurate estimates about the chances of a nuclear reactor meltdown, but no scientific risk analysis can answer the next question: Is the need for electrical power great enough and our concern about pollution from coal fired plants severe enough to justify building more nuclear power plants? While the scientific analysis of risk involves **questions of fact** (exactly how much risk does an activity present?), the act of deciding on which risks to embrace and which to avoid are **questions of value.** As we learned in Chapter 3, values are debated in political forums where people of different interests work out solutions to complex problems. Although risk communication uses the science of risk analysis as a starting point for debate, communication with the public cannot avoid concern for human values and choices.

Second, because it deals with values, risk communication is filled with **conflict.** People who do not share the same values will not agree on the risks to be approached or avoided. While secure employment is, for example, more important to some than the pollution exposure they and their family suffer from a manufacturing facility, others reject that risk out of hand. Some people gladly accept risks they control, such as smoking, but reject even minimal risks imposed on them by others, such as pollution. In fact, it is entirely possible that risk communication campaigns will increase rather than decrease conflict as community members state their divergent beliefs.

Finally, despite its tendency to create conflict, an open process of risk communication is still the most effective means of making complicated risk decisions. To remain democratic, our society must find ways to put technical information into the service of public choice. According to Marjorie G. Shovlin and Sandra S. Tanaka, employees of the Metropolitan Water District of Southern California,

"Public participation is the key to community acceptance of projects and positions. In order for people to support a project or position on an issue, they must be satisfied with the process by which the decision is made. This usually requires that the affected community have a voice in the decision-making process."[7] This does not, however, mean merely informing the public about a decision that has already been made. The "decide-announce-defend" approach of old-style risk communication is not sufficient for today's public. According to Peter Sandman, a noted expert in risk communication, community participation must come before the research stage, before the experts have assessed the risks, and certainly before any preferred solutions have been discussed. The public now expects a fair and open procedure for comparing options and for adding new ones. "This sort of genuine public participation is the moral right of the citizenry. It is also sound policy."[8] Sandman claims that when the public is involved, individuals show a surprising ability to master technical details and work their way through appropriate solutions. The next section explains the science of risk analysis.

The Scientific Process of Risk Analysis

Risk analysis is a relatively new science designed to provide quantitative estimates of the health and environmental risks posed by various hazardous substances and processes. According to M. Granger Morgan, "It is now possible to examine potential hazards in a rigorous, quantitative fashion and thus give people and their representatives facts on which to base essential personal and political decisions."[9] In this section we will explain the goal of risk analysis and then review the uncertainties always present in this science.

The Goals of Risk Analysis

Although it is beyond the scope of this chapter to explain the many intricacies of risk analysis, it's important that students of risk communication understand the goals that risk scientists pursue. Risk scientists attempt to quantitatively measure the risk posed by a particular hazard, or measure the costs or benefits of a specific risk.

Many risk studies assign a single number to the exposure level to a particular hazard and map the linear relationship between that exposure level and its consequences. For example, to describe the increased risk of cancer due to cigarette smoking, a scientist might set an exposure level of ten cigarettes a day and, after extensive study, conclude that this level of exposure increases the smoker's chances of contracting lung cancer by a factor of 25. A twenty-cigarette-a-day exposure level increases the chances of lung cancer by a factor of 50.2.[10]

Other studies analyze aggregate risks across large populations. The basic formula for calculating risk for a specific population is:

Potency of a particular hazard × the number of people in the affected population = risk

In 1996 the EPA concluded that if the nation could meet a stricter PM-2.5 standard of 15 micrograms per cubic meter of air (a 50 percent reduction from the current standard), it would produce the following results: 4,000 to 17,000 fewer premature deaths, and 63,000 fewer cases of chronic bronchitis.[11]

Finally, other forms of risk analysis examine the costs of reducing a risk. For example, while critiquing the EPA's proposed standards on ozone, The Center for the Study of American Business calculated that every dollar of benefit derived from ozone reduction provisions in the 1990 Clean Air Act costs consumers and taxpayers $3.30 to $5.10 in increased charges and regulatory expense.[12] Despite the apparent certainty in the results, risk analysis is always subject to a variety of constraints that make the conclusions less than definitive.

Risk Analysis as an Inexact Science

Although risk analysis has improved enormously in the past twenty years, it remains an inexact science. The sources of imperfect knowledge in risk analysis are numerous. To begin with, toxicity studies have not yet been done on a majority of industrial chemicals now in use in the United States. The financial resources do not exist to conduct all the studies that are needed. Second, once a study is initiated on a particular toxin, estimating exposure levels can be very difficult. Although measuring exposure in a laboratory is simple, exposure in the real world comes after toxins are diffused through the air, water, soil, and the food chain. The toxin comes into contact with other chemical compounds, where it may undergo physical and chemical transformations that may dilute the substance to unimportant proportions, make it inert, or combine to make the substance more dangerous. Additionally, once they enter the body, hazardous substances are altered by a series of chemical reactions that make a substance sometimes more dangerous and sometimes less dangerous. As a result, inferring exposure requires numerous assumptions on the part of the risk analyst.[13]

Third, estimating the probability of harm in a particular substance can be difficult. It is not easy to attribute a group of deaths or disease to a single cause. To make matters worse, many of today's hazards show up as ill effects only many years after exposure, which makes tracking extremely complicated. Finally, any estimates are complicated by the fact that toxic substances cannot be tested on humans. Scientists must rely instead on animals and computer models for their tests. Although there are various methods for making extrapolations from animal and computer data to inferences about human harm, each method includes a variety of assumptions, with various advantages and disadvantages.[14]

As a result of the problems just discussed, all risk assessments are characterized by substantial uncertainties. For example, "A study by the U.S. Nuclear Regulatory Commission estimated that the risk of a core meltdown at a nuclear power plant ranged between 1 chance in 10,000 and 1 chance in 1,000,000, depending on the assumptions that were made."[15]

The limitations of risk analysis pose an ethical dilemma for risk communicators. Should a speaker focus on the bottom-line conclusions of a risk study and omit a necessarily complicated discussion of limitations, or should the speaker cover a study's limitations even at the risk of confusing the audience and distracting them from important conclusions? The Ethics Brief in this section addresses this dilemma.

Finally, no matter how accurate a scientific analysis is, it cannot address the inevitable value and policy questions. Although scientists may conclude that it will cost the nation 23 billion dollars to reduce particulate emissions to a level at which 2,000 lives are saved, it is up to government leaders, industry, and the public to weigh the costs and benefits of the choice. Even if it were perfectly accurate, risk analysis is only the beginning of the process. In the next section we examine how audiences perceive various hazards.

Audience Perceptions of Risk

Risk managers and government officials often take a skeptical view of the public. The public, they say, is concerned about hazards that, according to mortality (death) and morbidity (disease) statistics, pose little real threat. On the other hand, the public ignores hazards that pose major risks.

At first glance, these concerns seem valid. For example, the EPA calculates that about 350 lives a year will be saved in Los Angeles if its new PM-2.5 standard is met, saving approximately one life per day. However, cigarette smoking kills over 350,000 people per year, and Los Angeles's share is about 12,000 deaths a year, or about 35 people a day. Obviously, smoking is a far more serious risk than airborne soot. In another example, *Consumer Reports* notes that people want the government to regulate pesticide residues on fruits and vegetables, which pose a minimal health risk, but most Americans haven't been persuaded to check for Radon gas in their basement, a hazard estimated to kill 14,000 people a year.[16]

However, the "experts" are wrong, because the public has a good sense of the magnitude of risk implied by various hazards. When people are asked to rank hazards by the number of people killed each year, they do so with remarkable accuracy.[17] However, when the question of managing risks comes up, a series of value choices serve to expand concerns beyond the number of illnesses and deaths that result. In this section we explain the perceptual issues that drive our level of concern about hazards. Understanding audience values makes it easier to predict concerns and tailor messages in risk campaigns for the greatest effect.

Researchers have discovered over twenty different factors that influence peoples' perception of risk.[18] Several of these factors are listed in Figure 12.1. If the hazard is perceived to involve factors on the left side of the figure, it will raise less concern than if it involves factors on the right side of the figure.

First, whether a hazard is **voluntarily** or **involuntarily** undertaken affects peoples' level of concern. We view even very hazardous activities such as mountain climbing, hang gliding, and smoking as less risky because they are done voluntarily, but we react with more concern to a hazardous waste dump in our community because we did not volunteer to live near the site. The next perceptual

Ethics Brief

As we described early in this chapter, risk analysis is an inexact science. Even the best study with the smallest margin of error and the most certain conclusions rests on a series of assumptions that are open to criticism. The temptation for many people in government or industry is to focus on the bottom line, omitting discussion of both how risk studies are conducted and the limitations of the scientific data. Many fear that such details will only confuse audiences, distracting them from bottom-line conclusions. Research indicates that succumbing to these temptations is both unethical and ineffective.

It's unethical to gloss over the technical complexities of risk assessments and their limitations. Democracy is based on helping people make informed choices, and risk communication is a field devoted to putting technology in service of democracy. The alternative is unattractive—technologically sophisticated people making judgments for others about the kinds of risk they will live with, the hazards they must accept or reject, and the technologies that will govern their lives. How would you like to be told that you are going to live near a potentially risky manufacturing operation, that you will have no say in the decision, but that experts (who, by the way, don't live near the facility) have deemed it safe and tell you your concerns are not supported by the data? When risk communicators gloss over the details and limitations of risk analysis, they are, in effect, taking decision authority away from an affected audience and reserving it for themselves. Risk communication should provide all the information audiences need to make informed decisions. It is unethical to tell people what risks they have to live with. It is equally unethical to appear to be giving people a choice, but covertly making a decision for them by withholding information.

In addition to being unethical, closed risk communication is less effective than open and complete risk communication. Most risk communication is conducted in an environment of competing interests and conflicting messages. If a communicator fails to cite the limitations of a study, it won't take long for a competing interest to hire its own scientists and make the omissions public. When uncertainties are exposed, the offending company or agency will lose credibility because it will appear as if they were covering up flaws in the study. Future messages won't be accepted, and the success of the effort will be jeopardized.

A Minnesota county learned this lesson the hard way. The plan for a waste-to-power incinerator passed all the appropriate permitting processes mandated by the state, and the county engaged in an extensive risk communication campaign with the public. However, that campaign did not discuss the minimal risks associated with the facility. When opposition to the incinerator did eventually arise, it focused on the project's potential risks. Because people hadn't heard about these risks, they concluded the county had acted deceptively, and this initiated strong resistance. Mary Anne Renz, who conducted a case study of the Minnesota incinerator incident writes:

> If the county had made the point from the beginning that the incinerator carried some degree of risk, the county could have had the upper hand. Not only would the issue have been debated on their ground, then, but also the element of openness implicit in an admission of risk would have added a perception of trustworthiness, creating a long-term gain in credibility."*

Although there is a temptation to gloss over scientific details and minor risks, this is an unethical and ineffective practice. Risk communicators should take pains to communicate the limitations of and be open about all the findings of risk studies.

*Renz, M. A., "Communicating About Environmental Risk: An Examination of a Minnesota County's Communication on Incineration," *Journal of Applied Communication Research,* 20 (1992): 9.

**FIGURE 12.1   Perceptual Factors Leading to
Different Degrees of Concern about Hazards**

Less Concern	More Concern
Voluntary	Involuntary
Control	No control
Natural	Unnatural
Familiar	Unfamiliar
Not memorable	Memorable
No dread	Dread
Fair	Unfair

factor is the degree of **control** over the activity. "People who hate to fly know perfectly well that it's among the safest forms of travel. The lack of control over the plane's mechanical upkeep and operation makes the small risk from flying feel intolerable to them."[19] However, people will happily accept a far higher risk of death or injury from automobiles because they have control over the vehicle's operation. Less control increases our concern about risk.

Referring again to Figure 12.1, **nature's** hazards are considered less risky than those created by humans. For example, although we want the government to control the use of industrially created pesticides on food, we ignore the far greater risks that natural toxins create in foods. In a similar vein, **familiar** hazards are of far less concern than the **unfamiliar.** The effluent from an obscure manufacturing process seems far more dangerous to us than the more concentrated exposure we get using household pesticides and herbicides.

A **memorable** accident, for example, the one at Three Mile Island, makes a hazard more vivid and easier to imagine than an event that is **not memorable,** such as daily pollution from wood stoves. **Dreaded** events create greater concern than events that imply **no dread.** The public's concern about recent ebola outbreaks rests mainly on the grotesque way the virus kills (massive internal hemorrhaging and external bleeding from every orifice), not on the number of people the disease kills. Such diseases as tuberculosis and flu kill far more people (by many orders of magnitude) than ebola.

Finally, **fairness** influences the degree of concern we feel. Do the people who bear the risks receive any of the benefit? If members of a community believe they bear the brunt of risks while a polluting company makes a large profit, concern over the pollution will increase. The converse is also true, and explains why small towns that benefit from a single plant for their livelihood are generally less concerned about pollution than would occur with the same plant in a city with many employers.

It's important to remember that the factors in Figure 12.1 are not irrationalities. The public's concerns are motivated by values greater than simple mortality statistics; and in a democratic society the public has a right inject these values in decisions. Whatever the goals of a risk campaign, they are easier to accomplish if the communicator understands the degree and source of audience concerns. But before we can address risk messages, it is important to consider credibility issues in risk communication.

Credibility and the Process of Risk Communication

Once a risk communication campaign is contemplated, credibility becomes both centrally important and highly problematic. Credibility is important because the goal of a risk campaign cannot be accomplished if the public doesn't trust the source. Several factors special to risk communication make credibility even more important than in mundane persuasive contexts.

Because the science of risk analysis is difficult to understand, the public will ignore details and make decisions based on source credibility. According to the National Research Council, "The reputation of the source, in terms of past record with regard to accuracy of content and legitimacy of the process by which it is developed, will be an important influence on the way recipients view particular messages."[20]

Although credibility is vital for risk communication, it is very difficult to achieve, for a variety of reasons. First, trust in almost all major institutions has declined since the 1960s. It is no secret that trust in major institutions—including the office of the president, Congress, labor unions, large corporations, the legal profession, the media, the armed forces, universities, churches, and the medical profession—declined from the mid-1960s to the mid-1980s.[21] Following the trend for other institutions, trust in science and technology has also declined, although not as precipitously. The cause of the decline for science could be related to unfulfilled expectations that world hunger, cancer, and AIDS might be solved, or to the environmental movement, which has successfully focused the public's attention on the ecological consequences of technology. As a result, the would-be risk communicator faces a credibility deficit. He or she probably represents a government or private institution that has less credibility than it did thirty years ago, and the science on which risk analysis is based is not only confusing, it may be distrusted.

A second credibility problem is created by conflict, which is inherent in the process. Almost all risk communication involves multiple parties and divided authority, where industry, federal regulators, and state and local authorities proffer multiple, often conflicting messages. The parties that create the most messages also have the most to gain by slanting information to suit their needs.[22] In these circumstances, it's difficult to identify reliable sources, and the credibility of all the competing parties is strained.

Although the challenges just described make it difficult to achieve high credibility, it is possible and vital for communicators to create adequate credibility. In this section we discuss ways to create and maintain individual, process, and institutional credibility.

Individual Credibility

The source of a message is an important context for building and maintaining credibility with an audience. As described in Chapter 11, individual credibility refers to an audience's perception of a speaker's competence, trustworthiness, and dynamism. Competence refers to the audience's assessment of the speaker's knowledge and expertise on the topic. Trustworthiness refers to the audience's estimate of the source's honesty, objectivity, fairness, and concern for the audience. **Dynamism** is the audience's perception of the speaker's energy, confidence, and enthusiasm. Figure 12.2 shows the factors that contribute to or detract from individual credibility.

If audiences detect hidden persuasive appeals, they will perceive the source as both untrustworthy and lacking in good will. Risk communicators should make their persuasive intentions clear to the audience from the beginning.[23] Of course, a source that is thought to be **objective** will be viewed as more trustworthy than a **biased** source. Slanting information to support organizational interests always hurts credibility and should be avoided. We do not mean to suggest, however, that complete objectivity is desirable or even possible in risk communication. The next factor in Figure 12.2, **fairness,** can compensate for bias. "Even if people are aware that the communicator has a vested interest in the issue and that s/he argues from a specific viewpoint, they may trust the message or develop confidence in the speaker provided that the information presented appears to be fair to potential counter-arguments and that it is presented with technical authority."[24] Credibility can be enhanced by addressing objections to the preferred position rather than making one-sided presentations. Risk messages that are structured

FIGURE 12.2   Factors that Lead to Positive or Negative Attributions of Individual Credibility

Positive	Negative
State persuasive intent (if any)	Hide persuasive intent
Objective content	Biased content
Fair to opposition viewpoints	Unfair to opposition viewpoints
Admit uncertainty	The absolute truth
Audience familiar with the source's education & experience	Audience unfamiliar with the source's education & experience
Liked	Not liked
Perceived similarity	Perceived differences
Citing sources	Vague or no sources
Clear and concise	Overly technical
Organized	Disorganized
Use of metaphors and similes	Literal presentation
Humor	Lacking humor

in ways to address objections, for example, the N-A-R structure or the balance structure are likely to improve the audience's perceptions of source trustworthiness and goodwill.

Admitting uncertainties in the risk analysis increases audience perceptions of source credibility. A speaker who adopts an attitude of informing the ignorant, correcting misinformation, and presenting the **absolute truth** diminishes credibility perceptions. Steven D. Perry, an environmental scientist based in Syracuse, New York, tells a story about attempts to site a low-level radioactive waste disposal facility in a community strongly opposed to the plan. At a meeting attended by several thousand citizens, a respected nuclear medicine researcher was scheduled to speak and "announced in a loud confrontational tone that he was there to tell the 'real truth' about LLRW risks. The audience responded with a roar of disapproval and disbelief, at which point the speaker shouted, 'If you don't want to hear the truth, then I won't say anything at all!' and stormed off the platform to the accompaniment of jeers and insults."[25] The audience was appalled by the speaker's display of arrogance. Years later, Perry reports, the state still has no site for storing low-level waste. Admitting uncertainty increases the audience's perception of source trustworthiness.

As mentioned in Chapter 10, when an audience believes that a source has **relevant education, credentials, and experience** with the topic at hand, this tends to increase perceptions of source competence. The source's credentials must be carefully presented so that they do not create psychological distance between the "all-knowing expert" and the "lowly, uneducated" audience members. This can be done by stating credentials matter-of-factly, with a sprinkling of humanizing information about the source's life, work, and family.

Looking again at Figure 12.2, research shows that **being liked** by an audience contributes to audience perceptions of trustworthiness.[26] Being liked involves being friendly, nice, and outwardly pleasant to others during meetings and presentations. The figure suggests that displaying **similarity** with the audience increases perceptions of source trustworthiness if the similarities are clearly related to the risk at hand. Unrelated similarities (we both like to go boating) contribute little or nothing to perceptions of trustworthiness.[27] To accomplish a relationship, risk communicators should clearly state the values and points on which they and the audience agree. For example, a statement such as, "I know that the fact that this change is being forced on you is of grave concern to many and I share that concern," helps to point out areas of similarity and improve credibility.

In terms of the content, **citing sources** increases the audience's perceptions of competence and trustworthiness, and specific citations increase credibility more than vague ones (e.g., many people argue that...).[28] In addition, messages that are **clear and concise** rather than complicated and technical improve audience perceptions of competence. **Organized** messages lead to greater perceptions of competence than **disorganized** messages. Use structures suggested in Chapter 7 and 10 to arrange written or oral presentations. Because **metaphors and similes** help listeners understand complicated risk data, their use improves perceptions of competence and trustworthiness over more **literal presentations.**[29]

Follow the instructions for the use of metaphors and similes in the chapter on technical presentations. Finally, the use of **humor,** if appropriate and not excessive, can lead to a small increase in audience belief about individual trustworthiness and dynamism.[30]

Process Credibility

The risk communication process is itself a source of increased or decreased credibility. Unlike source factors, however, **process credibility** factors are rarely in the hands of a single communicator; most risk campaigns are run by large institutions or government agencies that control the process. Nevertheless, if the process is to be considered credible it must be open and treat the public as an equal member of the decision-making team.

As you can see in Figure 12.3, there are three primary factors that influence the audience's perception of process credibility. Traditional risk communication uses the decide-announce-defend practice, wherein public input is not sought during the stages of problem definition, risk analysis, and decision making. The public becomes involved only after the solution is selected and then only to gather public reaction. According to Judy A. Shaw and Jeanne Herb, employees in the New Jersey Department of Environmental Protection, "A commitment to opening the decision-making process is vital. Although from a governmental agency's perspective this may appear to have the potential for making unsound decisions, case studies indicate that this is not necessarily true."[31] In fact, agencies have learned that **opening** the process pays off down the line in less public outrage and blocking.

Agencies have recognized that even minor lapses in openness can be disastrous. In Los Angeles, the Department of Water and Power decided to install air-stripping towers to remove TCE (trichlorethelene) that was contaminating about 50 percent of its wells. Risk assessments revealed that in the worst environmental conditions the cancer risk from the TCE off-gassing near the towers would be less than one in a million, assuming an uninterrupted seventy-year exposure—a very minimal risk. However, the community located near the site was not informed, and residents first learned of the project from a local newspaper article claiming that the project would spread toxins throughout the area. The damage to the

FIGURE 12.3   Factors Leading to Positive or Negative Evaluations of Process Credibility

Positive	Negative
Early and consistent openness	Closed (decide-announce-defend)
Remaining open to conflict	Stifling conflict
Allowing emotional expressions	Stifling emotional expressions

agency's credibility proved expensive. To minimize public concerns, the department installed scrubbers on the towers, increasing the project's cost by over 50 percent.[32] The public will have faith only in a project that involves them at the beginning, includes them consistently, and is open throughout.

Second, the process will be seen as credible only if **conflict is allowed** rather than suppressed. As we mentioned in the introduction to this chapter, risk communication is a process that increases rather than decreases conflict, at least in the short run. Attempting to stifle conflict by limiting access or suppressing opposition will backfire and cause the audience to question the process. Follow the guidelines in Chapter 5 for mediating various conflicts.

Finally, the process will seem more fair to people if they are allowed to talk in a language to which they are accustomed. For many people, this is the **language of emotion** rather than science. Risk communicators should not deny or rule out emotional expressions. Such statements as "We are only here to talk about the scientific facts of the matter" or "Unsupported emotional statements will not be allowed" serve to limit the public's ability to participate and reinforce the notion that individuals do not have a voice in the process unless they are scientists. Risk communicators should be prepared for personally directed emotional responses that may be insulting, or filled with invective. The goal is to turn these into clear positions on the issue at hand. Outlawing emotion is no solution and only makes people feel as if they are being shut out of the process.

Institutional Credibility

Finally, audiences will be more or less likely to accept risk messages based on the level of credibility they ascribe to the institutional source. The halo effect means that risk communicators fortunate enough to be working for a credible institution (in the eyes of the affected public) will see some of that credibility cover them and their messages. Of course, the opposite is also possible. The factors that contribute to **institutional credibility** are depicted in Figure 12.4.

The most important factor influencing institutional credibility is the audience's perception of the organization's policies. According to Peter Sandman, "Over the past several decades our society has reached a near-consensus that pollution is morally wrong—not just harmful or dangerous, not just worth prevent-

FIGURE 12.4   Factors Leading to Positive or Negative Evaluations of Institutional Credibility

Positive	Negative
Sound environmental policy	Unsound environmental policy
Consistent messages across time	Contradictory messages across time
Messages consistent with actions	Messages inconsistent with actions
Positive press or public relations	Negative press or public relations

ing where practical, but *wrong"*(emphasis in original).[33] A solid record of **pro-environmental attitudes and actions** will go a long way toward building credibility in the eyes of an affected public.

   Consistent messages from the organization also contribute to credibility. Changing or **contradictory messages** decrease audience perceptions of competence or trustworthiness. Referring again to Figure 12.4, messages need to be **consistent with actions.** Professing concerns for community health and the environment that are not backed by appropriate action results in intense outrage among affected audiences. Organizations must be ready to act on statements about both environmental clean-up and risk reduction with rapid and appropriate action.

   Credibility is centrally important because audiences will rely on assessments of individual, process, and, institutional credibility to make decisions. High credibility in these three contexts is likely to lead to greater acceptance of risk messages than will low credibility.

Creating Risk Messages

With an understanding of audience concerns and the various credibility factors, it is now possible to examine the goals of risk campaigns and learn ways to achieve these goals communicatively. Risk communicators must be perfectly clear about whether they are seeking private or public action. Asking for input about a new landfill or a waste incinerator, for example, involves **public debate and action.** On the other hand, attempts by a local health department to have people check their homes for radon gas or to get their children vaccinated are examples of **private action.** Whereas vigorous conflict and inconsistent messages from multiple sources are significant problems in public risk communication, overcoming apathy is a significant obstacle in private contexts.

   Be it public or private, risk communicators may have one or more **outcome goals** during a risk communication campaign. These outcome goals exist on a continuum ranging from attempts to decrease public or private concern about a risk, to remaining neutral and simply providing information about a risk, to increasing public or private concern about a risk. Figure 12.5 portrays these options on a continuum.

   In many cases, risk communication aims to **decrease public or private concern** about a risk; communicators explain the minimal extent of risks and calm fears. For example, a city's water department may wish to ease concerns about TCE contamination that is well within EPA limits. In the middle of the continuum a communicator presents the results of risk analysis studies **neutrally,**

FIGURE 12.5   Three Outcome Goals for Risk Communication

Decrease Concern	Neutral Information	Increase Concern

leaving the decisions to individual or public discretion. For example, a state regulatory agency contemplating stronger auto emission standards can clarify the benefits and costs of the new regulation, but leave the decision to citizens, voters, or elected officials. Finally, in some cases risk communicators want to **increase public or private concern** about various risks. For example, to increase the infant vaccination rate the local health agency may try to raise concerns about the return of such childhood diseases as polio, measles, or dyphtheria that can strike children. In this case, increasing concern may motivate private action. While providing neutral information is an **informative goal,** increasing or decreasing concern is a **persuasive goal.** It is, however, possible that a risk campaign may include two or more of the goals at different times. For example, early messages in a campaign may focus on neutral information, while later communication focuses on reducing concern among the now knowledgeable public. Let's examine the various methods of achieving both informative and persuasive goals in risk communication.

Katherine Rowan at Purdue University has created an excellent taxonomy of various goals, obstacles, and strategies for risk communication (see Figure 12.6). While goals 1 and 2 in Rowan's taxonomy are informative, 3 and 4 are persuasive.

Informative Risk Communication

Informative risk communication provides neutral information for its own sake or as a precursor to decreasing or increasing concern about a particular hazard. According to Rowan, two primary informative goals include **creating awareness** and **creating a deeper understanding** of risk (see Figure 12.6). Creating awareness alerts people to the existence of a potential hazard, which involves making messages detectable and decodable.

Detectable messages are **vivid or concrete,** and have some **surprise or startling elements** to them. For example, vividness is enhanced by demonstrating the information's effect on the receiver's life. Newspaper and television news reporters are skilled at finding ways to portray events vividly. For example, Idaho has one of the lowest childhood immunization rates in the country. A recent television news story portrayed a couple whose child came down with whooping cough and almost died. At the end of the story, the father implored the audience to have their children immunized or share the same near-death experience they faced. This story vividly demonstrated the risks involved in not immunizing children. Other ways to create a vivid message involve highlighting the surprising nature of the risk or finding startling statistics or stories to support the risk. Alerting people to risk also requires **brief** messages.

Creating awareness also requires **decodability**—meaning that a literate person is able to paraphrase the message easily.[34] Rowan recommends that, when referring to a hazardous substance by its technical name, a speaker should also relate that substance to the audience by **stating familiar products** made with the substance.[35] For example, "Liquefied phosphorus is a highly dangerous substance

FIGURE 12.6   A Summary of Goals, Obstacles, and Strategies in Risk Communication

---

Goal 1: Creating Awareness of Risk Information

Obstacle 1: Difficulties in Detecting a Message

Strategy 1: Make information psychologically vivid by emphasizing its effects on individuals, concretizing abstractions, giving many specifics about the nature and consequences of harms and benefits.

Strategy 2: Keep messages brief; highlight key elements.

Obstacle 2: Difficulties in Decoding a Technical Message

Strategy 1: In naming technical phenomena also describe familiar products they are associated with.

Strategy 2: Use simple, familiar language; keep sentences, words brief.

Goal 2: Creating or Deepening Understanding of Risk

Obstacle 1: Difficulty in Understanding a Word

Strategy 1: Define a word by its critical (always present) attributes.

Strategy 2: Give a range of examples and nonexamples (i.e., instances that people might think are examples but are not).

Strategy 3: Explain why examples and nonexamples have their respective statuses.

Obstacle 2: Difficulty in Envisioning a Structure or Process

Strategy 1: Use diagrams, analogies.

Strategy 2: Use devices to highlight text structure: titles, heading, preview statements, transitions, summaries.

Goal 3: Gaining Agreement

Obstacle 1: Disagreement about the Existence of a Condition

Strategy 1: Identify multiple signs of the condition's existence.

Strategy 2: Identify analogous situations in which similar signs lead to the same outcome.

Obstacle 2: Disagreement about the Condition's Likelihood or Severity

Strategy 1: Identify multiple signs of likelihood or severity or the lack of either.

Strategy 2: Describe ways in which these signs are already observable; or, question whether these signs are traceable to their supposed causes.

Strategy 3: Heighten perception of a condition's severity by emphasizing the risk's nature as involuntary, poorly understood, or as having capacity for irreparable damage.

Strategy 4: Minimize perception of risk's severity by emphasizing the risk's nature as voluntary, well understood, and as having capacity for minimal damage only.

(continued)

FIGURE 12.6   Continued

Strategy 5: If both risks and benefits exist, acknowledge both to avoid losing credibility.

Obstacle 3: Disagreement about the Best Solution

Strategy 1: Argue that problem is of a certain type and that all problems of this type require a certain solution.

Strategy 2: Argue that the solution allows the best balance of risks and benefits.

Strategy 3: Argue that the best solution meets the certain criteria and that a given solution most fully meets these criteria.

Goal 4: Motivating Action to Volunteer or Overcome Habit

Obstacle 1: Steps to Action Seem Unclear

Strategy 1: Urge a specific act, not a broad goal.

Obstacle 2: Action Seems Too Difficult, Expensive, Time-Consuming

Strategy 1: Make first step easy, not time-consuming, not expensive.

Obstacle 3: Doubt that One Person's Efforts Will Make a Difference

Strategy 1: Describe similar situations in which small acts of many individuals resulted in great success.

Adapted from Rowan, K. E., "Goals, Obstacles, and Strategies in Risk Communication: A Problem-Solving Approach to Improving Communication About Risks," *Journal of Applied Communication Research* 19 (1991): 300–329. Copyright by the National Communication Association, 1991. Used by permission of the publisher. The table omits "Strategy 1: Place information in familiar places, time slots," under Creating Awareness of Risk Information, and all the material under "Obstacle 3," under Creating Awareness of Risk Information. It also omits "Obstacle 3" under "Creating or Deepening Understanding of Risk," "Strategy 1: Account for an implausible notion by locating a broad, accepted belief that makes it seem reasonable," and "Obstacle 3" under Gaining Agreement. Finally, "Goal 4: Motivating Action in Emergencies," has also been eliminated.

that ignites on contact with air. However, when processed into phosphoric acid, it makes an excellent detergent additive and is also used in soda pop." Rowan also recommends using **simple, familiar language** for easy decoding.

Whereas awareness of risk is fine, if the public is to participate in decision making a deeper understanding of risk is needed. Goal 2 in Figure 12.6 suggests two obstacles to comprehending complicated risk information: difficult concepts, and difficult structures and processes. These obstacles should be familiar because they were explained in Chapter 9, on technical communication. Follow those guidelines when communicating technical information.

In addition to Rowen's obstacles, there are other unique constraints to creating a deeper understanding of risks. First, because probability statements are the foundation of most risk analysis, audiences must understand the nature of **probability.** Lay people often assume that probabilities change based on the previous occurrences of an event. Some believe, for example, that flipping a coin twenty times and getting heads every time increases the chance of tails on the next flip. Of course, this is incorrect; the chance of tails on the twenty-first flip are the same as in the previous twenty—50/50. Similarly, if a vessel containing ammonia is likely to rupture less than one time in 1,000 years of operation, some people mistakenly believe that every year that goes by without an accident increases the likelihood of a rupture. To help audience members understand probability, make analogies to everyday experiences of probability such as coin flipping, the weather forecast, and the stock market.[36]

In addition, because risk scientists believe the elimination of risk is an impossible goal, analysis is frequently couched in the form of **tradeoffs** in which the risks and benefits of various hazards are compared and contrasted. For example, it is useful to compare the risks of nuclear power with the risks of conventional power from coal-fired plants. Although conventional power eliminates the risk of radioactive releases and nuclear waste, it increases the risk of disease and death from airborne pollution and contributes greenhouse gases to the atmosphere. How can communicators help audiences understand the tradeoffs involved in a risk decision? Studies of risk campaigns in Germany and America suggest that referring to difficult tradeoffs people make in their everyday lives can help them understand the tradeoffs necessary in risk decisions. Consumers, for example, make a variety of tradeoffs when buying a car. Larger cars are safer, but they are more expensive to purchase and operate. Is the increased cost worth the added safety? Use everyday examples to help people understand the tradeoffs involved in risk analysis.[37]

Finally, **risk comparisons** are frequently employed to help people put various risks into perspective. For example, while miners have a four in 10,000 chance of dying in a mining accident annually, smokers have a two in 1,000 chance of dying from smoking annually. The comparison suggests that smoking is far more dangerous than mining. Another risk comparison calculates the chances of death from driving, flying, and living near a nuclear power plant. Your chances of dying in a motor vehicle accident are one in 4,000, in a plane accident one in 100,000, and in a nuclear reactor accident one in 5 billion.[38] Such comparisons can help a lay audience conceptualize risk by demonstrating relative dangers.

There are, however, a number of critical limitations to risk comparisons. First, it is important to remember that risk comparisons are limited by scientists' ability to model likely failures, to draw conclusions from low-level exposures or data derived from computer or animal experiments, or to understand synergistic and antagonistic effects of toxins.[39] It is important to fairly represent the uncertainties when presenting risk comparisons.

In addition, risk comparisons must be carefully made, based on similar rather than different activities and exposures. Comparisons of the risk of living near a nuclear power plant to that of suntanning, for example, appear patronizing to an audience. The activities are different in that suntanning is voluntary, and living near the power plant is not, and the catastrophic potential of the suntan is far less than that of the power plant (a tan can only kill one person at a time). The two also differ in terms of familiarity, personal control, and a host of other psychological factors mentioned earlier. Finally, unlike comparisons (referred to as false or inappropriate analogies in Chapter 10) can be insulting because they suggest that people who voluntarily engage in risk behavior, for example, sunbathing or smoking, surrender their rights to complain about other risks such as waste incinerators or nuclear power plants.[40]

When comparing risks, researchers in risk communication recommend the following: The best comparisons are those that evaluate the same risk at two different times (the cancer risk prior to TCE contamination and after TCE contamination) or relate the risk to a set standard (the contamination is well under the EPA's limit of ten parts per million). The next-best comparisons examine the risk of doing something as opposed to the risk of not doing anything, or an alternate solution (the risk that the incinerator poses versus the risk of siting a new landfill). The least desirable comparison is of two unrelated risks (nuclear power with driving during rush hour).[41]

Persuasive Risk Communication

Persuasive risk communication is very difficult to achieve. As previously mentioned, risk communicators from any institution have difficilty establishing credibility and campaigns are further jeopardized by risk campaigns that are typically filled with divergent interests and competing messages. Despite formidable obstacles, persuasion plays a vital role in risk communication. In Figure 12.6, persuasive communication involves Goal 3, **gaining agreement** about the existence and severity of a hazard and agreement about solutions to reduce the risk, and Goal 4, **motivating people to take action** to reduce a risk.

Under gaining agreement, three obstacles exist. First, parties to a risk campaign may disagree about the existence of a risk. Rowan suggests that risk communicators **identify multiple signs of the condition's existence** (argument from sign) and **identify analogous situations** (arguing from analogy) in which similar signs lead to the predicted outcome (see Figure 12.6). In towns where local health officials want people to test their homes for radon, they should point to the large number of homes that have tested positive for the hazardous gas.

In the second strategy, the risk communicator identifies similar radon exposures that have led to cancer. If reducing concern is the goal, the communicator identifies multiple signs that a hazard poses no significant risk and identifies analogous situations in which similar hazards produced no significant increase in disease or mortality. Electric companies, for example, can use studies that show no increase in leukemia for children living near high-voltage power lines as a sign that the lines are safe.

The second obstacle described by Rowan is a disagreement about a condition's likelihood or its severity. To overcome this disagreement, identify multiple signs of the likelihood or severity of the risk or the lack thereof. A community that wants to construct a waste-to-power incinerator should identify multiple examples of communities that have successfully installed this technology. In strategy 2, audience concerns can be increased by describing **signs that a risk is already causing problems** in the community, or by **denying that problems are caused by the risk** in question. This, of course, requires excellent causal reasoning, as described in Chapter 10.

In strategies 3 and 4, likelihood and severity can also be heightened or reduced by **emphasizing the perceptual factors** of the hazard identified in Figure 12.1. A communicator can, for example, heighten concern for the risk of radon by emphasizing its nature as involuntary, poorly understood, and having the capacity for dread diseases. Of course, communicators can also reduce concerns by educating people so the hazard is more familiar, by providing input into the process so they have more control, and so forth. In the case of a hazardous waste facility in North Carolina, the company's vice president made extensive efforts to involve the local community and continuously explained the nature of the hazards involved. This tended to increase the community's feeling of control, made the risks more familiar, reduced dread, and was more fair than if the company had made unilateral decisions.[42] These efforts reduced the community's concern about the site. Finally, in strategy 5, a speaker should **acknowledge both risks and benefits** to build credibility.

Another persuasive goal in risk communication is to **acquire agreement about the best solution.** In Figure 12.6 you can see three strategies to reach agreement. In the first strategy, the communicator argues that the problem is of a certain kind and **all problems of this type require a particular solution.** This form of reasoning represents the syllogism discussed in Chapter 10. The categorical syllogism uses a major premise to create a general category, the minor premise places the particular risk into that category, and the conclusion states that what is true of the major premise is true of the minor premise. For example, if TCE contamination levels exceed EPA standards, then the wells should be shut down. TCE contamination in three wells now exceeds EPA limits. The obvious conclusion is that the three wells should be closed down. The persuasive challenge is explaining the major premise to the group and then convincing them that the risk in question fits into that general category.

In the second strategy, a communicator **identifies and compares the risks and benefits of several solutions,** and the group selects the options with the greatest risk-to-benefit ratio. This is a conflict-prone form of risk persuasion because it is based on differing values over which costs and benefits to bear, who bears them, and so forth. Finally, **setting criteria for the best decision** means using the Reflective Thinking Sequence discussed in Chapter 5. In this process, leaders and citizens devise a series of criteria for the best solution and select the solution that meets most or all of the criteria. This, too, is difficult because multiple criteria will be debated, and it's likely that no single solution will meet all the criteria. Nevertheless, these are viable forms of persuasive risk communication.

Motivating action to volunteer or overcome a habit is a second form of persuasive risk communication. Rowen notes that such persuasion should **urge a specific action** rather than a general goal. For example, in the Great American Smoke Out, participants are encouraged to take a specific action (stop for a day) rather than a broad general goal, such as quitting altogether.[43] In addition, risk communicators need to do whatever is necessary to make action seem **easy, not time-consuming,** and **inexpensive,** and to **describe similar situations** in which the efforts of individuals acting alone have helped. For example, in Pocatello, the health department wants to discover the extent of radioactive slag in home foundations. To get people to test their homes, a brochure was created that uses clear, simple language to describe the testing process and the options homeowners have if radiation levels are found to be risky. A simple, one-page form allows someone to sign up for the test, which involves a quick walk-through by technicians with a Geiger counter. These efforts are designed to make the action clear and easy.

As you can see by the information in this section, risk communication messages, be they informative or persuasive, involve a complicated and conflict-prone process. It is doubtful one can enter a career in government, nonprofit advocacy, or business without needing to communicate with some group about risks.

Summary

Despite the fact that people live longer and healthier lives than at any time in the past, Americans are preoccupied by risk. As a result, risk communication has emerged as a means of exchanging information so the public is involved in democratic decision making about hazards.

The science of risk analysis provides quantitative estimates of the health and environmental risks posed by various hazards. Despite the advances made in risk analysis over the past twenty years, the results of this science are always inexact. The sources of imperfect knowledge include limited toxicity studies, estimating exposure levels after diffusion in the environment or the body, the difficulty of tracing results when effects occur years after exposure, and the inability to test toxins on humans. Despite its flaws, risk analysis is the only way to provide scientific judgment about relative risk.

Credibility is vital in risk communication campaigns because the public, lacking resources to adequately critique the results of a risk analysis, will rely on the reputation of the source to a greater extent than in other communication situations. Although vital to risk communication, the credibility of many institutions, including government, business, and science, has declined in recent years. Source credibility is the audience's perception of a speaker's competence, trustworthiness, and dynamism. The factors of source credibility are summarized in Figure 12.2. A credible process is created when the public is involved in the early rather than later stages of a project, when conflict is allowed rather than suppressed, and when the audience is allowed to express relevant emotions. Institutional credibility can be enhanced through sound environmental policies, consistent messages and actions across time, and positive press and public relations activities.

Risk communicators should decide whether they seek private behavior change or public debate. Communicators must also decide if they want to increase concerns, decrease concerns, or provide neutral information. Two primary informative goals include creating awareness of risk and deepening under-standing about that risk. Persuasive risk communication attempts to increase or decrease concern about a hazard. As such, it focuses on gaining agreement and motivating action.

QUESTIONS FOR DISCUSSION

1. What are the major risks in your community? What organizations or agencies communicate these risks to the public? Are messages aimed at changing private behavior or creating public dialogue? Are the messages primarily informative or persuasive? Are the persuasive messages trying to increase or decrease concern about the risk?

2. Think again about some of the important risks in your community. What agencies, organizations, or individuals are communicating these risks to the public? Use the credibility factors introduced in this chapter to analyze the relative credibility of the individuals, processes, and institutions involved in public communication. Are the risk messages in your community credible? Why or why not?

3. Throughout the chapter we emphasized that risk decisions always involve questions of value. The ongoing debate about automobile safety provides a case in point. According to scientific risk estimates, automobile travel is extremely risky, calculated as a one in 4,000 chance of dying annually. What to do about this problem, however, is a question of value.

   - Although seat belts were available in cars for years, few people buckled up.
   - Many states were then coerced into enacting seat-belt laws by the federal government's threat to withhold federal highway dollars from those states that refused.
   - State laws mandating seat-belt usage and expensive seat-belt campaigns eventually increased seat-belt usage in most states.
   - The introduction of airbags made cars safer but increased the cost of a new car.
   - Airbags have saved the lives of approximately 3,000 people but have been found to be dangerous to small adults and are estimated to have killed approximately thirty children.

   The position you take regarding each of the above statements implies a series of sometimes conflicting values. For example, the first statement implies that people who refused to wear seat belts value freedom of choice over safety. Discuss the values implied by each of the above statements or by your beliefs about them. Are these values consistent or are they contradictory? Which values should take priority? Why? Do your classmates agree with your prioritization?

ACTIVITIES AND EXERCISES

1. Your instructor may ask you to develop a risk presentation relevant to people in your community. Start by researching a relevant hazard in order to understand the kind of risk it poses. Analyze audience perceptions and decide whether individuals

are likely to be concerned or unconcerned about this risk. Decide whether your goal is private behavior or public debate. Decide whether your presentation should be informative or persuasive and apply the strategies depicted in Figure 12.6. Select an appropriate structure for the presentation and use solid evidence and reasoning throughout.

2. The following is an exercise in audience analysis. Using the factors of concern (voluntary, memorable, dread, etc.) shown in Figure 12.1, decide on the amount of concern each of the following three scenarios poses to an average audience. Which scenario is likely to pose the greatest concern to the public and which is likely to create the least concern? Why?

   a. The water department in Centerville has discovered various contaminants in three of twelve underground wells. The wells have been shut down because the contaminants are above EPA standards and are known to cause cancer. No contaminants have show up in the other nine wells, and provided the contaminants do not spread, the water department can provide adequate water for the city. The contamination is believed to be leaching into the groundwater from the local landfill. Because it is old, the landfill lacks the latest technology to prevent this kind of leaking.

   b. Fairfield is a town that is situated a hundred miles from a large nuclear research facility. The water for the town comes from an aquifer that passes under that nuclear station. Recent tests at the nuclear site have revealed trace levels of plutonium that was injected into the wells years ago when such practices were common. The plutonium is migrating toward the boundary of the site, although none has been detected past that boundary. Nevertheless, Fairfield residents are nervous because the aquifer is their only source of water. Although the site employs several thousand people, almost none live in Fairfield, and the residents gain almost no direct economic benefit from the site.

   c. Richfield Township, a suburban bedroom community next to a large city, often exceeds EPA maximum levels for ozone during the summer. Ozone is a by-product of automobile engines and becomes trapped close to the ground during hot, humid summer rush hours. Ozone produces short-term health effects such as wheezing, coughing, tightness in the chest, shortness of breath, and decreased lung function. The effects, however, are temporary and are usually eliminated by the body in less than twenty-four hours. Exposure can also be reduced by staying indoors or reducing exercise during rush hour.

3. In the section on persuasive risk messages, we noted that audience concern factors (voluntary, memorable, dread, etc.) can be used to increase or decrease concern about a risk. Imagine that your university or college is creating a campaign to encourage use of condoms. This requires increasing the audience's concerns about unprotected sex. Develop a brief list of arguments that use the audience concern factors to increase both concern about unprotected sex and condom use.

N O T E S

1. Ruckelshaus, W. D., "Risk, Science, and Democracy," *Science and Technology* 1 (1985): 31.

2. Renz, M A., "Communicating About Environmental Risk: An Examination of a Minnesota County's Communication on Incineration," *Journal of Applied Communication Research* 20 (1992): 1–18.

3. Ibid.

4. Shovlin, M. G., and S. S. Tanaka, "Risk Communication in Los Angeles: A Case Study," *Journal of the American Water Works Association*, November 1990, 40–44.

5. Morgan, M. G., "Risk Analysis and Management," *Scientific American*, July 1993, 32.

6. "Facing Our Fears," *Consumer Reports*, December 1996, 50–53.

7. Shovlin and Tanaka, 42.

8. Sandman, P. M., "Explaining Environmental Risk," Environmental Protection Agency, Document #0789, 20.

9. Morgan, 33.

10. Ibid.

11. Hopkins, T. D., "Proof? Who Needs Proof? We're the EPA!" *The Wall Street Journal,* 21 May 1997, A14.

12. Chilton, K. W., and S. Huebner, *Has the Battle Against Urban Smog Become 'Mission Impossible?'* (Washington University in St. Louis: Center for the Study of American Business, Policy Study Number 136, November 1996).

13. National Research Council, *Improving Risk Communication* (Washington, DC: National Academy Press, 1989).

14. Ibid.

15. Covello, V. T., "Risk Comparisons and Risk Communication: Issues and Problems in Comparing Health and Environmental Risks," in *Communicating Risks to the Public,* ed. R. E. Kasperson and P. J. M. Stallen (Boston: Kluwer Academic Publishers, 1991), 107.

16. "Facing Our Fears."

17. Ibid.

18. Sandman, P., Presentation to the Los Angeles Dept. of Water and Power (February 1989). Quoted in M. G. Shovlin and S. S. Tanaka, "Risk Communication in Los Angeles: A Case Study," *Journal of the American Water Works Association*, November 1990, 40–44.

19. "Facing Our Fears," 51.

20. National Research Council, 119

21. Renn, O., and D. Levine, "Credibility and Trust in Risk Communication," in *Communicating Risks to the Public,* ed. R. E. Kasperson and P. J. M. Stallen (Boston: Kluwer Academic Publishers, 1991), 175–218.

22. National Research Council.

23. Renn and Levine.

24. Ibid., 126.

25. Perry, S. D., "R_X for Risk Communication," *Civil Engineering,* August 1996, 62.

26. O'Keefe, D. J., *Persuasion: Theory and Research* (Newbury Park, CA: Sage, 1990).

27. Renn and Levine.

28. O'Keefe.

29. Renn and Levine.

30. O'Keefe.

31. Shaw, J. A., and J. Herb, "Risk Communication: An Avenue for Public Involvement," *Journal of the American Water Works Association*, October 1988, 44.

32. Shovlin and Tanaka.

33. Sandman, P. M., "Explaining Environmental Risk," 16.

34. Rowan, K. E., "Goals, Obstacles, and Strategies in Risk Communication: A Problem-Solving Approach to Improving Communication About Risks," *Journal of Applied Communication Research* 19 (1991): 300–329.

35. Rowan.

36. Renn, O., "Strategies of Risk Communication: Observations from Two Participatory Experiments," in *Communicating Risks to the Public,* ed. R. E. Kasperson and P. J. M. Stallen (Boston: Kluwer Academic Publishers, 1991), 457–481.

37. Ibid.

38. Covello.

39. Ibid.

40. Covello, V. T., P. Sandman, and P. Slovic, "Risk Communication, Risk Statistics, and Risk Comparisons" (paper presented to the Chemical Manufacturers Association, Washington, DC, 1988).
41. Ibid.
42. National Research Council.
43. Rowan.

CHAPTER

13 Crisis Communication

Any organization—be it an international conglomerate, medium-sized manufacturing firm, local government, government agency, or family business—is subject to crisis. The list of potential crises is daunting and includes terrorism, food poisoning, fraud, product recalls, hostile take-overs, employee injuries or deaths, environmental pollution, shootings at a plant, product liability lawsuits, and many others. Laurence Barton, a professor of management, defines an **organizational crisis** as "a major, unpredictable event that has potentially negative results. The event and its aftermath may significantly damage an organization and its employees, products, services, financial condition, and reputation."[1] Because the impacts of crisis are significant and the possibility of crisis is high in today's complex, interconnected world, this chapter covers communication strategies for organizational crises. We will do so by explaining the significance of crisis communication in modern organizations, describing the components of crisis communication, and the process of precrisis planning. The chapter then defines communication responses to organizational crisis, reviews ways these strategies can be employed for greatest effect, and closes with a discussion of structures for crisis communication.

Although the focus of this chapter is large—organization-threatening crises—the analysis methods and communication strategies we cover are also useful in less serious incidents, referred to as "problems" rather than crises. Problems could include minor accidents, employee injuries, small chemical spills, product liability complaints, and so forth, that do not threaten the organization's future, but still require effective responses. In addition, the methods and strategies described in this section are also useful for managers who need to restore their image inside the organization after a personal or team crisis or problem. In sum, although you may never plan for or manage a crisis in your organization, the material in this chapter is useful in a variety of other situations.

Before we begin, it is important to discuss the fundamental assumptions we hold about organizational crises. First, when crisis occurs, it is accepted that managers are responsible for two interdependent processes: crisis management and crisis communication. **Crisis management** focuses on solving the technical or human problems that precipitated the crisis. For a chemical company, a spill of several thousand gallons of ammonia would force managers to stop the leak, contain the spill, and clean up the affected site. If restaurant patrons contract food poisoning, management is responsible for identifying the source, contacting affected customers, disposing of the food in an appropriate manner, and preventing a recurrence. Because crisis management techniques differ for every industry, this chapter cannot provide specific crisis management advice. Instead, we offer suggestions for developing individualized plans for the most predictable crises.

Crisis communication, on the other hand, involves what the organization says to its employees, the media, the community, customers, suppliers, stockholders, and creditors during and after the crisis. Crisis communication has two primary goals: to protect affected publics and restore the organization's image. Thus, crisis communication includes the things the chemical company says to protect its employees, as well as how and when it notifies local, state, and federal emergency management agencies and the local community. Crisis communication also includes the things the organization says to explain the accident, and managers must do this in such a way that the organization's image is maintained or improved. These two goals are interdependent. If an organization does little to protect the public, the environment, and so forth, there is little that it can later do to restore its image.

A second assumption is that crisis communication depends on the audience. We have discussed the importance of audience beliefs and perceptions throughout this book, and the audience is no less important in crisis communication. Although from an organization's point of view, a minor chemical release may not represent a crisis, if an important audience (the community, local media, stockholders, consumers, etc.) sees a crisis, then a crisis exists. Although a company's management team may not believe it is responsible for a crisis, if an important audience does, then a crisis exists. Intel learned this in 1994 when problems cropped up in the Pentium microprocessor. A college professor (we're all trouble-makers) discovered that the chip made errors when performing complex mathematical calculations and he reported this to the company. "So confident was the company in its product that it reportedly gave the professor a polite brush-off. Turning to the Internet to see if others could confirm the problem he had encountered, he triggered an avalanche of some 10,000 messages…"[2] The media jumped into the fray and the result was a devastating flood of complaints to Intel. Although the error occurred only in extremely complicated calculations beyond the need of most users, and only 3 percent of affected consumers actually returned their chips, Intel made the mistake of assuming that a crisis is determined by objective measures of impact. Instead, problems can become crises because of the reaction of affected publics or the media. Understanding this principle is the beginning of good crisis communication.

The Significance of Crisis Communication in Business and the Professions

Because organizational crises have a severe effect on employees, products, services, and the financial condition of the organization, all managers should spend time preparing for crises. Look at Figure 13.1, which displays a selection of major crises to afflict organizations since 1982.

Organizational crises seem, from our point of view, both more frequent and more severe than they were thirty years ago. We believe this is true for several reasons. The increasing globalization of markets has forced business into more complex manufacturing, transportation, and financing arrangements than in the past. The increased complexity means that management errors or systemic breakdowns that could have been checked and limited to a single site or a small area can now reverberate throughout entire organizations and communities. These crises affect hundreds, perhaps even thousands of employees and people, costing millions of dollars. For example, in 1990, a simple filtering error caused the French company, Perrier, to recall 70 million bottles of water in the United States because traces of benzene were found in samples produced over a previous seven-month period. The recall cost 40 million dollars in lost sales, and Perrier's stock on the French market tumbled.[3]

Not only do complex manufacturing and global distribution processes increase the likelihood of crisis, the web of communication technology that now encircles the globe ensures that any major crisis will be widely reported. In the Intel case, the Internet served as a convenient rallying point for thousands of upset customers. In addition, print journalists are connected through modems and fax machines so that crisis information can be quickly and efficiently communicated to interested publics. Television can add vivid pictures to any depiction of organizational crisis. In 1986, the Chernobyl nuclear power plant exploded and released massive amounts of radiation into the air. Although the authorities of

FIGURE 13.1   Major Organizational Crises Since 1982

1. Tylenol pills are poisoned, resulting in seven deaths (1982).
2. Union Carbide disaster at Bhopal, India, kills over 2,000 (1984).
3. A. H. Robins files for Chapter 11 bankruptcy amidst lawsuits that its Dalkon IUD birth control device causes miscarriages and deaths (1985).
4. Morton Thiokol must explain its company's role in the explosion of the space shuttle *Challenger* (1986).
5. For a second time, Tylenol pills are poisoned, resulting in another death (1986).
6. Audi vehicles accelerate without explanation (1987).
7. The Park Service is accused of failing to prevent the massive Yellowstone Park Fires (1988).
8. Massive oil spill from the Exxon *Valdez* occurs along coast of Alaska (1989).
9. Veryfine products and other apple juice manufacturers face public scrutiny when the safety of using apples treated with the chemical alar is questioned (1989).
10. Traces of benzene found in Perrier water lead to a massive product recall (1990).
11. Sudafed capsules are tainted with cyanide, leading to two deaths (1991).
12. An interruption of long-distance telephone service blocks more than 5 million AT&T calls into and out of the New York area (1991).
13. Sears Auto Centers in California are accused of defrauding customers by performing unnecessary service and repairs (1992).
14. Dow Corning is targeted in an FDA probe that links its breast implants to cancer (1992).
15. NBC News is accused of ethical impropriety when it rigged a GM truck to blow up for footage in a *Dateline NBC* story (1993).
16. Consumers mount an Internet campaign against Intel for refusing to replace Pentium microprocessors that make occasional arithmetic mistakes (1994).
17. CBS News is accused of violating journalistic ethics when Connie Chung interviews Newt Gingrich's mother (1995).
18. The Army is rocked by scandal as five drill instructors in Maryland are charged with rape, forcible sodomy, and improper relations with female recruits (1996).
19. Texaco is accused of racism when audiotapes reveal upper management using derogatory language about minority employees (1996).
20. Reebok is embarrassed to learn that the name of its new line of women's shoes, the Incubus, represents a demonic figure that preys on sleeping women (1996).
21. ValueJet Airlines is grounded by a crash in the Everglades that critics charge was created by management policies that short-changed safety considerations (1996).
22. Employees at UPS go on strike, virtually halting deliveries throughout the nation and harming many small businesses (1997).
23. Nike is accused of being anti-Islamic when it uses a logo on its shoes that resembles the word "Allah" in Arabic (1997).

the former Soviet Union attempted to cover up the accident, despite their efforts, higher radiation levels were recorded in several European countries. Within a few days, international intelligence organizations and the press had exposed the problem to the world. As such, the Soviet Union was criticized not only for the crisis, but also for the attempted cover-up. Today, governments, multinational corporations, national manufacturers, and the family-owned business should spend time preparing for various crises.

In addition to greater interdependence, two public movements have made it next to impossible for organizations to hide disastrous events. The first involves government regulation. At the beginning of the twentieth century, U.S. business was largely unregulated. From 1909 until today, however, the government has exercised regulatory control through a variety of agencies, such as the USDA, the FAA, and the EPA, over many aspects of U.S. industry, including interstate trade, communication, food manufacturing, and pharmaceuticals.[4] These regulations came largely out of a populist desire to protect the citizenry from the excesses of large monopolies.

In the 1970s, the public also took an active interest in regulating organizations. Ralph Nadar, among others, organized a consumer movement that demanded higher quality, and safer, more thoroughly tested products from American business. As a result, the public began to influence the regulatory and reporting environment of U.S. business. The regulation of business was, in our opinion, necessary to eliminate the most destructive practices of unrestrained capitalism. The laws increased the reporting obligation for all organizations, meaning that any problematic situations or crises that occur must now be reported to local, state, and federal regulatory agencies.

The environmental movement, which also began in the late '60s and early '70s, is one of the most significant public movements of this century. Responding to years of hideous pollution from manufacturers, the environmental movement pressed organizations to consider the health of local populations, the local environment, and the long-term survivability of the planet in their manufacturing operations. As a result, even small organizational problems may become public knowledge and precipitate a crisis. Organizations must plan and prepare for crisis situations and must know what to say to affected publics in such situations.

Indeed, there is evidence that an increasingly large number of organizations are preparing plans for crisis management and communication. In a 1989 survey of 166 firms, over half reported having a crisis management plan in place.[5] However, the crisis plans seem to be concentrated in large organizations (over 10 billion dollars in sales) and midsize firms; those reporting between 100 million and 1 billion dollars in sales were significantly less likely to have a crisis management plan in place. The numbers decline even further when one considers smaller organizations.[6] Thus, despite the importance of crisis planning for all organizations, the message has reached only the largest companies. There is significant need for smaller firms to think about and prepare for potential crises.

Significant crises have severely tested managers at different organizations. Below are several examples of major organizational crises; some of these were

Global communications and marketing, combined with high technology manufacturing processes, have left organizations more vulnerable to crisis than ever before. Credit: Caryn Elliot

handled well by management, others not so well. We will refer to several of these examples throughout the rest of the chapter.

McNeil, a subsidiary of Johnson & Johnson, produced an extraordinarily successful pain reliever called Tylenol, which captured 37 percent of the nonprescription pain reliever market. On September 29, 1982, seven people in the Chicago area died when they ingested cyanide-laced Extra-Strength Tylenol capsules. Apparently, someone was able to remove bottles from store shelves, take apart the capsules, insert a lethal dose of cyanide, and replace the bottles without the knowledge of store employees. Victims did not notice anything unusual in the deadly capsules they were about to ingest. Within two weeks of the tragedy, 99 percent of the public became aware of the poisonings through the media.[7] As a result, Tylenol's position in the market fell from 37 percent to 12 percent and experts were predicting the company's demise. Four years later, in 1986, a second poisoning incident took place in Yonkers, New York, when a twenty-three-year-old woman was killed. No arrests have ever been made.

Johnson & Johnson's response to the crisis included several features. As soon as they were notified of the tainted capsules, the company suspended all Tylenol advertising and recalled 93,000 bottles from across the country. They established numerous communication ties with consumers through 800 numbers, as well as print and electronic media.[8] Johnson & Johnson executives appeared on a variety of television shows, from *Nightline* to *Today*. In response to the tampering, the company announced new triple-safety-seal packaging for Tylenol capsules and made free coupon offers. McNeil officials argued that a disgruntled employee could not have tampered with the product because the poisoned bottles came from plants in both Puerto Rico and Pennsylvania. In addition, it is very unlikely that, had poison been inserted at the two plants, those bottles would have ended up in several stores in one Chicago suburb. The location suggested that someone tampered with the product after it was on store shelves. Thus, the company blamed the incident on a madman intent on randomly killing innocent people. The FDA agreed with this reasoning. Soon after the incident, Tylenol regained an amazing 93 percent of its original market share.[9]

In the second Tylenol poisoning incident, the killer was able to defeat the three safety seals added to the Tylenol bottle. Subsequently, Johnson and Johnson decided to drop the manufacture of Extra-Strength Tylenol capsules in favor of caplets—solid, white pills that cannot be separated and would discolor if coated with a foreign substance.

For another model of crisis management and communication we turn to the Exxon *Valdez* oil spill, which occurred on March 24, 1989. The spill was caused when the *Valdez* struck a reef in Prince William Sound, Alaska, releasing 240,000 barrels (11 million gallons) of crude oil into the water, creating a slick the size of Rhode Island that threatened more than 600 miles of coastline.[10] Later, the public learned that the ship's captain, Joseph Hazelwood, was drunk at the time, ordered the ship put on autopilot, set a risky course, and left the bridge in the hands of a relatively inexperienced third mate. Exxon's first job was crisis management: cleaning up the spilled oil. But scientists and the media reported that Exxon was poorly prepared to handle the disaster. Supplies of dispersants were inadequate to the task, and equipment that was supposed to be available for such emergencies was missing. These revelations suggested that Exxon's crisis management plan was inefficient and lethargic.[11] In addition, Exxon sent a succession of lower-rank executives to Alaska to handle the problem. The company's CEO, L. G. Rawl, did not make his first comments about the incident until six days after the spill.[12] To sum up, Exxon failed to exercise visible, high-level leadership in managing the crisis.

Exxon attempted to shift the blame for the incident by scapegoating the captain. Later, however, it was reported that Exxon knew the captain had gone through an alcohol rehabilitation program but still put him in command of the *Valdez*. Exxon also blamed state and Coast Guard officials for not giving immediate authorization for clean-up operations to commence.[13] Finally, Exxon made unrealistic pledges to restore the fouled beaches of the Sound. When it became apparent that this would not be possible, the company was chastised for backing away from its promises.[14] Rather than helping to restore its image, these responses further hurt Exxon in the eyes of the public. Stockholders criticized Exxon's handling of the situation, consumers boycotted the company, and Exxon became the butt of jokes among the public.

In 1992, Sears auto repair shops were accused of performing unnecessary repairs. After a rise in customer complaints, the California Department of Consumer Affairs conducted a two-part investigation of the company. In the first phase, undercover agents took older cars to Sears auto repair centers with a spe-cific problem, but no other mechanical difficulties. The department found that Sears consistently replaced additional components that were not worn or dam-aged in the test cars. The agents were overcharged 90 percent of the time.[15] The Department notified Sears of their results and, in a follow-up investigation sev-eral months later, found that although the pattern of overcharging had dimin-ished, it continued 70 percent of the time. The Department of Consumer Affairs director, Jim Conran, went public with his allegation in June of 1992. He charged that the test cars represented a consistent pattern motivated by Sears's imposition of sales quotas on autoshop managers. By slashing hourly wages in favor of sales commissions, setting sales quotas, and sponsoring sales contests, Sears, the Department charged, had encouraged managers to sell parts and services whether they were needed or not.[16] One Sears mechanic said "he was recently instructed to sell $147 worth of parts and services per hour."[17]

According to William Benoit, Sears's early crisis communication strategy focused on denying the problem, and only later announced corrective action. Despite promises of correction, Sears never apologized for the incident. Sears chose to deny the charges through a California attorney rather than a corporate executive, which made the company look evasive. Sears's attempt at crisis com-munication was only minimally successful.[18]

In yet another major incident, on September 17, 1991, AT&T experienced an interruption of long-distance service that blocked more than five million calls into and out of the greater New York City area. This was worse than an inconve-nience: Because air traffic control depends on phone lines, all air service into and out of the New York metro area was halted. The shutdown occurred because AT&T had agreed to supply power for its New York City long-distance switching plant from its own generators to relieve peak demand on Consolidated Edison. When generators malfunctioned, the plant automatically switched over to battery power, which provided energy for about six hours. Alarms that notify workers that the plant was on battery support went unnoticed, and the system collapsed for want of power.[19] The shutdown affected airports as far west as Chicago and produced numerous problems in the eastern hubs of Boston, Philadelphia, and Washington, D.C. The breakdown also diminished the margin of safety for planes flying through the region. It is an excellent example of how increased interdepen-dence has the effect of spreading a crisis far beyond its point of origination. Rival phone services MCI and Sprint took out advertisements suggesting that AT&T was unreliable.[20]

Initially, AT&T blamed its employees and lower-level union workers at one of its plants for not noticing the battery alarms. However, the Communication Workers of America Union quickly refuted this attempt to move the blame. They said that the audio alarms did not go off because they were not working properly, and visual alarms were hidden behind recently installed equipment. They also blamed the problem on staff reductions that left the plant with fewer trained workers, while experienced workers were at a mandatory training session, ironi-cally, to learn about a new computerized alarm system. After hearing this response, AT&T changed strategies. In full-page newspaper advertisements in the *New York Times* and *The Wall Street Journal,* AT&T apologized for the error, promised to fix the problem, and announced a comprehensive review of all facilities, policies, and maintenance measures.[21] This effort (see Figure 13.2) worked. Soon after, competitor ads accusing AT&T of poor service ceased. As these examples suggest, the need for both crisis management and crisis communication skills is increasing in today's complex organizational environment.

The Components of Crisis Communication

Effective crisis communication involves several components. First, a crisis management team must be formed within the organization. Their job is to engage in precrisis planning to create a crisis management plan for the organization. This written plan details the kinds of crises the organization is most likely to face and develops management and communication plans for each individual crisis. In the next section we will explain how to form an effective crisis management team and discuss the precrisis planning process.

In the major section in this chapter, entitled "Communication Responses" we will cover a typology of image restoration strategies that organizations may use to restore their credibility during a crisis. These strategies form the core of crisis communication. In this work we are indebted to the efforts of William Benoit and his colleagues at the University of Missouri for their pioneering theory of image restoration. Finally, we will provide a series of guidelines for effective crisis communication, and we will help you format a crisis briefing presentation. By the end of this chapter we hope that you will be better prepared to think about and plan for organizational crisis, respond appropriately to various publics, and be able to manage crises in such a way that affected publics are protected and the company's image is restored.

Forming a Crisis Management Team and Precrisis Planning

Forming a crisis management team and precrisis planning involve several important steps and processes. Because this chapter focuses on crisis communication, our discussion of precrisis planning will be brief, focusing on three processes: forming a crisis team, reviewing and rehearsing crisis responses in advance, and formalizing these into a written implementation plan.

A **crisis team** is the group responsible for both precrisis planning and crisis management and communication during an actual emergency. In a large or mid-sized firm the crisis team should include several senior administrators such as the CEO, the chief financial officer, or various directors or upper-level managers. This is necessary so that the appropriate information and authority will be included in the plan. In addition, Laurence Barton recommends that operations managers be

"Apologies are not enough."

"I am deeply disturbed that AT&T was responsible for a disruption in communications service that not only affected our customers but also stranded and inconvenienced thousands of airline passengers. I apologize to all of you who were affected, directly or indirectly.

Apologies, of course, are not enough. We have identified the cause as a combination of mechanical and human failures. And, most regrettably, management practices were not followed that would have prevented the problem from affecting the public.

We have already taken corrective and preventive action at the affected facility. But the issue is a broader one. That's why I have directed a thorough examination of all of our facilities and practices, from the ground up. Perfect service continuity is our goal.

Through billions of dollars of investment and the skilled work of AT&T people, we have designed and built our systems to the world's highest standards. No communications systems have more backup or alternate routing. And we plan to spend billions more over the next few years to make them even more reliable.

I am also committed to working closely with government officials to satisfy concerns about the need for communications backup in situations that affect the public's welfare.

This is not a simple issue, though, because the depth of our technology and the breadth of our capabilities can't be backed up by anyone else in the marketplace. Ultimately, we have to be able to provide the certainty of service that is its own safety net. And we will.

We feel a deep sense of obligation not only to our customers, but to the public at large. The recent disruption underscored a fundamental truth: our services have a crucial impact across the economy, across society. They affect people's work and personal lives, in the most critical ways.

We built our business, in a far simpler day, on an unyielding ethic of service. With the incredible volume of communications handled by today's systems and with people so deeply dependent on communications, we know that service ethic is more important than ever.

I have great confidence in AT&T people. They have always set us apart from the competition and been the cornerstone of our customers' trust in us. You can count on our people's commitment to service to drive the management of this business more than ever in the years ahead."

R.E. Allen

Robert E. Allen, Chairman

FIGURE 13.2   Sample Image Restoration Advertisement from AT&T
Courtesy: AT&T

included because these people understand the manufacturing and technical aspects of the organization. The crisis team should include public and/or government relations employees who can anticipate and respond to the media, the public, and government agencies. In addition, the crisis team should include any individuals responsible for environmental, health, or safety engineering. People responsible for sales and investor relations can also provide valuable input to crisis planning and management. Finally, the crisis team should include legal counsel.[22] The individuals who form the crisis team and engage in crisis planning should also be the central management team during an actual crisis.

Once the team is formed, they must create a **crisis management plan** (CMP). The CMP is a written document that (1) anticipates the most predictable crises that could afflict the organization, and (2) plots management and communication responses. Developing the CMP involves two primary steps. First, the team should brainstorm a list of potential crises that could affect the organization. Norman R. Augustine, president of Lockheed Martin Corporation, recommends that organizations plan for crises that are both within and outside of their control. He states that simply because an organization can't predict or prevent the crisis "does not exempt you from living with its consequences."[23] However, because an organization cannot prepare for all fathomable crises on their brainstormed list, the team must focus on those that are more likely to occur and eliminate from the list the less likely crises.[24]

After the list has been narrowed, the crisis management team develops a written plan of crisis management and crisis communication for each disaster on the short list. This written document can be organized in a number of ways, but Barton suggests that the following information be included: The CMP should include an introduction and a brief letter from the president of the corporation encouraging or mandating that employees read the plan. The CMP should also include the names, phone numbers, fax numbers, and Internet addresses for all members of the crisis team. This section should also include the names of the people that are in charge during different crises and clarify who has authority in each situation. In another section, the team should include information about the appropriate community leaders, media outlets, and government agencies that need to be contacted in emergencies. This section should include updated phone, fax, and Internet information and the like for immediate use by employees in a crisis.

Barton suggests that the next section include crisis assessment, wherein the various crises on the team's short list are discussed. For each type of crisis, a series of crisis management and communication action plans should be detailed. Although the specifics of each crisis are different and cannot be anticipated, the team can suggest general actions for specific types of emergencies. For example, if an industrial accident involves employee injuries or fatalities, the crisis plan should specify how and when employee families are notified. Suggestions for how information will be communicated to the public can also be included in this section of the CMP.

Next, a media relations contact sheet must be included that has updated contact information for relevant media outlets. This section should also detail who handles the media and the preferred communication outlets for each crisis. Press releases, press kits, and news conferences are three typical ways of dealing with the media. A press release is a printed statement, faxed or e-mailed to media organizations, that details the nature of the crisis and the organization's responses. According to Barton, during a prolonged crisis, like the Tylenol tampering incident, several press releases each day may be issued. Press kits are packets of important background information about the company that may be sent along with a press release or prepared for the press when they attend a news conference. These may include fact sheets on key executives and the organization, data on the corporation and its history, and names and phone numbers for press contacts. "The preparation time involved in the generation of a press kit can be considerable, so many leading companies keep a 'boilerplate' press kit with essential corporate data that is already packaged and ready in boxes for distribution in case of emergency."[25] News conferences assure that representatives of the media get timely information from an appointed company spokesperson. The crisis briefing exercise in this chapter simulates a news conference wherein students act as organizational representatives responding to a crisis. In addition, many organizations set up 800 numbers so the public can contact the organization directly. Others use newspaper and television advertising to get their point across during or immediately following a crisis. The crisis plan should clarify, for each type of crisis, the types of media that should be used to communicate with the public and specify the employees in charge of public communication.

Finally, Barton recommends that financial and legal ramifications and options for specific crises be included in the CMP. Information may include how to reach consumers, how to temporarily suspend trading of a firm's stock, how to address stockholders quickly, or the various liabilities the organization has for each particular crisis.[26] In the next section we will examine crisis communication strategies.

Communication Responses to Organizational Crisis

Although management researchers such as Laurence Barton provide excellent advice for precrisis planning and crisis management, surprisingly little management scholarship has been devoted to crisis communication. Fortunately, in the communication discipline, several individuals have devoted themselves to understanding the effective use of crisis communication. This section will discuss the importance of maintaining a favorable image during a crisis and then list and exemplify William Benoit's typology of image restoration strategies.

Let's start our discussion by reviewing the importance of credibility to any communication event, either individual or organizational. In Chapter 10 we emphasized the importance of favorable credibility to a communicator's persuasive efforts. Credibility is also important for organizations. No employee wants to believe he or she works for a deceptive or failed organization that is responsible for environmental degradation or personal injury. These feelings diminish employee satisfaction. As a result, organizations spend millions on internal communication, part of which is devoted to building the credibility of the organization in the eyes of its employees. Image or credibility is even more important outside the organization. Organizations must have credibility in the eyes of various publics such as the local community, investors, customers, and stockholders. A tarnished image imperils an organization's ability to influence the surrounding environment. Thus, organizations spend millions on public relations campaigns for various audiences. For all the reasons we mentioned in the introduction to this chapter, organizations are prone to problems and crises that leave them open to attack. Because image is important, most organizations are compelled to respond to attacks.

Crisis communication strategies are messages that help restore an organization's tarnished image. The strategies we will discuss fall into the five general categories depicted in Figure 13.3.

The crisis communication strategies in Figure 13.3 should be applied with two primary goals in mind. The first and most important goal for managers is to do whatever is necessary to alleviate the human suffering or environmental harm caused by the crisis. If the organization is focused on managerial interests to the exclusion of the affected publics then it deserves all the derision that can (and probably will) be heaped on it. If for no other reason than self-interest, organizations should accept their responsibility to the public and act accordingly. Second, as the organization succeeds in the first goal it can then look to its own survival, which involves restoring its credibility in the eyes of various publics. Look at the Ethics Brief in this chapter for more information on the ethical responsibilities of organizations in crisis. We will now describe and explain the image restoration strategies in detail.

Denial

When using **denial,** the organization does not acknowledge performing a wrongful act or denies that a wrongful act occurred. For example, when Sears was accused of overcharging customers, it issued strong denials in response to the accusations. In various statements, Sears said that all employees involved in the controversial repairs were interviewed and the company was satisfied that there was no wrongdoing.[27] If this strategy is accepted by the audience, it should help restore the organization's image during the crisis. Denial strategies may take one of two forms.

In **simple denial,** the organization issues statements indicating either that no crisis has taken place or that the organization is not responsible for the crisis. In the early stages of the breast implant crisis (see Figure 13.1), Dow Corning released documents demonstrating that implants do not increase the risk of breast cancer.[28]

FIGURE 13.3   A Typology of Crisis Communication Strategies

Denial: Denies performing an act that precipitated the crisis or denies that a crisis occurred.

Simple Denial: Denies that a crisis happened, or denies that the organization is responsible.

Shifting the Blame: Provides a different target for the audience by applying blame to another party.

Evading of Responsibility: Evading or minimizing the organization's responsibility for the crisis.

Provocation: A crisis-precipitating act was performed in response to another wrongful act.

Defeasibility: The organization lacked information about or control over factors that precipitated the crisis.

Accident: Reducing the organization's responsibility for the crisis by appealing to factors that can't be controlled.

Good Intentions: Claim that the crisis was precipitated by actions that were done with good intent.

Reducing Offensiveness: Reducing the degree of ill or harm that various audiences experience because of the crisis.

Bolstering: Relating positive attributes of the organization that might mitigate the negative consequences of the crisis.

Minimization: Reminding an audience that the effects of the crisis are not as harmful or widespread as they might appear.

Differentiation: Distinguishing some acts from other similar, but less desirable acts.

Transcendence: Placing the crisis in a different context that directs attention to higher, more important values.

Attack the Accuser: Reducing the credibility of the source of an accusation.

Compensation: Remuneration to crisis victims to counterbalance the negative effects of the crisis.

Corrective Action: Vow to restore the situation to the state it was before the crisis or to prevent recurrence of the crisis.

Mortification: Admit responsibility for the crisis and ask forgiveness.

Ethics Brief

Crisis communication is a special form of persuasive communication. As we stated earlier in this chapter, the two primary goals of crisis communication involve protecting the health and well-being of affected publics and restoring the image of the organization. It is important to consider both ethics and effectiveness issues when involved in any form of persuasive communication. This is especially true in crisis communication.

What constitutes ethical crisis communication? Crisis communication strategies must meet several goals to be considered ethical. First, ethical crisis communication protects the health and well-being of affected publics. To fail at this is to fail at one's responsibility as an employer and member of your community. After that, ethical crisis communication persuades using evidence and logic, rather than appeals to ignorance or emotion. Finally, ethical communication is true to the facts as organizational members know them. It is unethical, for example, to try to blame others for a crisis that is your fault or to inappropriately minimize the harm of a very serious crisis. Thus, ethical crisis communication helps others affected by the crisis and makes an honest attempt to explain the crisis to the public.

What is effective crisis communication? Simply put, effective communication improves the organization's image during or after the crisis. This may be done to a greater or lesser degree, depending on the severity of the crisis. In most cases, ethical and effective crisis communication strategies are closely linked. By this we mean that the most ethical strategies are also the most effective strategies for improving the organization's image. Unethical strategies that do not protect the public and do not argue from the truth pose a double danger to the organization. If and when such things are exposed, the organization suffers not only for having precipitated the crisis, but also for lying or distorting information. The reason for the close connection between ethical and effective strategies is that, in most crises, the media, government regulatory agencies, and the public are watching the organization closely. Therefore, if the organization fails to protect affected publics or if its communication strategies are based on half-truths and distortions, it is likely that the public will be made aware of these indiscretions. Once that occurs, the organization's attempts at image restoration will have suffered a serious, if not fatal, blow. Thus, the scrutiny that organizations receive during crisis means that ethical communication strategies are also the most effective communication strategies.

Unfortunately, many examples in this chapter illustrate that the simple connection between ethical and effective communication eludes many managers in a crisis. For reasons that involve both personal embarrassment and legal liability for the organization, managers are reluctant to admit responsibility for a crisis and have engaged in numerous unethical approaches that later backfire. Perhaps it is human nature that encourages us to diminish, cover up, and distort the facts surrounding a crisis in order to minimize blame. Issues of legal liability are also involved. An open admission of guilt and an expression of remorse can lead to huge lawsuits. Perhaps managers are hoping that by using less than ethical strategies they can avoid short-term pain and, if the strategy is effective, accrue long-term benefits as well. Such rationalizations may be common in the heat of crisis.

Since there seems to be a lot of pressure on managers to try to have it both ways during a crisis, we suggest the following ethical guidelines. First, if you find yourself managing an organization's response to a crisis, you must avoid being trapped by the belief

(continued)

Continued

that unethical practices will produce a gain. Remind yourself of the inherent connection between ethical and effective communication during a crisis. Second, because the connection between ethical and effective communication in a crisis might elude other members of your crisis team, you must constantly remind people that the best, the safest, the most effective (for the organization) responses to a crisis are also the most ethical strategies. Third, if the situation calls for an admission of guilt and an apology to restore the company's image, but legal liabilities are too high, consider making an ambiguous apology. And, fourth, whether you decide to apologize or not, avoid attempts to distort information and cover blame. Although an ethical strategy may produce short-term pain, it is probably the most effective strategy for the organization over the long haul.

A second form of denial is **shifting the blame.** This strategy not only claims that the organization is not responsible, but shifts the blame to another target. For this move to be ethical, the target must be legitimately responsible for the crisis. Like denial, this claim may also be accompanied by various forms of reasoning and evidence. If the audience accepts the evidence, the organization's image should improve, because someone or something else is responsible. Early during its oil spill crisis, Exxon shifted blame for the accident to Captain Hazelwood, the *Valdez* skipper. Later, when accused of a slow response to the spill, Exxon attempted to move the blame to the state of Alaska and the Coast Guard for not immediately authorizing Exxon to begin clean-up efforts. Neither of these moves was accepted by the public, however.

As with all image strategies, there is nothing inherently unethical about denial if indeed no real crisis exists or the organization is truly not responsible. No one expects an organization to sit dumb and mute, accepting the blame for non-existent crises or those for which it has little or no responsibility. However, denial strategies will be both ineffective and unethical if not supported by the facts and strengthened with reasoning and evidence (see Chapter 10). For example, during the 1982 Tylenol poisoning, Johnson & Johnson claimed that neither they nor any of their employees could have introduced cyanide into the capsules. They provided evidence that the bottles came from two different plants and argued that it was unlikely the poisoned bottles from the two plants would end up in the same Chicago suburb. The company supported this logical appeal with testimony from the Food and Drug Administration (presumably perceived as an unbiased authority) confirming that the tampering could not have occurred in the plants.[29] Johnson & Johnson moved the blame to a "madman" who removed bottles from the shelves in order to randomly poison unsuspecting customers. This effort was persuasive because it was supported by the evidence. On the other hand, Sears's attempts to restore its image were less effective than Johnson & Johnson's. The denials had to overcome very convincing evidence of overcharges by officials in the California Department of Public Affairs. Because Sears offered little convincing evidence or reasoning, its image restoration strategies were ineffective.[30]

Based on these case studies, we believe denial strategies will be effective only if the organization can offer convincing proof.

In addition, crisis managers should think carefully before attempting to shift the blame to employees. Benoit states that shifting the blame is effective only when it is to someone clearly disassociated from the organization and plausibly responsible for the action.[31] Shifting the blame inside the organization does not meet these criteria. For example, in the *Valdez* oil spill, Exxon began by shifting the blame to Captain Hazelwood, who was reported to have been drunk at the time of the accident. In this instance, blaming an employee only casts doubt on Exxon's ability to hire, train, and supervise its workforce. Beyond being unethical, blaming employees who are not responsible for a crisis is often ineffective, because employee performance is a reflection of the organization's policies and decisions.

Evading of Responsibility

The second set of strategies for restoring an image during crisis is **evading of responsibility.** In this category the organization attempts to avoid or diminish responsibility for the crisis. Four specific strategies fall under this category.

Provocation responses claim that the act was performed in response to another wrongful act. Self-defense is the classic provocation defense. "I had to kill the person because he provoked a fight and threatened my life." It is unlikely that a provocation response would help restore a company's image during a crisis. Imagine your response to this reasoning: "We minimized our spending on safety equipment because our employees went on strike last month." We can think of no instances in which provocation would prove useful to an organization in crisis.

More useful in organizational crises are appeals to **defeasibility.** Defeasibility is the claim that the organization lacked information about or control over important factors, thus shouldn't be held fully responsible for the crisis. When AT&T blamed employees for the long-distance failure, the union responded with several defeasibility arguments. They said that audio alarms were not working and the visual alarms were hidden behind newly installed equipment. The employees didn't know the alarms sounded and shouldn't be blamed for the failure. Apparently, these arguments were effective because AT&T recanted.

Like denial, defeasibility is effective only if information was truly unavailable or situational factors were truly out of the organization's control. For example, rather than blaming the Coast Guard and state officials for withholding permission to commence clean-up (a charge that doesn't sound reasonable), Exxon could have blamed water conditions that were too calm and cold for oil-dispersing chemicals to work effectively. Even if Exxon personnel could have been there earlier, the effect of the oil dispersants would have been negligible.[32] For defeasibility to work, conditions must truly be out of the organization's control and the case must be strongly made with solid evidence and reasoning.

An appeal to **accidents** helps to reduce the organization's responsibility by appealing to factors that cannot be controlled. We generally do not hold organizations responsible for events that cannot reasonably be controlled. For example, part of NASA's early strategy for repairing their image during the *Challenger* accident was to remind audiences of the complexity of space travel, claiming that some accidents are inevitable and uncontrollable. However, this strategy was undercut when it was reported that Morton Thiokol engineers advised that the cold weather launch might result in catastrophe. As such, the "accident" was preventable. If an appeal to accidents is to be effective, the crisis must be an unpredictable event that cannot be controlled.

Sometimes organizations can reduce responsibility for an event by citing their **good intentions.** If the act was done with good intentions, audiences may be willing to reduce the organization's responsibility for the crisis. In late 1992, NBC News was accused of irresponsible journalism on its *Dateline NBC* program about C/K pickup trucks manufactured by General Motors. The trucks have a tendency to catch fire in high-speed side collisions because their gas tanks are mounted on the outside of the truck frames, rather than the inside. The *Dateline* story claimed that 300 people had died in these accidents and included a 57-second sequence showing a GM truck bursting into flames after a side collision. GM hired detectives who accused *Dateline* of attaching miniature rocket motors to the gas tank to produce the explosion. In addition to apologizing, NBC could have responded by saying that they made the errors while dramatizing the real dangers the C/K pickup trucks presented to the public. Sometimes audiences will forgive errors in pursuit of a noble goal. Rather than trying to reduce responsibility, the next category of responses attempts to reduce the offensiveness of the crisis.

Reducing Offensiveness

If the organization can reduce the degree of ill or harm experienced by the affected public it may succeed in **reducing offensiveness** of the crisis. In this way, the organization's image may be restored. This strategy has six variations.

Bolstering involves relating positive attributes of the organization or actions it performed in the past that might mitigate the negative consequences of the crisis. While the guilt for the crisis remains, increased positive feelings about the organization may offset negative feelings about the crisis. For example, when AT&T created a long-distance service interruption, their newspaper advertisements used bolstering to restore their image. Chairman Allen cited the billions AT&T had spent on customer service and the billions it planned to spend improving its system. If the audience perceives the comments to be sincere, it may reduce the offensiveness of the crisis.

To be effective, bolstering should be directly related to the charges made against the organization. For example, when accused of overcharging customers, Sears bolstered its case by referring to the thorough technical training Sears's mechanics receive. However, even if true, the claim is not very effective because technical training does not make a mechanic ethical.[33]

Minimization is an attempt to reduce the amount of negative affect associated with the crisis or to convince the public that the crisis isn't as bad as it might appear. After the Los Angeles riots the police department responded to criticism by stating that, despite what people saw on television, the rioting and looting were limited to an area of only several city blocks. The effectiveness of minimization depends on the magnitude of the crisis. Organizations should avoid trying to minimize large crises that are well publicized in the media. For example, Exxon tried to minimize the effects of the spill by claiming that the company did not expect major environmental damage, and it talked of record salmon catches in Alaska, not mentioning that these statistics were not from the spill area.[34] This strategy was especially ineffective given the nightly television pictures showing oil-soaked beaches, fouled habitat, and birds and marine life killed by the oil. Attempting to make a serious problem seem trivial is unethical and ineffective.

Differentiation distinguishes an act performed from other similar, but less desirable actions. In comparison, the action that precipitated the crisis seems less offensive. For example, in responding to charges of unnecessary repairs, Sears characterized its "sales quotas" as "sales goals" or guidelines based on surveys of the public's needs.[35] Sears hoped that goals or guidelines would be perceived as less offensive than "sales quotas." Of course, the public must share the organization's perception if this strategy is to be effective.

Transcendence places the crisis or actions related to the crisis in a different context that directs attention to higher values. The higher values justify the act and explain the crisis. Robin Hood, for example, would probably refuse to define his actions as theft. Instead, he might reframe his acts as helping the downtrodden victims of an unfair economic system. When Martin Luther King was asked how he dealt with the contradiction that he wanted people to follow civil rights laws, but that he purposely refused to obey laws of segregation, he referred to a higher law. He said, "A just law is a man-made code that squares with the moral law of God. An unjust law is a code that is out of harmony with the moral law. Any law that uplifts human personality is just. Any law that degrades human personality is unjust. All segregation statutes are unjust because segregation distorts the soul and damages the personality."[36] Violating unjust laws is not wrong, it is the responsibility of every moral person. Of course, the ethics of transcendence depends on the existing evidence and on moral judgments supporting the value of the strategy.

Transcendence was used by Volvo when it responded to charges of false advertising in 1989–90. Volvo ran a TV commercial claiming its vehicles could survive being run over by a monster truck but that other vehicles would be crushed. In reality, the Volvo used in the ad was reinforced with a steel roll cage, making it stronger than the other cars depicted. The Texas Attorney General sued Volvo for deceptive advertising. In their response, Volvo attempted to reduce the offensiveness of the act through transcendence. An advertisement in *USA Today* made the following claim: "On October 30 Volvo management learned for the first time that the film production team had apparently made modifications of two of the vehicles [referring to the steel support cages]. There were two reasons for the modifications: first to enable the filming to be done without threatening the safety of the production crew, and second, to allow the demonstration Volvo to withstand the number of runs of the "Monster Truck" required for filming."[37]

In this response, Volvo explains the charge by saying the steel roll cages were installed to protect the film crew, an appeal to the importance of safety.

During a recent Christmas holiday season, American Airlines was in the midst of a long contract negotiation with its pilots. Many pilots called in sick as part of the protest, and American was forced to cancel over 10 percent of its flights. In newspaper advertisements American apologized to its customers and attempted to reduce the offensiveness of the event through transcendence. The company said it would continue to negotiate with the Allied Pilots Association but would not accede to demands that would create high costs. The airline cited its duties to reasonable fares for customers and reasonable profits for stockholders.

In some crises, if the credibility of the source of the accusations can be reduced, the damage to one's image from the accusations may be diminished. Thus, **attacking the accuser** may divert attention away from the undesirable act. When Dow Corning was accused of selling silicon breast implants that caused cancer, the company attempted to reduce the offensiveness of the safety issue by attacking the Food and Drug Administration, the agency investigating the implants.[38] If one can show that the accuser is trying to create a crisis for personal gain, then attacking the accuser becomes a viable strategy. Of course, such a strategy is likely to be ethical and effective only when supported by appropriate evidence and reasoning.

When offering **compensation,** the organization remunerates the victim to offset the negative effects of the crisis. The redress can be made in valued goods and services or a monetary reward. In effect, compensation represents a "bribe" to lessen the effects of the crisis.[39] Of course, the degree to which the organization follows through on such claims is an important determinant of the success of this strategy.

To conclude, none of the six strategies just covered denies that the organization committed the bad action or diminishes the organization's responsibility for the crisis. Instead, they attempt to reduce unfavorable feelings by increasing audience esteem for the company or decreasing the audience's negative feelings.

Corrective Action

Corrective action entails a vow to correct problems created by the crisis. This can work in two ways. The organization can vow to restore (**restoration**) the situation to the conditions that existed before the crisis, or the organization can make changes in its operation to prevent (**prevention**) recurrence of the crisis. Benoit helps clarify the difference between this strategy and compensation. While corrective action addresses the source of the crisis (rectifying damage or preventing future crises), compensation consists of a gift designed to counterbalance, rather than correct, the source of the crisis.

For example, Exxon promised to clean up the oil and restore Prince William Sound to its original state. When AT&T's long-distance service failed, the company said it had already corrected the problems to prevent similar incidents in the future. Whether corrective action helps restore the organization's image depends on the degree to which promises are supported by action. If similar service outages happened to AT&T, the company's image would suffer severely.

THE IDAHO STATE JOURNAL

SUNDAY, OCTOBER 1, 1995 B3

Sheriff credits officers with heroic action at Ligertown

By Bill Lynn
Bannock County Sheriff

Please allow me the opportunity to express some feelings on the events which have taken place at Ligertown.

Much has been written in the Journal, and much more has been presented by the national and international media. It is easy to see that the stories involving animals are popular, and I think on the whole, the news of the incident has been reported very responsibly, and I thank you for your balance and understanding.

I do not want to dwell on the negative, but feel obliged to use the Journal to explain to those who may not understand why we did not "dart" the animals escaping from the compound instead of euth-

GUEST OPINION

anizing them.

The darting of animals is a very precise talent which requires specific skills and very specific equipment. Even the Fish and Game Department usually only has one person per district who is fully trained in the practice, and the equipment is scarce. I suspect many people assumed that any rifle could be used and you would just put in a drug dart and shoot.

In actuality, the darter must use very exact amounts of numerous compounds, and each dart must be made up individually. Beyond the one dart per shot problem, the type and gender of the animal, the

weight of the animal, and many other factors would determine the serums used in each darting.

Beyond the above problems, the darter must get to within about 10-20 feet of the animal to be darted, and then the animals, if they are lions, take from 15 minutes to 1 1/2 hours to knock down. During this 15-minute to 1 1/2-hour time frame, the lions would have the ability to injure or kill the darter, other officers, or wander downstream to Lava Hot Springs which was less than one mile away. While the lions begin to get lethargic, they are still very aggressive and capable of inflicting injury or death.

At the worst time, about 2 a.m., even if we had had a darter with a dart ready, little could have been

done, as we had at that time as many as 14 lions on the loose. And we had them on all four sides of the compound

The fact that we were able to put down the lions without them escaping to town or injuring anyone was a miracle in itself, which we are grateful for. While we wish that darting would have been an option, it simply was not, and the Humane Society of the United States as well as the lion experts from California both confirmed that we did all that we could do, and praised us for our response and for maintaining the public well-being.

As for the officers who responded to Ligertown that Wednesday night and Thursday morning, let me make comment. During the

worst time, we had many brave men and women, from numerous agencies, putting their very lives on the line for the public well-being.

As for those who would say that it is their job to put their lives on the line, I would say you are right to a point, but no responsible set of individuals, no community, or no person can expect its law enforcement officers to have to deal with an escaping pride of lions, and consider it anything but heroic.

It is hard to express to you, the public, as well as to the officers themselves, how very proud I am of them. I have tried by private letter, but anything I say falls short.

All of you must know the bravery of those who were in harm's way, but further you must know

that few groups of people in the world could have pulled off this situation with so much class, so much calm, and so much courage.

Many officers have said before that they would follow each other across the threshold of Hell, and indeed, that is exactly what they have done for each other. I not only count them as friends, I count them among the heroes I have known.

I believe that in life we find heroes very seldom, but when we do, we find them in the most unlikely places. I found so many that night in Lava Hot Springs, and I am honored to count them as friends, but even more honored to walk by their side. Perhaps as their leader, that makes me the luckiest man in the world, and that is exactly how I feel!

Reprinted by permission of *The Idaho State Journal.*

Recovering from Ligertown

By Newt Lowe
Mayor of Lava Hot Springs

GUEST OPINION

As a lifelong resident of Idaho, a resident of Lava since 1950, and Mayor for the last 10 years, I am compelled to respond to the spate of unfavorable publicity that the Ligertown situation has forced upon us.

Since the Ligertown owners first arrived, it has been apparent that they did not aspire to "good citizen status." Soon after their arrival in 1986, they presented the City with a spurious claim for damages and threatened a law suit. Things went down hill from that point. It was soon apparent to anyone with a sense of smell and an eye for beauty that Ligertown was rapidly deteriorating into a blight, a cancerous growth that needed excision.

The various government agencies that control such problems were duly alerted, each in turn fulfilled their legal responsibility to a point. All agreed that a problem existed but that until something additional — i.e. some further violation occurred, their hands were tied. A classic case of "bureaucratic shuffle."

This is not an attempt to place blame on any agency. There is enough for all to share, including the City of Lava. I'm suggesting that a situation such as this should not have gotten to this deplorable state. Hindsight is wonderful, isn't it?

Ligertown has been a "Sword of Damocles" hanging over us. The Sheriff's Department and the City of Lava have been aware of the problem. It didn't come as a surprise.

Kudos to the Sheriff's Department and all others for the professional way in which the recent catastrophe was handled. The circumstances precluded the use of tranquilizers and in protection of the public they acted appropriately.

In our society, everyone is entitled to an opinion. The aftermath has brought the kooks and bleeding hearts crawling out of the woodwork. The hate mail to Lava City is astounding, but easily dismissed.

The Ligertown owners now claim that their "rights" have been violated and threaten all sorts of litigation against anyone involved. They have forgotten the judicial admonition that "You have the right to swing your fist until it collides with your neighbor's nose." Don't get downwind from the compound or your nose will be violated.

I'm sure that there is an aspiring Kunstler out there, who for the publicity or on a contigency will take the people of Bannock county to court for a multitude of alleged damages. Count on it. An oxymoron for sure.

There is no defense for the maltreatment of animals or the endangerment of the public that Ligertown has posed. The drama has almost played out. Thanks, that no innocent person has yet been injured. Now that the cancer has been defined, let's hope that it can be controlled. If it takes legislative action, so be it. Let's back that approach. Idaho could use a "Fieber" law, along with Oregon.

It is my sincere hope that the authorities do not let this matter slip "under the rug." Now is the opportune time to make Lava a better place.

Think of the money that has been and will be spent in rectifying this problem. Who pays? We do.

Whose rights have been violated?

Reprinted by permission of *The Idaho State Journal.*

Mortification

Mortification means that the organization admits responsibility for the crisis and asks forgiveness. If the audience sees the apology as sincere, it may forgive the organization for its role in the crisis. Mortification is one of the strongest image-restoration strategies available. However, many companies avoid this strategy, especially early in a crisis. This avoidance may be based on two things. First, most organizational crises are characterized by a lack of information, and managers may not know what precipitated a particular event. Thus, it is wise to wait before apologizing until more information is available and clear attributions of responsibility are possible.

Unfortunately, although temporarily withholding mortification may be prudent, many organizations make the mistake of opening with denials that must later be recanted after the facts are known. A belated apology often follows. Mitsubishi initially denied charges that female employees were subject to sexual harassment on its assembly lines, but later recanted and settled a large lawsuit brought by the government. Although sometimes effective, belated mortification can do more harm than good for an organization's image. When the first strategy, be it denial, shifting the blame, attacking the accuser, or whatever is refuted, the organization looks as if it tried to cover up the facts. Mortification looks forced on the organization by circumstances rather than as a sincere request for forgiveness. If you must delay mortification because of a lack of information or legal concerns, don't compound the problem by issuing denials or blaming others based on inaccurate information.

Legal liability is the second reason organizations avoid mortification. Mortification is not a problem in less severe crises where no one is killed, injuries are minor, and the damage to the environment is contained and relatively easy to clean up. However, in severe crises, managers are torn between the demands of two audiences. Although the public insists on a sincere apology, managers also have an obligation to consider the damage that liability lawsuits will produce for employees, stockholders, and creditors. Admitting an error implies guilt, inviting lawsuits and providing ammunition to plaintiffs in court. After all, if the organization isn't guilty, why did their executives apologize? In severe crises, corporate managers are trapped because—much as they might like to apologize to meet the demands of the public—they cannot apologize without violating their fiduciary responsibility to stockholders.[40] Lisa Tyler, a professor at Sinclair Community College, suggests that ambiguous apologies are one solution to this problem.

As you may recall from Chapter 1, ambiguity occurs when there is low correspondence between the intention of the sender and the interpretation of the receiver. Ambiguous mortification omits important details and asks the audience to infer that an apology has been made without a clear admission of guilt. There are several methods of making an ambiguous apology. First, Exxon's response to the *Valdez* grounding admitted that the spill was the company's responsibility, but continued to refer to the incident as an "accident," thus, suggesting it was an "unavoidable act of God rather than a preventable result of human error."[41] The apology is ambiguous because it makes contradictory claims: that Exxon is both responsible and not responsible for the spill. Another method of ambiguous mortification is to express regret for the crisis without admitting guilt. Avoiding admission of guilt provides legal protection, while regret puts a human face on the corporation. Finally, a third method is to focus on prevention measures without admitting any responsibility for the event. As such, the company promises to correct whatever it is that it hasn't admitted doing.[42] In Western cultures, ambiguity detracts from the value of mortification.[43] Thus, clear mortification is more ethically pure and preferable from the standpoint of the organization's image. However, when legal liability is high, ambiguity may be the only way to mediate the conflicting demands of various audiences.

Effectively Employing Crisis Communication Strategies

In this section, we will present general guidelines for the effective use of organizational image restoration strategies. Of course, no set of rules can guarantee successful image restoration. Instead, these guidelines provide signposts for reasoned choices when communicating to various audiences.

Use Multiple Strategies in Concert with One Another

Rarely will an organization focus its image restoration campaign on a single strategy. Rather, the best campaigns use multiple strategies in concert with one another. AT&T used mortification, corrective action, and bolstering to rebuild its credibility.[44] However, it is vital that the strategies do not contradict one another or contradict vivid and accurate media accounts. Unfortunately, these two prescriptions are often violated.

For example, Sears's image restoration strategy went through contradictory phases. The company started by attacking the accuser, the California Department of Consumer Affairs, but later dropped these attacks and promised corrective action. In addition, Sears opened with sharp denials and then backed off, saying there had been incidents of unneeded repairs.[45] Rather than improving the company's image, contradictory strategies make the problem worse by creating a second problem of confidence and trustworthiness. Although it is wise to use multiple strategies, they should be consistent with one another.

In addition, multiple strategies should not contradict vivid and accurate media portrayals of the crisis. Such portrayals are more likely to be seen and believed by the audience than the organization's PR efforts and will make the organization look disingenuous.

Support All Strategies with Strong Reasoning and Evidence

All image strategies must be supported with strong reasoning and evidence. A crisis means that something negative has happened and at least some audiences see the organization as responsible. The organization will begin management efforts from a credibility deficit. Crisis communication is, by definition, a "come-from-behind" game. The organization must marshal all the evidence and reasoning it can to support its positions and make this information available to the public repeatedly through the media.

How does an organization do this? It is best to think of the image restoration strategies as claims that require support if they are to be believed. As we mentioned in Chapter 10, a claim is a statement that the organization believes is true or a simple statement that concludes an argument. However, claims by themselves are rarely convincing. They require inductive and deductive reasoning, and appeals to credibility, and emotion to persuade. Thus, it is not enough to say "This was an unavoidable accident," or "We had good intentions," or "The crisis is not as bad as it seems," or "Corrective action will be taken." These claims must be backed up by appropriate appeals to logic, credibility, and emotion. Although Sears issued strong denials that it overcharged customers, the company presented little evidence to this effect. Sears said its quotas were easy to meet and denied that the quotas might induce managers to overcharge. But when the Sears spokesperson was asked to provide an example of an easy quota, he was stumped. "This was a particularly poor choice in the face of the concrete and detailed charges against the company. Because specific autos, individually identified auto repair service centers, and exact details of unneeded repairs and charges were documented by a credible source, it was a mistake to deny the accusations."[46] If they are to be believed, image restoration strategies must be supported.

Exercise Visible Leadership from the Highest Executives

Effective image restoration requires that the highest executives handle the crisis in a visible manner. This means that owners or managers should go to the scene as soon after the crisis as possible. They should personally speak with the press on a regular basis and they should be forthcoming at all times. Sending lower-rank employees to the scene suggests that management isn't concerned about the crisis. Exxon was criticized, for example, for sending lower-rank managers to the scene in Alaska. This failed to show the company taking control of the situation in a visible, forceful way.[47] In addition, higher-rank employees should communicate with the press, and the same members should communicate throughout the crisis. Johnson & Johnson executives did this throughout the 1982 and 1986 Tylenol poisoning incidents. In both cases, two higher executives handled the media. McNeil Chairman David Collins and CEO James Burke of Johnson & Johnson, McNeil's parent company, were regulars on various TV news shows. Consistent communication reassures the public that the problem is being handled effectively.

Finally, organizations in crisis must be forthcoming with all relevant information. Withholding data hurts the organization in the eyes of the media, who pass their suspicions to the public. Such practices result in more scrutiny, distrust, and bad publicity.

Identify the Target Audience and Select Strategies Accordingly

As we mentioned at the beginning of this chapter, it is the audience's perception of the crisis that counts. The audiences for organizational image restoration may be numerous, and they include the federal government, local government, the general public, stockholders, suppliers, sales outlets, creditors, and customers. The concerns, needs, and interests of these groups differ widely and require different image restoration strategies. For example, although a chemical leak may pose an extremely severe crisis to an audience of local residents, stockholders may see this as an aberration that doesn't affect their larger interests. The communication challenge is therefore different for each audience.

The strategies you select depend on the specific audience's perception of two important factors: the organization's responsibility, and the severity of the crisis. Placing these two perceptions together creates a two-by-two matrix that depicts four different kinds of audiences for organizational crisis communication (see Figure 13.4). Each category in the matrix represents a different kind of audience, and each audience requires different strategies for effective image restoration.

Category A represents what we refer to as an **animated audience,** who believe the crisis is severe but that the organization's responsibility is minimal. These audience members pay attention to news reports and experience emotional feelings of concern and regret for victims. However, for whatever reason, they do not believe the organization is primarily responsible for the tragedy. As such, they are concerned for the victims or for their own interests if they are affected.

Denial and shifting the blame are unnecessary for the animated audience because they don't hold the organization responsible for the crisis. It may be useful on occasion to remind the audience that the organization is not responsible, but this is all that is necessary for the animated audience. On the other hand, strategies that reduce the offensiveness of the event (e.g., bolstering or compensation) may have a positive effect on the animated audience perceptions. The organization is likely to appear humane because it is trying to solve a problem it did not create.

Early in the Tylenol crisis, Johnson & Johnson effectively employed denial strategies to demonstrate that tampering couldn't have taken place in their facto-

FIGURE 13.4   The Different Audiences for Crisis Communication

High	Category A High Severity, Low Responsibility **Animated Audience**	Category B High Severity, High Responsibility **Antagonistic Audience**
Severity	Category C Low Severity, Low Responsibility **Bemused Audience**	Category D Low Severity, High Responsibility **Concerned Audience**
	Low	Responsibility High

ries. They shifted the blame to a madman who tampered with the product after it was on the shelves. Once this was accepted, the public became an animated audience. Further attempts to deny or reduce responsibility for the crisis were unnecessary. Johnson & Johnson then focused on corrective action by pioneering the safety seal security system that is now found on many consumer products. During the second poisoning, Johnson & Johnson ended the production of capsules in favor of caplets because caplets cannot be separated or opened. The corporation took corrective action despite the fact that few blamed them.

Mortification should be avoided for such a reactive audience. An organization that is not responsible for the crisis should not apologize. However, there is no problem in reminding the audience that everyone is sorry the event occurred, and expressing concern for the victims is both expected and appropriate.

Category C represents a **bemused audience,** one that perceives both the severity of the crisis and the organization's responsibility as minimal. Bemused audiences look at the situation as a problem rather than a crisis. Despite the inconsequential nature of events, the bemused audience can become more concerned or antagonistic if the media or competitors attempt to publicize the problem. In 1991, for instance, Earth's Best Baby Food, of Middlebury, Vermont, accused Beach-Nut Nutrition Corporation of deceiving customers with its new line of organic baby food. Whereas Earth's Best used foodstuffs from farms that have not used synthetic fertilizers or pesticides for three years, Beach-Nut used the California Organic Food Act of 1990, which requires that farms be free of synthetic chemicals for only one year. Beech-Nut maintained that it was doing nothing deceitful or against the law.[48] Although committed environmentalists might be concerned about Beech-Nut's interpretation of "organic" foods, we suspect the average audience member doesn't see the incident as a crisis. If such situations merit a response, denial, shifting the blame, attacking the accuser, and minimization may be effective strategies. In addition, taking time to respond to the problem can provide an opportunity for extensive bolstering, which amounts to public relations for the organization.

Referring back to Figure 13.4, you can see that low-impact, high-responsibility perceptions create a **concerned audience,** category D. Although the audience believes that the harm to people or the environment is minimal, individuals are concerned because a weakness in the organization has been revealed that could cause a more serious crisis later. Such an incident occurred in 1987 when Beech-Nut paid a two-million dollar fine to the federal government for selling "apple juice" that was nothing more than sweetened water, chemicals, and preservatives. Although the incident was not a threat to public safety, the company was fully responsible.[49] In this case, although no one was physically harmed, the public's belief in the company's competence and trustworthiness was diminished. These concerns must be addressed if the company is to weather the storm.

The concerned audience is difficult to convince with denial. The audience already believes the organization is responsible, and attempts to change this perception must be well documented and based on the truth. The same is true of reducing the responsibility strategies. For the concerned audience, the combination of minimization, bolstering, and some form of corrective action is likely to be effective. Minimization reminds the audience that the severity of the event is low. Bolstering reinforces the credibility of the organization, and corrective action reassures the audience that the problem is unlikely to recur. Mortification is also effective for the concerned audience and poses small legal liability since the severity of the crisis is minimal.

Finally, the **antagonistic audience,** category B, believes the organization is mainly responsible for a very severe crisis. In such a crisis, denial strategies are unlikely to be effective unless supported by overwhelming evidence. Also, avoid knee-jerk denials that must later be recanted. Reducing responsibility strategies can be effective for the antagonistic audience if the action is well supported and constantly repeated in the media and through paid advertisements. Appeals to defeasibility, accidents, and good intentions may also work to help reduce the organization's responsibility for the crisis. Because the impact of the crisis is perceived as severe, reducing responsibility strategies should be combined with reducing offensiveness strategies. To be effective, all strategies must be well supported with evidence and reasoning.

Finally, two of the most important image restoration strategies for the antagonistic audience are corrective action and mortification. Corrective action helps reassure the public that the situation will be restored or, at the very least, the organization will prevent its recurrence. Mortification can also be vital in these circumstances. As we discussed previously, there may be legal reasons that prevent an organization from offering mortification. However, refusing to offer an apology, even after the organization has been firmly and convincingly blamed for the crisis, makes the organization look both guilty and unrepentant. Ambiguous mortification may be required to minimize legal liability.

Our suggestions provide reasonable guidelines for selecting image restoration strategies during a crisis. However, each audience is different, including many shades and hues of opinion that can't be categorized by a single descriptive label. These differences may necessitate altering or violating any or all of the guidelines. They are meant as a starting place for analysis, not a concluding summary of what is correct in all circumstances. Crisis communication is an art rather than a science; messages must be adapted to particular circumstances.

Recognize the Limits of Persuasive Communication

William Benoit emphasizes that the power of persuasive communication is limited.[50] When organizations are responsible for egregious errors, overlook standard procedures, or make inept decisions there may be little that communication itself can do to help. Although damage can be mitigated, the best solution to this problem is to avoid the crisis in the first place. This is why risk management, following government regulations, and paying attention to in-house health and safety experts is a good idea. Vigilant crisis prevention is always the best form of image protection.

Structuring Organizational Crisis Communication

Finding an appropriate structure for organizational crisis communication is a difficult task. Most communication research is devoted to content rather than structure. Most of the written image restoration advertisements that we have seen and the ones included in this chapter follow the topical structure discussed in Chapter 7. You can also see this structure in the case study included in the exercises of this chapter. The topical pattern moves through a series of image restoration claims and associated evidence in a point-by-point manner. Although this pattern is acceptable, it may not be very persuasive. There is nothing in the content of the image restoration strategies that prevents the use of other organizing structures.

Despite the fact that almost any pattern can be used for crisis communication, we believe the N-A-R structure has special utility. The narrative section allows the speaker to review details of the crisis in a way that is beneficial to the organization. The arguments section allows the organization to deploy and support image restoration claims. Finally, the refutation allows the organization to correct inaccurate information that affected audiences, regulatory agencies, or the media might have. For example, the Demonstration Crisis Briefing in this chapter works from the point of view of Michael Gartner, President of NBC News, who needed to justify the *Dateline NBC* story on GM pickup trucks. This briefing was never presented by NBC, rather, your authors created it as a demonstration of what NBC could have said to restore its image. We structured this briefing using the N-A-R pattern:

Introduction

Narrative (tells story that uses minimization, moving the blame, and apology)

Refutation (denies and minimizes certain claims made by GM)

Arguments (explains NBC's good intentions, apologizes, attacks the accuser)

Conclusion

As you can see, we modified the structure slightly by reversing the refutation and arguments sections. We felt that this was necessary in order to first deny inaccurate claims before making arguments that include good intentions, apologies, and attacking the accuser. This reversal is perfectly acceptable if it makes a stronger case for the organization. It is possible that network lawyers would omit our attacks on GM (since NBC was so clearly negligent, lawyers would counsel against further antagonizing GM). However, we believe that the public for this event represented a concerned audience that would be persuaded by reminders of GM's responsibility to the public. The exercise was a useful one for us in learning how to structure and support image restoration speeches.

Demonstration Crisis Briefing

Background

I am playing the role of Michael Gartner, President of NBC News, and I am under pressure to explain and justify the handling of a story on General Motors's trucks by my division's *Dateline NBC* program. The program was broadcast on November 17, 1992, and dealt with the controversy surrounding the design of General Motors's C/K pickup trucks. Six million of these trucks were produced between 1973 and 1987 and have demonstrated a tendency to catch fire in high-speed side collisions because of their "sidesaddle" gas tanks—tanks that are mounted on the outside, rather than the inside, of the truck's frame rails. Between 300 and 600 people have died in these crashes, prompting more than 100 product-liability lawsuits.

In a recent press conference (mid-February 1993), GM accused NBC of irresponsible journalism and presented evidence to refute almost every major point made in the *Dateline* story—especially a fifty-seven-second sequence showing a GM truck bursting into flames after a side collision. GM revealed that it hired detectives who learned the crash sequence was rigged. GM charged that *Dateline* had said incorrectly that the truck's gas tank had ruptured when it hadn't and, more serious, had used explosive miniature rockets to make sure the truck would burst into flames—two important facts NBC's viewers were not told.

I am holding this press conference in mid-February 1993 for members of the media who will disseminate information to the general public.

Crisis Briefing

Specific Purpose: To explain the errors NBC News made and to work to restore the image of the news division.

Strategic Summary: Minimization and apology followed by attacking the accuser.

INTRODUCTION

 I. To a journalist, nothing is more important than credibility. If the audience doesn't believe in the facts of our reports, we have no reason to exist.
 II. People rely on the media to report both the actions of our government and unsafe business practices. Because of problems in a *Dateline NBC* story in November, we have damaged our credibility, and this concerns us here at NBC News.

(Trans. Let me open by providing some background information on the events in question.)

NARRATIVE

Many of you already know the story. In November of 1992, while trying to alert people to an important danger to public safety on our highways, the staff at *Dateline NBC* made a mistake. *Dateline's* November 17 show featured fourteen minutes of balanced debate capped by our mistake—fifty-seven seconds of crash footage that showed how the gas tanks of certain GM trucks could catch fire in side-on collisions.

Despite my previous comments defending the segment, the crash footage, conducted by the Indiana-based Institute for Injury Reduction, now appears to have been a mistake. Ultimately, I am troubled by two primary problems. First, our story reported that the gas tank had ruptured when it had not, and second, we did not fully disclose the nature of the crash test to *Dateline NBC* viewers.

(Trans. Let me explain these two errors through reference to claims GM has made against us).

REFUTATION
I. First, according to GM, our segment claimed that the gas tank ruptured when no such damage occurred, and that the fire was caused by an ill-fitting gas cap that was not original equipment. These claims are partially true.
   A. It is true that we made an error in falsely reporting the gas tank rupture and for this we are chagrined and embarrassed.
   B. In addition, GM is correct in its claim that the gas cap was not original equipment (Henry, 1993).
      1. However, it was an after-market replacement cap similar to those found on many vehicles on the road today.
      2. The fire was not, as GM claimed, caused by an ill-fitting gas cap.
         a. Instead, the force of the collision blew the cap off the filler tube and gas was ejected from the crushed tank.
         b. It was the ejected gas that caught fire and caused the explosion.

(Trans. In addition to criticizing our report on the gas tank rupture, GM has made another claim against NBC).

II. GM also claims that *Dateline NBC* purposely used incendiary devices to ignite the 1977 Chevy pick-up used in the crash test; again, this claim is partly true.
   A. While incendiary devices were wired to the truck, these would cause a fire only if fuel was spilled from the tank (Henry, 1993).
   B. In addition, our investigations reveal that the cause of the fire in the test crash was a spark from a broken headlamp, not the incendiary devices (Henry, 1973).
      1. Nevertheless, it is the responsibility of reporters to explain all the relevant details behind video demonstrations such as this.
      2. We did not tell the public about the presence of the incendiary devices as we should have.

(Trans. Having explained the background of the events in regard to GM's claims, I would now like to make three additional points.)

ARGUMENTS
I. First, although we acknowledge serious errors in creating this story, we began the investigation with good intentions.
   A. Our nation's founders intended the media to serve as a check on the actions of government, and in this century, this watchdog function has been extended to big business.
   B. The safety of GM trucks is exactly the kind of issue that a popular news program such as *Dateline NBC* should address (Henry, 1993).
   C. Any product whose design injures or kills a significant number of people is worthy of investigation.
      1. Estimates suggest that 600 people have died in side-impact crashes in GM trucks, and many lawsuits have been filed against GM (Multinational Monitor, 1994).
      2. As a result, these trucks deserve the scrutiny of news programs like ours, and such scrutiny is necessary to protect public safety.
      3. I firmly believe that in this matter our intentions were honorable and in keeping with journalistic traditions.

(Trans. Our good intentions aside, we did commit significant errors that I have discussed above and we would like to apologize for these.)

(continued)

Continued

II. As I stated above, we made two major errors in judgment, and for these we wish to apologize.
  A. First, we were in error reporting that the tank ruptured when it did not, and we were in error when we failed to report the presence of the after-market gas cap.
   1. There is no excuse for these omissions in a network news organization.
   2. We wish to offer our sincere apology to our viewers.
  B. Second, we were also negligent in failing to report the full details of the crash test, including the presence of the incendiary devices on the gas tank.
   1. NBC News presents 225,000 minutes of news each year.
      a. We don't wish to be defined by the errors in this fifty-seven-second crash test (Henry, 1993).
      b. We ask the public's forgiveness for these errors.
   2. To prevent such errors in the future, we have created the following policy:
      a. In the future, no unscientific demonstrations will be used in hard news stories.
      b. In the future, no simulations of real events will be produced (Byron, 1993).
      c. In the future, we will report all relevant details about how scientific demonstrations are produced and edited.
      d. We believe that strict adherence to these guidelines will prevent the errors we made for the GM segment and hope this will help restore the public's faith in NBC News.

(Trans. Finally, although we apologize for our errors, we regret the use of these errors to divert attention from an important public safety issue.)

III. It is unfortunate that our errors have allowed GM to divert attention from the central issue, that there may be a fundamental flaw in the safety of C/K pickup trucks (Diamond, 1993).
  A. Automotive research clearly demonstrates the safest location for fuel storage tanks.
   1. According to Richard Alexander, of the San Jose–based Alexander Law Firm, auto industry researchers have known for years that placing the tank between the frame rails, rather than outside the rails, and forward of the rear axle is the safest location (Alexander, 1998).
   2. That fuel tanks should never be put in the crush zone, for example, outside the frame rails, was well understood when the 1973 GM pickups were in their design stage (Alexander, 1998).
   3. According to Department of Transportation Secretary Federico Pena, "The record clearly shows that there is an increased risk associated with GM C/K series pickups and leads me to conclude at this point that the risk is unreasonable. This case involves not only serious injuries, but a significant number of fatalities, in crashes that were otherwise survivable" (Multinational Monitor, 1994, p. 7)
  B. Some people claim that the flaw in the C/K truck designs has lead to unacceptable injuries and deaths.
   1. Clarence Ditlow, director of the Center for Auto Safety, estimates that more than 600 persons have been burned to death in GM pickup fire crashes and thousands more have been injured (Multinational Monitor, 1994).
   2. This past week in Atlanta a jury awarded a $105.2 million judgment against GM for a Georgia teen who died when his truck was struck from the side, the fuel tanks ruptured, and the vehicle exploded in flames (Henry, 1993).

3. "Joe McCray, a San Francisco–based trial lawyer who has handled 19 GM pickup truck injury and death cases, estimates that about 300 such cases have been brought against GM" (Multinational Monitor, 1994, p. 8).

C. Finally, evidence exists that GM has known about the dangers of the C/K pickups since the late 1970s.

    1. According to Secretary Pena, "Of critical importance in this matter is the evidence that GM was aware, possibly as early as the mid-1970s, but certainly by the 1980s, that this design made these trucks more vulnerable and that fatalities from side-impact fires were occurring…However, GM chose not to alter the design for 15 years" (Multinational Monitor, 1994).

    2. It is possible that GM has violated provisions of the National Traffic and Motor Vehicle Safety Act.

        a. The act states that, if a company becomes aware that its vehicles are dangerous, it must notify the government and consumers and repair the defect.

        b. If GM was aware of the problems with its "sidesaddle" tanks since 1978, it has also been in violation of the law.

        c. Did we make errors in our November 17 story? Without question.

        d. But GM has arguably made errors with its C/K pickup trucks as well.

(Trans. Having made my arguments and apologies, let me conclude this briefing.)

CONCLUSION

I. Today I have explained the circumstances behind our errors and again wish to acknowledge these errors and apologize for them.

  A. For a news organization, credibility is vital.

  B. We hope that by admitting our errors and creating a policy to prevent future incidents we can move toward restoring our credibility with viewers.

II. However, we don't want our errors to obscure other issues.

  A. You can't put a price on safety.

  B. We at NBC News will continue to pursue product safety stories in the belief that this is one of the most important services a news organization can provide.

References

Alexander, R. (1998, June 19). "Gas Tank Fires." The Consumer Law Page: Articles [On-line]. Available: http://consumerlawpage.com/article/gm-exploding-tank.shtml

Byron, C. (1993, February 22). "Crash and Burn." *New York, 26,* 19–20.

Diamond, E. (1993, March 15). "Auto-Destruct." *New York, 26,* 18–19.

Henry, W. A. III. (1993, February 22). "Where NBC Went Wrong." *Time, 141,* 59.

Multinational Monitor (1994). "10 Worst Corporations of 1994." [On-line]. Available: http://www.ratical.com/corporations/mm10worst94.html

Summary

Be they public or private, large or small, all organizations are susceptible to crisis. Organizational crisis is defined as a major, unpredictable event that has potentially negative consequences. When a crisis occurs, managers are responsible for crisis management—solving the technical or human problems that precipitate the crisis—and crisis communication—interacting with various audiences to protect affected groups and restore the organization's image. For a variety of reasons, including more complex manufacturing, transportation, and financing arrangements, as well as such public responses as the consumer and environmental movements, organizational crisis is more common and more difficult to hide than ever before.

In order to manage crises, organizations should form a crisis team and develop a crisis management plan. The crisis team should include the CEO; the chief financial officer; public and government relations officials; health, environmental, and safety engineers; investor relations specialists; and legal counsel. The team should brainstorm a list of potential crises and narrow that list to cover the most likely scenarios. A media relations sheet should including updated media contact information. The crisis team should select an individual or a few individuals to handle media contacts during various crises. Press releases, press kits, and news conferences are three typical means of communicating to various audiences.

A variety of image restoration strategies are available to organizations during a crisis. In denial strategies, the organization denies performing acts that caused the crisis. These strategies include simple denial and shifting the blame. Reducing-responsibility strategies diminish or avoid responsibility for the crisis. This category includes provocation, defeasibility, accident, and good intentions. In provocation, the organization claims the precipitating action was performed in response to another wrongful act. An appeal to defeasibility claims the organization lacked important information about or control over factors that led to the crisis. Because an accident cannot be controlled, it reduces the organization's responsibility for the crisis. An organization can also claim that the crisis was precipitated by well-intended actions.

A third category of image restoration is reducing the offensiveness of the event. This includes bolstering, minimization, differentiation, transcendence, attacking the accuser, and compensation. Bolstering involves relating positive attributes of the organization that might mitigate the negative consequences of a crisis. Minimization suggests that the effects of the crisis are not as severe as they appear. Differentiation distinguishes some precipitating actions from other similar, but less desirable actions. Transcendence places the crisis in a different context that directs attention to higher values. Attacking the accuser reduces the credibility of the source of the attacks. Compensation provides remuneration to victims. Corrective action is a strategy that vows to restore the situation to its state before the crisis or to make changes that prevent recurrence of the crisis. Mortification is a strategy that admits responsibility for the crisis and asks forgiveness. Ambiguous mortification may be necessary when legal liability is high.

To effectively employ the image restoration strategies, an organization must follow several guidelines. Multiple strategies can and should be used as long as they do not contradict one another. The organization should exercise visible leadership from the highest executives. It should be sure to identify the nature of the target audience and adapt image restoration strategies to them. Audiences may be animated, bemused, concerned, or antagonistic, and each suggests a different approach. Finally, managers should recognize that persuasive communication can only do so much in restoring an organization's image. Prevention is the best image insurance. Although crisis communication can be structured in any number of ways, the N-A-R structure is a promising way to present an organization's case to a variety of audiences.

QUESTIONS FOR DISCUSSION

1. Examine again the advertisement from AT&T in this chapter (Figure 13.2). Label the specific image restoration strategies used in the ad. What combination of strategies are used in the ad? Discuss which strategies are effective and which are ineffective. Why do you feel this way? What do you think about the ethical implications of the advertisement? Are there some strategies that strike you as especially ethical or unethical? Why?

2. Examine the Demonstration Crisis Briefing for NBC News near the end of this chapter. Label each of the image restoration strategies throughout the speech. What, if any, strategies seem most effective? Why? What strategies seem ineffective? Why? What legal ramifications do you think the briefing might create? What ethical issues does the briefing raise? Does the briefing help restore your image of NBC News? Why or why not?

3. Our belief that ethical image strategies are also the most successful strategies may be controversial. Can you think of examples in which an individual or organization used unethical image restoration strategies that, nevertheless, succeeded? What made these strategies unethical? Why did these succeed rather than fail? What role, if any, did the media play in the crisis? Can you think of more ethical strategies that would have accomplished the same goal?

ACTIVITIES AND EXERCISES

1. On the night of September 20, 1995, in the small town of Lava Hot Springs, Idaho, nineteen hungry African lions were shot to death by county sheriffs after escaping from Ligertown, a ramshackle, squalid game farm less than a mile east of the city. The incident attracted national news attention. The game farm, owned by a recluse couple from Oregon, had been an eyesore to Lava citizens for years, but little was done because there were no county or state laws against keeping exotic pets. When a neighboring farmer saw one of the animals loose, he killed the lion and called the sheriff. By 2 A.M. a perimeter was set up around the compound, and wandering lions that had managed to escape their pens were shot to death before they could move into the town itself. After the incident, the sheriff's department was attacked in several editorials and phone calls for killing the lions rather than tranquilizing them. The "Guest Opinion" of Sheriff Bill Lynn is a response to the accusations made during the crisis. Read the response from Sheriff Lynn and label the image restoration strategies used in the response. What is the primary image restoration strategy employed? Was it effective? Why?

2. In the Ligertown crisis just described, Lava Hot Springs also came under attack from animal rights activists who claimed the town had not done enough to close down the Ligertown operation. They cited articles in the newspaper demonstrating that many of the twenty-seven surviving lions and forty wolf hybrids were

suffering from disease and malnutrition. The town, the accusations said, should have done more to prevent the animals' suffering. By failing to act, the critics claimed the city of Lava Hot Springs was partly responsible for the escape and the deaths of nineteen lions. The second "Guest Opinion" is from the mayor of Lava Hot Springs, Newt Lowe, who responds to the criticism the town received. Read the response from Newt Lowe and label the image restoration strategies that he uses. How effective was the mayor's attempt to restore Lava's image? Why? Compare this opinion to the Sheriff's above. Which was the most effective? What characteristics account for the relative effectiveness or ineffectiveness of each article?

3. Create a newspaper advertisement based on a case study of a particular organizational crisis. The goal of this newspaper ad is to restore the organization's image following its crisis. You may select an organizational crisis from the list depicted in Figure 13.1 or develop your own ad from a crisis with which you are familiar. Conduct research to learn about the background and causes of the crisis. Examine what this organization said in response to the crisis and any critiques that commentators made about the organization's response. This information will form the backbone of your response. In your ad, select image restoration strategies based on the kind of audience (animated, bemused, concerned, antagonistic) that this organization is trying to persuade. Provide appropriate support for your claims.

4. Create a crisis briefing based on a case study of a particular organizational crisis. The goals of this briefing are twofold: to protect the public and restore the image of the organization. You can select an organizational crisis from the list depicted in Figure 13.1 or develop your briefing from a crisis with which you are already familiar. Thoroughly research the crisis to discover the background and precipitating events. Examine what this particular organization did and said in response to the crisis and any critiques that commentators made about the organization's response. This information will form the backbone of your crisis briefing.

Assume the role of a corporate executive in the organization you have studied and create a six-to-seven minute briefing that responds to the crisis, using several of Benoit's image restoration strategies. Decide on the kind of audience (media, employees, community, stockholders, etc.) and time (month and year) that you are delivering this speech. Select strategies that are most appropriate for the kind of audience (animated, bemused, concerned, or antagonistic) that you face. Provide appropriate support for your claims. Try to limit the information in your briefing to that available to organizational leaders at the time of your briefing.

N O T E S

1. Barton, L., *Crisis in Organizations: Managing and Communicating in the Heat of Chaos* (Cincinnati: South-Western Publishing Co., 1993), 2.

2. Augustine, N. R., "Managing the Crisis You Tried to Prevent," *Harvard Business Review,* November–December 1995, 152.

3. Barton.

4. Ibid.

5. Wisenbilt, J. Z., "Crisis Management Planning Among U.S. Corporations: Empirical Evidence and a Proposed Framework," *SAM Advanced Management Journal* 54 (Spring 1989): 35.

6. Barton.

7. Clare, D. R., "The Tylenol Story: From Crisis to Comeback," *Cross Currents* 12 (1983): 38–43.

8. Benoit, W. L., and J. J. Lindsey, "Argument Strategies: Antidote to Tylenol's Poisoned Image," *Journal of the American Forensic Association* 23 (1987): 136–146.

9. "Company Turnarounds: Johnson and Johnson Reincarnates a Brand," *Sales and Marketing Management,* 16 January 1984, 63.

10. "Oil Slick Spreads Toward Coast: FBI Begins Probe," *Los Angeles Times,* 2 April 1989, Part I, 1 & 24

11. Benoit, W. L., *Accounts, Excuses, and Apologies: A Theory of Image Restoration,* (Albany: State University of New York Press, 1995).

12. Tyler, L., "Ecological Disaster and Rhetorical Response: Exxon's Communications in the Wake of the Valdez Spill," *Journal of Business and Technical Communication* 6 (1992): 149–171.

13. Benoit, *Accounts, Excuses, and Apologies.*

14. Tyler.

15. Benoit, W. L., "Sears' Repair of Its Auto Service Image: Image Restoration Discourse in the Corporate Sector," *Communication Studies* 46 (1995): 89–105.

16. Ibid.

17. Gellene, D., "Sears Offered Prizes, Trips: State Also Alleges Mechanics Were Under Quota System," *Los Angeles Times,* 13 June 1992, D1.

18. Benoit, "Sears' Repair of Its Auto Service Image."

19. Benoit, W. L., and S. L. Brinson, "AT&T: 'Apologies Are Not Enough,'" *Communication Quarterly* 42 (1994): 75–88.

20. Benoit and Brinson.

21. Benoit and Brinson.

22. Barton.

23. Augustine, 149.

24. Barton.

25. Barton, 129.

26. Barton.

27. Gellene, D., "New State Probe of Sears Could Lead to Suit," *Los Angeles Times,* 12 June 1992, D4.

28. "Breast-Implant Maker Releasing Data to Back Safety Claim," *New York Times,* 18 July 1991, A16.

29. Benoit and Lindsey.

30. Benoit, "Sears' Repair of its Auto Service Image."

31. Benoit, *Accounts, Excuses, and Apologies.,*

32. Ibid.

33. Benoit, "Sears' Repair of Its Auto Service Image."

34. Benoit, *Accounts, Excuses, and Apologies.*

35. Benoit, "Sears' Repair of Its Auto Service Image."

36. King, Martin Luther Jr., *Why We Can't Wait* (New York: Harper & Row, Publishers, 1963), 77–100.

37. Volvo Advertisement, *USA Today,* 6 November 1990, 2B.

38. Brinson, S. L., and W. L. Benoit, "Dow Corning's Image Repair Strategies in the Breast Implant Crisis," *Communication Quarterly* 44 (1996): 29–41.

39. Benoit, *Accounts, Excuses, and Apologies.*

40. Tyler, L., "Liability Means Never Being Able to Say You're Sorry: Corporate Guilt, Legal Constraints, and Defensiveness in Corporate Communication," *Management Communication Quarterly* 11 (1997): 51–73.

41. Ibid, 61.

42. Rothchild, J., "How to say you're sorry," *Time,* 20 June 1994, 51.

43. Tyler, "Liability Means Never Being Able to Say You're Sorry."

44. Benoit and Brinson.

45. Benoit, "Sears' Repair of Its Auto Service Image."

46. Ibid., 99.

47. Tyler, "Ecological Disaster and Rhetorical Response."

48. Miller, C., "Competitor Rips Beech-Nut Organic Line," *Marketing News,* 10 June 1991, 1 & 12.

49. Henriques, D. B., "10% of Fruit Juice Sold in U.S. Is Not All Juice, Regulators Say," *The New York Times,* 31 October 1993, A1 & A24.

50. Benoit, *Accounts, Excuses, and Apologies.*

INDEX